D0219509

THE BRITISH SYSTEM OF GOVERNMENT

The tenth edition of this acclaimed text continues to provide a lively, comprehensive and up-to-date account of British political institutions, of the way in which they operate, and of what they reveal of the society in which they developed.

The British System of Government explores recent political developments without losing sight of the underlying structure of governmental institutions and its relationship with political ideas and behaviour. Anthony H. Birch examines in detail the political actors in British politics and their roles. He portrays them at work, pursuing political objectives and facing social, economic and diplomatic problems. His approach enables students to gain an excellent understanding of the institutional context of political change and of the process of government in Britain.

This tenth edition has been thoroughly revised and updated. It includes new sections on key areas, such as the 1997 general election and the extraordinary results, the transformation of the Labour Party, the judicial system, the recent restrictions of rights and the growth of judicial activism, the state of the monarchy and the House of Lords, Europe, Northern Ireland, foreign policy in the post-Cold War era, and the problems and merits of British government, including devolution and Britain's future in Europe. *The British System of Government* is an ideal introductory text for those students approaching British politics, its institutions and the processes of government for the first time.

Anthony H. Birch is Emeritus Professor of Political Science at the University of Victoria, Canada. He has worked in the British Civil Service, has taught political science in both Britain and North America, has served as Vice-President of the International Political Science Association, and is a Fellow of the Royal Society of Canada.

By the same author

FEDERALISM, FINANCE AND SOCIAL LEGISLATION

SMALL-TOWN POLITICS

REPRESENTATIVE AND RESPONSIBLE GOVERNMENT

REPRESENTATION

POLITICAL INTEGRATION AND DISINTEGRATION IN
THE BRITISH ISLES

NATIONALISM AND NATIONAL INTEGRATION

THE CONCEPTS AND THEORIES OF MODERN DEMOCRACY

THE BRITISH SYSTEM OF GOVERNMENT

Tenth edition

Anthony H. Birch

London and New York

First published 1967
by Allen and Unwin
Tenth edition published 1998
by Routledge
11 New Fetter Lane, London EC4P 4EE

Simultaneously published in the USA and Canada
by Routledge
29 West 35th Street, New York, NY 10001

Typeset in Goudy by Florencetype Limited, Stoodleigh, Devon
Printed and bound in Great Britain by
T.J. International Ltd, Padstow, Cornwall

British Library Cataloguing in Publication Data
A catalogue record for this book is available from the British Library

Library of Congress Cataloguing in Publication Data
Birch, Anthony Harold.
The British system of government / Anthony H. Birch – 10th edn.
Includes bibliographical references and index.
1. Great Britain – Politics and government – 1945–. I Title.
JN231.B57 1998
320.441 – dc21   97–33484

ISBN 0–415–18389–8

To my beloved daughter Tanya

CONTENTS

ILLUSTRATIONS

FIGURE

TABLES

PREFACE TO THE TENTH EDITION

This book has been extensively revised for this edition.

It includes analyses of the disaster that has befallen the Conservative Party, the transformation of the Labour Party, the extraordinary election of 1997, the aftermath of the Maastricht Treaty, the problems of enlarging the European Union, and the emerging problems of constitutional change in Britain.

I should like to thank my former colleague and good friend Bernie Wainewright of London for his invaluable help, Rob Clements of the House of Commons Library for statistical data on the 1997 election, and the staff of the Inter-Library Loan division of the University of Victoria Library for their exceptional efficiency and courtesy.

I am also, as always, grateful to my wife Dorothy for her support and assistance.

Anthony H. Birch
Victoria, B.C.
1997

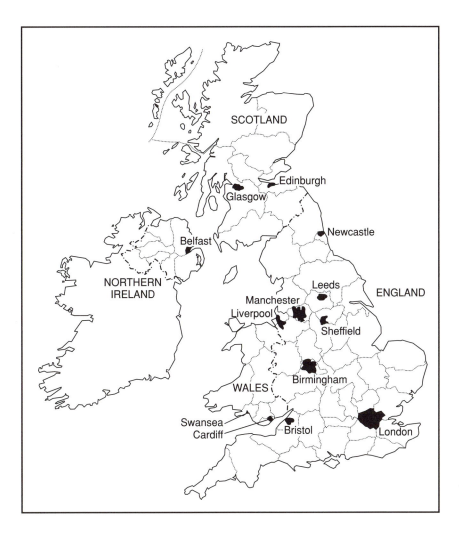

Part I

THE SOCIAL BASIS

1

BRITISH SOCIETY AND THE BRITISH PEOPLE

This book is concerned with the nature of British political institutions and the way in which they operate. Both the institutions and their mode of operation have been shaped to a large extent by the nature of the society in which they have developed, and they reflect and embody the habits and assumptions of the people who operate them. This is a general truth about political systems that applies not only to the government of Britain but also to the government of other nations; and not only to the government of nations but also to the government of small societies within nations. It can be seen as clearly as anywhere in the government of voluntary societies. Thus, student organizations tend to be ultra-democratic because students dislike authority, and to have elaborate rules of order because of the ingenuity with which student politicians exploit any ambiguity or loophole in the rules. Church organizations, on the other hand, tend to be dominated by a few leading personalities and to have very loose rules of procedure that reflect the belief that relations between members should be characterized by mutual trust and good faith. Nations are similar to voluntary societies in this respect; how they are governed depends to a large extent on the beliefs and habits of their citizens and the social relations between them. The most appropriate introduction to a study of British government is therefore a short discussion of some of the salient characteristics of British society and the British people.

The component parts of British society

The term 'Britain' is slightly ambiguous, being used sometimes as a shorthand equivalent of the political entity called the United Kingdom of Great Britain and Northern Ireland, sometimes as a short version of the social entity called Great Britain, and frequently (by the English) as a synonym for England. As 83 per cent of the people of the United Kingdom live in England, the whole political system is heavily influenced by the character of English society. However, as the state is, strictly speaking, multinational, it is appropriate to begin by saying a word about Ireland, Wales and Scotland.

Ireland is best regarded as England's oldest colony, having been invaded by the English in the twelfth century and governed in colonial fashion until 1800, with a Governor responsible to London and a local Parliament (in the eighteenth century) composed almost entirely of Anglo-Irish landowners and merchants. Between 1800 and 1922 Ireland was legally part of the United Kingdom, and subject to laws passed by the Westminster Parliament. In the latter year, after a limited but bitter campaign of guerrilla warfare, the greater part of Ireland became an independent country known first as the Irish Free State and now simply as Ireland, leaving the six north-eastern counties as a partially self-governing province of the United Kingdom.

Irish society and Irish politics have always been very different from English society and English politics, and strictly speaking they are outside the scope of this book. However, the political violence that broke out in Northern Ireland in 1969 has been kept within bounds only by a large contingent of British troops, and since 1972 the Belfast Parliament has been suspended and the Province has been governed directly from London. In view of these developments the political character and problems of Northern Ireland will be summarized briefly in an appendix (see pp. 264-75).

Wales, like Ireland, was invaded by the English in the twelfth century. It was politically integrated with England in 1536, and from then onwards the two countries were governed as one, with no significant differences between their political institutions until a measure of decentralization was introduced in 1964.

The social integration of Wales and England has inevitably been a more gradual process than their political integration. Until the nineteenth century, the Welsh language was spoken by the great majority of people, although English had been the language of government since 1536 and the Welsh middle classes had adopted both the English language and many aspects of English culture. During the nineteenth century the development of coal-mining and industry in south Wales brought a large influx of English workers, while the development of state education was accompanied by an official campaign to establish English as the universal language of discourse. By 1981 only 19 per cent of the people of Wales claimed any knowledge of Welsh, and it is only in rural areas and a few small towns that the language is used. Traditional Welsh culture has declined along with the language, and it would be easy to conclude that Welsh society will be completely integrated with English society within two or three generations.

Such a conclusion may not be warranted, however. For one thing, a vigorous campaign is being promoted to revive the Welsh language and culture, and the Welsh nationalist party, Plaid Cymru, has had some significant electoral successes since 1967. As a result of its campaigns, the fourth television channel in Wales uses Welsh as its medium. Secondly, there are in fact subtle differences between Welsh and English society, quite apart from the language and the traditional culture of rural Wales. Lacking their own aristocracy, the Welsh tend to be more egalitarian than the English and are considerably more reluctant to vote Conservative. Since the franchise was extended to most working-class men in 1867, the Conservative Party has always had difficulty in winning more than a handful of the Welsh parliamentary constituencies. In the twenty-four elections held between 1900 and 1992, excluding the 'coupon election' of 1918, Conservatives gained an average of 5.9 Welsh seats out of a total that varied between 34 and 38. Until 1922 Wales was overwhelmingly Liberal in sentiment and since then it has been overwhelmingly Labour. In addition, Welsh people tend to show more emotion than the English, and this affects their political attitudes and behaviour. A leading student of Welsh politics has observed that 'Welsh political culture is . . . shot through with Welsh cultural and national values and is thus inherently conducive to anger and conflict' (Madgwick 1977: 236–7).

The position of Scotland is different again. For several centuries Scotland was an independent state, and when it joined in political union with England and Wales in 1707 it did so by agreement, not by conquest. Moreover, although the Scottish Parliament voted itself out of existence, other Scottish institutions remained intact, including a distinctive legal system, a somewhat distinctive educational system and the Presbyterian Church of Scotland. With this history, it is not surprising that the Scottish people have a secure sense of national identity, which has survived nearly three centuries of political union with England and is now the basis of a lively nationalist party that seeks to regain Scottish independence.

It follows that there is a real sense in which British society is multinational. However, the differences between England, Wales and Scotland are limited in extent. The Industrial Revolution has had a similar impact on each, and they are all highly urbanized. Engineering is the largest single industry in each. There is a high level of personal mobility between the various parts of Britain, and communication statistics reveal an exceptionally high degree of integration between England and Wales and a considerable degree between England and Scotland (see Birch 1977: ch. 3). The centralized nature of British government has further reduced the social differences between the various parts of the country.

It is therefore reasonable, in a brief treatment, to outline the characteristics of British society as if it were one society, even though occasional reservations have to be made to allow for Welsh and Scottish differences. Table 1.1 gives some basic facts about the constituent territories, with Northern Ireland included for comparative purposes.

Some characteristics of British society

As the resolution of conflicts is one of the main functions of government, the nature of the divisions and cleavages in society has a major influence on the character of the political system. Cleavages vary in kind, and one of the most important lessons to be drawn from a study of politics is that conflicts deriving from linguistic, religious or racial cleavages are usually more difficult to resolve

Table 1.1 The constituent territories of the UK in 1991

	Population (millions)	Population %	Relative income per head %	Roman Catholics %	Gaelic speakers %
England	47.8	83.3	102	9	–
Scotland	5.1	9.0	98	16	1.6
Wales	2.9	4.9	87	7	19.0
Northern Ireland	1.6	2.8	78	38	–
United Kingdom	57.4	100.0	100	11	1.1

than conflicts deriving from economic cleavages, whether the latter be between regions of the country or classes within society. There are two reasons for this difference. The first is that people are locked into their linguistic, religious and racial groups, usually having no wish to change even if they could, whereas people can hope to escape from a depressed region or class by individual mobility. If they themselves cannot escape, they can hope that their children will do so. The second reason is that it is easier for governments to mitigate economic conflicts, by a process of incremental adjustment, than it is for them to mitigate linguistic, religious or racial conflicts.

The contemporary world provides ample evidence for these generalizations. Linguistic conflicts have created constitutional crises in both Belgium and Canada. Religious conflicts have led to prolonged violence in Northern Ireland, Lebanon and India. Racial conflicts have led to riots in American cities and to bloodshed in many African and Asian states. Economic conflicts, though present in all countries, are normally resolved peacefully by bargaining, wage increases, price controls and adjustments to the tax system.

In this perspective, Britain can be counted as fortunate in that modern British society is relatively free from the most troublesome kinds of cleavage. There is no linguistic cleavage in Britain except in some parts of Wales, and as the Welsh-speakers comprise only 1 per cent of the British population (and can virtually all speak English as well) this does not pose a serious threat to political stability. Religious divisions are no longer of any general significance, largely because of the decline of religious conviction. Only about 5 per cent of the population attend church on a normal Sunday, and the attitude of the great majority of people towards religion is one of indifference. There are a few constituencies in and around Glasgow and Liverpool where the concentration of Roman Catholic voters is so great that the Labour Party, at least, normally nominates a Catholic candidate; but these are areas of heavy Irish immigration, so that the religious dimension to political life there can be regarded as an importation from across the water. In addition to its nominally Christian population, Britain has about 400,000 Jews, 600,000 Hindus and Sikhs and over a million Muslims. However, no statistics are available regarding attendance at synagogues, temples and mosques. The fact that a minority of the

Muslims are fundamentalists raises the possibility of social conflict over religious issues, as became apparent in 1989 when the Ayatollah Khomeini of Iran called upon militant Muslims to murder the British author Salman Rushdie on account of some allegedly blasphemous passages in a novel he had written. However, it remains true that, in general, religious loyalties have little impact on British political life. The contrast with Northern Ireland is obvious and there is also a marked difference between Britain and the United States on this matter. In America, politicians are apt to be judged on moralistic grounds, while the strength of religious feeling about the control of abortion was demonstrated by the bombing of twenty-eight abortion clinics by religious zealots during 1986. In Britain, political and religious issues are normally kept separate and the great majority of British voters neither know nor care what religious views (if any) are held by candidates for political office.

The question of race is rather more delicate. For many centuries Britain has had a high degree of ethnic homogeneity, with immigrants arriving only in a trickle and thus easily assimilated. In the nineteenth century, the arrival of large numbers of Irish settlers sometimes created tension in industrial areas, but did not lead to any permanent social problems. In the present century British society has easily absorbed several contingents of European immigrants seeking refuge from the political problems of their own countries. In round numbers, these contingents comprised 150,000 Russian Jews in the years before the First World War, 65,000 German Jews in the 1930s, 100,000 Polish ex-servicemen who stayed on in 1945, and 30,000 Hungarian refugees in 1956. In the late 1950s, however, social tensions and problems resulted from the arrival of considerable numbers of Pakistani, Indian and West Indian immigrants, who until 1962 had unrestricted right of entry to Britain as citizens of Commonwealth countries. As soon as this development came to the attention of the general public, opinion polls showed that over 80 per cent of the public were opposed to it, and in 1962 immigration of this kind was restricted by the Commonwealth Immigrants Act. Subsequent measures have tightened the controls, but by 1997 Britain had 3.1 million Commonwealth immigrants and their descendants and it is officially estimated that by the end of the century the number will be about 3.3 million.

The existence and growth of these ethnic minorities, largely concentrated in a few cities, has given rise to various types of concern. First, there has been concern that the minorities may suffer from racial discrimination. The promotion of good race relations is a matter upon which all the major political parties are agreed, and overt discrimination in almost all fields of activity has been made illegal by successive pieces of legislation, but some covert discrimination in employment undoubtedly occurs. Secondly, there has been concern that the minorities might not become integrated into the British economy and British society, sharpened by the revelation that black children have (for whatever reason) done markedly less well in the British educational system than white children and Asian children have. Thirdly, there have been fears that areas containing sizeable ethnic minorities might be marked by violent conflicts between races, or between minorities and the police. There have in fact been violent clashes between young black citizens and the police in Bristol, Liverpool, Birmingham and parts of London, but few direct clashes between blacks and whites.

Economic divisions with a geographical (as distinct from a class) basis fall into two categories: divisions between urban and rural areas, and divisions between more prosperous and less prosperous regions. Divisions between urban and rural areas are relatively unimportant in Britain because the country is more urbanized than any other country in the world apart from city states like Singapore. The proportion of the total male workforce engaged in agriculture was only 1.8 per cent in June 1996 (the seasonal peak) and is lower than in any other country apart from Kuwait. One of the consequences is that in British politics there is no sharp clash between representatives of urban and rural inter-ests. The farming industry is an important pressure group, but its influence depends on the goodwill of the government and the fact that the country could not easily afford to increase its imports of food, not upon the voting power of people dependent on agriculture for their livelihood.

Regional disparities in prosperity are inevitable in any sizeable country, and in Britain they have been accentuated in recent decades by the decline of several older staple industries such as coal-mining, shipbuilding and textiles. These industries are mainly situated in Wales, Scotland and the north of England, and a political consequence of this is that these regions are more pro-Labour than southern England. This difference has grown significantly since 1980, but it can hardly be called a conflict.

A factor that reduces the impact of regional issues is the centralization of the mass media. There is no other country of Britain's size in which the press is so dominated by national newspapers. The choice is wide, there being eleven national morning papers that can be delivered to the doorstep throughout Britain; but they are all edited in London. Five of these constitute the serious, 'quality' press, with a combined circulation of 2.5 million in 1992. The other six are popular tabloids, with a combined circulation of 11.2 million. It is esti-mated that 75 per cent of the population over the age of sixteen read one or more of these eleven national dailies. With a handful of exceptions, Welsh and provincial English papers are read in addition to national papers rather than as alternatives to them, and people tend to look to the national press for political news and to their local papers to find out what is on at the cinema. The only papers that can be regarded as alternatives to the national press are the *Yorkshire Post* (with a circulation of 89,000), the *Western Mail* (circulation 77,000), the *Liverpool Daily Post* (circulation 78,000) and the *Birmingham Post* (circulation 28,000). It will be seen that their combined circulation is insignif-icant compared with that of the national dailies. The Sunday press is similarly centralized, a readership survey showing that 87 per cent of the population over the age of sixteen read one or more of the nine national Sunday papers, with a combined circulation of 16.2 million.

However, Scotland is an exception to this general rule. It has three important daily papers of its own in the *Scotsman*, the *Glasgow Herald* and the *Daily Record*, as well as several smaller independent dailies and the Scottish editions of British national papers. Statistics show that in Scotland the total circulation of the Scottish-owned daily papers is about the same as that of the London-owned papers, and the Scottish editions of the latter contain a high proportion of Scottish news even though they are now all edited in England.

It is, of course, also important that the main national radio network is owned by the government and that the two main television news programmes are produced by national agencies, one by the BBC and the other by an independent organization that provides a news service for all the commercial television companies.

The consequence of all these factors is that political news is much the same all over the country. In the United States, where sectional differences are considerable, and all newspapers and radio stations are local, it often happens that at any one time people in different parts of the country are concerned with quite different political issues. In the south-western states a prominent issue might be the position of Mexican immigrants; in Texas, the politics of the oil industry; in the midwest, the federal government's policy towards agriculture; in the north-east it might be foreign policy. As a result, in an election the fortunes of the parties may vary between regions, the Democrats gaining in one part of the country and the Republicans gaining elsewhere.

In Britain, the combined effect of the smallness of the country, the absence of marked sectional differences and the existence of national newspapers is that political localism of this American kind rarely occurs except in Scotland. Local issues do not often make newspaper or television headlines, and when they do they usually make headlines all over the country – at any rate in England and Wales. This state of affairs is partly responsible for the fact that, from 1945 until the 1980s, movements of political opinion were remarkably uniform over the whole of the country, apart from Scotland. If the government of the day lost popularity, the general tendency was for it to lose popularity almost everywhere. If there was a swing from one main party to the other in a general election, this was reflected in all the regions of England and Wales, with minuscule variations.

Scotland followed the general trend from 1945 to 1955, but after that date it veered slowly but steadily to the left, putting the Conservative Party into the position of a permanent minority north of the border. In the 1983 election the Conservatives won only twenty-one of the seventy-two Scottish seats, despite getting a large majority in the country as a whole, while in the 1987 election they held only ten Scottish seats and in 1997 none at all.

In England and Wales uniform swings continued until 1983, when the intervention of the new Social Democratic Party (SDP) made a difference. The SDP, acting in electoral alliance with the Liberal Party, took many more votes from Labour in the south of England than it did in the north. The consequence was that in most of southern England the main battle was between the Conservatives and the Liberal–SDP alliance, with Labour coming third, while elsewhere the traditional Conservative/Labour conflict continued to dominate the polls except where there were local pockets of Liberal strength. In the 1987 election the alliance gained slightly fewer votes, but regional differentiation in voting became even more marked as a consequence of the contrast between the prosperity of much of southern England and the relative poverty of the older industrial areas of northern England and Wales. The Labour Party gained votes in these areas without making any impact on the southern counties, where its record was even poorer than that of the Conservative Party in Scotland. In this way regional economic and social differences have now come to have a very significant impact on the party system.

The class system

It has sometimes been observed that the British are more conscious of considerations of social class in their relations with one another than citizens of other western societies, and some account of the class system is essential in any discussion of the characteristics of British society. However, when people talk of a class system they do not always refer to the same phenomenon. There are in fact three quite different models of what a class system consists of. In one model the difference between classes is conceived as being a difference of power; in another it is a difference of status; and in a third it is a difference of interests.

The view of the class system in terms of power derives from the theories of Karl Marx. In the Marxist model of society the ownership of the means of production determines class identity and class relationships. In an agricultural society the owners of land dominate the landless, who are forced to work on the land for low rewards. In an industrial society the owners of capital become the dominant class, with the landowners relegated to the position of a small *rentier* class and the great majority of people forced to sell their labour to the capitalists. The majority, known to Marxists as the proletariat, are exploited by the capitalists and cannot escape from their condition of exploitation except by a revolution that would transform society by expropriating the possessions of the capitalist class and establishing a socialist form of industrial organization. Revolution will be difficult, because the dominant class in any society controls the machinery of government and can use the coercive power of the state to crush incipient revolts. Class relationships in a capitalist society are therefore relationships of conflict, with democratic institutions (if they exist) serving the pacifying function of giving the workers the illusion of popular control without actually giving them political or economic power.

Marxists would acknowledge that the class system of modern Britain is not usually viewed in this way, and is in any case much more complex than this bare model suggests. They would insist, however, that the model reveals the realities of power that underlie the day-to-day controversies and compromises that are the stuff of democratic political debate.

A second model of the class system, much favoured by social commentators and journalists, views class differences as essentially differences of status. In modern Britain, it is said, people categorize one another by a variety of indicators, such as accent, clothes, manners, type of school attended, recreations pursued and type of car driven. At an immediate practical level, this is undoubtedly a more useful model than the first one. When British people meet strangers in a pub or on a train, this is exactly how they go about classifying one another. It is in terms of this model that the British may be more conscious of class than the Germans or Dutch or Americans are. However, from the political point of view, status differences may be only a superficial guide to behaviour. People from quite different status groupings can be found sharing political ideals and interests, while people of similar status may be committed to opposing political parties. In so far as we are concerned to use the class system as an explanatory factor in understanding political behaviour, the most useful model of the class system is neither the one based on power nor the one based on status, but the one based on interests.

What is of crucial importance is that people with different sources of income and different occupations have different economic interests, and that these differing interests are reflected in the party system and the policy-making process. People who derive much of their income from rents or investments, as an example, have a long time-perspective. They have little need to worry about unemployment, unless there is a major slump, and relatively little need to worry about inflation, which will increase the value of their property and investments. Their most direct political concerns will be to minimize or avoid having a capital gains tax and to minimize or avoid having effective death duties.

Professional and business people whose income depends on their individual talents and efforts are in a different position. They characteristically own little property apart from their house, so that they will not be particularly concerned about capital gains tax but will have a direct and strong interest in the continuance of tax relief on mortgage interest payments. They will be very upset by inflation, which is apt to cut their net income because salary-earners are not so well protected against inflation as either the propertied classes or the unionized wage-earning section of the workforce. They have less direct reason than wage-earners to be worried about the level of unemployment. They are less concerned about death duties than the propertied classes but may be particularly concerned about the quality of the educational system, as they want their children to have at least as good an opportunity as they had to acquire professional qualifications. Like the propertied classes, people in this category are very much more likely to support the Conservative Party than the Labour Party, because they see the Conservatives as more likely to protect their economic interests.

The third distinctive category comprises manual workers, whose economic position has always been less secure than that of people in the two categories so far mentioned. In the nineteenth century Britain produced a large industrial proletariat whose members suffered not only from relatively low incomes but also from various kinds of insecurity and hazard. They were often hired by the day and subject to unemployment without notice. Their working conditions often posed threats to their health. Unlike most salary-earners, they were not paid when sick. They usually lived in rented housing and were thus at the mercy of possibly rapacious landlords. Having small incomes and little property, they were not worried about the level of taxation. Knowing that their incomes depended on collective action, they were concerned about the legal position of trade unions. Without superannuation schemes, and unable to save, they depended on their unions and the state for pensions in old age.

To itemize the concerns of manual workers in this way is to draw up what became the main agenda of the Liberal government of 1905–14 and the Labour Party from 1918 onwards. The Liberal government gave unions immunity from legal action in respect of industrial disputes and also authorized them to collect a political levy from their members for donation to a political party, which in practice meant the Labour Party. The Liberals also launched state insurance schemes to provide for benefits in case of sickness or unemployment and for pensions after retirement. The Labour Party promised to extend these benefits, to establish a free and universal system of health care, to provide municipal housing for workers at subsidized rents, to enact measures to cut the rate of industrial accidents, and to use the budget to tax the rich and help the poor. It therefore follows that manual workers have had good economic reasons to support the Labour Party, as (until the 1980s) the majority of them have done.

In this model of the class system, white-collar workers occupy an intermediate position, having better working conditions and more security of employment than manual workers but not being nearly so well off as professional people or business executives. It is therefore not surprising to find that in the elections of 1950 and 1951, the first in which voting behaviour was analysed by sample survey techniques, white-collar workers split about fifty-fifty between voting Conservative and voting Labour.

In recent years the British class system, viewed as a system of differing economic and social interests, has undergone marked changes. In the first place, economic and technological changes have led to a move from manufacturing to service trades, while within industry the growth of automation has increased the number of technicians and computer operators but brought about a reduction in the number of manual workers. The proportion of the workforce in manual occupations fell from 70 per cent in 1951 to 52 per cent in 1981 (see Halsey 1987: 15) and has fallen to well under 50 per cent since 1981. Secondly, the measures of social security and industrial safety promised by the Labour Party have all been achieved and are accepted by all parties. Thirdly, the widespread (though not universal) growth of affluence has led to a reduction in the differences in living conditions that were apparent in the immediate postwar period. When people come to own their own house, to have central heating and to own a car they reach a plateau of comfort that takes the edge off the feelings of resentment that were once common. This development has been paralleled by the equalizing effects of supermarkets and television, which reduce differences in lifestyle and tastes. The spread of comprehensive schools has had a similar impact. The general trend of the past two decades has been for British society to become more egalitarian, even though the unemployed and certain other disadvantaged minorities remain trapped in poverty.

This does not mean that class differences are no longer of any importance. At the top of the social scale there is an upper class, constituting a fraction of 1 per cent of the population, whose members are born into it and possess (or have expectations of possessing) substantial inherited wealth. Next, there is an upper-middle class, of about 4 or 5 per cent of the population, whose members can afford to send their children to good fee-paying schools and thus secure for them the probability of going to Oxford or Cambridge and acquiring substantial advantages in the market for well-paying careers. At the bottom of the social scale there is an underclass, of between 10 and 20 per cent of the population, whose members suffer from unemployment or other crippling disadvantages, have poor housing conditions, and became relatively, in some cases absolutely, poorer during the 1980s. It is among the remainder of society, about three-quarters of the population, that class distinctions which used to be important have become much less so. These people became appreciably more prosperous during the 1980s; they almost all own their own homes and possess one or more family cars; they mostly have central heating and own VCRs; they have a lifestyle which in the 1950s was enjoyed by no more than about a quarter of the population.

The consequence of these economic and social changes, which have brought the British social structure much closer to the social structures of Canada and the United States, is that class consciousness has decreased. Surveys in the past decade have shown that fewer than half of the population identified themselves with a particular class. And in parallel with this decrease in class consciousness, there has been a decrease in the correlation between the occupation of voters and their behaviour at the polls. As will be shown in Chapter 6, the 1970s and 1980s were marked by a class de-alignment in partisan allegiance and voting behaviour.

Political attitudes and values

The British system of government is determined not only by the history and social characteristics of the country but also by the political attitudes and values of the British people. Some of these have been mentioned already and many others will emerge during the course of the book. However, one or two of them have played such an important part in shaping political institutions that they merit a special place in this opening chapter.

The first of these is a very strong attachment to personal liberty. This is so well known that it hardly needs explanation, but a few contemporary examples may

13

reinforce the point. The British would never accept the widespread security checks for bureaucratic posts that are taken for granted in the United States. The British would not agree to a proposal to ban extremist parties in times of peace, as communist and fascist parties were banned in West Germany. If it were revealed that the British police had conducted several hundred illegal break-ins, a British Prime Minister would not feel able to tell Parliament that such actions were justified in the campaign against potential terrorists and criminals, as the Canadian Prime Minister did in 1978. Equally, it is inconceivable that a British government would instruct the security police to compile files on the political affiliations and activities of all candidates for political office, irrespective of party, as the Canadian government has done. Another British attitude is very strong opposition to identity cards, which would surprise visitors from many other European countries, who are required to carry 'papers' to show to the police on demand, or visitors from North America, who are accustomed to constant demands to show their 'I.D.', not only by police but by private institutions such as banks.

Even in minor matters of everyday life, similar contrasts can be found. British drinkers would not like the situation in most Canadian provinces, in which it is a legal offence to consume alcoholic beverages in the open air, and a glass of beer at a picnic can lead to prosecution. British swimmers would hardly put up with the situation on American beaches, where the provision of life-guards is immediately followed by rules making it an offence to swim anywhere except in a small roped enclosure in front of the life-guard. British sailors of yachts would be appalled by the detailed regulations about safety equipment that their French counterparts have to cope with. In all kinds of ways Britain is still a land of freedom, and any readers who doubt this should move overseas and find out for themselves.

A second generalization that can be made about British attitudes to government is that they are endlessly pragmatic. The British do not have a written constitution and they have no coherent theory of the state. They have inherited a set of political institutions and their instinct is to adapt and modify these rather than to replace them by new ones. One consequence of this is a rather extreme kind of institutional conservatism, which has allowed a medieval body like the House of Lords to survive into the late twentieth century. Another consequence is that British administrative arrangements are labyrinthine in character, like an old building that has been continually improved and extended, but never redesigned.

Proposals for radical reform are sometimes made, but they are invariably blocked, diverted or undermined by this preference for incremental adjustment. A national economic plan was commissioned in 1964 but abandoned in 1967. Radical proposals to reform the civil service in 1968 resulted in small piecemeal changes, leaving the structure of the service intact. The Civil Service College was established to train senior administrators, but it has turned out to be a rather small college offering very short courses. The campaign to create national assemblies for Scotland and Wales in the 1970s collapsed in the face of political resistance and public apathy. The British are no longer particularly smug about their institutions, as they were until the 1960s, but dramatic changes in structure would be out of character.

A third generalization that can be made about British political attitudes is that people have a long-standing preference for being governed by a united party under a strong, or apparently strong, leader. The repeal of the Corn Laws in 1846 'broke up the Conservative Party and so put the Whigs into power, with short intervals, for twenty years' (Trevelyan 1929: 645). Gladstone's advocacy of Home Rule for Ireland in 1886 'broke up the Liberal Party and greatly weakened it for twenty years to come' (Trevelyan 1929: 688). The divisions among Labour ministers about how to deal with the depression in 1931 led to their party's massive defeats in the next two elections so that they were out of power until 1945. The division among Conservative ministers and MPs about policies towards the European Community in 1992–7 led to the party's defeat in the 1977 election and do not bode well for its future.

The preference for strong Prime Ministers is also quite clear. In the early years of Queen Victoria's reign Sir Robert Peel made the following comment on this topic:

> I could not admit any alteration in any of these bills. This was thought very obstinate and very presumptuous; but the fact is, people like a certain degree of obstinacy and presumption in a minister. They abuse him for dictatorship and arrogance, but they like being governed.
>
> (Rosebery 1899: 67)

That was a long time ago, but in 1967 Harold Wilson displayed a similar attitude when interviewed by a political scientist who was also a Labour MP. When presented with a list of possible cases of backbench influence on policy, the Prime Minister did not say – as government leaders in many other democracies would have done – that he had taken account of the views of his parliamentary colleagues and the movements of public opinion they represented. On the contrary, he went through each example carefully 'to demonstrate that on no occasion was he consciously deflected from his original purpose, even over mode of presentation or timing, by any estimate of what dissident groups on his back benches might say' (Mackintosh 1977b: 85).

Evidence that British voters like the appearance of firm leadership is to be found not only in scattered public opinion polls but also in the striking effect that the 1982 war in the Falkland Islands had on the popularity and esteem of Margaret Thatcher. Public assessments of her performance as a Prime Minister increased markedly during the conflict and remained at a higher level after it was concluded. She had displayed strong leadership and this commanded public admiration. Her party's continuing lead at the polls and in elections throughout the 1980s, despite the unpopularity of many of her social policies, reveals the degree to which political leadership is respected.

It does not follow from this that the British people always experience strong government. On the contrary, compromise and concessions to pressure groups have been regular features of government policy in many areas. On the occasions when bold initiatives have been taken, governments have often had to modify or withdraw their measures in the face of opposition. In 1969 the Labour government had to abandon both its plan to reform the House of Lords and its proposal to regulate industrial relations. The Conservative government's decision in 1970 to give no more subsidies to declining industries was abandoned within two years. The 1971 Industrial Relations Act was effectively sabotaged by trade union opposition. Three plans to build a third airport for London were given up in the face of public hostility in the areas chosen for its location. The Callaghan government showed notable weakness over the issue of devolution to Scotland. Margaret Thatcher's plan to liberalize shop trading hours was rejected by the House of Commons. The Thatcher government was more determined than any other government since 1950, but the general postwar record indicates that caution and compromise have been as common as bold initiatives carried through in the face of strong opposition.

A fourth generalization that has been made is that the British people are more trusting in matters political than citizens of other democracies. A famous international survey conducted in 1959 showed that the British were more certain of receiving equal and considerate treatment from bureaucrats and the police than were Americans, Germans or Italians. They were also more confident then Germans and Italians, though not Americans, of their ability to do something about regulations they regarded as unjust (Almond and Verba 1965: 70, 72, 142, 181). The organizers of the survey described the British as deferential and allegiant.

The adjectives have always been open to question, and there is scattered evidence that British attitudes have changed since that time. In the 1959 survey 83 per cent of respondents said they expected equal treatment from bureaucrats, but in a 1972 survey of teenagers only 18 per cent agreed (Hart 1978: 44). In 1959, 59 per cent said they expected 'serious consideration of their point of view' from government officials, whereas in a 1973 national survey the figure had gone down to 30 per cent (Marsh 1977: 118). There is also evidence of an increased readiness to resort to various forms of direct action to achieve political objectives. The 1973 survey revealed that 15 per cent approved of street blockades and the occupation of buildings in furtherance of a political objective, 18 per cent thought it would be 'justified to break the law' to 'combat excessive rent, tax or price increases', and 12 per cent thought this was right 'as a generalised means of furthering a legitimate cause' (Marsh 1977: 45, 53). These attitudes were reflected in the riots in twenty-seven urban districts in 1981, in the violence that accompanied the prolonged miners' strike of 1983–4, when three people were killed, in the riot in central London in 1990 to protest against the poll tax for local government, when well over a hundred police officers and demonstrators were injured, and in the demonstrations by animal-lovers at ports in 1995, which physically prevented the export of British calves for slaughter on the continent.

The 1990s have seen a decline in public confidence in the government's ability to defend British interests *vis-à-vis* the European Community, in the integrity of MPs following revelations that some of them have engaged in unethical behaviour, and in the judicial system because it has failed to prevent innocent people being convicted of murder and other serious crimes. The British are still trusting in that they believe their politicians and public servants to be honest and free from corruption, being somewhat more confident in this respect than Americans and much more confident than Italians. But it would be stretching the evidence to say that their present-day political attitudes can be regarded as deferential.

Further reading

For a fuller discussion of social structure and political attitudes see Moran (1989) *Politics and Society in Britain*, chs 1 and 2.

Part II

THE CONSTITUTIONAL FRAMEWORK

2

THE NATURE OF THE CONSTITUTION

Nearly all modern states apart from the United Kingdom have written constitutions that set out the nature and powers of their institutions of government. It does not follow from the absence of such a document in Britain that the country lacks a body of constitutional law or that this law is based entirely on custom and precedent. There are numerous statutes concerning the composition and powers of particular institutions. Thus, the powers of the monarchy are limited by the Bill of Rights of 1689 and the Act of Settlement of 1701; the powers of the House of Lords are defined by the Parliament Acts of 1911 and 1949; and the modern electoral system is regulated by the Representation of the People Acts of 1948 and 1949. There is no lack of statutory provisions regarding the various institutions of government, considered individually. What is lacking is a documentary and authoritative statement of the relations between these institutions.

The consequence of this lack is that when writers and speakers describe the British constitution they produce accounts that are often significantly different from one another. These differences will be explored, but before moving to this topic it is important to note that there is one feature of British constitutional arrangements about which little disagreement is possible. This feature is the limited political influence of the courts of law. They have developed Common Law over the centuries and by doing so have helped to define the liberties of the citizen. However, where statutes exist the courts normally have no power to challenge them. Judges cannot declare statutes to be unconstitutional on the ground that the statute infringes a declaration of personal rights, as they can in the United States, Canada and those states that have incorporated the European Convention on the Protection of Human Rights into domestic law. Nor can courts declare that a statute is unconstitutional because it regulates an area of activity that is outside the jurisdiction of the national legislature, as can be done in all federal states. Britain has a unitary system of government, not a federal one, as was very clearly demonstrated in 1972 when the Parliament of Northern Ireland was suspended by the British Parliament within forty-eight hours of the Prime Minister's decision that this would be desirable. The system is not only unitary, but highly centralized. Borough and county councils have no entrenched rights, and their area, powers and even names can be and have been changed at will by the national government.

In Britain, Parliament is sovereign, in the sense that there are no constitutional limits to its authority. Since 1973, part of this authority has been handed over to the European Community, but this is a grant of power that could legally be rescinded by a future Parliament. All in all, the British constitutional system is unusual among democratic systems in its absence of checks and balances and the very great power that it gives to the party that wins most votes in a general election. More will be said on this question in Chapter 18.

The constitutional questions about which commentators differ relate to the balance of practical power and influence between Parliament and the administration. Granted that Parliament can, in law, do whatever it likes, the question remains of whether parliamentarians actually run the country or merely act as a rubber stamp for decisions taken by ministers and civil servants. The answer to this question, which should be determined by empirical investigation, is sometimes implied by the language in which constitutional matters are discussed. And it often seems that participants in constitutional discussions are using two quite different languages.

The languages of the constitution

The predominant language at the present time is best called the 'liberal language', because it embodies a number of ideals associated with the liberal reform movement of the nineteenth century. In this language the central concept is 'the sovereignty of Parliament'. It is emphasized that in the British system of government, supreme power lies with Parliament, which has direct and exclusive control over legislation and indirect control over the actions of the executive and the central administration. In respect of legislation, Parliament is said to be both omnipotent and omni-competent: there is no constitutional restriction on its authority; and other law-making bodies in the country (such as local councils) exercise their powers only so long as Parliament authorizes them to do so. In respect of administration, Parliament is said to have ultimate control by virtue of the convention that ministers are responsible to Parliament both for their own decisions and for all the actions of their departments. Government policy may be framed in the Cabinet, but Cabinet ministers have to answer to Parliament for all that they do and may be forced to resign by a vote of no confidence in Parliament if their actions do not meet with parliamentary approval.

In this view of the constitution British political life is dominated by a chain of command that leads from the electorate to the House of Commons, from the Commons to the Cabinet and other ministers and from the ministers to the civil servants who carry out their instructions. Since civil servants have some authority over citizens, the chain of command eventually completes a circle. The system is said to be democratic because it ensures that government policies reflect 'the will of the people'.

This is a crude and over-simplified version of the view of the constitution that appears to command most general acceptance and to underlie most of the comments on political affairs that are to be found in the popular press. It is by no means universally accepted, however. If the average higher civil servant were asked to comment on it, they would probably say that it gives an unrealistic picture of the flow of power. British civil servants do not see the role of the departments as being confined to the implementation of policies that are made by politicians, bending to the will of the electorate. They know that policy and administration are intimately related and that many, perhaps most, changes of policy are initiated in the departments as the result of memoranda written by civil servants, not by politicians.

A good example to support this bureaucratic view of the constitution is afforded by the reform of the gambling laws in 1960. This major reform, which permitted the establishment of betting shops, involved issues that many people regarded as issues of moral or political principle. It was proposed immediately after a general election and had clearly been in the pipeline before the election, but the government had carefully refrained from raising it as an electoral issue. The movement for the reform was in fact generated within the administration, using this term in a wide sense to include the police.

Until 1960, the law had prohibited off-the-course betting on horse-races for cash, although this was permitted on credit. Since most manual workers were unable to secure credit, the consequence was that a large-scale illegal industry had developed, with an annual turnover of tens of millions of pounds. The unsuccessful efforts of the police to stamp out this industry took time that the police thought could better be devoted to other purposes and also tended to bring the law (and possibly the police) into disrepute with the betting public. Chief Constables had therefore frequently pointed out to officials in the Home Office that there was a case for the reform of this law, and when a reforming Home Secretary was appointed, he took up this suggestion. The next step was the appointment of a Royal Commission, which consulted various affected interests and mustered the evidence for reform; after that the Home Secretary persuaded his Cabinet colleagues that a reform was both administratively desirable and politically feasible; officials in the Home Office made the first draft of a new law on the subject; and then, but only then, the government informed Parliament of its intentions. It remained for ministers to persuade backbench MPs that the reform was desirable and for the MPs to defend the proposal when it was criticized by their constituents.

Other examples could be cited to support the view that in practice many political reforms are initiated from within the administration rather than by party politicians in Parliament, but it is unnecessary to give them because the liberal model of the constitution is in fact open to objections that are far more radical than this. The most important of these is its failure to depict the role of the Crown in the British system of government. In the liberal language there is no indication that both ministers and civil servants are servants of the Crown, not of Parliament. Nor is there any indication that the House of Commons can meet only when it is convened by the Crown, acting on the advice of the Prime Minister. It is true that the House must be convened at least once every twelve months, but a great deal can happen in twelve months and a body that lacks the power to convene itself cannot properly be described as the centre and source of authority. In 1963, when Lord Home took office as Prime Minister, he advised the Queen to postpone the opening of Parliament until he had had time to divest himself of his title, fight a by-election, and take a seat in the House of Commons. The Opposition was annoyed by this, but had no power to do anything about it.

Equally, the liberal view of the constitution fails to take account of the independence enjoyed by the executive in the conduct of foreign policy and the making of war. There are other countries (notably the United States) in which treaties are made subject to ratification by the legislative assembly, and if the British Parliament were really as powerful as the liberal language implies it would be reasonable to assume that this situation obtained in Britain. In fact treaties are concluded by ministers in the name of Her Britannic Majesty; they are not subject to ratification by Parliament; and they cannot be disowned by Parliament. Declarations of war are made in a similar fashion, and Parliament is told that war has been declared, not asked whether war should be declared.

People who are conscious of these features of the constitution, including most ministers, top civil servants and constitutional lawyers, rarely use the liberal language when discussing constitutional matters. Instead, they use a language that may for convenience be called 'the Whitehall language', both because many of those who use it are connected with the departments in Whitehall and because in this language it is Whitehall rather than Parliament that is depicted as the centre of government.

The Whitehall language emphasizes the importance of the Crown in the British constitution and the fact that ministers and civil servants are servants of the Crown, responsible for governing the country according to their view of the public interest and not obliged by law (though to some extent they are by convention) to take account of opinions expressed in Parliament. In this language Parliament appears not as a corporate entity wielding power but as a pair of debating chambers in which public opinion is aired and grievances are ventilated. It is noted that Parliament is convened and prorogued by the Queen, acting on the advice of her ministers, and it is suggested that the political process consists in part of a debate or conversation between Parliament on the one hand and the government on the other. Parliament has the right to criticize the actions of the administration, to withhold assent to legislation and in the last resort to pass a motion of no confidence in the government of the day. But it does not have the right to participate in or to control the administration. In this view of the constitution, there is clearly something like a separation of powers between Parliament and the executive, and there is no chain of command except that within the administration itself.

The coexistence of these different views of the constitution raises two questions that must now be answered. The first question is: should one view be regarded as right and the others as wrong, or do both views contain aspects of the truth? If the answer to this is that both views contain aspects of the truth, as will be suggested, a second question follows. This is: how can we account for the fact that an adequate explanation of the British system of government apparently requires the use of two rather different languages?

The constitution in practice

It is suggested that both views of the constitution embody aspects of the truth. Taking the second view first, it is certainly true, as a matter of constitutional principle, that the monarch (acting on the advice of the Prime Minister) decides when and when not to convene Parliament, that ministers are servants of the Crown, not of Parliament, and that Parliament does not have the right to control the activities or expenditures of the executive, but only the right to call ministers to account for what the executive has done.

This view of the constitution is not only correct as a matter of principle but is also a helpful guide to practice. The British administration conducts its affairs in substantial independence of Parliament, in respect of not only defence and foreign relations but also of many domestic matters. An example is the decision to bring about a major expansion of higher education that followed the publication of the Robbins Report in 1963. The first point to note about this is that the report was not made available to MPs until the government had considered its contents and formulated a policy in regard to its recommendations. This policy was in fact announced by the Prime Minister the day after the report was published. The second point to note is that the application of this policy was entirely a matter for executive action. The amount of money made available for university expansion was decided by the Treasury and the Ministry for Higher Education, with the Cabinet acting as arbiter in case of dispute. It is true that Parliament had to authorize this expenditure, but the British Parliament has no power to increase financial estimates presented to it and has never been known to decrease them. When new universities were established in the 1960s and in 1992, these universities were granted degree-giving powers by royal charter, no parliamentary action being required. By the same token, the reductions in public grants to universities between 1979 and 1984 were also decided upon within the administration, without effective control by Parliament.

However, this view of the constitution is clearly incomplete. Its most crippling omission is that it takes no account of the fact that the composition of the House of Commons determines which party or parties will form the government. In the twentieth century the normal situation has been for one party to have an absolute majority of seats in the Commons and for members of this party to fill all ministerial appointments. There were exceptions during both world wars, when coalition governments were formed for the sake of national unity even though the majority party could have kept its monopoly of ministerial posts had it chosen to do so. There were also exceptions in 1923–4, 1929–31 and 1977–9, when no single party had a majority of seats in the Commons. In these periods the country was ruled by minority Labour governments that depended for their parliamentary majorities on the support of the Liberals (and in 1977–9 on support from Scottish and Welsh nationalists also). Each of these minority governments came to a sticky end. In 1924 the Liberals withdrew their support; in 1931 the Labour government collapsed with internal divisions; and in 1979 both the Liberals and the Scottish Nationalists voted against the government on a motion of confidence. In each of the ensuing general elections the Labour Party was defeated.

A corollary of this weakness in the Whitehall view of the constitution is that no adequate account is given of the importance of elections in the British political system. A general election is not simply a way of choosing the people who will conduct debates in one of the Houses of Parliament; it is the institution that determines which party or parties will govern the country. And the prospect of the next general election is rarely far from the minds of politicians and has an influence on government policy as well as on parliamentary debates.

The other weaknesses of the Whitehall view of the constitution flow from the fact that, by focusing attention on the conduct of administration, it tends to underestimate the role of Parliament in the political life of the country. In the first place, Parliament is the training-ground for political leaders. The great majority of ministers achieve ministerial office because they have made a mark in parliamentary debates, and as a consequence of this they tend to remain parliamentarians at heart, with a special sensitivity to parliamentary criticism even though they know there is no danger of it leading to an adverse vote. Then again, the attention of the press is focused on Parliament and for this reason parliamentary criticism of the government may have an effect on public opinion that is out of proportion to the real weight of the criticism. And, even if it does not have such an effect, ministers, being human, may sometimes fear that it will do so, and may moderate their actions accordingly. The behaviour of civil servants is also affected by their wish to avoid provoking parliamentary questions about their departments.

It follows that both these views of the constitution embody aspects of the truth, and that both are necessary to a balanced account of how government is conducted in Britain. Both views exist because each is based on a set of political values, and each has a basis in British history. To put the matter in its simplest form, the Whitehall view reflects those features of the constitution that have remained fairly constant from the eighteenth to the twentieth centuries while the liberal view reflects the ambitions and achievements of nineteenth-century reformers who transformed the political system from one of oligarchy to one of democracy. Both views remain valid because the reformers did not abolish institutions but merely changed their nature to a greater or lesser degree. To understand the present constitution it is therefore necessary to know something of both eighteenth-century institutions and nineteenth-century reforms, and these will be discussed in the following two chapters.

Before moving to these historical chapters it may, however, be helpful to give advance notice of the constitutional matters that are still subject to change and controversy. One of these, to be mentioned in Chapter 3 and discussed more fully in Chapter 8, is the recent decline in the effectiveness of party discipline in Parliament. This raises questions about the factors underlying party discipline and the reasons for its decline. A second issue, to be discussed in Chapter 4, is that of the powers of the monarch in regard to the appointment of the Prime Minister. It is an issue that might become critical in the event of an election in which no one party won an overall majority of seats. A third issue, also to be discussed in Chapter 4, is that of the composition and role of the House of Lords. It is by no means a new issue, having been on the agenda for most of the twentieth century, but it has become more critical now that the House has displayed a greater readiness to amend or defeat government measures and the Labour Party has proposed to transform the House. A fourth issue, to be discussed in Chapter 18, is whether there is now a good case for constitutional change, to create a Scottish National Assembly and/or to give Britain a Bill of Rights. These constitutional questions are all very much alive today, and the brief account of historical developments that follows in the next two chapters will place them in perspective.

Further reading

For a brief but valuable analysis of the constitution see Waldron (1990) *The Law*, ch. 4; for a full account of constitutional conventions see Marshall (1984) *Constitutional Conventions*; for a full discussion of alternative models of the constitution see Birch (1964) *Representative and Responsible Government*; for an analysis of some recent constitutional issues see Jowell and Oliver (1989) *The Changing Constitution* and Oliver (1991) *Government in the United Kingdom*; for a sceptical view see F. F. Ridley (1988) 'The is no British Constitution: a dangerous case of the emperor's clothes'.

3

THE DEVELOPMENT OF
LIBERAL INSTITUTIONS

The central institutions of British government are extremely old. The monarchy has an almost unbroken history dating from before the Norman conquest, and the two Houses of Parliament both have medieval origins. The development of these and other institutions in the medieval and early modern periods is a subject for historians; the student of modern politics can safely begin at the end of the seventeenth century.

In this period three events of great importance took place in quick succession. The first was the revolution of 1688, in which a group of politicians invited William of Orange to bring an invading army to England in order to depose James II from the throne. It was a bloodless revolution because, when it came to the point, James's lieutenants would not fight, but it was a revolution nevertheless. The success of this venture greatly strengthened Parliament's position in relation to the monarchy, and it was immediately followed by the Bill of Rights of 1689. In this Bill it was declared, among other things, that henceforth the monarch could neither make nor suspend laws without the consent of Parliament; could not raise money except by parliamentary grant; could not maintain a standing army without parliamentary authority; and could not restrict the right of free speech within Parliament. A few years later the Act of Settlement of 1701 decided the immediate succession to the throne, declared that no future monarch could either be or marry a member of the Roman Catholic Church and deprived the monarch of the power to dismiss judges, who henceforth could be removed from office only by a resolution of both Houses of Parliament.

The eighteenth-century constitution

This Revolutionary Settlement inaugurated a period of stable government and gradual constitutional evolution that continued without any major legislative change until the great Reform Act of 1832. The eighteenth-century constitution was one in which the mass of the people had little direct influence; it was a system of government by a small ruling class. However, it was distinguished from the autocratic systems of continental Europe (and of England under the Tudors) by some vitally important features.

First, and of most importance to the ordinary person, it gave its citizens a considerable degree of liberty. True, punishments were harsh and people could be hanged for stealing a sheep. But they could not be punished except for a clear offence against the law; they were entitled to a fair trial; and, most important of all in terms of its political effects, they were free to criticize the government as much as they pleased so long as they kept within the laws relating to libel and sedition. Only those who value political liberty but do not enjoy it can appreciate just how much it means. It is not surprising therefore that some of the most eloquent praise of the eighteenth-century British constitution came not from Britons but from foreigners who visited the country. One of these was Voltaire, who, in his *Dictionnaire Philosophique*, published in 1764, wrote in the following terms of the rights of the subject in Britain:

> To be secure on lying down that you shall rise in possession of the same property with which you retired to rest: that you shall not be torn from the arms of your wife, or from your children, in the dead of night, to be thrown into a dungeon or buried in exile in a desert; that when rising from the bed of sleep you will have the power of publishing all your thoughts; and that, if you are accused of having either acted, spoken, or written wrongly, you can be tried only according to law. These privileges attach to everyone who sets his foot on English ground.

The explanation of this liberty lay partly in the nature of British society, which was both more tolerant and less rigidly hierarchical than that of France and many other continental countries. But another French observer, Baron Montesquieu, suggested that a good part of the explanation was to be found in the structure of the central government. The basis of British liberty, he declared, was the separation and balance of powers between the executive, the legislature and the judiciary. In France the king dominated all three and the result was despotism; in Britain the executive was restricted on the one hand by the fact that it did not control Parliament and on the other by the independence of the judiciary, and the result was freedom. The same view was put forward by the English constitutional lawyer Sir William Blackstone, who made the following comment on the independence of the judiciary:

> In this distinct and separate existence of the judicial power in a peculiar body of men, nominated indeed, but not removable at pleasure, by the crown, consists one main preservation of the public liberty; which cannot subsist long in any state, unless the administration of common justice be in some degree separated both from the legislative and also from the executive power.
>
> (Blackstone 1809: 268)

And elsewhere in the same treatise Blackstone noted that 'the total union' of the executive and legislature 'would be productive of tyranny' and commended the balanced nature of the British constitution, in which the executive was a part of the legislature but was not identical with it (ibid.: 153).

At the time when Blackstone wrote, the executive consisted of the king and six or seven ministers. The ministers were chosen, and could be dismissed, by the monarch, so that he was able to exercise a good deal of influence over government policy if he chose to do so. On the other hand, neither he nor his ministers could control Parliament. They could influence its behaviour through the distribution of patronage and the formation of cliques and parties, but MPs were jealous of their independence and were not willing to be dominated by the executive. Neither the executive nor the legislature could control the actions of the courts, in which judges held office for life once they were appointed.

This system of government could be described as both constitutional and parliamentary. It was not in any sense democratic. The House of Commons was elected on a very narrow franchise, and until the 1832 Act less than 5 per cent of the adult population enjoyed the right to vote. This franchise was based on property qualifications that varied from one area to another, and the constituencies themselves were wildly unequal in size and number of electors. There was no machinery for the redistribution of seats to take account of population movements, with the result that some constituencies retained the right to send representatives to Parliament even though their population had dwindled so that only a handful of electors lived there. These constituencies were known as 'rotten boroughs'. Such a representative system was easily manipulated by those who possessed social influence and wealth, and their task was made easier by the absence of any effective laws against bribery and other corrupt practices at elections. Wealthy landowners could put their nominees into seats that were normally uncontested, and it has been estimated that in 1793 about 150 landowners (many of whom were themselves in the House of Lords) controlled almost half the seats in the House of Commons. The Duke of Newcastle alone controlled eleven seats. Moreover, the Treasury could control up to a hundred seats by the careful distribution of patronage, so that the governing group at the time of a general election was normally safe from defeat. Ministries were brought to an end as the result of intrigue among the ruling élite, intervention by the monarch, or failure to get parliamentary support for their policies, but not by the verdict of the electorate.

This system of government was democratized during the course of the nineteenth century. However, no legislative change was made in the powers of the monarch, the two Houses of Parliament and the judiciary. The representative system was transformed by successive extensions of the franchise, and the result was to transform the working of the governmental system without changing its structure, which remains today very similar to that of the eighteenth-century constitution.

The movement for reform

The changes brought about by the Industrial Revolution were the basis of the movement for political reform that developed in the last two decades of the eighteenth century and eventually resulted in the Reform Act of 1832 and the numerous other reforms that followed the Act. The development of industry led to the growth of classes whose fortunes depended on industry, notably mill-owners and manufacturers but also including merchants, tradesmen and skilled artisans. These groups grew in numbers, in wealth and in social influence, but the political system denied them both adequate representation in Parliament and influence over local administration. Their under-representation in the House of Commons was thrown into relief by the growth of large industrial towns that had no parliamentary representative of their own, including Manchester, Birmingham, Leeds and Sheffield.

The campaign for political reform was waged by a number of largely unrelated groups who differed in both their arguments and their methods. There were spokesmen for the industrial and commercial interests who advocated a redistribution of parliamentary seats to take account of population movements and the establishment of franchise qualifications that would be uniform over the whole country, though it was assumed that a property qualification would be retained. There were middle-class societies devoted to political reform who proposed changes of a more sweeping nature, using arguments drawn from the writings of intellectual reformers like Joseph Priestley, Richard Price and Jeremy Bentham. And there were the new political unions, composed mainly of skilled workers, who adopted the revolutionary ideas that Tom Paine had advanced in his pamphlets and in his book *Rights of Man*.

The reformers won their first and most crucial victory in the passage of the Reform Act of 1832. This Act increased the electorate from 5 per cent of the adult population to 7 per cent, which in itself was hardly a revolutionary change. However, this quantitative change in the franchise was less important than two other features of the Act. One of these was that the Act abolished the system of local franchises, which varied from one constituency to the next, and replaced it by a uniform national franchise. The implication of this was that representation was being granted not to areas and municipal corporations but to individuals. The change made further demands for reform inevitable and also deprived the opponents of reform of some of their more persuasive arguments. Until 1832 they had been able to produce the familiar British argument that, although the system might not be logical, it was hallowed by tradition. It would be wrong to deprive boroughs of a right to parliamentary representation that they had long enjoyed; since nobody wanted to increase the size of the House this made it difficult to give direct representation to the new industrial towns; and in any case the residents of these towns should regard themselves as 'virtually represented' by the members for older industrial towns, which had similar interests. After 1832 these points lost all their force, and the opponents of further reform had no firm ground on which to take their stand.

The other feature of the Act that was of considerable significance was the way in which it was passed. In the election of 1831 the proposed reform was the only important issue, and in constituencies up and down the country reformers demanded that the candidates pledge themselves to support it if they were returned. The result was a sweeping victory for the reformers, and the subsequent Parliament was the first one whose members could claim that they had been given a mandate by the electors to pursue a specific policy. Strengthened by this development, the Prime Minister persuaded the King to agree to create sufficient new peers to secure the passage of the Bill through the House of Lords. The threat proved sufficient and the Lords eventually let the Bill go through. The potential supremacy of the people over the Commons was thus made clear for the first time in the election of 1831, and the supremacy of the Commons over the Lords was asserted for the first time just twelve months later. It was this that led Disraeli to remark that 'the aristocratic principle has been destroyed in this country, not by the Reform Act, but by the means by which the Reform Act was passed'.

The immediate effects of the Act on the working of the political system were important even though they were not dramatic. The main consequence was that the choice of government was effectively placed in the hands of the Commons. Some discretion remained with the monarch but the limits within which it could be exercised were narrowed. When a ministry was defeated in the Commons on an issue of confidence, the Prime Minister felt obliged to resign or to ask for a dissolution. If he resigned, the monarch rarely had any choice but to offer the post to the leader of the largest opposition group. In case of a dissolution the question of who should form a government was effectively settled by the votes taken in the first few meetings of the newly elected House. In short, the convention that the government should be collectively responsible to Parliament, and in particular to the House of Commons, was firmly established as a principle of the constitution.

This principle assumed considerable prominence in the middle years of the nineteenth century because the nature and distribution of party loyalties resulted in a series of government defeats. The Irish party consisted of a group of about eighty MPs on whose support no government could rely with any confidence; the Conservatives were split by the repeal of the Corn Laws in 1846 and for many years after were divided into protectionists and free traders; and the Liberal Party had Whig and Radical wings whose differences were occasionally reflected in the division lobbies. Most governments in this period had to depend on more than one group for support, and in any case the discipline within groups was very slack. The consequence was that in the thirty-five years between the first and second Reform Acts ten governments were brought to an end by defeat in the Commons and no government succeeded in staying in office for the entire life of a Parliament, from one general election to the next.

It was in this period that writers with liberal sympathies laid stress on the supremacy of Parliament in the British constitution. Gladstone described the House of Commons as 'the centre of our system' and said that the supremacy of the Commons over the administration was 'the cardinal axiom of the constitution'. Walter Bagehot described the Cabinet as 'a committee of Parliament'. The Duke of Devonshire said that Parliament 'can dismiss a ministry if it is too extravagant, or too economical; it can dismiss a ministry because its government is too stringent or too lax. It does actually and practically in every way, directly govern England, Scotland and Ireland.' Certainly it seemed in this period as if the reformers' aim of parliamentary control of the executive had been achieved. Not only were ten governments brought down in thirty-five years, but also it was established as a convention that each minister should answer to Parliament for the blunders of his department, the first ministerial resignation for this reason occurring in 1855. However, with the franchise extended to less than 10 per cent of the adult population, it could not be said that the House of Commons yet represented anything like the whole nation. In the late 1850s and 1860s the attention of liberals was therefore focused on the need for a further reform of the electoral system.

This reform came in 1867, when Disraeli introduced an Act that almost doubled the electorate in one stroke. For a Conservative leader to seize the initiative in reform in this way was a surprise, and it was said that he 'stole the Liberals' clothes when they were bathing'. It was also an extremely shrewd and far-sighted move; Disraeli realized that the progressive extension of the franchise was inevitable, and that it would relegate his party to the position of a permanent minority unless something could be done to attract lower-class voters to the Tory banner. Few of his colleagues had much confidence in this possibility, but, as R. T. McKenzie once said, Disraeli 'saw the working-class Tory in the British proletariat as the sculptor sees the angel in a rough lump of stone'. History has vindicated his judgement.

Besides extending the franchise, the 1867 Reform Act deprived the House of Commons of the right to decide on the validity of elections in cases of protest, and put questions of this kind within the jurisdiction of the courts. This was a move towards the elimination of corrupt practices in elections, which was carried a great deal further by the adoption of the secret ballot in 1872 and the establishment of effective controls on electoral expenditure, and sanctions against bribery, by the Corrupt Practices Act of 1883.

In 1884 there was yet another extension of the franchise, which increased the electorate by 67 per cent and gave the vote to the great majority of adult men. Perhaps equally important, the Redistribution Act of the following year was the first important step towards the equalization of territorial constituencies. Before this Act the electorates in the most populous constituencies in England were over forty times as big as those in the smallest constituencies; after the Act the ratio was only seven to one.

The result of this second wave of reform, when five major acts were passed in eighteen years, was an electoral system that could reasonably be called democratic. True, it was not until many decades later that the liberal reformers' objective of 'one man, one vote; one vote, one value' was finally achieved. Complete manhood suffrage did not come until 1918. Women acquired the vote in two instalments, those over thirty being grudgingly given the rights of full citizenship in 1918 and their younger sisters getting the same privilege ten years later, when it had become clear to even the most suspicious male that they were not likely to subvert the constitution. The second vote enjoyed by university graduates and some business proprietors was not abolished until 1948. But these later changes, important as they were to the groups concerned, made relatively little difference to the working of the representative system. After 1885, this system ensured that Members of Parliament, and therefore the government, had to keep the support of the greater part of the population if they wished to stay in office, just as the system before 1832 had made it necessary only for them to keep the support of the aristocracy and the country gentry.

The development of party management

Liberal reformers had assumed that the extension of the franchise would make the House of Commons more representative of the nation without in any way diminishing its influence over the administration. Indeed, many reformers thought that the authority and the power of the House would be enhanced if it could claim to reflect all sections of society. However, at this point there occurs a twist in the story. The assumptions of the reformers were not borne out by events, because the most significant political development in the years following the 1867 Reform Act was one that few had foreseen. This was the development of large-scale party organization and a form of party management that made it possible for the government of the day to ensure that its parliamentary supporters would toe the party line on important issues.

Up to 1867 the political parties were simply parliamentary groupings, with some organization inside Parliament but without mass memberships or branches in the constituencies. Elections were fought by individual candidates, not by a party organization. To some extent the candidates gained or lost support according to the popularity of their parties, but generally speaking the main determinants of a candidate's fortunes at the polls were his popularity in the constituency and the success of his personal campaign. It followed that party leaders had very little power over their parliamentary supporters, who could be sure of keeping their seats so long as they kept control of the situation in their constituencies. Sanctions for party discipline did not exist, and backbench revolts were common.

This situation changed after the reforms of 1867 and 1872. The extension of the franchise meant that the more populous constituencies contained several thousand voters, too many for the personal appeal and influence of the candidate to be sufficient to carry the day. The limitations placed on electoral expenses made it impossible for candidates to go on buying large numbers of votes by bribery, lavish entertainment and free beer all round. And the adoption of the secret ballot in 1872 made even the most discreet forms of corruption less effective, since the candidate had no clear way of checking that the voters had honoured their side of the bargain. These changes created a clear need for party organization, at any rate in the urban areas, and the need was quickly met.

This development of party organization in the constituencies might have led to the growth of local party bosses, as in the United States. In fact, for a variety of reasons (of which one was that the political scene happened at that time to be dominated by the two outstanding party leaders of the century, Gladstone and Disraeli) the development led to the emergence of national party organizations in the shape of the National Liberal Federation and the National Union of Conservative Associations. These organizations came to acquire a strategic place in the political system as parliamentary candidates became increasingly dependent on organized support for their election campaigns.

The relationship between these new national party organizations and the parliamentary leaders was not immediately settled. In both parties there was an attempt by ambitious politicians (Joseph Chamberlain on the Liberal side and Lord Randolph Churchill among the Conservatives) to build up the power of the organizations in order to promote their own political aims. But both these attempts failed, and their failure settled the question in favour of the parliamentary leaders. The same period, namely the twenty years following the 1867 Reform Act, also saw the development of efficient party bureaucracies, staffed with professional organizers and propagandists and under the direct control of the parliamentary leaders. It was these bureaucracies, by name the Conservative Central Office and the Central Liberal Association, that undertook to find candidates for local party organizations in need of them, and so were able to hold out the promise of a tangible reward (in the shape of a safe seat) for the loyal party man.

These developments laid the foundation of the party loyalty that has been so conspicuous a feature of the British political scene in the twentieth century. While MPs were entirely dependent on their own efforts and popularity for re-election, they could vote against their party leaders without risking their seats. When they became dependent on organized support for re-election, and the organizations that provided this support were controlled (directly or indirectly) by the party leaders, the independence of backbenchers was sharply diminished.

As it happened, the strength of the government in relation to backbenchers in the House of Commons was also increased by the procedural reforms of the early 1880s, which were introduced in order to frustrate the attempts of the Irish MPs to disrupt government business. The most important of these reforms was the introduction of the Closure, which gave the government effective control over parliamentary time. All these developments, taken together, transformed the relationship between Parliament and the government in the last third of the century. The nature and extent of the transformation is indicated by Table 3.1. As can be seen, the relationship that had developed

Table 3.1 The growth of party loyalty in Parliament

Period	Number of government defeats	Defeats per year (average)
1856–61	52	8.7
1862–7	60	10.0
1868–73	50	8.3
1874–85	70	5.8
1886–91	13	2.2
1892–7	9	1.5
1898–1903	2	0.3
1904–70	34	0.5

by the 1890s continued, without significant change, throughout the first seven decades of the twentieth century. However, it has to be added that in the 1970s the pattern changed again. For reasons that will be examined in Chapter 8, this decade saw a remarkable increase in the frequency of government defeats, yielding sixty-five defeats in the nine years up to the 1979 election (7.2 per year). In the 1980s the number of defeats fell again, with only three in the first ten years of the Thatcher government (0.3 per year), this being the result partly of larger government majorities and partly of Margaret Thatcher's highly effective style of leadership.However, her government had to make repeated concessions to backbenchers to keep their support, to an extent that was unknown before 1970 (see Norton 1985: 29–36).

Conclusion

The democratization of the House of Commons did not strengthen the position of the House in relation to the executive, as might have been expected. Instead, it was the main cause of developments in the party system that gave the executive the means of controlling the House of Commons. The executive remains responsible to Parliament, but since Parliament has become fully representative of the nation the practical significance of this has changed. The nature and significance of ministerial responsibility to Parliament in the twentieth century will be examined in later chapters, but it must not be assumed that they can be summarized in terms of the 'chain of command' implied by liberal views of the constitution.

Further reading

For the ideas of the reformers see Birch (1964) *Representative and Responsible Government*, chs. 3–5; for an examination of the changing relationships between Commons, Lords, Cabinet and monarch see Mackintosh (1977a) *The British Cabinet*, chs. 2–9.

4

THE SURVIVAL OF MEDIEVAL INSTITUTIONS

The development of liberal institutions changed the British political system without completely transforming it. The 'chain of command' concept of government was superimposed on the older system of balance, but the old institutions were not abolished. It is not part of the British political tradition to do away with established institutions, and the modern constitution abounds with practices and offices that have survived from medieval times. Some of these are symbolic and perhaps picturesque but have little or no practical importance; a good example is the procedure by which members of the House of Commons are summoned to the House of Lords for certain formalities by a gentleman dressed in medieval clothes who bears the title of Black Rod. It is not our purpose to discuss formal procedures of this kind, so practices and institutions that no longer play a significant role in the working system of government will be ignored in this book.

There are, however, two surviving medieval institutions that are of considerable importance in the political system. One is the House of Lords, much less powerful than it was but still playing an active part in government. The other is the monarchy, the existence of which affects the whole pattern of government even though the personal powers of the reigning monarch are a pale shadow of what they used to be. The role of these two institutions in the modern political system will now be considered.

The monarchy

Britain has not experienced a political revolution since 1688, when the powers of the monarch were effectively curtailed, and in consequence the institution of the monarchy has survived intact into the age of democracy. In this respect Britain resembles its neighbours in Holland, Belgium and Scandinavia. The main political advantage of retaining a monarchical system in a democracy is that it provides a head of state who has been insulated from party politics since childhood and can therefore be accepted as neutral between the contending parties.

The monarchy has symbolic and social roles as well as a political role, and in its social character the British monarchy differs sharply from its neighbours in northern Europe. Unlike them, it is surrounded by pomp and ceremony that are almost medieval in nature. When combined with the British gift for organizing ceremonial events, this has made the monarchy a considerable tourist attraction as well as generating excitement and admiration among the British people. The British style of monarchy is, however, very much more expensive than the Scandinavian style, and this aroused a good deal of public controversy in 1991 and 1992. Members of the royal family are paid out of public funds for the performance of royal duties, the maintenance of their palaces and castles, and the costs of the royal yacht, royal train and royal aircraft. When Windsor Castle was severely damaged by fire in 1992, a poll showed that most people believed the Queen should pay at least half the cost of the repairs. At the request of the Public Accounts Committee of the House of Commons, the National Audit Office launched an inquiry into the cost to the public of maintaining five of the seven royal palaces and castles.

In 1992 polls showed most citizens believed that the Civil List allowance, the official payment for the performance of royal duties, was being paid to too many members of the royal family. An even larger proportion of citizens, together with many MPs, also objected to the fact that the Queen was paying no income tax on her enormous private income, which comes from investments and is quite distinct from the Civil List payments. The history of this is that from the 1840s (when income tax was introduced) until the late 1930s the monarch paid tax on his or her private income, but that in 1937 this obligation was secretly removed. A newspaper poll in 1992 indicated that over 80 per cent of respondents felt that this concession was inappropriate. In response to these criticisms, it was announced in November 1992 that the Queen would henceforth pay tax at the normal rate on her private income, and that the Prince of Wales would do the same on his income from the Duchy of Cornwall. At the same time, it was stated that Civil List payments would henceforth be paid only to the Queen, the Duke of Edinburgh and the Queen Mother, leaving them to pass some of the money on to other members of the royal family if they wished.

One controversy leads to another, and the Queen's role as employer has also been called into question. It seems that she has demanded and secured exemption from British regulations and conventions about fair employment practices, and has taken advantage of this to maintain a staff that is predominantly male and almost entirely white. In 1992 it was revealed that all the forty-nine top officials at Buckingham Palace were white and all but four of them were male, which critics thought inappropriate in view of the current composition of British society. It was also revealed that the Queen has secured exemption from environmental regulations for royal houses and estates, which displeased critics who believe that these regulations should apply equally to all buildings and estates in the country. The failure of the Prince of Wales's marriage also caused intense public debate about the royal family and the social role of the monarchy, to such an extent that polls in 1996 showed that over a fifth of the British public thought that the country might become a republic after the death of Queen Elizabeth while over half thought it would do so within a further fifty years.

The failed marriage of Prince Charles and Princess Diana received so much publicity around the world that details here would be superfluous. It is sufficient to say that the great majority of the British public regard Prince Charles as mainly to blame and find it difficult to excuse his behaviour in marrying an innocent young women while he was actually in love with another woman, namely Camilla Parker-Bowles. In other ways too he treated Diana badly, such as by not congratulating her on her success in teaching herself how to carry out her royal duties and clearly becoming jealous when she became more popular with the crowds than he was.

In terms of public relations he has also shown up poorly. While Diana became extremely popular with the press, Charles has tended to treat journalists with contempt, as when he was accompanied by a planeload of them on an official visit to Asian countries but refused to speak to them for nine consecutive days. He has sometimes seemed to show a certain contempt for the public also, as when he invited press photographers to portray him teaching his younger son how to shoot birds, when he must, or anyway should, have known that this upper-class pastime is widely unpopular and the Royal Society for the Protection of Birds had over a million members.

In an attempt to restore his popularity, Prince Charles arranged to have an hour-long interview on nationwide television, conducted by one of his supporters, and he commissioned the same man to write a long biography of him. Neither the interview nor the biography was well received by critics or public, partly because some of their contents put him in a poor light and partly because it seemed undignified for him to appear to be 'running for king', as *The Economist* put it. In the interview he said he thought it necessary for the royal family to have a royal yacht and a royal train for their exclusive use, and he has let it be known that the cost of the monarchy does not seem to him to be excessive. It is not easy to discover the overall cost of the monarchy, as many of the figures are buried in the budgets for various government departments. However, when *The Economist* set a team of researchers on the task, they produced Table 4.1 for total public subsidies given to support the British and several other European monarchies, and this speaks for itself.

In January 1997 the royal family, after a much-publicized family conference, embarked on a campaign with three fairly clear objectives, namely to marginalize Princess Diana, to improve the popularity of Prince Charles and if possible to make Camilla Parker-Bowles acceptable to the British public and commonwealth governments as the future Queen Camilla. For the second of these objectives a new team of public relations experts was appointed. It is certain that Charles will become King unless he unexpectedly changes his mind and decides to abdicate, and it is difficult to imagine that a future government would actually take the initiative in converting the country to a republic. The constitutional problems involved in such a change could not easily be

Table 4.1 Public subsidies to European monarchies in 1993

Country	Name	Subsidy in £m
Belgium	King Albert II	5.6
Denmark	Queen Margret II	3.6
Norway	King Harold V	5.1
Sweden	King Carl XVI Gustaf	6.8
United Kingdom	Queen Elizabeth II	54.5

Source: The Economist, 10 December 1994

surmounted, and the whole process, involving agreement on Britain's first written constitution, would take so much Cabinet and parliamentary time that the government would be forced to accept the postponement of the numerous policy changes to pieces of legislation that every government wishes to promote.

It is more likely that there will be a reduction in the extravagant lifestyle of the royal family, with its enormous palaces, castles and houses, vast retinue of personal servants, and four royal aircraft in addition to the yacht and the train. Some Labour MPs would certainly like to see a drastic reduction. However, it is difficult to make firm predictions about this matter. In 1996 John Major announced that his government had decided not to authorize the construction of a new royal yacht after the present one is decommissioned in 1998, as the expense could not be justified. In January 1997, presumably after intense pressure on the government from the royal family, the Minister of Defence told Parliament that a new though smaller royal yacht would be built after all, with a contribution from the Queen towards the cost of furniture and fittings in the royal apartments. In April 1997 the sentence said to be most likely to receive tumultuous applause at Tony Blair's campaign meetings was his promise not to spend £60 million on a new royal yacht while patients were lying on trolleys in hospital corridors (*Sunday Times*, 4 May 1997). Time will tell.

The political role of the monarch has changed dramatically since the beginning of the nineteenth century, though without any legislative measure or other overt action to which a date can be given. To explain how this change took place it will be helpful to distinguish the nature of the Royal Prerogative from the personal discretion enjoyed by the reigning monarch.

The Royal Prerogative is a term that denotes the authority resting with the Crown, as distinct from that resting with Parliament or the courts. Thus, it is within the Royal Prerogative to enter into diplomatic relations with other states and to conclude treaties with them; to command the armed forces, to declare war and to make peace, to appoint judges, to initiate criminal prosecutions and to pardon offenders; to summon, to prorogue and to dissolve Parliament; to appoint ministers, including the Prime Minister; to confer honours, to create peers and to appoint bishops of the Church of England. All these acts, and others, are acts performed in the name of the Crown, and the way in which they are performed cannot be questioned or controlled by the courts. Most of them are equally free from parliamentary control, though some of them are now subject to the influence of parliamentary opinion because ministers themselves are subject to that influence.

The extent of the Royal Prerogative has not diminished appreciably during the last two hundred years. What has happened is that, whereas two hundred years ago the reigning monarch performed many or most of these acts at their own discretion, today the monarch performs the acts on the advice of ministers or other persons. The acts are performed in the name of the Crown, but except in a few special cases the decision is no longer taken by the monarch. The conduct of foreign affairs is in the hands of the Prime Minister and the Cabinet, as are decisions about defence policy; judges are appointed by the monarch on the advice of the Prime Minister or the Lord Chancellor; ministers are appointed on the advice of the Prime Minister, and on that advice alone; honours are conferred and other appointments are made on the advice of a variety of persons.

These changes have not come about as the result of crises or been marked by formal declarations, but have simply emerged over the course of the years. It is not easy to give precise dates for them because the monarch's powers have not been taken away, but have merely fallen into disuse. Thus, with the advantage of hindsight we can now say that the royal power to veto Bills passed by both Houses of Parliament was last used in 1707, but in the 1720s it was not known that this power would never be used again. Equally, we can say that during the latter part of Queen Victoria's reign the monarch lost the power to exercise a positive influence on the Prime Minister's choice of ministers, but Queen Victoria would not have acknowledged that this was the case. At the present time there remain one or two powers of the Royal Prerogative of which the exercise is surrounded by a penumbra of doubt, at any rate in the popular mind, and these will be discussed in the following section.

The powers of the monarch today

An understanding of the position of the monarch today may possibly be helped by drawing on the analogy of the position of a referee at a football match. In one sense the referee is in charge of the match; he tosses the coin to decide which captain shall have choice of ends, he determines the start and finish of the game and only he can declare that a goal has been scored. But the referee exercises this control within strict rules that he did not make and cannot influence. He has the power to give orders to players, but in his exercise of this and other powers he has less freedom of action than anyone else on the field. There are two indiscretions that the referee must at all costs avoid. The first is interfering with the natural course of the game, except when some rule has been violated. The second is partiality to one of the teams, or even the appearance of it. If a referee fails to avoid these mistakes, he will find himself in difficulties, and serious failures of this kind may result in the termination of his career as a referee.

This is a crude analogy, but it may serve to focus attention on some of the difficulties of the monarch's position. She is expected to play a daily part in the government of the country without ever showing the slightest sign of partiality towards one party rather than another or one policy rather than another. Action by her is required at most crises and turning-points of politics, but must never be thought to be interfering with the natural course of political events. The task of the monarch is clearly one of extreme delicacy and it is only by the strict observance of convention that it is possible to keep the monarchy from becoming involved in political controversy. One important convention is that normally only the Prime Minister has access to the monarch, their discussions being entirely secret. When a Prime Minister resigns, other conventions are brought into play, which result in the appointment of a successor.

To delineate the role of the monarch more precisely it will be helpful to give examples of events in recent years that have led to public speculation about the extent of royal discretion. The powers that have been under discussion in this way in the twentieth century are the power to create large numbers of peers, the power to dissolve Parliament and the power to appoint a Prime Minister. After the questions arising from these have been dealt with it will be a fairly simple matter to outline the normal pattern of royal activities in relation to government.

The power to create sufficient new peers to change the majority in the House of Lords is one that has been used once and invoked on two other occasions. It was used in 1712 when Queen Anne created twelve Tory peers to secure a majority in the House of Lords that would support her government's proposals to end the war with France. It was next invoked in 1832, when the King agreed to accede to the Prime Minister's request to create sufficient new peers to swamp the House of Lords if that House refused to pass the Reform Bill. A similar pledge was given by the King in 1910 in connection with the proposal to restrict the powers of the upper chamber over legislation. The government of the day was successful in an election that turned on the issue and once again, as in 1832, the threat of the creation of a large number of new peers was sufficient to induce the House of Lords to pass the Bill in question.

It could be said, therefore, that there is a convention that if the government of the day asks the monarch to overcome the opposition of the Lords to a constitutional reform (or possibly to any important reform) in this way, the monarch is entitled (and perhaps ought) to insist that a general election be held to test the popularity of the government but should accede to the request if the government is successful in the election. In practice, however, this convention is unlikely to be used again. The Parliament Act of 1911 contained its own procedure for overcoming the opposition of the Lords to a legislative measure, after a delay of two years, and the Parliament Act of 1949 (passed under the provisions of the 1911 Act) reduced the period of delay to one year. It is difficult to envisage a measure that would be so urgent that it could not wait twelve months and for this reason it is now unlikely that any government will find it necessary to invoke the threat of swamping the House of Lords with new members.

The existence of the royal power to dissolve Parliament raises two possible questions: whether the monarch could dissolve against the advice of the Prime Minister and whether he or she could refuse to accede to a Prime Minister's request for a dissolution. The answer to the first question is, in all conceivable circumstances, in the negative. In the crisis over Home Rule for Ireland between 1912 and 1914 several Conservative leaders argued that the King had the right, and even the duty, to dissolve Parliament and call for a general election before letting the government proceed with a measure that would put some of His Majesty's loyal subjects under the rule of a government that they would regard as alien. King George V made no public comment on this suggestion, though he wrote to the Prime Minister at length about the prospect of civil war in Ireland and suggested that it would be desirable for a general election to be held before the Home Rule Bill was put through Parliament. The Prime Minister could not accept this suggestion, and it is clear from the correspondence that the King, though extremely anxious about the course of events, did not feel that he could dissolve Parliament any more than he could dismiss his ministers or refuse assent to the Home Rule Bill. If he had done any of these things, he would have provoked a constitutional crisis that would have jeopardized the position of the monarchy itself. Since it is difficult to envisage a situation in which the arguments for royal intervention would be stronger than they were in regard to Home Rule, it is reasonable to conclude that dissolution against the advice of the Prime Minister is not a practical possibility.

The question of whether a monarch can refuse to dissolve when asked to do so is slightly more complex. The key to the question lies in the need for the monarchy to retain its reputation for impartiality between the parties. If the monarch were to refuse a dissolution and the Prime Minister were to resign, it would presumably be necessary to ask the Leader of the Opposition to form a government. If this government were quickly defeated in Parliament, dissolution would be the only possible way out of the ensuing crisis. But this would mean that the monarch would be granting to one Prime Minister what had been refused to another, which would inevitably tend to damage the esteem in which the monarch was held by supporters of the original government. It follows that the practical rule is that the monarch can refuse to grant a dissolution only if it is known that a viable alternative government can be formed. This situation will obtain only when no one party has a majority in the House of Commons, so that there is the possibility of varying coalitions. If one party has an absolute majority and the leader of the party, being Prime Minister, asks for a dissolution, the most that the monarch can do is to express the opinion that the move might be unwise and ask the Prime Minister to give the proposal further consideration. If the Prime Minister adheres to the original position, the monarch has no real choice but to accede to the request.

These points were illustrated by the events of 1923 and 1924. The general election of 1922 had given the Conservative Party a parliamentary majority, and Bonar Law had become Prime Minister. In 1923 Bonar Law became ill and Stanley Baldwin, who succeeded him, wished to call a general election after only a few months in office. The King was unhappy at the prospect of an election when Parliament was only about a year old and he asked the Prime Minister if he would think about the matter further and discuss it with his colleagues. But Baldwin insisted on a dissolution, and the King therefore agreed to his request.

The result of this election was that no one party had a majority in the Commons, and a minority Labour government was formed with the support of the Liberals. Ten months later the Liberals withdrew their support and J. Ramsay MacDonald, the Prime Minister, asked the King for a dissolution. On this occasion the possibility existed of a viable alternative government being formed with Liberal and Conservative support, and the King (anticipating MacDonald's request) had consulted the Liberal and Conservative leaders to see if they would be willing to join in a coalition. As they were not so willing, MacDonald's request was accepted, but it is to be assumed that if a Liberal–Conservative government had been possible the King might have refused to dissolve Parliament and would have been entitled to do so. However, the longer the time that elapses without a monarch exercising this constitutional right, the greater is the likelihood of controversy if it were done.

The third royal power that has sometimes led to uncertainty about the role of the monarch is the power to appoint a Prime Minister. As both main parties now have settled procedures for the election of their leaders no problem can arise if the leading party has a secure majority in Parliament. If the need for a new appointment is created by the defeat of the existing government in an election, the outgoing Prime Minister would advise the Queen to appoint the leader of the victorious party. If a Prime Minister wishes to retire for personal reasons, he or she could be expected (health permitting) to announce that intention so as to give the party time to elect a successor. This was the procedure Harold Wilson followed in 1976. If a Prime Minister should die in office, the Queen would simply wait until the governing party chose its new leader, which need take only a few days. The Queen would then invite the new leader to form a government.

The only circumstance that might require a greater degree of initiative on the part of the monarch would be a general election producing no clear majority for any party. When this occurred in February 1974 the Prime Minister delayed his resignation until after he had tried, but failed, to secure a promise of support from the leader of the Liberal Party. If he had been given this, and had felt that he could also depend on support from the Ulster Unionists, he would presumably have remained in office. Upon his resignation the Queen sent for Harold Wilson, as leader of the Parliamentary Labour Party, and asked him to form a government. She took this step although Labour had thirty-four fewer seats than the other parties combined and could not be certain of getting parliamentary support. Ten days later Wilson told the leaders of the smaller parties that if they did not support his new government he would ask the Queen to dissolve Parliament again and hold another general election. This was a surprising threat for him to make, but it had the desired effect. His government survived without being defeated on a vote of confidence until it gained an overall majority in the election of October 1974.

As there is always the possibility of an indecisive general election, it is worth asking whether the precedent of February 1974 ought to be followed on future occasions. In parliamentary democracies in continental Europe where indecisive elections are the norm, it is common for the Head of State to give a party leader a provisional rather than an outright mandate: to ask that leader to see if he or she can secure parliamentary support and to delay appointing him or her as Prime Minister until an affirmative answer is received. A good case can be made for saying that this is the procedure that ought to be followed if a future British election produces an indecisive result. Wilson's tactic worked well enough in 1974, but on another occasion the smaller parties might not be willing to fall into line. In that case, would the monarch be obliged to dissolve Parliament immediately? It might be thought that the monarch has a duty to the newly elected House of Commons, as well as to the person who has just been asked to form a government. If a second election also produced an indecisive result, would it be proper for the leader of the biggest party to secure yet another dissolution, with the prospect of exhausting the funds of the smaller parties and inducing their supporters to give up in despair?

It can well be argued that if an election produces a Parliament without a majority for any one party, the procedures ought to encourage the formation of a coalition government, which might take time. The appointment of a minority government endowed with the immediate power to threaten the other parties with the prospect of a repeat election does not seem, in principle, to be desirable on democratic grounds. This is a constitutional question on which the experience of other European democracies might be a better guide than the precedent of February 1974.

The normal role of the monarchy in government

The preceding section has outlined the role of the monarch at the various turning-points of politics: when a Prime Minister dies or resigns; when a dissolution of Parliament is proposed; and in cases of acute conflict between the two Houses of Parliament. In addition the monarch plays a small but continuous part in the normal process of government. She opens and closes Parliament each year and delivers the 'speech from the throne' setting out the legislative policy of the government at the beginning of each session. She assents to Bills after they have been passed by both Houses, this assent marking the formal completion of the legislative process. She receives ambassadors from foreign countries. She confers honours of varying degree. And as Head of State and Head of the Commonwealth she occasionally makes state visits to foreign or Commonwealth countries.

In none of these activities does the monarch have much personal discretion. The Prime Minister will always listen respectfully to the monarch's views, but the effective decisions are made by members of the government. The speech from the throne, for instance, is written by the Prime Minister even though it is read by the monarch. It is in this way that the ancient institution of monarchy has been adapted to meet the requirements of a democratic age.

In private discussion the monarch has an opportunity to present her views to the Prime Minister. It is the custom for the monarch to be sent copies of Cabinet papers and to have a brief weekly meeting with the Prime Minister to discuss current issues. The rights of the monarch in these discussions were summarized about a century ago by Bagehot as 'the right to be consulted, the right to encourage, and the right to warn'. But the monarch is not a politician and it should not be thought that the government of the day is likely to be deviated from its chosen course by royal influence.

It is evident that in the twentieth century the monarch is a figurehead rather than an active political force. However, it does not follow that the existence of the monarchy should be regarded as a formality that makes no difference to the political process. On the contrary, the institution of monarchy is extremely important in two different ways.

First, the existence of the Royal Prerogative gives the British government a substantial degree of independence of Parliament in some fields, without giving it so much independence that it cannot be called to account. Thus, the conclusion of international treaties is within the Royal Prerogative, and British diplomats can conduct negotiations and reach agreements without any fear that their work might be undone and their future position undermined by a refusal on the part of Parliament to ratify the agreements made. At the same time Parliament has the right to question the Foreign Secretary and the Prime Minister about their conduct of foreign policy so that these ministers have to explain and justify their actions in public – and to suffer a loss of reputation if their justifications fail to convince.

The institution of monarchy is also important in that it provides a Head of State who constitutes a symbol of the identity and unity of the nation. There is no evidence that a monarchical system of government is in any objective sense better than a republican system, but there can be no doubt that the continued existence of the British monarchy symbolizes in a direct and personal way the continuity and stability of the British political community, and by so doing acts as a focus for the loyalty of British citizens.

The House of Lords

While monarchies are still quite common in the world, the House of Lords is unique among legislative assemblies because of its hereditary element. It has approximately 1,200 members, of whom about 800 are hereditary peers, about 390 are life peers and 25 are Law Lords. Members do not receive a salary, though when they attend debates they can claim expenses, which in 1997 amounted to £66 a day for subsistence and secretarial services, plus £75 for overnight accommodation if they stay away from home. The average attendance is around 300. The composition, powers and activities of the House have been the subject of intermittent controversy throughout the twentieth century.

The House has been in a relatively weak position ever since the passage of the 1832 Reform Act, to which it had agreed only under duress. The fact that the House of Commons could henceforth claim to be based on a national suffrage gave it a degree of moral and political superiority over the second chamber. The convention of collective governmental responsibility to Parliament, as it developed, involved the Commons rather than the Lords. Ministers had to answer questions put to them by peers, but the government was not expected to resign if it was defeated in the Lords.

From the 1880s until the 1960s the House of Lords had a clear Conservative majority, and the use of that majority to defeat legislation promoted by Liberal and Labour governments has inevitably caused controversy. The rejection of the Liberal budget in 1909 particularly outraged the government of the day, which proposed to curtail the legislative power of the Lords and succeeded (with its Irish allies) in winning an election in which this proposal was the only important issue. There followed the Parliament Act of 1911, which abolished the rights of the Lords to hold up Finance Bills and reduced its power of delay over other Bills to a period of two years.

In 1945 the first majority Labour government took office. As the Labour Party had fundamental objections to hereditary peers wielding political power, it has to be asked why this government did not use its large majority in the Commons to abolish the House of Lords and replace it by a more representative second chamber. The answer to this question falls into three parts.

First, the Conservative leader in the Lords announced that his party would abide by a new convention when considering controversial legislation promoted by the Labour government. If the measure had been mentioned in Labour's election manifesto the Conservatives would not use their power in the Lords to obstruct the Bill. They would discuss the details and might suggest amendments, but Bills in this category would not be held up.

Secondly, the Labour Party had no agreed plan for a reformed or new second chamber, and it was clear that any proposal would be highly controversial and would take up a great deal of time. As the new government had a full programme of social and economic legislation to introduce, and it was clear that the Lords did not intend to delay measures of this kind, the government had a strong incentive to put the issue of constitutional reform on one side for the time being.

The third answer is that Labour politicians contemplating a radical reform of the Lords had to face the probability that a reformed House would have more prestige and more influence than the existing House. Since most Labour politicians felt that parliamentary power should be concentrated in the hands of the Commons, they jibbed at the prospect of creating a second chamber that might be an effective rival to the Commons. This dilemma was stated very clearly by Herbert Morrison, who was Lord President of the Council in the 1945 Labour government and had a general responsibility for steering legislation through Parliament:

> The Labour government was not anxious for the rational reform or democratisation of the second chamber, for this would have added to its authority and would have strengthened its position as against that of the House of Commons. Changes which gave the House of Lords a democratic and representative character would have been undemocratic in outcome, for they would have tended to make the Lords the equal of the Commons. . . . The very irrationality of the composition of the House of Lords and its quaintness are safeguards for our modern British democracy.
>
> (Morrison 1954: 194)

The Labour government of 1945–51 therefore made no attempt to change the composition of the Lords, though the 1949 Parliament Act reduced its power of delay from two years to one. It was in fact a Conservative government that made the first attempt to modernize the composition of the House, in the form of the Life Peerages Act of 1958. This measure enabled the Prime Minister to appoint persons of either sex to peerages that are not hereditary. By 1997 the House contained about 390 life peers, many of whom have enjoyed distinguished careers in other walks of life and have improved the quality of debates. As many of them are Labour supporters or Liberal Democrats, the party bias of the House has also been partially corrected.

Another Conservative reform that affected the composition of the House was the Peerage Act of 1963, which enables peers to disclaim their peerages and thus to stand for election to the Commons. In the autumn of 1963 this step was taken by the Earl of Home, upon his being invited to succeed Harold Macmillan as Prime Minister. He could not have accepted this invitation had it not been possible for him to renounce his earldom and acquire a seat in the Commons. In the first ten years after the passage of this Act twelve peers disclaimed their peerages. The Act also admitted women holding hereditary peerages to membership of the House.

These reforms, although welcomed by all parties, did nothing to change the central anomaly of the House, namely the right of hereditary peers to vote on legislative proposals for no better reason than that one of their ancestors had been included in a royal honours list. In 1969, however, a radical reform was proposed by the Labour government and was actually supported by the House of Lords. This Bill provided for a House that would contain 230 working members, all of whom would be appointed and paid, and for a process whereby the hereditary peers would gradually be phased out.

This scheme had been worked out in confidential talks between representatives of the main parties. However, some time before the Bill was drafted the Prime Minister had broken off these talks and in consequence the reform was sponsored by the government alone, so that, although the Conservative front bench gave it tacit support, it did not feel under any obligation to employ party discipline to assist its progress. At the Committee Stage in the Commons it ran into a determined campaign of obstruction from backbenchers on both sides of the House. Labour left-wingers joined in an unprecedented alliance with Conservative right-wingers to frustrate a plan that they disliked for contrasting reasons. For ten days the business of the House was held up by protracted manoeuvres, skilfully planned and executed, until the government simply gave up in disgust and withdrew the Bill. Since this débâcle there have been no more attempts at reform. The Conservatives have no real wish for change, and the Labour Party has had more than one policy. In 1992 Labour proposed that the House should be replaced by an elected chamber representing the various regions of the country, while in the 1997 election manifesto it was stated that reform would be accomplished in three steps if Labour were returned to power. First, the right of hereditary peers to sit in the House would simply be abolished. Second, the criteria for appointing life peers would be revised so that they would 'more accurately reflect the proportion of votes cast at the previous general election', though without giving any one party a majority. Third, a committee of both Houses of Parliament would be appointed to bring forward proposals for further change.

The present role of the Lords

The present functions of the House of Lords are of four main kinds. First, its members question ministers about the activities of the government and stage debates on general issues of national policy. The Lords can discuss issues in a broader frame of reference than is possible in the Commons and they conduct their debates in a less partisan way. As the House includes peers with a wide range of experience, the level of debate is often high. There are top surgeons and physicians to discuss health services, retired generals and admirals to discuss questions of national defence, bishops and archbishops to discuss religious affairs, senior judges to discuss legal issues. However, it is difficult to assess the extent of the practical influence of these debates.

Secondly, the House saves the time of the Commons by giving a first hearing to non-controversial Bills, which subsequently go through the Commons with a minimum of discussion. Since 1945 something like a quarter of all government Bills have had their first reading in the Lords, and in a fair number of cases this has resulted in an appreciable saving of time in the Commons. This way of routing Bills is particularly appropriate when the legislation is complex in a technical sense, such as Bills dealing with company law or the law relating to copyright.

Thirdly, the House of Lords revises the details of Bills sent to it by the Commons. This function has become increasingly important in the twentieth century as the activities of the state have been extended. Legislation has become more voluminous and more complex without any commensurate increase in the amount of time that the House of Commons can devote to it. Many Bills are necessarily pushed through the Commons with less discussion than they need. Detailed consideration of such measures by the Lords is usually welcomed by the Commons, by the government and by the various organizations representing interests likely to be affected by the legislation in question.

Sometimes the Lords make amendments that the Commons subsequently strikes out or revises again, but in most cases detailed amendments in the Lords are acceptable to the government of the day and are endorsed by the Commons when the Bill is referred back. In some cases the amendments are initiated by the government, using discussions in the Lords as an opportunity to refine the original draft. It would be difficult to question the value of this work of revision.

The fourth and most controversial function of the House of Lords is that it occasionally rejects Bills sent to it by the Commons, or amends them in ways that are unacceptable to the majority in the Commons. As it happens, this has been done with increased frequency in recent years. In most cases the Commons majority has reconfirmed its original decision and the Lords have accepted this, but there have been a number of cases since the botched attempt to reform the second chamber in 1969 when opposition in the Lords had led to the abandonment or significant modification of legislative proposals.

These cases can be divided into three categories: cases in which the original proposal was perceived to violate norms about the public interest; cases in which the proposal was thought to be excessively doctrinaire; and cases in which the Lords simply took a more liberal view of the issue than the government and the Commons had done. Before enumerating these cases it must be pointed out that the House of Lords no longer has a working majority of Conservatives. A survey conducted in 1988 indicated that the House contained approximately 525 Conservatives, 125 Labour supporters, 85 Liberals and Social Democrats and 465 peers who described themselves as independent. D. R. Shell has produced a valuable analysis of the affiliations of those members who attended at least one-third of the sittings in earlier sessions, and this is summarized in Table 4.2.

In considering these figures two points should be stressed. One is that the independents are genuinely independent, with voting behaviour that is rather

Table 4.2 Party affiliations in the House of Lords

| Party | Affiliations of members attending one-third of sittings | | |
	1967/8	1975/6	1981/2
Conservative	125	140	153
Labour	95	105	77
Liberal–SDP	19	22	44
Independent	52	63	57
Total	291	330	331

Source: Shell 1985: 20.

unpredictable. The other is that party discipline among Conservative peers is weaker than it is among peers affiliated to the other parties, or for that matter among Conservative MPs; in all the cases mentioned below, Conservatives recorded votes on both sides of the question.

The first category comprises three proposals that were widely perceived to be outrageous, in the sense of being concerned solely to further partisan or sectional interests and being indefensible in wider terms. One of these was advanced in 1969, when the Labour government realized that the outdated system of electoral boundaries was biased in Labour's favour and promoted a Bill to release the Home Secretary from his legal obligation to present an extensive set of boundary revisions for parliamentary approval before the next election. The revisions had been drawn up by impartial commissions and this attempt was immediately perceived to be no more than a blatant move to gerrymander the electoral system. The Lords frustrated this move. In the event the government got its gerrymander anyway, because the Home Secretary persuaded his parliamentary colleagues to reject the revisions he proposed, but at least the government's behaviour was exposed in its true colours.

The second proposal in this category was put forward in 1977, when the Labour government introduced a Bill at the behest of the Transport and General Workers' Union that would have had the effect of extending the control of the dockers' section of this union to workers engaged in packing and unpacking containers at any location within five miles of a registered dock. This was clearly an attempt to further a sectional interest at the expense of the public interest; it would never have passed the Commons on a free vote; and it was rejected by the Lords. When it was reconsidered in the Commons abstentions by Labour MPs prevented it being passed a second time.

The third proposal of this sort was put forward in 1984, in regard to the Conservative government's plan to abolish the Greater London Council and the councils of the other six metropolitan areas. This plan was mentioned in the 1983 Conservative election manifesto and it was made clear that the Lords would not oppose it. However, in 1984 the government proposed an interim measure, pending the adoption of legislation for the abolition of these authorities, whereby the elected members of their councils would be replaced by members nominated by lower-tier authorities. The effect of this proposal, in London and possibly elsewhere, would have been to replace Labour majorities by Conservative majorities without an election. This was perceived to be a partisan move with no general arguments in its favour, and the Lords rejected it. The rejection was reluctantly accepted by the government.

Between 1969 and 1989 there were seven other occasions on which the House of Lords successfully challenged measures that were seen as excessively doctrinaire. In 1975 it secured modifications in a measure that would extend the principle of the closed shop to the profession of journalism, for fear lest a trade union should secure influence over opinions expressed by journalists and editors. In 1980 it rejected a proposal to impose charges for the transport of children to and from school in rural areas. In 1980, and again in 1984, it prevented the sale of municipal housing that was specially designed for the elderly. In 1981 it reduced the scale of financial cuts aimed at the overseas broadcasting services of the BBC. In 1983 it prevented the privatization of the Ordnance Survey, the department responsible for producing all Britain's official maps. In 1984 it prevented the sale of municipal housing that had been specially designed or adapted for handicapped people. The fact that five of these reversals of government policy affected the Conservative government of Margaret Thatcher reflected the tendency of Conservative peers to be suspicious of the right-wing neo-liberal attitudes of this government. Not surprisingly, Conservative peers tend to be traditional Conservatives in their political orientation. (See Shell 1985, for fuller accounts of these and other government defeats in the Lords.)

Finally, there have been several instances since 1969 when the Lords have insisted on liberalizing government measures. In 1971 they secured an amendment of a Bill on nationality so as to protect the rights of immigrants. In 1973 they insisted that free contraceptive services should be made available by the National Health Service. In 1973 they passed an amendment to protect areas of natural beauty from spoliation by reservoirs. In 1984 they secured a limitation on the right of the police to stop citizens in the street to search for incriminating evidence. In 1987 they abolished the use of corporal punishment in state schools, instead of just restricting it as the government had proposed. In 1988 they passed an amendment to the Education Reform Bill guaranteeing university teachers freedom to put forward controversial or unpopular opinions without endangering their jobs or academic privileges. These moves, like the other examples mentioned, illustrate the extent to which the House of Lords has become a moderating influence in British party politics. While the two main parties in the House of Commons both adopted more extreme policies in the 1970s and 1980s, the peers moved towards the centre.

This brief account of the current role of the House of Lords indicates that the House performs valuable functions. It is only because of this that such an anomalous medieval institution has been able to retain influence and respect

Table 4.3 Preferred policy of British electors regarding the House of Lords, 1983

| Preferred policy | Party identification | | | All |
	Conservatives %	Liberal–SDP %	Labour %	electors %
Remain as it is	72	55	44	57
Abolish it and				
replace by nothing	3	6	15	8
Replace by				
different body	6	12	14	10
Some other change	13	21	19	16
Don't know	6	6	8	9

Source: Jowell and Airey 1984: 31.

in the last third of the twentieth century. It remains to be seen whether a reformed second chamber will do better. The general public have been reasonably content with the existing chamber, as is shown by Table 4.3, but are not likely to offer any strong opposition to reform.

Further reading

For a brief analysis of the constitutional powers of the monarch see Marshall (1984) *Constitutional Conventions*, ch. 2; for a discussion of the role of the monarch in the formation of governments, with some European comparisons, see Butler (1983) *Governing without a Majority*; and Waldron (1990) *The Law*, ch. 4; for a summary of relations between the monarch and the Cabinet see Mackintosh (1977a) *The British Cabinet*, ch. 9; on the House of Lords see Shell (1985) 'The House of Lords and the Thatcher government'.

Part III

THE ACTORS AND THEIR ROLES

5

POLITICAL PARTIES

The political actors in a democratic system of government include electors and voters, pressure group spokesmen and lobbyists, political parties, candidates and elected politicians, government ministers, civil servants and local officials. In modern Britain the political parties are so visible, and an understanding of their role is so essential for an understanding of the system, that it is appropriate to deal with the parties before discussing the various other actors.

The nature of the party system

The main characteristics of the party system can easily be outlined. First, it has been dominated for well over a century by two major parties (though not always the same two), with smaller parties playing only a minor role. This is partly because of the relative unimportance of social cleavages other than the horizontal cleavage of class, partly because the electoral system favours the larger parties and discriminates against the smaller ones.

Secondly, the major parties are parties of mass membership, having branches throughout the country and collecting monthly or annual subscriptions from their members. In the 1950s the parties had well over 3 million individual members between them, in addition to about 5 million 'affiliated members' of the Labour Party, who subscribed through their trade unions. As a consequence of the growth of other leisure-time activities party membership has been falling steadily since that time, but in 1997 the total of individual members was still about 1 million. Many members (including nearly all of Labour's affiliated members) do nothing for the party apart from subscribing; many others take part in social and fund-raising activities; and a minority are active in party organization or electoral campaigning. Local studies suggest that about 1 per cent of the electorate are willing to do voluntary work during elections, which would produce an average of about 500 workers per constituency if this were the general pattern. The number who actually turn out is probably a little less than this in most areas, but as there are no paid canvassers in British elections these party workers fulfil an important function during the campaign.

Thirdly, the parties are highly centralized in spite of their mass member-ships. In the United States the real party managers operate at state and local level, the national parties being loose alliances formed for electoral purposes. But in Britain the local party branches have little real power except over the nomination of candidates. Local branches are encouraged to discuss questions of policy and they send in resolutions for debate at the annual conference, but in practice their influence on national party policy is for the most part rather slender.

Fourthly, both main parties, and some of the smaller ones too, are extremely active in publishing, producing a steady stream of policy proposals and pamphlets for discussion. In this way also they are quite unlike their American counter-parts, which publish practically nothing.

Until 1918 the two main parties were the Conservative and Liberal Parties, but the latter was displaced by the Labour Party shortly after that date. The rise of Labour was probably inevitable, given the extension of the franchise in 1884 and 1918 to large numbers of working-class citizens who had not formed loyalties to either of the other parties. Socialist parties have come to play a major role in all industrial democracies in the twentieth century, with the sole exceptions of the United States and Canada. However, why Labour displaced the Liberals rather than the Conservatives is a question that deserves a word of explanation.

One factor is social. Between the 1880s and 1918 the Liberals lost much of their basic constituency, the ambitious entrepreneurial class of the nineteenth century, whose members felt themselves to be relative newcomers on the social scene and who wanted reforms. They were gradually transformed into a pros-perous business class, with a sense of being part of the British establishment. They transferred their allegiance to the Conservative Party, partly for social reasons and partly because the Conservatives seemed better prepared to defend business interests against the threat posed by the trade unions. Another reason is that the 1914 war deprived the Liberals of one of their policy planks; having stood for generations as the party of international peace and friend-ship, they had led Britain into that disastrous conflict and could no longer sustain the role.

Other factors were tactical and personal. The Liberals encouraged the infant labour movement, when their party's interests would have been better served by an attempt to throttle their rival at birth. During the war the party was badly split by a conflict between its two leading figures, Asquith and Lloyd George. By 1918 the Liberal Party was doomed to decline. That it had become a small third party by 1924, with only 40 MPs to Labour's 151, demonstrates that the British electoral system does not necessarily act as an obstacle to the realignment of the party system. On the contrary, the system hastened the process of transition in this period; under a system of proportional representa-tion the Liberal Party would have retained far more seats than it did in 1924 and would have remained a force to be reckoned with right up to the present day. However, the Liberals did not become converted to the principle of proportional representation until just after they had lost the power to establish such a system – which was not just a tactical error but a major strategic blunder.

Since 1924 the party system has been dominated by the Conservative and Labour parties, which are very different in their doctrines and organization. However, the Labour Party has not been as successful as the Liberal Party was before its decline. From 1860 until 1918, the Liberals were in power more frequently than the Conservatives, while from 1924 to 1997 the country had Labour governments for twenty years but Conservative governments or Conservative-led coalition governments for fifty-three years. In the remainder of this chapter the two main parties will be analysed in turn, followed by a discussion of the smaller parties.

The Conservative Party

The Conservative Party has existed under that name since the 1830s, though it was first simply an organized group of MPs and peers and did not develop local branches until the extension of the franchise in 1867. In that year local Conservative associations were formed and a body called the National Union of Conservative Associations was established. Large numbers of supporters quickly rallied to the cause and by 1875 there were already 472 branches in the constituencies (Norton and Aughey 1981: 204).

In discussing the structure and working of the party it is necessary to distinguish between the party at Westminster and the party in the country. At Westminster the party has a Central Office staffed by professional organizers, which was established in 1870, a committee of backbench MPs that first met in 1922 and is known simply as the 1922 Committee, and the Conservative Research Department, which was formed immediately after the Second World War. In the country there are 640 constituency associations, with a membership that was estimated to be about 1.5 million in 1974 (Pinto-Duschinsky 1985: 331) but had fallen to no more than a third of that by 1997. There are also numerous branches of the Young Conservatives, which had a membership of 157,000 in their peak year of 1949, but have declined since. In 1978 they were said to have approximately 27,500 members (Norton and Aughey 1981: 213), and in the 1990s fewer still.

The income of the party has come mostly from individual members. The Conservative associations (largely middle class in their membership) are highly sociable groups, devoting much energy to regular whist drives, occasional dances and garden parties, and innumerable coffee mornings and sherry parties in members' houses. All of these activities are so arranged that they contribute in some degree to party funds. In 1975/6 the local associations raised about £4.5 million, of which about 5 per cent came from business firms and the rest from individual subscriptions and fund-raising activities. In 1990/1 they raised about £15 million.

The national head office of the party had an income of just under £2 million in 1975/6, of which it is estimated that about two-thirds came from business firms (Norton and Aughey 1981: 216). Overall, business contributions in that financial year therefore amounted to between 20 and 25 per cent of total income. The smallness of this proportion is significant. Although the party tends to favour business interests as against labour interests, it has never been captured by business interests. As has often been noted, business firms need the support of the Conservative Party more than the Conservative Party needs business support.

It may fairly be observed that this organization has proved itself to be very efficient over the years. Throughout the period 1924–92 the Conservative Party had more members than all the other parties put together, and for much of this period it had twice as many as the rest. It has also been able to employ far more full-time paid constituency organizers, the figures in 1979 being 365 for the Conservatives compared with 80 for the Labour Party and 15 for the Liberals (Rose 1980a: 255). However, in the past decade the party has been faced with a declining membership and a worsening financial situation.

One reason for this is that the average age of members has increased substantially, with the party finding it difficult to recruit young people to replace those dying or too old to participate. The Young Conservatives have declined in numbers from about 150,000 throughout the 1950s to between 6,000 and 9,000 in 1993 (see Seldon and Ball 1994: 275). The Federation of Conservative Students was the scene of ideological squabbles in the 1980s and received so much bad publicity that it was disbanded by Central Office in 1986. It has been replaced by a body called the Conservative Collegiate Forum, but this has no more members than the Young Conservatives (ibid.: 276). Another social factor has been the tendency, greatly increased since the 1970s, for wives to pursue careers of their own, which has been particularly damaging to the Conservative Party as, unlike Labour, it has long had more women members than men.

Another important reason is the growth of ideological disputes within the party. In the 1980s many members were upset by Thatcher's move to the right and withdrew from their local party branches. In 1990 many of Thatcher's supporters were upset by her dismissal and regarded Major as an uninspiring successor. Since 1992 the ever-increasing split in the parliamentary party about Britain's role in the European Community has led to a further drainage. As no official membership figures are published it is impossible to be precise about the present situation, but it appears that the party had fewer than half a million members at the time of the 1997 election and the number has declined further as a consequence of defeat. By 1998 the party, for the first time in history, had fewer members than Labour.

The decline in membership, combined with the greatly increased costs of publicity and the salaries of officials, has led to serious financial difficulties. At the end of the 1992 election campaign the national party was heavily in debt.

One consequence of this has been a marked decline in the number of full-time constituency agents. This went down from 365 in 1979 to under 230 in late 1983. The number rose to 299 for the 1992 general election, but fell again after that to 230 in December 1993 (see Seldon and Ball 1994: 285).

The leader of the party is elected by Conservative MPs. This is a relatively new procedure, as up until 1965 the leader 'emerged' as the result of discussions between a handful of senior figures in the party, who consulted wider groups only in an informal way. In 1965 Edward Heath became the first leader chosen by election. Ironically, in 1975 he also became the first leader to be overthrown by the vote of his colleagues, having put himself up for re-election to stem complaints about his leadership, only to find himself defeated by Margaret Thatcher.

The present procedure is open and democratic to a degree that is surprising in view of the élitist procedures that were used before 1965. There has to be a leadership election between three and six months after each general election, with provision for annual elections thereafter if formal challenges are mounted. Thatcher easily defeated a challenge in 1989, by securing a large majority on the first ballot. In 1990 she got a majority on the first ballot, but failed to get the 15 per cent margin over her challenger, Michael Heseltine, that the party rules require. After consulting her Cabinet colleagues, she stood down two days later, and on the second ballot John Major defeated Heseltine. Major became Prime Minister only thirteen days after Heseltine's challenge was announced, with minimum disruption of government.

Policy-making within the party is formally the responsibility of the leader, who is not bound by resolutions of the annual conference and does not have to report to anything in the nature of an executive committee. The leader controls the Central Office and appoints the party chairman. On paper the powers of the leader are formidable, and far greater than those of the leader of the Parliamentary Labour Party. In practice the Conservative leader has to be careful to retain the support of a majority within the party, and would therefore be unwise to ignore substantial currents of opinion among colleagues.

Even under the old procedure, the party had ways of putting a leader under pressure. Austen Chamberlain was effectively ditched as leader in 1922, Neville Chamberlain was forced to resign from the office of Prime Minister in 1940, Eden and Macmillan had to cope with criticism, and Douglas-Home was gently persuaded to step down after agreeing to the new selection procedure in 1965. The fate that overtook Heath and Thatcher has driven the lesson home. The Conservative leader has enormous scope for leadership, but if it is not exercised effectively the leader will face trouble.

Conservative doctrines

Conservative doctrines have become a topic of controversy since Margaret Thatcher became leader, as in the crucial sphere of economic policy she took the party along unfamiliar paths. This will become clear if I first outline the main tenets of traditional Conservatism and then indicate the nature of Thatcher's departure from these tenets.

Traditional Conservatism is a coherent doctrine that can be summarized under six main headings. In the first place, there is a conservative view of human nature that is best described as sceptical. Liberals have always taken an optimistic view of human nature, believing that people are naturally good and well intentioned, though often corrupted by society. Socialists dislike the whole concept, believing that human behaviour is shaped by social forces rather than by anything as intrinsic as human nature. Conservatives believe that children are naturally selfish and greedy and need to be educated out of this condition by socializing institutions and procedures. For this reason they support the nuclear family, emphasize the importance of education and stress the social role of religion. The argument is that the more people are socialized, the more co-operative they will be and the less need there will be for police, courts and prisons.

Secondly, Conservatives have a view of what society is or should be like. Liberals believe that society is (or should be thought of as) a collection of individuals, each pursuing his own interests in a peaceful way. Socialists believe that under the capitalist system society is divided into classes, with interests that necessarily conflict. Conservatives, on the other hand, believe that a society, if it operates properly, is an organic unity of people and groups who are bound together by feelings of mutual obligation. This belief leads Conservatives to a constant emphasis on the importance of national unity. In the two decades following the Second World War, the theme of 'one nation' was stressed in their propaganda. In the 1983 election they used large posters depicting a black man, with the slogan 'Labour says he's black. Tories say he's British'.

Thirdly, Conservatives are not egalitarians. They regard human inequality as an inescapable fact of life, and insist that those more fortunate in their birth or more successful in their careers have a social and moral obligation to help fellow-citizens who are less fortunate or less successful. This belief has led in the past to an emphasis on the duty of the upper classes to give part of their time to unpaid public service and on the duty of landowners to look after their tenants. In the modern era it has led the Conservative Party to join the other main parties in supporting social services, and to the slogan 'the ladder and the safety net'.

Fourthly, Conservative theorists and leaders have a theory of political knowledge derived from the writings of Edmund Burke. In summary, they believe that individual human reason is not adequate to the task of working out a theory of good government from scratch. Instead of attempting this, people should build on the wisdom of past generations, which is embodied in the political institutions and traditions that the present generation has inherited. Burke was unusual among politicians of his day (he was an MP for many years) in supporting the revolution in the American colonies while being vehemently opposed to the French Revolution. His reason for drawing this sharp distinction was that the American colonists were defending their existing rights to legislate for themselves (particularly regarding taxation) whereas the French revolutionaries were insisting on the importance of theoretical, non-existing rights and attempting to remodel society in the light of theories devised by intellectuals. He predicted that the American Revolution would succeed while the French Revolution would lead to a reaction and the restoration of the old regime, which is just what happened.

Fifthly, and following directly from this fourth point, Conservatives are opposed to radical changes in institutions and policies. It is necessary to adjust to technological and social changes, but politicians should do this in a pragmatic way. They should avoid the temptation to prepare a blueprint of the future. The government should respond to social changes and popular pressures, but should not try to impose its own vision of the future on society.

Finally, if Conservatives had to define the proper role of government in a word, they would say it is protective. Political leaders should use their authority to protect the weaker members of society against exploitation. Conservative theorists point proudly to the fact that in the nineteenth century it was the Conservative Party that promoted laws protecting women and children against exploitation by industrialists, and regulating the length of the working day in factories. The Liberals of that period were representing the interests of the factory owners, while Conservatives, representing the traditional ruling classes, had attitudes that were in some respects more humane. A recent Chairman of the Conservative Party, referring in his memoirs to the protective role of the state in society, said that Conservative attitudes 'may be stigmatized as paternal, but why not? We are, or should be, a family. I don't find paternal an offensive word' (Carrington 1988: 375).

In another sense of being protective, political leaders should protect the institutions and traditions of society against groups who seek radical change. They should also, of course, protect the interests of the national society against threats from outside. Whereas nearly all Liberals and some socialists stress the ideals of international friendship and brotherhood, Conservatives stress the importance of national defence and skilled diplomacy. Labour governments reluctantly spend money on arms but Conservative governments do so gladly. The level of expenditure does not vary greatly, but the attitude tends to be different.

These beliefs have led Conservative governments in the past to accept most of the reforms introduced by previous Liberal and Labour governments, while rejecting those that seemed excessively radical or doctrinaire. When the Conservatives returned to power after the dynamic Labour government of 1945–51, they denationalized road haulage and the steel industry, ended food and petrol rationing and scrapped Labour's plans to modify the rights of land-owners. However, they left four other major industries (gas, electricity, railways and coal-mining) in public ownership, accepted Labour's extensions to the social services and continued the policy of maintaining full employment by exercising control over the monetary and fiscal system. The elements of continuity were greater than the elements of change.

Among postwar leaders, Churchill, Eden, Macmillan and Douglas-Home embraced all the tenets of conservative theory outlined above. Edward Heath was slightly different, in that he adopted the role of a rational planner in several spheres of policy. Heath created the Central Policy Review Staff as a high-powered planning unit reporting directly to the Cabinet. He introduced a legal framework for the conduct of industrial relations. He modernized local government and merged traditional authorities to create larger units. He introduced a national policy for the control of wage and salary increases. Most of these innovations have since been scrapped, but they certainly mark Heath as a planner – some would say a technocrat – rather than a traditional conservative.

The decisive break came, however, with the election of Margaret Thatcher as party leader. She believed passionately that her role was to lead the country in a new direction rather than to conserve existing values and practices. The direction in which she pointed, both by policy and by exhortation, was towards the restoration of the entrepreneurial spirit that flourished in Britain from the beginning of the Industrial Revolution in the 1760s until its maturity in the 1880s. As an individualist, Thatcher believed that the British people had gone soft and must be stimulated into recovering the adventurous risk-taking attitudes that the industrialists and merchants of earlier generations displayed. A necessary step in this stimulation was to reduce the dependence of citizens on government by reducing the extent of state intervention in economic affairs. In 1977 the party published a booklet called *The Right Approach to the Economy*, which contained the following statement, signifying an attitude different from that of all previous postwar governments.

> We believe that government knows less about business than business-men, less about investment than investors, and less about pay bargaining than trade union negotiators and employers. We think we understand the limitations on what a government alone can do.
>
> (Quoted in Layton-Henry 1980: 26)

These attitudes are those of an old-fashioned liberal rather than those of a conservative. In her economic policies Thatcher was undoubtedly a neo-liberal, and in her style she was (as she herself proclaimed) a radical. She declared more than once that she was 'a conviction politician', and convictions on the part of the Prime Minister about how society should be changed are not really compatible with traditional conservative beliefs about the proper role of government. Margaret Thatcher was therefore a controversial leader whose economic policies had numerous critics among the parliamentary Conservative Party. It is significant that the event that established the clear control she acquired over the party was the Falkland Islands war, for in this conflict she behaved exactly as Conservative leaders are expected to behave, rallying the country behind her in a powerful defence of national interests against a challenge by foreigners.

Controversial or not, Margaret Thatcher had acquired a very firm grip on the party by 1983 and she promoted colleagues who shared her views. Her economic policies, including a very extensive programme of privatization, have changed the British economy in the way that she wanted and have contributed to a period of growth that began in 1982 and continued without check throughout the 1980s. She is the only Conservative leader to have given her name to a doctrine, namely 'Thatcherism', and it is fair to conclude that she has modified the character of conservative doctrine in respect of economic issues.

Her influence on social policy is more difficult to assess. She talked in disparaging terms of 'the nanny state', which seemed to imply a less caring and protective attitude towards the social services. In practice, however, expenditure on the social services increased in real terms during her period of office. This is even true of the health service, which is underfinanced in comparison with the services in other advanced industrial societies. Britain does not spend enough or have enough doctors to provide a service as good as those of France, Germany, Switzerland or Canada. The administrative reforms introduced in 1989, though described as radical by both supporters and critics, did not make significant improvements, nor, on the other hand, did they involve any retreat from the postwar commitment by all British governments to a universal system of health care. The policy statements produced during the 1997 election campaign revealed no real differences between the parties in respect of health service finances, although the British Medical Association has predicted that the hospital system will be in a severe state of crisis unless expenditure on it is quickly boosted to a much greater extent than either main party is committed to.

The educational reforms launched in 1988 were considerably more radical, involving more control of the curriculum by the national government, more variety in types of school and more parental choice regarding the schools attended by their children. However, it cannot be said that these reforms are out of line with traditional conservative views about education. As Thatcher was a whole-hearted conservative in respect of law and order, foreign affairs and defence, the overall conclusion must be that Thatcherism involved a changed emphasis in economic policy but the maintenance of traditional conservative approaches in other fields of policy.

John Major had a more consensual style than Thatcher and was more willing to spend government money on the arts, sport and other good causes, but in his seven years in power his government's policies on the economy, privatization, education and health were essentially the same as the policies pursued by the Thatcher government of which he had been a member.

In 1992 the Conservatives won a narrow election victory, but in the five following years the party developed an internal schism that ruined its chances of re-election. Its massive defeat in the election of May 1997 ended exactly eighteen years of power, the longest period than any party has governed the country without a break since the Reform Act of 1832.

The cause of this schism was a disagreement over Britain's policies regarding the European Community. Between June 1990 and February 1992 the heads of government of all EC states held a series of meetings designed to further the objective of increasing economic and political unity that had always been supported by the original six members. The final result was the Maastricht treaty signed in the Dutch town of that name. This was an immensely long and complicated treaty made even more difficult to understand than it needed to be by the fact that it was poorly drafted. To simplify matters drastically, the Treaty provides for reforms in the existing European Community to take it farther along the road to economic and monetary union (EMU), together with the two other 'pillars' of a new over-arching organization called the European Union. The second pillar is concerned with foreign policy, defence and security while the third deals with citizenship, justice and domestic affairs. The Treaty made steps towards the objective of its sponsors by proposing co-operation and unity within each pillar, and it also regulated the relationships between the organizations responsible for negotiations and policies within the pillars.

The British government, reflecting the wishes of most British electors, dragged its feet in the moves towards unity in all three spheres of policy, with John Major particularly determined to avoid Britain being committed to the provisions designed to promote EMU. One of these provisions, in the Social Chapter, would compel the governments of all member states to harmonize their economic policies and gradually to surrender control over most aspects of economic policy, the labour market and budgetary policy to the European Commission, subject to guidelines to be established by weighted majority vote in the Council of Ministers. The other provision was that following the harmonization of budgetary policy and the achievement of various specified objectives about the rate of inflation, the national debt and so forth, the states would then agree to the establishment of a single European currency and central bank by January 1999.

After much patient negotiation, Major succeeded in watering down some of the provisions in the second and third protocols and in persuading the other leaders that Britain could be permitted to opt out of the Social Chapter and the commitment to a single currency. He then signed the Treaty, subject to ratification by the British Parliament, which had the advantage that Britain would continue to be represented on all the committees, including those dealing with the establishment of a single currency, and would also have the chance to opt in to the Social Chapter if a future government decided to do so. This aroused little enthusiasm, but in the first major parliamentary vote on the issue, in May 1992, the Treaty was nevertheless given approval in principle by 226 votes to 92, with the dissenters (including 23 Conservatives) drawn from all parties apart from the Liberal Democrats, as were about 220 abstainers. However, to secure this positive vote Major promised that the detailed provisions of the Treaty would also be put to parliamentary votes in the coming months.

This concession had serious consequences, for in the following months there were two significant changes in the attitudes of parliamentarians which spelled the beginning of disaster for the Conservative Party. One of these changes was that a group of Conservative backbenchers came to the view that the future of Britain as a more-or-less independent state required the rejection of the Treaty (over which Britain, like all member states, had a veto) and decided to vote accordingly in Parliament. Their reasons are entirely understandable. It had become clear in statements made in (or leaked from) Brussels that the European Commission had elaborate plans to take over completely the direction of economic policy, financial policy and industrial relations in the member states in the years after the Treaty came into effect.

In June 1992 the Danish electorate had rejected the Treaty in a referendum, which led *The Times* to produce a banner headline on the front page reading 'Denmark's no vote leaves Maastricht Treaty in tatters', and *The Economist* to declare that 'the gamble of the Treaty on European Union has failed'. While much of the British popular press expressed pleasure in this development, Major played a leading part in persuading other governments to let Denmark have a similar kind of opt-out from the Social Chapter and the single currency that he had secured for Britain and persuading the Danish government to hold another referendum to get a positive vote, which duly happened. When French electors endorsed the Treaty by only 51 to 49 per cent it became evident that the French public did not share the enthusiasm for European integration shown by their governments. When a reliable national poll in Britain revealed that the opponents of Maastricht among the electors were twice as numerous as its supporters, it became evident that if Major held a referendum the Treaty would in all probability be rejected, and that if he had held it before the French referendum a negative vote in Britain might have persuaded 1 per cent of the French electors to change their minds, so that the whole Treaty would have been killed and, happily for Britain, the Franco-German partnership which dominates Community policy would have been undermined.

The other significant change is that the Labour Party withdrew the support it had originally given to the Treaty, in the form negotiated by Major, on the ground that Britain should not opt out of the Social Chapter. Their reasons for this are also entirely understandable. British trade unions pressed the party to favour the Social Chapter when they realized that the European Commission, under pressure from Germany, had plans to force member states to follow the German example of placing a legal limit on the hours of overtime worked, discouraging part-time work and giving workers in large firms the right to be represented on boards of management, given detailed information on company policies and consulted on lay-offs. All these were objectives of British unions which they had absolutely no chance of securing under Conservative governments. Any doubts by party leaders were swept away by union pressure and by the realization that if they joined with Conservative dissidents in parliamentary votes they might be able to bring down the government.

The result of these developments was that, when the detailed provisions of the Treaty were presented to Parliament for ratification, Major and his immediate colleagues found themselves faced with opposition from both flanks, with each set of opponents expressing straightforward and sometimes passionate support for clear positions of principle. In response, Major's constantly reiterated argument was that as he had enabled Britain to opt out from the most objectionable provisions, ratifying the Treaty as a whole would do no harm. This sounded like a feeble argument when compared with the clear convictions of his opponents.

As the protracted debates dragged on, the government frequently faced defeat and on two issues was defeated, with Major avoiding a general election after the second defeat only by holding another debate on a motion of confidence and getting the support of the Ulster Unionists. The Treaty was eventually ratified in full, but the result of the whole affair for Major was that in little more than twelve months his image had changed from that of triumphant campaigner who had snatched an electoral victory from the jaws of defeat into that of a rather weak Prime Minister.

In the following four years the position of the party moved from poor to bad to worse. The debates over Maastricht had led many other MPs to sympathize with the small group of active dissenters, and several developments that could not have been predicted led the European Union to become increasingly unpopular within both the party and the country as a whole. One of these was Britain's fishing dispute with Spain, when the Union refused to prevent Spanish trawlers from using part of the fishing quota that had originally been allocated to British fishermen. While this bald statement oversimplifies a complex issue, this was how most British mass media presented the matter. Another and more serious question was the response to mad cow disease.

This disease was and is surrounded with scientific puzzles. While it is generally accepted that it was caused by a new kind of cattle feed introduced in the 1980s, nobody knows for certain why it has affected over 100,000 British cattle but only a handful of cattle in other European countries and North America that were given almost identical feed. Nor is it known for certain whether it can be passed on from cows to their calves, or why, assuming it can be transmitted to humans, it had affected only 17 young people by May 1997 and not the 30 or 40 million other British residents who had been eating beef over the critical years.

What can be said for certain is that the matter has been handled clumsily by almost all the politicians involved. The British Ministers of Agriculture and Health were badly at fault for having made no adequate contingency plans for handling the announcement that a neurologist had identified ten cases of people who had contracted a rare and deadly disease linked with mad cow disease. This announcement produced a panicky reaction from British tabloids and a savage decision by a committee of the European community, which immediately banned the export of British beef not only to the rest of the Community but also to the rest of the world and covered not only beef itself but all products containing components derived from beef, such as cheese and numerous cosmetics.

There was no scientific justification for such a wide coverage of the ban, and a committee of veterinary scientists and doctors appointed by the European Commission duly recommended, after studying the matter, that the ban be relaxed. However, when this recommendation came before a committee of politicians for ratification, the committee decided by a majority vote to reject the advice of their experts. This decision, made under German influence, seemed to be simply vindictive. None of this was Major's fault, but he assumed partial responsibility for it by refusing to dismiss the Minister of Agriculture, which would have been the natural thing to do when it emerged that the Ministry had been lax not only in public relations but also in enforcing its regulation that all British cattle affected by the disease should immediately be sent for slaughter separately from healthy cattle and in ensuring that all British abattoirs maintained acceptable standards of hygiene. Then Major took the issue to a special meeting of European heads of government in June 1996 and signed an agreement for the relaxation of the ban that he described as a victory but was in fact extremely harsh, involving the immediate slaughter of another 100,000 British cattle that remained healthy. A little later, following a new scientific report by a research team at Oxford University suggesting that only 40,000 more cattle need be slaughtered, Major repudiated his agreement, a move that infuriated other heads of government and led a spokesman for the European Commission to suggest that in Brussels they were considering some form of financial retaliation.

These developments widened support among Conservative MPs for the Eurosceptics, as they came to be called, as did two other developments that undermined the government's position that, given the opt-out, signing the Maastricht Treaty would 'do no harm' to British interests, as the government perceived them. One was that a ban limiting overtime in Britain, as in the other countries, was passed under the 'health and safety' provisions of the Treaty, over which Britain had no veto as a majority vote was enough. A case can be made for limiting overtime, and the impact of the rule on Britain has been greatly reduced by the success of British civil servants, working behind the scenes in advance of the vote, in securing exemption from the rule for groups, such as junior hospital doctors, for whom a strong case can be made. Nevertheless, the decision showed that the opt-out from the Social Chapter can be circumvented. The other development was that when Britain appealed to the European Court of Justice against the ban on beef exports to countries outside the European Union the appeal was rejected, partly on the ground that whereas the commitment to European unity was only in the preamble to the Treaty of Rome, and therefore not binding, it had been transferred to the main text of the Maastricht Treaty. The British judge on the court broke his normal silence to complain that the position of British ministers seemed to be that they had not really meant what they did when they approved that part of the Treaty.

The consequence of these various developments was that more and more Conservative MPs moved to the Eurosceptical position. At one point eighty declared themselves to have done so, and a number of them, including Major's first Chancellor of the Exchequer, adopted the radical view that Britain should withdraw from the European Union altogether. The Cabinet became visibly split, and Major emphasized this by describing the four Eurosceptical Cabinet ministers as 'the four bastards' at a BBC party where his remarks were recorded by a concealed microphone and subsequently published. In June 1995 one of the dissidents, John Redwood, competed with Major in a party leadership election and won 89 votes. From that time onwards it seemed that the Eurosceptics had given up hope of a Conservative victory in the next general election and were manoeuvring instead to replace Major as party leader after defeat.

The party as a whole was greatly weakened by the Eurosceptical stance adopted by influential right-wing newspapers, which repeatedly drew public attention to the nefarious plans being made in Brussels and kept giving head-lines to the divisions in the Conservative Party. Between 1995 and 1997 British Conservatives seemed to be bent on a kind of collective suicide, so that their defeat in the general election became almost inevitable. Labour might well have won in any case, of course, as the government looked rather tired and there was a widespread feeling in the country that it was time for a change, but it was Maastricht that wounded the Conservative Party, perhaps for many years to come.

As the foregoing paragraphs have been by implication very critical of John Major, it is fair to add that he is a highly talented and honest politician who was very unlucky during his tenure of 10 Downing Street from 1990 to 1997. The non-partisan The Economist observed in December 1992 that 'the main snag for Mr. Major is that Britain is lumbered with this ghastly mess called Maastricht but all the alternatives are worse' (The Economist, 19 December 1992). A reasonable case can be made for saying that he was wise to keep Britain's options open. As a constitutionalist, he was scrupulous in making it easy for a future government to reverse his policies. It is not clear how any Prime Minister could have coped with the hostility towards Britain shown by other European leaders when it emerged that mad cow disease could be trans-mitted to humans.

The whole story illustrates the generalization about British political attitudes made in the first chapter of this book, that the British people like to be governed by a united party presided over by a strong leader. Millions of electors expressed hatred for Margaret Thatcher for her attitudes and policies, but they respected her for her dominant leadership, and her party won large majorities in three successive general elections. Hardly anyone hates John Major, but he is perceived as politically weak and has suffered accordingly. As Crewe has pointed out, the dramatic fall in his personal standing in the polls was more a consequence than a cause of his party's fall in popularity (Crewe 1996: 433), but it remains true that he presided over an increasingly divided and tired Cabinet and acquired the reputation of being a likeable, well-intentioned but rather ineffective national leader.

The overwhelming defeat of the Conservatives in the 1997 election led to Major's immediate resignation as leader, leaving the field for his succession wide open as his Deputy Prime Minister, Michael Heseltine, was unable to compete because of bad health, the man said to be Major's favourite, Chris Patten, was out of the country as Governor of Hong Kong and the most prominent of the Eurosceptics, Michael Portillo, lost his seat in Parliament. Malcolm Rifkind, who had been a canny Foreign Secretary, might have drawn support from both wings of the party, but he also had lost his seat. The competition was therefore between Ken Clarke, the very talented former Chancellor of the Exchequer who was pro-European, and the three remaining outspoken Eurosceptics who had been Cabinet ministers, Michael Howard, Peter Lilley and John Redwood, with William Hague, the former Secretary for Wales (although he comes from Yorkshire) as a somewhat Eurosceptical candidate who had the advantage in many eyes of being only thirty-six so that he would still be relatively young if Labour stays in power for a decade or more. In the third ballot Hague defeated Clarke by 92 votes to 70.

The Labour Party

The Labour Party differs from the Conservative Party in its origins and structure as well as in its ideology. The party has its origins in the Labour Representation Committee, established in 1900 by a group of trade unions and socialist organizations to secure the election of working-class candidates to Parliament in order to protect and promote the interests of labour. The committee changed its name to the Labour Party in 1906 and adopted a constitution in 1918.

The 1918 constitution, which was hardly changed until 1981, gave the party a unique form of organization that reflected the assumptions of the trade union leaders who dominated the conference at which the constitution was drawn up. There are two types of membership in the party, individual members who join constituency branches and affiliated members who pay a political levy to their trade union, which the union then hands over (in whole or in part) to party funds. The arrangement is that the trade union members pay this levy (which is very small) automatically unless they sign a document to 'contract out' of doing so. After the 1926 General Strike the Conservative government changed these rules by legislation, to provide that the levy would be payable only if members took the intitiative to 'contract in'. This reduced the number of affiliated members by over a third, and in 1946 the Labour government understandably changed the rule back again.

The Annual Conference of the party has, in principle, supreme control over policy, and it also elects the National Executive Committee, which takes policy decisions between conferences. Until 1993, the method of voting at the Annual Conference was by 'card vote', whereby the leader of each delegation from a party branch or a trade union has a card indicating how many members he or she represents and therefore how many votes he or she can cast. There were two controversial aspects of this procedure. One was that each local branch was credited with 1,000 members unless it claimed more. As fewer than a hundred branches had as many as 1,000 members this rule meant that there was no clear relationship between membership and voting power; very small branches had as many votes as large ones.

The other and more important aspect of the system was that the leaders of the large trade unions had enormous powers at the conference. For many years the leader of the Transport and General Workers Union had a card with 1,250,000 printed on it, so that his vote alone counted for more than the votes of all the 633 party branches put together. In the 1960s the five largest unions had half the votes at the conference. This arrangement was criticized on various grounds. One was that the number of votes given to a union corresponded simply to the number declared by the unions to be 'affiliated members', with no independent check on this figure. A government report in 1984 showed that in 1983 the engineers' union had declared 850,000 affiliated members although it had actually had only 542,000. Other unions also registered either more or less than the true number, either to buy votes or to save money, and there was nothing in Labour Party rules to prevent this (Ewing 1987: 52–4).

Another problem was that the internal politics of the unions varied greatly. Some had democratic procedures while others left a great deal of discretion in the hands of their leaders. In the later 1960s 'the emergence of left-wing in place of right-wing leaders in just four unions was decisive in shifting the position of the entire party' (Crouch 1982: 180).

Since 1993 all this has been changed. The present position is that the unions and other affiliated organizations, such as the co-operative societies, have only 50 per cent of the total votes at the Annual Conference, no matter what their membership, and that their votes must represent the views of their members (however determined) so that instead of a single card vote the delegates must vote separately according to their instructions. The other half of the total votes is given to the constituency branches of the party, with their delegates also dividing according to their instructions. These changes ended the trade union domination of the Conference that had existed from 1918 to 1993.

Labour MPs belong to the Parliamentary Labour Party, which is charged with the duty of advancing party policy in Parliament. For most of the party's life the parliamentarians have elected their own leader, who becomes Prime Minister if Labour wins an election. In a formal sense, the leader's powers are much weaker than those of the Conservative leader. The Labour leader does not control the professional organization of the party, which is run by the National Executive Committee (NEC). The leader is a member of the NEC but does not chair its meetings and does not have the power to appoint any of its members. In practice the Labour leader has usually acted in Parliament in a manner similar to that of the Conservative leader, and of course enjoys exactly the same powers when Prime Minister. However, the structure of the Labour Party leaves room for internal arguments about who controls policy. As in 1981 such arguments led four leading party members to resign and form the Social Democratic Party, where they were quickly joined by twenty-six other MPs, it is appropriate to out-line the nature of the structural problem at this point.

The central organization was modelled on that of British trade unions, in which there is always an executive committee with the responsibility for promoting the general policies laid down by the Annual Conference. The differ-ence is that in the unions the executive committee has the practical power to do this, by conducting (or supervising) negotiations over pay and working conditions. In the Labour Party, in contrast, the NEC lacks the practical ability to do anything except control the professional organizing staff and prepare publicity. Labour policy is advanced by the Parliamentary Labour Party (PLP), which is jealous of its independence and does not take orders from either the NEC or the Annual Conference. Over the decades, there have been inter-mittent rumblings of discontent because the PLP has been perceived by some as disregarding conference policy.

Certain conference resolutions over the years have simply been ignored by parliamentarians. In 1960 a resolution was passed that had generated so much passion that it could not be ignored, namely a resolution opposing British possession of nuclear weapons. The then party leader, Hugh Gaitskell, refused to accept this as binding. He stated that he would not be content until he persuaded the party to reverse this policy, and at the 1961 conference he succeeded in doing this. However, the incident left a good deal of resentment among the left wing of the party, which surfaced again after the 1979 electoral defeat and led to a revision of the constitution in January 1981.

Under the new rules the leader of the PLP was to be chosen by an electoral college in which the affiliated trade unions had 40 per cent of the vote, the constituency Labour parties 30 per cent and the MPs the remaining 30 per cent. Another change was adopted providing that sitting MPs would have to submit themselves for reselection by their branch parties before each election, instead of being automatically renominated as had hitherto been the case. These changes were perceived by all commentators as a victory for the left (which was stronger in the unions and in the local branches than in the PLP), and they led to the resignation of the four leaders on the right of the party who established the rival Social Democratic Party. The nature of the ideological conflicts within the party will be discussed in a later section.

In the country, the local Labour Party branches perform the same functions as the Conservative associations, namely collecting subscriptions, holding meetings and social events, raising funds and providing voluntary workers in election campaigns. Their social life is not as active as that of their Conservative rivals, but they conduct lotteries as an alternative fund-raising device. However, the branches, having far fewer members than their Conservative counterparts, have naturally collected much less money.

Because of this, the Labour Party is heavily dependent on the trade unions for financial support. Whereas less than a half of the Conservative Party's regular income has come from business firms, over four-fifths of the Labour Party's regular income has come from trade unions. Labour's income in non-election years has been much smaller than the Conservative Party's income, but the unions provide large grants to the party for each general election campaign. The party is therefore not seriously handicapped in its campaigning by shortage of funds, though its activities are run on a tighter budget than those of the Conservatives and, as noted, it has fewer local organizers.

Labour Party doctrines

In the realm of doctrine, it is for two reasons more difficult to set out the theoretical foundations of Labour's policies than it is to do this for the Conservative Party. One reason is that the trade unionists who have always played such a large role in the party have generally been uninterested in political theory. As Drucker has pointed out, the unions have an ethos rather than an ideology (Drucker 1979). This ethos arose out of the experience of the working class in the industrial areas of Britain. It emphasizes the values of class solidarity, loyalty to leaders, plain living and plain speaking, and establishing a reserve fund to safeguard the group against unspecified disasters or attacks that the future may bring. It is the ethos of a group that feels itself vulnerable and exploited, is instinctively cautious and believes that its only real strength lies in the unity of its members. In terms of practical policies, this ethos has stressed the importance of legal rights for trade unions, of laws to guard against industrial accidents and of measures to protect workers against the misfortunes of unemployment, poor health and old age.

The second problem about identifying Labour doctrines is that the theoreticians of the party have differed rather widely among themselves. On a left–right dimension, they have varied from groups working for the abolition of capitalism to groups who merely want to improve the operation of the capitalist system and to provide social security for citizens. What nearly all Labour theorists and leaders have had in common until recently is agreement on two basic assumptions. First, they have agreed that society is divided into classes whose interests conflict. This is undesirable, but is a fact of life. Secondly, they have been egalitarians, constantly urging that measures should be taken to reduce the inequalities that flow from the economic system and the status system.

The translation of this working-class ethos and these socialist doctrines into a set of practical policies has always involved discussion and argument within the Labour movement. From the early years of the century until the late 1960s, these arguments were always won by the moderate wing of the movement. Communist and certain other Marxist organizations were proscribed (i.e. their members were ineligible for membership of the Labour Party), while non-Communist left-wingers were outvoted. Equally, the groups favouring centralized control always won over groups favouring local democracy or workers' self-government in industry.

In the late 1960s, two developments took place. First, some of the larger unions fell under the control of leaders with Marxist sympathies, with the result that at Labour Party conferences their votes were swung to the support of left-wing causes rather than to the support of the mainly moderate parliamentary leaders. Secondly, the New Left movement came into being, under the leadership of students who were radicalized by their opposition to the American role in the Vietnam war. During the 1970s these young radicals moved into Labour Party branches, and became more influential there with the passage of time. In 1981 these two groups of left-wingers pushed through the organizational amendments already mentioned, though this was against the wishes of most parliamentary leaders.

In the early 1980s, the moderates lost the grip on the party that they had held ever since the 1920s. When Michael Foot, a left-winger, became leader of the parliamentary party in 1981 he radicalized its policies and took it into the 1983 election with commitments to renationalize privatized industries without necessarily paying full compensation to the owners, to withdraw Britain from the European Community, and to move towards unilateral nuclear disarmament. These policies were far too radical for the electorate to accept and the result was that Labour secured a smaller proportion of the votes than it had at any election since 1918.

Foot resigned and was replaced by Neil Kinnock, a Welsh miner's son who had been on the left of the party but who realized that he had to moderate its extremist image if he were to have any chance of leading it to victory. This was not at all easy and his efforts were undermined by the success of extremists in gaining control of local authorities in several large cities, including London, Manchester and Liverpool. In some London boroughs funds were diverted to set up 'lesbian workshops', while committees were established to root out 'heterosexual prejudice' among municipal employees. The press promptly coined the term 'the loony left' to describe the sponsors of these activities and gave them a great deal of publicity. In Liverpool, Trotskyites gained control of the city council, overspent the council's budget by a large margin, borrowed money from a consortium of Swiss banks to cover the deficit, and thus burdened the people of Liverpool with a large debt at a rather high rate of interest. In the 1987 election Labour went down to another heavy defeat, though it recovered some of the votes it had lost four years earlier.

After this election Kinnock became absolutely determined to lead the party towards a more moderate position. He waged a campaign against a Trotskyite faction called Militant Tendency, which got a good deal of favourable publicity for him and was moderately successful. More important, he disavowed his own previous belief in nuclear disarmament and gradually persuaded the party to drop its commitment not only to this but also to the renationalization of the industries that were privatized by the Thatcher government. By 1990 he had won his battles within the party and the result was that Labour entered the 1992 election campaign with the most moderate manifesto it had ever presented to the people. This strategy was so successful that Labour was tipped by all the pollsters to win the election, and its eventual defeat was a crushing blow to Kinnock, who immediately gave up the leadership.

His successor, John Smith, a Scottish lawyer who was also on the moderate side of the party, persuaded it to accept a system of 'one member, one vote' at the Annual Conference, but did not have time to make other changes before his sudden and untimely death in 1994. The really significant figure is Tony Blair, who took Smith's place. Blair is young and dynamic, and quickly showed himself to be a shrewd and courageous party leader. Knowing that the main reason for Labour's surprising defeat in 1992 was the feeling among many electors, when it came to the point of voting, that they could not trust a Labour government to handle the economy as well as the Conservatives, he decided that the only sure way to make Labour electable was to abandon all the economic and fiscal policies that distinguished it from its opponents. This meant abandoning policies that the party had always stood for, and were dear to the hearts of many MPs, trade unions and party members. His first major step in this direction was to remove the notorious Clause 4 of the party's constitution, drafted under Marxist influence in 1918 and committing the party to 'public ownership of the means of production, distribution and exchange'. This was always too extreme for the majority of the party and became obsolete in the late 1950s, when nearly all the social democratic parties of Europe, following the German lead of 1957, deleted Marxist phraseology from their constitutions. As leader, Hugh Gaitskell had tried to persuade the Annual Conference to change it in 1959, but failed badly, and the conventional wisdom after that time, accepted in turn by Wilson, Callaghan, Kinnock and Smith, was that any subsequent attempt to change or remove it would be so controversial as to be not worth trying. To almost universal surprise, Tony Blair tried it in his first few months as leader, and won a resounding victory. It was a remarkable demonstration of leadership ability. The new Clause 4, which he drafted, is so long and platitudinous that it is practically meaningless.

In the following two years Blair persuaded a majority of Labour MPs and members voting at annual conferences to abandon the party's proposal to renationalize some of the industries that the Thatcher and Major governments had privatized and to play down the party's traditional commitment to promote economic and social equality. He announced that the next Labour government would continue the Conservative policy of restraint in public expenditure and low rates of income tax. He said that he admired much that Margaret Thatcher had done as Prime Minister, though it had been fiercely opposed by Labour at the time, and she even said that she admired him. Thatcher had indeed been the only person of note to have predicted that the Labour Party would eventually abandon its socialist principles and become the British equivalent of the American Democratic Party. In a *Financial Times* interview of 19 November 1986 she 'forecast that it would take perhaps two more terms of Conservative government to get rid of socialism as a second force in British politics' (Grant 1989: 153). She was right on both counts, for Blair has led his party, despite internal opposition, to accept competitive capitalism. He calls himself a social democrat but his policy preferences are more those of a Christian democrat, on the lines pursued by the German Christian Democratic Union. It was an astonishing achievement for a young and inexperienced leader in his first three years of office.

Needless to say, his policies have not met with unanimous support within the party. His achievement has been to remodel the party to what he and his supporters have called New Labour, and the media naturally came to bracket his critics under the name of Old Labour. Some Old Labour supporters are traditional socialists who deeply dislike his sharp move to the right. Others have a fair amount of sympathy for his policies but dislike his somewhat authoritarian style of leadership and have accused him of dictatorial tendencies. Many have commanding positions on city councils and have threatened to obstruct the implementation of his proposed educational reforms, as has the largest teachers' union. He is likely to find that getting his policies accepted and implemented as Prime Minster is more difficult than achieving that office, but his performance within the party has been brilliant.

The smaller parties

Under this heading we shall outline the roles of the centrist parties (the Liberals, the Social Democrats and, since 1988, the Liberal Democrats) as well as, more briefly, the nationalist parties in Scotland, Wales and Northern Ireland.

The Liberal Party, after a long and successful history, fell to the position of a small third party between 1918 and 1924. In the 1950s and 1960s its parliamentary representation was reduced to six, leading journalists to suggest that its caucus meetings might be held in the back of a taxi. In view of this, the first question to be asked about the party is how it has managed to survive for over seventy years with only a minimal degree of influence at the national level.

The main answer to this question is that the party has been kept going by its grass-roots members, who have rarely numbered fewer than 100,000 and are not primarily interested in issues of national policy. These members may be divided into two broad categories. First, there are a considerable number of older members, mainly drawn from the professional classes, who are attached to the internationalist ideals to which the party has always subscribed. They tend to run the local branches of the United Nations Association and to be active in other organizations concerned with international issues. Secondly, many Liberals are involved in what has come to be known as community politics. They are active in housing associations, groups concerned with environmental issues, committees to improve race relations and similar local good causes. If Conservative or Labour councillors propose that an unused church or church hall be demolished, it is a fair bet that Liberals will form a pressure group to demand that the building be preserved and turned into a day-care centre.

Neither of these groups is primarily concerned with economic affairs or even with the activities of the national government. They tend to focus on international or local issues rather than on the policies of the national state. In this respect they faithfully reflect the history and ideological orientation of their party. They are descendants of the politicians who campaigned against the slave trade, against slavery in the British Empire, in favour of free trade, in favour of international peace and the League of Nations. British Liberals have only sometimes had their main concerns at the level of the national state.

On the one hand, Liberals are idealists, believing in the possibility of international peace and justice. On the other hand, they are individualists, concerned with the liberties of the private citizen. Certainly Gladstone was a Liberal leader who reformed the financial arrangements of the national government, but he was also the leader who campaigned in a British general election on the issue of Bulgarian atrocities in the Balkans. It is noteworthy that it is the Liberal Party that promoted Home Rule for Ireland, that genuinely believes in the principle of devolution to Scotland and Wales and that favours decentralization of government within England. In principle, Liberals would like to see the United Kingdom turned into a federation.

The electoral system has deprived the Liberal Party of fair representation since it became a third party. However, after 1970 the Liberals made something of a comeback. This was not because of any change of philosophy or dramatic innovation in policy. It was mainly because voters showed signs of disenchantment with the two main parties. In 1974 voters turned to the Liberals in England at the same time as they turned to the nationalist parties in Wales and Scotland. In the February 1974 election the Liberals got 19 per cent of the total British vote, comprising just over 6 million voters. After the Social Democratic Party was formed in 1981 the two small parties established an electoral alliance, and in 1983 this alliance got 25 per cent of the vote – though winning only 3.5 per cent of the seats.

The Social Democratic Party was formally established in March 1981. In January 1981 the Labour Party held a special conference in London at which the rules were changed regarding the election of the parliamentary leader and the reselection of MPs. On the very next day four of the party's leaders announced the formation of the Council for Social Democracy, which was turned into the Social Democratic Party (SDP) two months later. The four leaders were Roy Jenkins, a former Chancellor of the Exchequer just returned to Britain from four years as President of the European Commission, David Owen, a former Foreign Secretary, William Rodgers, a former Minister of Transport and Shirley Williams, a former Minister of Education. They were supported by nine other Labour MPs.

While the immediate issue that led to this development was the change in Labour Party rules, the move had been envisaged before that and three main reasons for it were explained in the declaration made in January. One was what the four leaders called 'the drift towards extremism in the Labour Party'. Another was the belief that the increasingly adversarial character of British politics, leading to sharp changes in economic policy when the government changed hands, was bad for the economy. A third was concern lest a future Labour government should take Britain out of the European Community and weaken the British ties with NATO. It was also important, and was spelled out later, that the founders of the SDP wanted a left-of-centre party that would not be shackled to the trade unions.

The SDP was an instant success. It got extensive publicity in all the mass media and it is reported that within ten days of its formation it had 43,588 paying members (Zentner 1982: 10). Intellectuals, lawyers and doctors supported it in large numbers. Its leaders travelled tirelessly around the country addressing public meetings. Within a month the Gallup Poll reported that, if the SDP formed an electoral alliance with the Liberal Party, the alliance would be likely to win the next general election (Zentner 1982: 14). All this happened before the SDP had a constitution, a single designated leader or a set of specific policies. Its sudden popularity was the political sensation of 1981.

Throughout its first year the SDP gained strength. It won two important by-elections and attracted the support of several more Labour MPs together with one Conservative MP. By June 1982 it had thirty MPs and had also gained a fair number of members in the House of Lords. It had acquired about 70,000 members in the country. Its conferences drew an enthusiastic body of supporters, who were described as overwhelmingly white, male, middle class and in their middle years (Stephenson 1982: 111). It was the most fashionable party in Britain and was in some respects the most modern, staging dramatic media events and being the first party to encourage its members to pay their subscriptions by credit card.

However, when the SDP published a statement of its policies these were not particularly novel. It wanted to retain existing policies towards Europe and NATO, to maintain and improve social services, to drop some of the rather harsh financial policies of the Thatcher government and to try once more to establish a government incomes policy in spite of the failures of both Conservative and Labour governments in this field in the 1970s. *The Economist* immediately offered the new party an electoral slogan, namely 'The SDP promises you a better yesterday.'

The SDP and the Liberal Party fought the 1983 and 1987 general elections as partners. The partnership was rather strained, however, because there were both policy differences and personality clashes between the leaders. The election results were a disappointment for the Liberals and a disaster for the SDP. Although the alliance candidates won over 25 per cent of the vote in 1983 and 23 per cent in 1987, they won only 23 seats in the earlier election and 22 in the later one. The Liberals won 17 seats each time, with the SDP taking the remainder. This meant that of the 28 MPs who crossed the floor of the House to join the SDP in its early days, 22 lost their seats in the ensuing election. This was a chilling lesson to other MPs who might have considered following their example.

Three days after the 1987 election, the Liberal leader, David Steel, sprang an astonishing surprise on his allies (and on the nation). He proposed that the two parties should merge and a new leader should be chosen by a vote of the combined rank-and-file members. As the Liberals had about twice as many members as the SDP, this meant that the new leader would almost certainly be a Liberal. The proposal immediately divided the SDP leaders. Roy Jenkins and Shirley Williams, who had both lost their parliamentary seats, came out in support of a merger, while David Owen was vehemently against it. The five MPs divided, with the two from Scotland favouring the merger and the three from southern England opposing it. After much anguished debate, the issue was put to a postal ballot of SDP members, of whom 78 per cent responded and who voted to support the merger by a majority of 57 per cent to 43 per cent. At this point the SDP split down the middle, with both halves claiming the party's name.

There followed several months of negotiation between the Liberals and the pro-merger half of the SDP. One result of these negotiations was agreement upon a title for the new merged party, which now calls itself the Liberal Democrats. Another result was agreement on a fairly ambitious statement of policy objectives, but this was immediately repudiated by rank-and-file Liberals and several Liberal MPs. A third result was the resignation of David Steel, who was replaced by Paddy Ashdown.

The effect of these developments on public opinion was unfortunate for the centrist parties. Whereas they got 23 per cent of the vote at the 1987 election, their combined support fell during 1988 to about 12 per cent. Both parties suffered a substantial loss of members and in the European elections of 1989 the two parties actually got fewer votes than the previously minuscule Green Party. In April 1990 the rump of the SDP was wound up. In 1992 the Liberal Democrats secured 18 per cent of the votes and won 20 seats, of which 9 were in Scotland, 4 in Wales and 6 in the south-west of England. It seems that in national politics, as distinct from municipal politics, they only have strength in the peripheral areas of the country.

The other small parties are the nationalist parties of Scotland, Wales and Northern Ireland. The Scottish National Party (SNP) represents a nationalist movement with a long history, but the party did not make a serious impact on a general election until 1970. Its rapid growth in the early 1970s reflected widespread disenchantment with the handling of British economic policy by successive Conservative and Labour governments, leading to the claim that Scotland could do better if it had its own independent government. This claim was greatly strengthened by the discovery of a large oilfield off the Scottish coast in the North Sea. If an independent Scotland were to control North Sea oil, it would clearly be a wealthy state.

In 1970 the SNP gained more than twice as many votes as in any previous election and won a seat in Parliament. In the election of February 1974 its proportion of Scottish votes rose to 21 per cent and the number of seats won rose to seven. In the election of October 1974 the proportion of votes went up to 30 per cent and the number of seats won to eleven.

This rapid growth of public support for the SNP threatened to undermine the position of the Labour Party in Scotland. Largely for this reason, the Labour government of 1974–9 prepared an elaborate scheme for the devolution of government, under which Scotland would be given a National Assembly with legislative powers in many fields, though without the power to levy taxes. While this proposal fell far short of nationalist demands, opinion polls indicated that it would satisfy the apparently large number of Scottish people who had some sympathy for the nationalist cause without endorsing the demand for full independence.

Legislation to establish a Scottish Assembly was passed by the British Parliament, but its implementation was made conditional upon its securing the support of at least 40 per cent of Scottish electors in a referendum. This referendum was held in March 1979 and resulted in an affirmative vote of only 33 per cent of the electors. In consequence, the legislation was repealed. This was a devastating blow to the SNP, which secured only 19 per cent of the votes in the general election of May 1979 and saw its parliamentary representation fall from eleven to two MPs.

There followed a period of internecine conflict within the party and in the 1983 and 1987 elections its share of the Scottish vote fell to 12 per cent and 14 per cent respectively, securing first two and then three seats. In 1992 it did better, securing 21 per cent of Scottish votes, but it still won only three seats. In 1997, with a small increase in votes, the SNP doubled its representation to six seats.

In Wales Plaid Cymru (the Welsh Party) has a basis that is different from that of the SNP. Plaid Cymru is more concerned with the preservation of the Welsh language and culture than with the management of the economy, and its leaders want a large measure of cultural and political autonomy for Wales rather than full independence as a national state. Like the SNP, Plaid Cymru gained support in the early 1970s but suffered a severe reverse in the referendum of 1979. The proposal for a Welsh Assembly was accepted by only 12 per cent of Welsh electors. However, because the party's support is based on an enduring concern for the Welsh culture – a concern that has no significant Scottish equivalent – its rise and decline have both been less dramatic than the rise and decline of the SNP.

In the two elections of 1974 Plaid Cymru secured 10 and 11 per cent of the Welsh vote, winning two and three seats respectively. In 1979 the proportion of votes declined to 9 per cent and by 1987 it was reduced to 7 per cent, but the party still won three seats. In 1992 the votes went up to 9 per cent and four seats were won; this result was replicated in 1997.

In Northern Ireland the position is different again. The majority of parliamentary seats in Northern Ireland have always been won by the Ulster Unionist Party, which stands for the continuation of the union with Great Britain and for a policy of keeping the social services in parity with British social services. In a real sense, this can be regarded as a nationalist party for the Protestant majority in the province. The Catholic community have supported various opposition parties, such as Sinn Fein, the Republican Party and the Social Democratic and Labour Party.

From 1922 until 1972 the Ulster Unionists had an informal alliance at Westminster with the British Conservative Party, and because of this their MPs were usually counted as Conservatives when a tally was made of the results of each general election. In 1972 this alliance was broken off by the Unionists when the Conservative government abruptly suspended the Northern Ireland Parliament, which had certain devolved powers of legislation in the Province. The Conservatives paid a heavy price for this action at the next general election. In February 1974 they secured more votes than the Labour Party but four fewer seats. Had the alliance still been effective, the ten Ulster Unionist MPs would have been counted in with the Conservatives and the latter would have been declared the election winners. As it was, they emerged as losers and had to give way to a minority Labour government.

In the 1997 general election the Ulster Unionists – now divided – won thirteen of the Irish seats, while the Social Democratic and Labour Party won three and Sinn Fein won two.

In Britain there are also several fringe parties, none of which gets more than a very small share of the votes. In 1997 the nine fringe parties got 3 per cent of the votes between them.

Further reading

The best recent book on the party system is Ingle (1987) *The British Party System*; on the Conservative Party see Norton and Aughey (1981) *Conservatives and Conservatism*, Seldon (1996) *How Tory Governments Fall*, chs. 8, 9 and 10, and, for a detailed history, Seldon and Ball (1994) *Conservative Century*, selected chapters; on the Labour Party see Kavanagh (1982) *The Politics of the Labour Party*, Jeffreys (1993) *The Labour Party since 1945* and Shaw (1996) *The Labour Party since 1945*; on the Liberal Party see Bogdanor (1983) *Liberal Party Politics*; on the SDP see Crewe and King (1995) *SDP*; on the Scottish and Welsh nationalists see Birch (1977) *Political Integration and Disintegration in the British Isles*.

6

ELECTORS AND VOTERS

In a liberal democracy decisions about which political party or parties shall govern the country are made by electors, casting votes in free elections. The object in this chapter is to outline the nature of the British electoral system, to discuss contemporary criticisms of it and arguments for reform and to provide a brief guide to British voting behaviour.

The electoral system

The way in which an electoral system works depends partly upon the methods adopted of dealing with certain practical problems of electoral organization that arise in every democratic country. These include the compilation of a register of qualified electors, the delimitation of constituency boundaries, the nomination of candidates, the control of expenses and the method of translating votes cast into seats won. These problems, and the British ways of dealing with them, will now be outlined.

The first problem is that of compiling an electoral register. The main question here is whether the initiative and responsibility should rest with individual citizens or with the government. If individual citizens are made responsible, and they have to register to vote in advance, those people who are apathetic, ignorant, forgetful or sick will find themselves unable to vote on polling day, when their interest might have been awakened by the campaign or they themselves might be in better health. If the government is made responsible, it is essential to ensure that the opposition parties have no reason to think that the politicians in power are taking more care over the registration of their own supporters than they take over the registration of their opponents.

In Britain this problem is dealt with by placing the responsibility for compiling the register on permanent municipal officials, who are not political appointees. In each county or borough the clerk to the council has the duty of ensuring that all adult citizens are registered. This is done by sending a registration form to each householder for completion, followed by a door-to-door canvas of those who do not return the form promptly. The register is compiled afresh each autumn and is a record of those qualified to vote on 10 October. It is published by January and comes into force on 16 February for a period of twelve months. This means that the register may be as much as sixteen months old when the election is held, but the effects of this are mitigated in two ways: persons within eight months of their eighteenth birthday on registration day are placed on the register even though they are not allowed to vote until they reach 18; and persons moving out of the constituency can vote by post (as can invalids).

This is a reasonably good system, but not quite as good as is generally thought. Official surveys showed that the registers compiled in 1987 and 1991 were only 91–93 per cent accurate at the date of compilation, so that about 3 million potential electors were actually disfranchised (Leonard 1996: 21–2). The system is better than the American system but not as efficient as the Canadian one, which requires a new register to be compiled by door-to-door canvass a few weeks before each federal election.

The second problem is that of dividing the country into constituencies. This caused a good deal of controversy in Britain from the early part of the nineteenth century until 1944, when an attempt was made to take the matter out of politics by establishing permanent Electoral Boundary Commissions. The Commissions that were set up in that year (one each for England, Wales, Scotland and Northern Ireland) have the task of surveying the country at periodic intervals and of making reports and recommendations to the House of Commons. The first reports of the commissions were adopted (with some amendments) in 1948 and changed the boundaries of over 80 per cent of the constituencies.

The impartiality of the Boundary Commissions has never been questioned. They are instructed to take into account a number of social and geographical factors, including the desirability of making constituency boundaries coterminous with local authority boundaries wherever possible. But they take no account of political factors and their proposals tend to irritate members of all parties. There is a problem about the frequency of redistribution, because infrequent changes result in growing inequalities of size that violate the principle of 'one vote, one value' whereas frequent ones are inconvenient to both MPs and local party branches. The 1944 legislation had required redistribution to take place at intervals of between three and seven years, but this caused so many difficulties that in 1958 the intervals were extended to between ten and fifteen years. In 1992 the law was changed again, this time to reduce the intervals to between eight and twelve years.

During the 1970s two fresh concerns about constituency boundaries were manifested. One was concern among English commentators about the deliberate overrepresentation of Scotland and Wales that was written into the 1944 Act. The official explanation of this is that these territories have a lower density of population than England, but this cannot justify the extent of the overrepresentation, which results in cities like Glasgow and Cardiff getting more parliamentary seats than cities of the same size in England. The situation is clearly anomalous, but no changes had been made by 1977.

The other concern related to the disparity in constituency sizes even within England, which was so great that in the United States the courts would have declared them to be in violation of the constitutional right of citizens to equal representation. These disparities resulted not from partisan bias but from the intense local pressures put upon Boundary Commissioners to respect municipal boundaries when drawing up their plans.

When the commissions reported in 1982 it was clear that they had made a considerable effort to meet this last criticism. However, this did not stop the Labour Party from challenging the plans in court on the ground that unnecessary variations in constituency population in the London area would operate to the disadvantage of Labour. The court rejected this appeal. If the appeal had been accepted, this might have delayed the implementation of the plans so that the government would have had either to postpone the next general election or to fight it on the basis of the 1970 constituency boundaries (which would have helped Labour in view of the movements of population that had occurred since 1970). However this may be, it seems clear that in terms of a democratic principle of 'one vote, one value' there is a good case for a revision of the instructions given to the Boundary Commissions so as to place less emphasis on respect for municipal boundaries and more emphasis on equality of population in constituencies.

The third problem is that of establishing a procedure for the nomination of candidates. In some countries where the names of the parties are printed on the ballot papers, it has become necessary to pass legislation defining what constitutes a political party and establishing rules for the resolution of conflicts between rival candidates, each claiming to be the official candidate of the same party. In the United States the need to resolve disputes of this kind has led the state governments to lay down procedures for the nomination of candidates by parties and thus to pass legislation regulating the internal organization of the parties.

In Britain these legal complications have been avoided, by the wish of all concerned. Candidates stand as individuals, simply requiring the support of ten local citizens to be nominated. There is therefore no need for rules about the internal procedures of parties. Until 1969 there was no provision for the names of parties to be printed on the ballot paper. In response to a demand that more information be permitted, Parliament then agreed to a new rule that gives candidates permission to add any slogan of their choice after their names, provided it does not exceed six words. This enables a candidate to give the name of a party while preserving the principle that each candidate stands as an individual. In practice there has been no problem about two candidates claiming to represent the same party.

The other problem about nominations is to prevent the ballot paper being extended by a long list of frivolous candidates. In some American states candidates have to be supported by a petition signed by a large number of electors unless they are nominated by parties that were included on the ballot in the previous election. That kind of arrangement is both administratively complicated (because signatures can be forged) and open to political objections (in that it may be a difficult hurdle for new parties or independent candidates to surmount).

In Britain the rule is that candidates must pay a deposit, which is forfeited if the candidate fails to secure a certain proportion of the votes cast. The size of the deposit was unchanged at £150 from 1918 until 1985, and because of inflation the effectiveness of the deposit as a deterrent steadily decreased. In the seven inter-war elections an average of 36 candidates lost their deposits; in the elections between 1945 and 1959 the average was 71; in the elections of the 1960s the average was 121; in those of the 1970s the average was 438; and in 1983 the number was 739. In 1984 an Act was passed raising the deposit to £500, while simultaneously lowering the threshold for saving the deposit from one-eighth of the votes cast to one-twentieth. The object of this change was to deter frivolous candidates and those from small extremist groups, while bearing less hardly on the smaller parties than the previous rule. In the 1987 election only 290 candidates lost their deposits, but in 1997 the number shot up to 1,592. This included 505 of the 547 Referendum Party candidates, 193 of the 194 UK Independence candidates, and all of the 196 Natural Law candidates.

The fourth problem is that of establishing control over electoral expenses, with the dual objects of preventing corruption and keeping wealthy candidates or parties from having an untoward advantage over others. In Britain electoral expenses were first regulated in 1883 and control was tightened in the early part of the twentieth century.

The controls operate at the local rather than at the national level and they depend on a simple but extremely effective device. Each candidate is required to appoint an official election agent; all expenditure designed to promote the interests of the candidate during the campaign has to be authorized by the agent; and at the end of the campaign the agent has to submit a statement of account showing how the money was spent and also showing that the total sum expended did not exceed the permitted maximum. The maximum allowed is determined by a formula and in 1992 it worked out at between £5,000 and £6,000 per candidate. This is a very small sum compared with election expenditures in North America, but British election campaigns are short, candidates get one free postal delivery to each elector, and in practice most candidates spend appreciably less than the maximum.

The central expenses of the parties are not controlled, but they are minimal compared with the equivalent expenditures in the United States and Canada. One reason for this is the shortness of the campaign period – normally between three and four weeks. The other main reason is that the parties cannot buy advertising time on television or radio. They get a certain number of free broadcasts each and a great deal of free news coverage, which has to be balanced and impartial between the main parties. Central publicity is therefore confined to press advertising, posters and pamphlets, and to personal appearances and news conferences by party leaders.

In the 1987 election the Conservatives spent £9 million centrally (two and a half times as much as in 1983) compared with £2.8 million locally, while Labour spent £4.2 million centrally (almost twice the 1983 total) compared with £2.5 million locally (Butler and Kavanagh 1988: 235). Central expenditure therefore rose sharply, in part because both parties employed expensive public relations firms. However, these sums are still fairly modest by international standards, and the general conclusion of nearly all commentators is that money has only a marginal impact on election results in Britain.

The fifth problem, which is currently the most contentious in Britain, is that of the method of converting votes cast into seats won. The British system, like the American and Canadian systems, is that of simple plurality in single-member constituencies. It is sometimes called a 'first past the post' system. This system helps the two main parties and particularly helps the most successful party. It bears hard on the smaller ones, though the extent to which smaller parties suffer from the system depends on how far their support is geographically concentrated. The nationalist parties in Scotland, Wales and Northern Ireland do not come off too badly, but the Liberal Democrats are seriously affected because their supporters are dispersed around the country. The extent of their disadvantage is indicated by Table 6.1. It is clear that in recent elections most Liberal and Social Democratic votes have been wasted because of the way the electoral system works.

The question of proportional representation

Ever since 1922, the Liberals have favoured replacing the simple plurality system by a system of proportional representation. Most European democracies have proportional representation (PR) in one form or another. With the revision of the French electoral system in 1985, Britain became the solitary member of the European Community not to have PR. Several polls since 1983 have shown that a majority of British electors believe that PR would be a fairer system. In view of this the case for and against PR deserves examination.

There is one general argument commonly advanced in favour of PR and two other arguments commonly advanced against it. The argument in favour is simply fairness. If democracy implies not only 'one person, one vote' but also 'one vote, one value', it is manifestly undemocratic for the supporters of smaller parties to be effectively denied fair representation in the legislature by the workings of the electoral system. The most vehement opponents of PR cannot deny this; they merely say that other factors make a degree of unfairness acceptable.

The main general argument against PR is that it leads to a reduction in the accountability of governments to the electorate and a loss of control by the electors over the composition of the next government. If government is in the hands of a single majority party that party cannot escape responsibility for what has gone wrong during its term of office. In contrast, parties in a coalition government can always try to lay the blame on their partners.

Table 6.1 General election results, 1974–97

Date	Party	Number of votes (millions)	Number of seats won	Percentage of votes	Percentage of seats won
Feb.	Conservative	11.9	297	37.9	46.8
1974	Labour	11.6	301	37.1	47.4
	Liberal	6.1	14	19.3	2.2
	Others	1.8	23	5.6	3.6
Oct.	Conservative	10.5	277	35.8	43.6
1974	Labour	11.5	319	39.2	50.2
	Liberal	5.3	13	18.3	2.1
	Others	1.9	26	6.6	4.2
1979	Conservative	13.7	339	43.9	53.4
	Labour	11.5	268	36.9	42.2
	Liberal	4.3	11	13.8	1.7
	Others	1.7	17	5.5	2.7
1983	Conservative	13.0	397	42.4	61.1
	Labour	8.5	209	27.6	32.2
	Liberal–SDP	7.8	23	25.4	3.5
	Others	1.4	21	4.6	3.2
1987	Conservative	13.7	376	42.2	57.8
	Labour	10.0	229	30.8	35.2
	Liberal–SDP	7.3	22	22.6	3.4
	Others	1.4	23	4.4	3.5
1992	Conservative	14.1	336	41.9	51.6
	Labour	11.6	271	34.4	41.6
	Liberal Democrats	6.0	20	17.8	3.1
	Others	2.0	24	5.8	3.7
1997	Conservative	9.6	165	30.7	25.0
	Labour	13.5	418	43.2	63.4
	Liberal Democrats	5.2	46	16.8	7.0
	Others	2.9	30	9.4	4.4

Another common argument against PR, frequently deployed in Britain, is that the establishment of multi-member constituencies would deprive voters of the close ties with their elected representatives that they can enjoy in single-member constituencies. However, the validity of this argument depends on which of the various possible systems of PR is adopted. It is not essential to have multi-member constituencies under PR. In the German system half the members are elected in single-member constituencies while the other half, so composed as to give a proportional balance to the total, are elected on a regional basis. In the Irish system, which does depend on multi-member constituencies, there is no lack of closeness in the relations between constituents and representatives. As candidates within each party have to be placed in order of preference by the voters, the system produces a positive incentive for candidates to cultivate the constituency and maintain close relations with local voters after they are elected.

It may be concluded that in general a system of PR scores in terms of fair representation but is open to criticism on the ground of accountability. However, in the specific circumstances of contemporary Britain these general and theoretical arguments have faded from importance. The distribution of party support means that in most postwar elections the Liberals would, under PR, have held the balance of power in Parliament, and until recently Liberal leaders refused to say which main party they would support in that case. There were small minorities among the members of both main parties who favoured PR, particularly in the 1970s. However, in the early 1990s Paddy Ashdown, the leader of the Liberal Democrats, made it crystal clear that his party would always support Labour, so that Conservatives are now united against PR. Labour leaders and MPs are divided between those who support it because it could be expected to put their party almost permanently into office and those who oppose it because they prefer the chance of complete power for Labour to the probability of having to share it with the Liberal Democrats. Tony Blair has not come down openly on either side, but has promised that the reform would not be introduced without a referendum on the proposal.

Election campaigns in Britain are short in comparison with campaigns in most other democratic countries. Polling takes place only seventeen working days after the Proclamation summoning a new Parliament, which is made by the monarch on the advice of the Prime Minister. It is usual for the Prime Minister to announce the date of the election about a month before polling day. The government of the day has some tactical advantage in being able to fix the date of the election, and it is normal practice for a government to make the most of this by calling the election at fairly short notice some time before the end of Parliament's term.

The development of public opinion polls has increased the importance of this advantage, but the polls are not an infallible guide. In 1970 the Conservatives won the election even though the pollsters had predicted a few weeks earlier that Labour would win. In 1974 the Conservatives were trapped into calling a snap election when the polls showed a swing in their favour that turned out to be transitory, the advantage being lost during the campaign. In 1992 the Conservatives won the election although every poll had predicted a Labour victory or a hung Parliament.

The shortness of the campaign period stands in sharp contrast to the very long campaigns that are conducted in the United States. This brevity is uncontroversial because a British election campaign is not generally regarded as an occasion for interest groups to press their views on politicians, for parties and leaders to formulate attitudes and policies, and for candidates to meet the people and subject themselves to cross-examination regarding their records and ambitions. Instead, it is regarded as essentially an occasion when the parties should be given a fair and equal opportunity to rally their followers and persuade them to go to the polls, it being assumed that both the policies of the parties and the allegiance of most of the electors are established before the campaign opens.

These assumptions are largely valid. Party programmes are generally prepared well in advance of the campaign and are rarely changed during it. And the surveys that have been made of voting intentions and behaviour show that most voters generally make up their minds in advance of the campaign. In this respect the 1974 and 1992 elections were exceptional.

The voting behaviour of the minority who are uncertain may of course be of crucial importance. If it were possible for the parties to design policies and propaganda specially calculated to influence these 'floating voters', this would almost certainly be done. If the floating voters were mainly women, or pensioners, or the unemployed, the campaign might be dominated by propaganda directed particularly at these groups. This has not been the case in postwar British elections, however. Surveys in the 1950s and 1960s showed that, broadly speaking, floating voters were a cross-section of the electorate, not distinguished from their fellow-citizens by any particular social characteristics. The parties had, therefore, to aim their appeals at the whole electorate. More recently, as will be explained later in this chapter, the opinions and loyalties of the electorate have become more volatile. This has opened up the possibility of selective appeals to target groups. In the 1979 election campaign the Conservative Party made a considerable effort to win support from manual workers, with 'specific commitments to abandon wage controls, further restrict immigration, and oblige local authorities to offer to sell council houses at favourable terms to their tenants' (Sarlvik and Crewe 1983: 49). This policy met with some success, as the swing to the Conservatives was greater among manual workers, at 9 per cent, than among non-manual workers, at 5.5 per cent (ibid.: 83). Further efforts to cater for the assumed interests of particular groups can be expected in future elections, but it must be emphasized that this has not become a major feature of British campaigns, as it has of American campaigns. British electors are not so ready as many Americans are to change their votes on the basis of a single issue, and it is to be expected that British parties will continue to place most emphasis on appeals directed to a wide cross-section of the community.

At the local level, the main object of party organizers is to make sure that as many as possible of the party's supporters turn out to vote. Canvassers concentrate almost entirely on supporters and try to avoid being drawn into argument by opponents. Supporters who have not gone to the polls by early evening on polling day will be telephoned or called for with a car.

Candidates are expected to make numerous personal appearances at meetings, but the personality and political views of the candidate rarely have more than a marginal effect on the result, except sometimes in the case of smaller parties. The attitude of most voters was neatly summarized by an elector in Birmingham who said: 'I'd vote for a pig if my party put one up.' It remains true that a good candidate may advance his or her cause by promoting the growth of a large and active local party, and this is particularly true of the smaller parties. However, this is work that has to be done between campaigns rather than during the campaign itself.

At the national level the campaign is increasingly dominated by television. Each party is allocated a few free broadcasts, five each for the main parties and one or two for the others in 1992. However, what is undoubtedly more important is that the whole campaign gets a great deal of news coverage, with the broadcasting authorities carefully respecting their legal obligation to provide a fair balance between the parties. Each of the national party leaders normally gives a news conference in London every morning, and these conferences are the opportunity for a running debate between the parties on policy issues. Because of this, there is no need and no demand for a direct confrontation between party leaders on television, as is staged in American and Canadian elections.

British election campaigns, though short and inexpensive by international standards, are relatively effective at getting out the vote. The turn-out at general elections averages about 75 per cent of the electorate. It does not vary much between elections, the postwar extremes being 78 per cent in 1992 and 71 per cent in 1997. This turn-out figure is slightly lower than the norm in most other European democracies, but appreciably higher than the norm in American elections.

Voting behaviour

To explain British voting behaviour two questions have to be asked, as follows. First, how is voting behaviour influenced by social factors such as sex, religion and occupation? Secondly, how is voting behaviour influenced by individual values and attitudes to political issues raised during the campaign? The answers to each question have to be couched partly in historical terms, for it would be a mistake to slip into the assumption that voting behaviour is determined by timeless and immutable laws.

The significance of sex and religion for voting can be dealt with briefly. In the early postwar surveys it was reported that women favoured the Conservative Party in slightly larger numbers than men. However, by 1979 this statistical tendency had virtually disappeared. Its significance for an understanding of voting was in any case never very clear. Women have different opportunities in the labour market, are more likely to be non-employed and have a more direct interest in certain social issues like abortion. There is every reason to expect that particular categories of women, having to cope with particular social situations and problems, may have distinctive political attitudes not shared by so many men. These are the proper subject of detailed inquiries (see Dunleavy and Husbands 1984). But there is no obvious reason why women, taken as a whole, should be more right-wing or more left-wing or more centrist than men in their political sympathies.

The political significance of religion is somewhat greater, though it is declining. At the beginning of the twentieth century there was a clear and important relationship between religious affiliation and voting, with Anglicans tending to support the Conservative Party and members of other churches

91

supporting the Liberal Party. This relationship has gradually lost its significance, partly because of the disappearance of religious issues in politics and partly because of the decline in religious faith and observance. In the 1960s it was still true that Anglicans who claimed to attend church once a month or more were significantly more likely to vote Conservative than other citizens, but only 16 per cent of nominal Anglicans made this claim (Butler and Stokes 1974: 157). Moreover, most of these practising Anglicans had middle-class occupations, which also inclined them towards Conservatism. The statistical relationship is evidence of a syndrome rather than of a causal relationship between religion and voting.

The other relationships between religion and voting that emerge from some of the surveys are essentially relationships between ethnicity and voting. Thus, Irish voters (of whom there are over a million) are nearly all Catholics and mostly Labour, but the basic reason for this is that the Irish dislike the Conservative Party for historical reasons. Welsh rural voters are mostly Methodists and mostly anti-Conservative (being Liberal Democrats, Labour or Plaid Cymru), but this is also for historical and social rather than for purely religious reasons. Most Muslim and Hindu voters support Labour, but this is because of the assumption (not necessarily correct) that a Labour government might be more generous than the Conservative government has been about the immigration of relatives from Pakistan and India.

The relationship between occupation and party preference has been much more significant in postwar elections, though its importance has diminished recently. The relationship is not surprising since categorizing voters according to the type of occupation they follow is broadly equivalent to categorizing them according to their life experiences in material terms. Some people are fortunate or successful in their encounters with the educational system, are able to find interesting and secure employment and earn enough to satisfy their material expectations. Others are inadequately educated, face insecurity in their employment and find that their lives are dominated by a struggle to maintain acceptable living conditions for themselves and their families.

It is not surprising to learn that members of the first category have tended to favour the Conservative Party, while members of the second category have tended to favour the Labour Party. The general image of the Conservatives has always depicted them as in favour of maintaining the existing pattern of economic and social relationships, while the general image of Labour depicts it as favouring measures designed to increase the security and welfare of the less fortunate members of the community. The figures in Table 6.2 show the relationship between occupation and voting in the 1951 election, this election being chosen because the relationship was stronger in the 1950s and early 1960s than before or since, and the 1951 election was one in which the two main parties were evenly balanced.

These figures establish a broad relationship between type of occupation and voting, as shown in the final column. However, they also indicate two other

Table 6.2 Occupation and voting in Britain, 1951

Occupational group	Number of Conservative voters (millions)	Number of Labour voters (millions)	Conservative percentage of two-party vote
Business and professional	4.6	1.0	82
White-collar and intermediate	2.6	1.6	62
Manual	6.2	11.3	35
Total	13.4	13.9	49

Source: Bonham 1954.

points of interest. One is that the relationship in 1951 was much stronger among business and professional people than among the remainder of the voters. Business and professional people were pro-Conservative in the ratio of 4.6 to 1. Manual workers were pro-Labour in the ratio of only 1.8 to 1. The other point is that, while the Labour Party got 81 per cent of its support from male manual workers (and their wives, who were categorized according to their husbands' occupations in this study), the Conservative Party got only 34 per cent of its support from business and professional people and only 54 per cent of its support from non-manual workers of all types.

What general interpretation should be given to these figures? A widespread tendency among social scientists in the 1950s and 1960s was to interpret them in terms of a class-conflict model of politics. The middle classes, it was suggested, would naturally vote Conservative to protect their economic interests, while the working classes would naturally vote Labour to advance their very different economic interests.

A great deal of intellectual energy was then devoted to explaining the behaviour of the working-class Conservative voters, who were cast in the role of deviant cases. It was said that they were in the grip of deferential attitudes, misguidedly voting Conservative because they liked to see the government of the country in the hands of the traditional ruling classes. Another explanation stressed the relative youth of the Labour Party, suggesting that voters supported the Conservatives partly because they retained an allegiance they (or their parents) had acquired before Labour was a credible alternative. Yet another line of argument invoked the residual influence of religion on party preference. The implication of all these explanations was that working-class Conservatism could be expected to fade away with the passage of time.

There were several difficulties about this interpretation. For one thing, it implies that political behaviour is determined (or ought to be determined) by occupational status, which makes it difficult not only to account for the working-class Conservatives but also to explain why there are so many floating voters, who change parties between elections or are undecided until the campaign.

On this determinist view, it is hard to understand why voting behaviour varies so much from one election to the next.

Secondly, there have always been too many working-class Conservatives for it to be reasonable to regard them as deviants. There is something wrong with a generalization that has to account for 6 million deviant cases. Thirdly, the relationship between occupation and voting has not become stronger with the passage of time but less pronounced. From 1966 onwards there has been a process of de-alignment in British politics, with the relationship between type of occupation (or class) and partisan support becoming weaker and more complex. Statistics show that the class alignment in British politics, never so clear as was frequently asserted, has been withering away for the past thirty years or more. If the two Labour victories of 1966 and October 1974 are compared, it emerges that Labour lost about a sixth of its support among manual workers over the period, but won the 1974 election nevertheless because the Labour vote among non-manual workers held steady. If the two Conservative victories of 1970 and 1979 are compared, it emerges that the Conservatives did better in 1979 because, relative to Labour, they got a higher share of the votes cast by manual workers despite getting a smaller share of the vote cast by non-manual workers. It remained true, and still is true, that the class relationship has continued at the extremes of the social scale, with the top 10 per cent of income earners being largely pro-Conservative and the bottom 20 per cent largely pro-Labour, but among the majority of the electors class is no longer the most important factor.

This trend is not in the least surprising in view of the changing character of British society outlined in Chapter 1 of this book. Apart from the unemployed, almost everyone in Britain has become a good deal more prosperous since the 1960s. Most people have achieved lifestyles that were previously enjoyed only by a privileged minority. The equalizing effects of television, supermarkets and car ownership have been very marked. At the same time as this process of levelling up has taken place, there has been an interesting movement of a quite different kind. This is the growth of trade union membership among white-collar and professional workers, with bank clerks, nurses, hospital doctors and senior civil servants threatening to strike in support of their pay claims. The sense of distance between manual workers who strike and middle-class people who would not consider such a degrading tactic has been somewhat eroded by this development. The result of these and similar changes, as noted in Chapter 1, has been a marked decline in class consciousness. It is entirely logical that this should have been accompanied by a weakening of the relationship between class membership and voting behaviour.

While this relationship has declined, another relationship became increasingly important in the 1980s. This is the relationship between area of residence and voting behaviour. It has always been true that area of residence had some influence, with white-collar workers, for instance, tending to be more pro-Labour in industrial areas than workers in similar occupations in rural or

94

Table 6.3 General election results by region, 1992 and 1997

| Region | MPs elected in 1992 | | | | MPs elected in 1997 | | | |
	Cons.	Lab.	Lib.Dem.	Other	Cons.	Lab.	Lib.Dem.	Other
South West	38	4	6	–	22	15	14	–
London	48	35	1	–	11	57	6	–
Rest of South East	106	3	–	–	73	36	9	–
East Anglia	17	3	–	–	14	8	–	–
Midlands	57	43	–	–	28	74	1	1
North	53	107	3	–	17	138	4	1
Scotland	11	49	9	3	–	56	10	6
Wales	6	27	1	4	–	34	2	4
Northern Ireland	–	–	–	17	–	–	–	18
Total	336	271	20	24	165	418	46	30

suburban areas. There is a long-standing tendency for electors without firm partisan allegiances to conform to the majority viewpoint in their area. In the 1980s, however, Britain experienced a period of continuous economic growth in the southern half of England combined with virtual stagnation in many of the older industrial areas of northern England and western Scotland. This was partly a result of the Conservative government's economic policies, and it is not at all surprising that the political consequence of it has been an increasing gap between the pro-Conservative tendencies of the southern counties and the pro-Labour tendencies of the northern industrial areas. In 1987 Glasgow and the seven largest cities in northern England returned forty-three Members of Parliament of whom thirty-nine were Labour, three Conservative and one Liberal in affiliation. In contrast, London returned fifty-eight Conservatives to twenty-three Labour MPs, one Liberal and two Social Democrats. The rest of southern England was overwhelmingly pro-Conservative.

The events of the 1990s have slightly modified this geographical skew, partly because the economic recession of 1990–2 had a rather worse impact on the south than on the north, partly because non-economic factors produced a dramatic swing to Labour over the entire country in the 1997 election. A regional breakdown of the results in 1992 and 1997 is given in Table 6.3, from which it can be seen that the Conservative advantage in Greater London and the Midlands was swept away in that five-year period. At the same time, the Conservative Party was left without any MPs at all from Scotland and Wales, for the first time in history in the case of Scotland and the first time since 1910 in the case of Wales.

In addition to these social and geographical changes, there have also been some attitudinal changes in recent decades. There is scattered but persuasive evidence that the British people have become more sceptical about the performance of their governments. Between the 1950s and the late 1970s, successive failures by both Conservative and Labour governments to promote economic growth as fast as that in Britain's main competitors undermined the confidence people once felt in their chosen party. Repeated survey have shown that feelings of loyalty towards both main parties have weakened. Voters have become more detached, more fickle in their political sympathies and more volatile in their voting behaviour. Butler has attributed this increased volatility not only to disillusionment but also to weakened class loyalties, higher educational levels and the impact of television on election campaigns (Butler 1989: 65–6).

All these developments have tended to make electors more likely to pursue individual – as opposed to collective – interests when they participate in politics, and also more sensitive to particular issues of policy. Surveys show that in 1979, and again in 1983, Labour did poorly (by its own earlier standards) among manual workers as a whole, but nevertheless maintained its support among workers in public enterprises. The reason is that Labour was seen as the party that supported public enterprises and was willing to subsidize them from general revenue, whereas the Conservative Party wanted them to pay their way and had a policy of selling them back to private ownership where possible. White-collar workers and managers in the public sector were much more inclined to vote Labour than their equivalents in the private sector, for exactly the same reason (see Dunleavy and Husbands 1984: 14).

In regard to the influence of policy issues on voting, we are fortunate that a study has been published revealing the political attitudes of a panel of Londoners who were interviewed repeatedly, and in depth, between 1951 and 1974 (Himmelweit et al. 1981). The information made available by this study is far richer than the information gathered by the ordinary single-interview or double-interview surveys, with interviews conducted on the doorstep. The study suggests that individual values and attitudes to political issues have had a greater influence on voting behaviour than has commonly been believed, and that this kind of influence has been of growing importance in recent years. The sample of electors interviewed in this study was small, but doubts on this score about the reliability of the results have been largely resolved by the statistical analysis made by Rose and McAllister and published under the title *Voters Begin to Choose*. These authors draw their data from several national surveys based on large samples and they show that voters have indeed become more volatile in the last two decades, more likely to be influenced by attitudes to particular policies and more likely to be influenced by the campaign (Rose and McAllister 1986: *passim*).

Himmelweit and her colleagues believe that British voting behaviour is better explained by a model depicting electors as consumers than by the more familiar model of class conflict. In the Himmelweit view electors are individually motivated, spending time to gain information about what the parties have to offer and 'buying' whichever package appears to them to be most advantageous. This implies that the 'floating voter', who seriously considers changing votes (or abstentions) between one election and another, should be regarded as normal rather than as a deviation from the assumed norm of partisan loyalty.

The statistics derived from the study support this model. Only 30 per cent of the respondents made the same voting decision in all the six elections covered by the study (ibid.: 34). A fair number changed more than once. They confirmed the findings of one of the earlier studies, namely that many of the floaters are keenly interested in politics, and the floaters as a category should not be regarded as apathetic (see Benewick et al. 1969; Himmelweit et al. 1981: 239). They showed that the floaters were significantly more likely than the consistent voters to be undecided at the beginning of the election campaign and that many of them made up their minds only in the last few days (Himmelweit et al. 1981: 47, 241). They also showed that electoral volatility and indecisiveness increased over the period covered by the study, with a third of the sample in 1974 undecided at the beginning of the election campaign (ibid.: 193).

This increase in volatility was associated with the increased support for the Liberal Party (though not associated only with this). It appears that this support has been surprisingly lacking in constancy. There have been few faithful Liberal voters. Even in the two elections of 1974, separated by only eight months, there was an astonishing degree of movement into and out of the Liberal camp. Sarlvik and Crewe report that 48 per cent of the Liberal supporters in February 1974 – about 3 million voters – had defected by October, but over 2 million new voters had been attracted (Sarlvik and Crewe 1983: 46).

What attracted voters to the Liberals? The conclusion of the Himmelweit study is that this is the wrong question to ask. The Liberal Party got most of its support from voters who were disenchanted with the party they previously supported but not ready to go over to the other main party. 'The Liberal vote is a vote of disaffection; it represents movement away from a party rather than movement to the party; it is a vote signifying departure rather than arrival' (Himmelweit et al. 1981: 159). In view of this we should not be surprised that Liberal voters have been so inconstant, apt to move on to the other main party or back to their former love after dallying with the Liberals.

A detailed examination of the attitudes of the Himmelweit panel to political issues revealed that these attitudes did indeed prove to be good predictors of voting at the next election, as the consumer model of voting implies (ibid.: 83). It was also shown that there is 'a causal chain from attitude to vote and from attitude shift to vote defection' (ibid.: 101). It seems that there is a kind of political market-place in which party propagandists and other moulders of opinion try to shape popular attitudes to issues of the day, while electors weigh these messages against their own perception of what would be good for them and what would be good for the country as a whole.

What are the most important issues? There are several more or less permanent issues on which the Conservative Party has had an advantage, in the sense of being viewed by most electors as having the better record and/or the better policies. These are foreign affairs, defence, the protection of law and order, and the control of prices and inflation. Equally, there are two more or less permanent issues on which the Labour Party has an advantage. These are the delivery of social services and the control of unemployment.

There are also issues on which a party can only lose. One is the nationalization of industry, to which the great majority of electors have always been hostile. This issue has repeatedly lost votes for Labour. Another losing issue is industrial relations, associated with the prevalence of strikes and the power of trade unions. This hindered the Conservatives in 1974 and Labour in 1979, both parties being blamed for the strikes that occurred while they were in power.

Issues rise and fall in their significance for the electorate, partly because of events but also because of deliberate efforts by party leaders to promote them or neutralize them. The control of immigration became an important and emotional issue in the 1960s, but is no longer significant. The introduction of comprehensive schools became salient in the 1970s, but is now a *fait accompli*. In the 1979 election the Conservatives successfully promoted the reduction of taxation as an issue. The Falkland Islands war of 1982 promoted defence to the forefront of public attention, and as this was to the advantage of the Conservatives, it was exploited accordingly.

An interesting example of issue manipulation is provided by policy towards municipal housing. As the Labour Party has supported extensive housing provision with subsidized rents, this has been one of Labour's better issues. When Conservative governments made legislative changes to housing policy in 1957 and 1972, they incurred widespread unpopularity on each occasion. A poll taken in 1983 indicated that only 19 per cent of municipal tenants supported the Conservative Party (*Guardian*, 13 June 1983). In the face of this, the Thatcher government promoted a new and ingenious policy. Local authorities have been compelled to offer their houses for sale to tenants at advantageous prices. As nobody is compelled to buy, tenants' interests are not infringed. However, those who take up the option are thereby transformed from tenants into owner-occupiers, and lose their interest in maintaining rent subsidies. Surveys indicate that most owner-occupiers usually vote Conservative.

The whole field of voting behaviour has therefore to be regarded as a field of tactical and strategic operations, in which political leaders and news editors have the initiative but the electors decide the outcome of the battle. In doing this they are influenced partly by their personal and family situations; partly by their economic interests; partly by their political and social values; and partly by their perception of current political issues, as these are presented to them through the mass media.

Recent elections and the future

The 1983 election was not an exciting contest, because the victory of the Conservative Party was a foregone conclusion from the beginning of the campaign. It was, however, a very interesting event because the Conservatives won in spite of having presided over the greatest growth of unemployment since the slump of the early 1930s. The Conservatives did not pretend to have a remedy for this development; on the contrary, they predicted that mass unemployment would remain for the foreseeable future. Their strategy was to disown responsibility for unemployment, saying on the one hand that it was produced by international economic forces that had affected other countries equally; and on the other that the situation would be improved only if the British people became (under Conservative guidance) more enterprising and the British economy more competitive. The message was stern rather than optimistic.

The 1987 election was also a walkover for the Conservatives. Unemployment was much reduced and weighed seriously against the government only in the industrial areas of the north, which were in any case overwhelmingly pro-Labour. The Conservatives were able to claim that their economic strategy had been successful and made much of the fact that in 1986 the British economic growth rate was actually higher than that of France (for the first time since 1958) and that of West Germany (for the first time since 1945). The result of the election was never in doubt, with Margaret Thatcher achieving her third successive victory and saying that she intended 'to go on and on'.

The 1992 election was more interesting, as the Conservative Party won against all the odds and all the pollsters' predictions. Many of the policies pursued by the Thatcher government after its 1987 victory proved to be unpopular with the electorate. A MORI survey for the *Sunday Times* in November 1988 showed that 75 per cent of electors disliked the plan to privatize the water authorities, 69 per cent disliked the plan to privatize the electricity industry, and 60 per cent disliked the idea of replacing grants to university students by loans. A further plan that aroused vigorous hostility was that to replace property taxes as a source of local government revenue by a fixed 'community charge' to be paid equally by every adult living within the boundaries of a local authority, no account being taken of ability to pay. This charge became known as the poll tax and it was a disaster for the government. Demonstrations against it were held, including one in central London which led to hundreds of demonstrators and policemen being injured. Getting on for 2 million people refused to pay the tax, with the result that local authorities lost a good deal of revenue. Thousands of non-payers were prosecuted and fined, which was a time-consuming business for police and courts. By the autumn of 1990 the Conservatives were fifteen points behind the Labour Party in the polls. It was largely because of this that Thatcher was ditched by her colleagues.

John Major's appointment as leader and Prime Minister revived the government's popularity, and for some months the Conservatives enjoyed a slender lead in the polls. However, in 1991 the onset of recession, a series of bankruptcies that had no precedent since the early 1930s, and rising unemployment caused the lead to evaporate. The election was delayed as long as possible, but when it was called all the polling organizations predicted a Conservative defeat. Both parties then waged clever campaigns, Labour's being more flashy and more expensive while the Conservative effort was more modest. Major himself went from city to city carrying a small soap box, which he set up in the city square for highly informal meetings. The main theme of Conservative propaganda was the burden that would be imposed on taxpayers by the tax increases that Labour proposed to levy. It was shown that higher incomes taxes would be paid by everyone earning over £21,000 a year. Seven thousand large posters were put up on hoardings all over the country to ram home this point that Labour stood for higher taxes. It was also claimed that Labour's plan to introduce a payroll tax on industry would cause employers to reduce their labour force, and that the proposed minimum wage would have the same effect. In the last week of the campaign Major also attacked Labour's plan to create a Scottish Parliament, which he said would weaken the unity of the United Kingdom.

Right up until polling day the opinion polls predicted a Conservative defeat, but when the votes were counted Labour trailed the Conservatives by 7.5 percentage points and the latter were returned to power with an overall majority of twenty-one seats. The General Secretary of the Labour Party, in his report to the party, said that this could only be explained by postulating that numerous voters, while sufficiently critical of the government to say that they intended to vote against it, found when it came to the point that they did not actually want to see Labour in power. A wildly enthusiastic Labour rally in Sheffield, held and partly televised a few days before polling day, was said to have put floating voters off; they did not actually want to be governed by 'that lot'.

As the 1997 election produced a dramatic shift in party support, it deserves more attention than has been given to particular elections in previous editions of this book. The election campaign had, in fact, three extraordinary features.

One of these features was that it was the first campaign for nearly fifty years not to be dominated by economic issues, namely the performance of the government in office, the economic and fiscal promises made by the two main parties, and public expectations about their competence and probable success in economic matters. The Conservatives won most of the elections from 1951 to 1992 largely because electors trusted their competence in economic affairs more than they trusted that of the Labour Party. They lost office in 1964 mainly because the public realized that British economic growth in the previous thirteen years had been slower than that of France, Germany and several other European countries. Labour got in by promising to revitalize the economy, but they were so conspicuously unsuccessful in this that they were thrown out in 1970. In 1974 the Conservatives lost again because they proved unable to control the trade unions, and British industry was reduced to a three-day working week by the government's failure to cope with industrial strife. However, the ensuing Labour government secured industrial peace only by giving in to excessive union demands, so that in 1975 the rate of inflation rose to 25 per cent in twelve months, much the highest rate in British history. In 1978–9 industrial peace was again shattered by the unions, and the Conservatives returned to power for eighteen years, the longest period of single-party rule since the eighteenth century.

Why, then, were economic issues insignificant in 1997? To this crucial question there are two answers. The first is that, although the Conservative government of 1992–7 had been extremely successful in its economic policies, reducing the unemployment rate to the lowest in the European Union while retaining a very low rate of inflation, the majority of electors refused to believe in this success. The polls indicate that the main reason for this scepticism was the effect on public opinion of the day in September 1992 when Britain, along with Italy, was forced to withdraw from the Exchange Rate Mechanism (ERM) of the European Community that Britain had joined two years earlier. This did not really matter, as the slight devaluation of sterling that followed the withdrawal helped the economy by making British exports more competitive. However, the withdrawal was embarrassing at the time because the government had promised to stay within the ERM, and the press called the day of withdrawal 'Black Wednesday'. Gallup Polls showed that the Conservatives, always previously thought better than Labour at handling the economy and leading by 11 points on that question in the spring of 1992, suddenly lost public confidence so that they trailed Labour by 10 points by the spring of 1993. Despite the government's excellent economic record in the following years, its reputation with the general public never recovered from this setback (Crewe 1996: 429).

The second answer is that Blair's transformation of Labour Party policies left no important gap between the parties on economic issues. He promised not to renationalize privatized industries, not to raise public expenditure except on education, and not to increase rates of income tax. Labour could no longer be accused of being a tax-and-spend party. The only real economic difference between parties was Labour's promise to introduce a legal minimum wage, but this never became an election issue as the Conservatives did not think they would gain votes by attacking it.

The second extraordinary feature of the election was that no other policy issues of substance arose to divide the parties. The main reason for this was the absolute determination of Blair and his supporters not to permit it. When the government promised to continue their insistence on a whole package of educational reforms that were highly unpopular with teachers and Labour local counsellors, Blair and his shadow minister of education promised to continue them too. When the government introduced a policy of 'zero tolerance' for even minor forms of street crime and to insist on sending even more people to prison, the Labour spokesman on home affairs endorsed both policies and promised to be even tougher. When the Labour spokesman on Northern Ireland rashly suggested that she would like to see Sinn Fein rejoin the peace talks, she was quickly repudiated by Blair, greatly helped by a series of IRA bomb attacks and bomb scares in England. The only significant policy differences were Labour's commitment to constitutional reform in Britain and to endorsing the Social Chapter of the Maastricht Treaty on European integration. However, English electors showed no interest in the first of these matters, and if the

101

Conservatives had laid much emphasis on the second this would have drawn further public attention to the divisions within their party. The Conservative manifesto contained one or two novel ideas on taxation policy, but these aroused little public interest.

This almost complete lack of policy conflicts, combined with Labour's overwhelming lead in the polls, meant that the 1997 election campaign was bound to be boring to anyone with a serious interest in politics. However, a third extraordinary feature was that it was saved from that fate for the rest of the population by a development that turned it into the most sordid campaign of the twentieth century. This development was the emergence of a series of sexual and financial scandals, or alleged scandals, involving Conservative MPs.

Allegations of sexual misconduct, never before significant in British elections, had first become prominent in 1994. At the Conservative Party annual conference in October 1993 Major had said that his slogan for the coming year was 'Back to Basics', by which he was thinking mainly about educational reforms. Several newspaper editors realized that the slogan could also be said to cover what American Republicans of that period were calling the restoration of family values, so that the government might be damaged by revelations of adultery on the part of Conservative MPs and ministers. The editors proceeded to secure such revelations by a variety of methods, including hiring private detectives to conduct secret surveillance of MPs and offering very large payments to girl-friends who were willing to disclose embarrassing details of the sexual behaviour of their lovers. A junior minister was disclosed as having six mistresses as well as a wife, which one national newspaper reported by covering its entire front page with the words 'Yes, Yes, Yes, Yes, Yes, Yes Minister'. Then one of the ablest ministers in the Cabinet was embarrassed into resigning when his girl-friend revealed some comical details of their relationship, notably that on one occasion he had answered questions in Parliament while wearing the outfit of his favourite football team under his formal suit and had then repaired to her flat and scored four goals. The press did not fail to point out that his post was Minister for the National Heritage.

In the same period it emerged that one or two Conservative MPs had accepted money from outside groups to ask parliamentary questions designed to illicit information from ministers that would help the groups. This is not illegal but is contrary to parliamentary ethics. The Prime Minister responded by appointing a committee under Lord Nolan, with a membership acceptable to all three national parties, to investigate the whole issue of the outside earnings of MPs. This committee produced a report, showing a greatly increased incidence of unethical or questionably ethical practices by MPs, that led to the adoption of a new law requiring MPs to report outside earnings. In 1995 and 1996 questions of this kind were driven from the headlines by other issues, but in the 1997 election campaign they came back with a bang.

In the second and third weeks of the campaign newspapers opposed to the government made a carefully-timed series of allegations against Conservative candidates that enabled them to call the party 'the party of sleaze'. In a period of ten days the public learned that: (1) a Conservative MP had withdrawn from the campaign because he had been forced to admit receiving a large wad of bank notes from an Egyptian multi-millionaire who had vowed to take revenge on the government because Department of Trade officials had accused him of making dishonest financial statements, and did this in part by first giving money to Conservative MPs and then, months or years later, accusing them of accepting bribes; (2) a former minister had withdrawn from his candidacy for a safe seat in Scotland because of newspaper allegations of a former love affair with a married woman; (3) the candidate due to replace him, the Chairman of the Scottish Conservative Party, resigned because he wanted to protect his family from threatened allegations (which were made anyway) about a sexual misdemeanour (said to be homosexual) in his past; (4) a former minister standing for a safe Conservative seat was alleged to have accepted another large wad of bank notes from the Egyptian, though he denied this charge; and (5) a junior minister was said by a pro-Labour tabloid to have had 'a sex romp' in a park with a young hostess from a Soho strip joint, who had been paid by the newspaper to invite him into the park, where they were duly photographed by press photographers who had followed them.

The last two of these allegations proved to be particularly damaging because some top ministers let it be known that they thought the accused MPs should withdraw from the campaign for the good of the party. In the 'sex romp' case two senior Cabinet ministers expressed this view while two other senior Cabinet ministers contradicted it and urged the MP to stay and fight. In both cases the local branches of the Conservative Party held emergency meetings at which their candidates were supported; a result that could have been predicted as local branches jealously guard their right to choose their candidates, the only important power they possess. This made the party leaders look a little silly.

It is impossible to say how many voters were directly influenced by these events, but the revelations damaged the Conservative campaign because they were carefully timed to take the headlines on days when official statistics (produced by civil servants, not influenced by politicians) were published showing that the unemployment rate and rate of inflation had declined. Major had provided for the longest campaign period since 1945 so that he would have time to change public opinion by stressing his government's successful economic performance, and the sleaze allegations frustrated this. With the same aim in mind, he challenged Blair to a televised debate, on the lines of the presidential debates in America, but this was also frustrated because Blair wisely refused to accept the challenge.

Four other factors contributed to the scale of the Conservative defeat. One was the entry of the new Referendum Party, formed a year or so earlier by a multi-millionaire with the single policy of demanding a referendum before any government agreed to further measures of European integration. This party fielded no fewer than 547 candidates, of whom 505 lost their deposits. It is difficult to say how many constituency results were directly affected, but it is likely that most of its supporters were previously Conservative voters, and its presence and propaganda gave continuing publicity to Conservative divisions over the European Community.

Another factor was the behaviour of the national press. At the beginning of the campaign Britain's largest-circulation newspaper, the *Sun*, announced its conversion to the Labour cause on the instruction of its Australian proprietor, whom Blair had thoughtfully flown out to visit a few weeks earlier. The *Sun* had definitely helped the Conservatives in 1992 by its sensational last-minute warnings of the dangers posed by Labour, and it helped Labour in 1997 by its scorn for the Conservatives and its promotion of the 'sex romp' scandal. In the last week of the campaign the *Financial Times* cautiously came down on Labour's side. Several pro-Conservative newspapers continued to damage their favoured party by harping on its divisions over Europe.

A third factor was that, for the first time since 1945, Labour's campaign was more efficiently organized than that of their opponents, who appeared to be somewhat demoralized by the near-certainty of defeat. And the fourth was the development of tactical voting, with Labour and Liberal Democratic supporters in some areas switching to the candidate most likely to defeat the Conservative.

The overall result was a record-breaking victory for Labour, better described as a tidal wave then a landslide as it swept across the whole of Britain. The Conservative share of the vote, 31.4 per cent, was the lowest since 1832, and the number of their candidates to be elected was the lowest since 1906. The swing from Conservative to Labour, 10 per cent, was the largest since 1945, and the number of Labour MPs elected, 418, was the largest ever. Other features of the result were that the Liberal Democrats doubled their parliamentary representation, which rose from 20 in 1992 to 46 in 1997, their best result since 1929, and that the number of women elected rose from 59 to 120, of whom 101 were Labour MPs. It was altogether a sensational election, which may usher in a new era in British history.

Further reading

The best account of electoral procedures is that in Leonard (1996) *Elections in Britain Today*; for discussions of the case for electoral reform see Jowell and Oliver (1989) *The Changing Constitution*, chs. 4 and 13; for analyses of voting behaviour see Sarlvic and Crewe (1983) *Decade of Dealignment* and Himmelweit et al. (1981) *How Voters Decide*; after each general election David Butler and a colleague publish a valuable analysis of the issues, campaign and results, of which the most recent is Butler and Kavanagh (1992) *The British General Election of 1992*; for an overview and analysis of changes since 1945 see Butler (1989) *British General Elections since 1945*.

7

PRESSURE GROUPS

Seen in the light of democratic theory, the citizen is first and foremost an elector, having general views about government and expressing preferences between one political party and another. Seen in another light, the citizen is not so much a whole political individual as a bundle of specific interests and values, having definite views about particular issues of policy. A citizen with children will be concerned about education and the maintenance of child allowances; one with a widowed mother will be worried about the level of widows' pensions; sports enthusiasts will want more playing fields; trade unionists will have views about the law relating to trade unions; animal lovers will be concerned about animal welfare. The list could be extended almost indefinitely.

While some citizens are active in political parties that embody general attitudes to government, others are active in defence of their particular interests and values. The British political scene is populated by a vast number of pressure groups, whose spokesmen are engaged in the business of exerting influence on government policies. Pressure groups are highly varied in character but they can be usefully categorized into three broad types. As so often in political science, the categories are not watertight compartments and a few groups straddle two of the categories. But this fact does not destroy the utility of the classification.

Types of pressure group

In the first place, there are innumerable permanent associations that are concerned to defend and promote the interests of their members. Trade unions and trade associations are the most obvious of these, but the category also includes groups concerned with religion, sports, motoring and other activities. Nobody has ever taken a census of interest groups, and their multiplicity and variety are perhaps best illustrated by a random selection of titles, as follows:

The Small Pig Keepers' Council
The National Union of Railwaymen
The Society of Authors

The Bookmakers' Protection Association
The Royal Yachting Association
The National Union of Students
The Free Church Federal Council
The Take Away Fast Food Federation
The Royal Automobile Club
The British Limbless Ex-Servicemen's Association
The British Insurance Brokers' Association
The National Federation of Pakistani Associations

Very few of these organizations are concerned exclusively with political action. The majority of them provide services of various kinds for their members and many of them regard this as their main function, turning to politics only when the interests of their members are threatened by government action or by the activities of other groups in a way that can be prevented only by government action. But the range of government activities is now so great that most interest groups take on a political role from time to time, acting in ways that will be discussed in a later section.

The second category comprises organizations that are concerned not with the protection of their members' interests but with the promotion of some kind of social, moral or political cause. Groups of this kind are best called promotional groups, and a complete list of the promotional groups that play a role in the British political process would be just as varied, though not so long, as a complete list of interest groups. Some examples follow:

The Royal Society for the Prevention of Cruelty to Animals
The Lord's Day Observance Society
The Council for the Preservation of Rural England
The Campaign for Nuclear Disarmament
The Noise Abatement Society
The Organization Against Sexism in Software (OASIS)
The Howard League for Penal Reform
The Friends of the Earth

Promotional groups tend to have smaller memberships than interest groups and, unlike the latter, to draw their members largely from the upper and middle classes. Some promotional groups are well financed – there really are people who leave their money to animal welfare societies – while others have to spend a good deal of energy trying to raise funds. But the success of promotional groups in their political activities does not depend either on their ability to claim a mass membership or on their ability to mount an expensive campaign; it depends rather on the quality of their arguments, the energy they put into their activities and the existence or otherwise of a group opposed to the cause they are supporting.

A third category consists of groups that spring into existence to fight a particular proposal and are wound up after the issue has been decided. Government authorities propose to build a new highway, power station or airport; local residents feel that their interests are threatened by the proposal and hold a meeting to protest against it; and within days or weeks a new pressure group is in business. S. E. Finer called such groups 'fire-brigade groups', which is self-explanatory (Finer 1966). A more neutral way of describing the members of this category would be to call them temporary defence groups. They have become increasingly prominent in recent years, partly because of the power of example; the news that a spontaneous association of citizens has wrecked the plans of a county council or government department spreads quickly, and encourages the formation of groups in other parts of the country with similar objectives.

Pressure groups and the administration

Group spokesmen engage in politics in various ways. They write to newspapers; they organize public demonstrations; they speak in Parliament; they sit on government advisory committees; they negotiate directly with government departments. As a broad generalization it is probably true that the more conspicuous their activities are, the less influence they are likely to exert. Public demonstrations and speeches in Parliament are only occasionally effective, while representation on official committees is always helpful, and informal negotiations with government departments pay more dividends than any other form of activity. It is a generalization to which exceptions can be found, particularly in the realm of moral issues. But the point is true enough for it to be sensible to pay most attention in this chapter to the relations of group spokesmen to government departments.

It would be a complete mistake to assume that there is anything sinister about the influence of group spokesmen in Whitehall or to imagine that they usually have difficulty in gaining a hearing. On the contrary, government departments think it both proper and necessary to consult the 'affected interests' in the normal process of administration. They think it proper because the affected interests, broadly defined, will include nearly all those likely to have an informed opinion on any issue that may be in question. They will know best how the existing arrangements work and what their shortcomings are; they are in the best position to judge how effective any proposed changes are likely to be; they can draw attention to the particular difficulties involved in the introduction of reforms. Of course, the responsibility for government policy rests with the minister, and he should not allow himself or herself to be 'captured' by the affected interests, but in the British political tradition it is thought entirely proper that the minister and the permanent staff should consult fully with these interests before notifying Parliament of any modifications in policy that he or she proposes to introduce.

The tradition of constant consultation with the affected interests is strengthened by two further considerations. One is that, as will emerge in Chapter 10, British civil servants are not specialists. They are intelligent people with a good education who acquire a facility for familiarizing themselves with specific problems, but they need advice on technical matters and they often find that they can get it most conveniently by consulting the spokesperson for the industry or activity with which they are concerned. The other consideration is that government departments need the co-operation of the relevant sections of the public if administration is to be efficient and government policies are to be successful. No government could be happy with a situation in which it had constantly to rely on its powers of coercion. Economic policies need the co-operation of both sides of industry if they are to succeed; educational policies need the co-operation of teachers and local authorities; health policies need the co-operation of the medical profession. Consultation does not guarantee co-operation but its absence would almost certainly cause resentment; it is a necessary even though not a sufficient condition of successful administration.

Not all group spokesmen are consulted by government departments because not all groups are recognized as having a legitimate interest in the matters at stake. The Ministry of Defence does not consult pacifist groups, who have to resort to other means of bringing their views to the attention of those in authority. But government departments are generally liberal in their attitudes to this matter, and many promotional groups enjoy fairly close contacts with the relevant departments. Certainly this is true of the groups concerned with social welfare and with penal reform.

There are some groups that are thought so useful by the government that their position has been strengthened by financial support from public funds, or even by legislation requiring certain categories of persons or firms to join them. One is the Pharmaceutical Society of Great Britain, charged with certain regulatory powers and duties. Others include the National Council of Social Service, the Royal Society for the Prevention of Accidents and the Central Council of Physical Recreation.

The complexity of the consultative process varies from one field of activity to another and depends largely on the number of interest groups involved. In most aspects of economic and industrial policy, the government department concerned will have to balance conflicting pressures from the trade associations on one hand and the trade unions on the other. In regard to agricultural policy, the situation was for many years more straightforward because the National Farmers' Union (NFU) was the only group involved. From 1947 until 1972, the level of government support for agriculture was determined by lengthy negotiations between officials of the NFU and officials of the Ministry of Agriculture and Fisheries, which resulted in a 'global award' for the industry. Although the NFU was not always happy with the size of the award, it was rarely willing to jeopardize its good relations with the civil servants involved by attacking the ministry in public. A somewhat cosy relationship therefore developed, which was transformed in January 1973 by Britain's membership of the European Community. Since then, the most important decisions regarding British agriculture have been taken in Brussels, and the relationship between group spokesmen and decision-makers has become more complex.

For some years, the British Medical Association (BMA) enjoyed a relationship with the Ministry of Health that was rather similar to that between the NFU and the Ministry of Agriculture and Fisheries. However, this relationship also has become more complex recently, primarily because other spokesmen for groups within the National Health Service have challenged the virtual monopoly of the BMA. Some of the general practitioners are now represented by another organization and some of the junior hospital doctors have formed a third organized group. Moreover, the nursing profession has become unionized and hospital porters have attempted to influence government policy through the National Union of Public Employees.

The situation regarding universities has always been rather complex. In Britain higher education is largely financed by the government but funds are distributed by the University Funding Council, a body whose members are drawn largely from the academic profession. The network of organizations dealing with the government of universities is illustrated in Figure 7.1, in which the writer's former university is taken as an example.

Messages, inquiries and proposals flow constantly in all directions along the lines of communication indicated in this diagram. The universities are engaged in what seems to be an almost continuous process of framing and revising plans for the future. Such plans have financial implications and have therefore to be

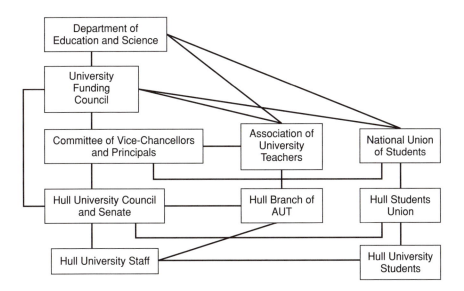

Figure 7.1 The university network

communicated to the Funding Council, which in its turn constantly bombards the universities with requests for information about their activities.

The Association of University Teachers, while out of the mainstream, is not without influence. It speaks for an extremely articulate group of people who also speak for themselves, in a never-ending flow of letters, articles and talks in the mass media. Governments are apt to ignore academic opinions about foreign policy but they cannot easily ignore academic views about higher education. The National Union of Students also enjoys a degree of influence. When the Department of Education and Science proposed in 1971 to abolish the system whereby student unions enjoy substantial autonomy in their expenditure of the public funds given to them, opposition from the students (supported by the Vice-Chancellors' Committee) induced the department to drop the proposal.

This network of institutions and channels of communication is paralleled by similar networks for colleges of education, for technical colleges and for the world of adult education. In the case of technical colleges the local authorities are also involved, and they have their own influential spokesmen in bodies like the County Councils Association. Those responsible for higher education in the ministry have to deal with all these numerous spokespersons on whom, indeed, they rely for information and for guidance about what is feasible. Since higher education cannot be entirely separated from secondary education, they have also to consider the views of the various and influential spokesmen for both state and private schools.

It follows that civil servants in the ministry dealing with education have to deal with a great variety of spokesmen for the various sections of the educational world, who are usually in disagreement with one another. Partly because of this, the ministers responsible for education are given to appointing advisory committees that will hear evidence from all interested groups and contain representatives of many of them, in the hope that the committee will relieve the minister of the difficult task of balancing rival claims and assessing conflicting proposals.

Action through Parliament

Parliament is somewhat less important than the administration as a focus for group pressures in most fields. As the great majority of Bills are drafted by civil servants and sponsored by the government of the day, it is clearly better to apply pressure while the legislation is being planned than to wait until after the Bills are published. Governments dislike major amendments to their legislative proposals and can usually rely on party discipline to prevent such amendments being passed. For this reason, Parliament is less important as a channel of group pressures than is the United States Congress.

It is also noteworthy that in Parliament there is nothing like the level of lobbying on foreign affairs that is accepted as normal in Congress. In 1974, for instance, the Greek–American lobby, representing only a very small proportion of the population, was powerful enough to secure an arms embargo on Turkey following the fighting in Cyprus – a decision that weakened the entire western alliance and caused anxiety in the State Department, the Pentagon and the White House. It is inconceivable that any pressure group could have this kind of impact on defence or foreign policy in Britain.

However, Congress is unique among legislative assemblies in its constitutional separation from the executive and in the weakness of party discipline within it. Pressure groups are highly active in the British parliamentary process even though they are less successful than their American equivalents.

In the first place, a large number of MPs receive financial help from pressure groups. Between 1945 and 1997, between 40 and 50 per cent of Labour MPs were sponsored by trade unions, which paid most of their electoral expenses and in some cases also paid the MP a retainer. In 1966, when Labour won a comfortable majority, the proportion was 41 per cent and in 1979, when Labour lost, it was 49 per cent. However, in February 1996 the party's National Executive Committee decided to discontinue this arrangement, in view of the report of the Nolan Committee which criticized the extent of outside payments to MPs and recommended that they should in future be required to report all such payments for inclusion in the register of Members' interests. It followed that in the 1997 election no Labour candidates were officially sponsored by unions. Many unions have continued to make payments to local party branches, but these are contributions to the local party, not to the MP.

The other parties have not had sponsorship arrangements in the same formal way, and do not permit outside bodies to pay the election expenses of their candidates. However, many individual MPs in all parties act as consultants or advisers to pressure groups and some get a retainer or honorarium for doing so. Business groups and farmers have Conservative MPs active on their behalf. The National Union of Teachers always has at least one Conservative MP acting for it as well as two or more Labour MPs.

It is not thought in any way wrong (as it would be in Congress) for MPs to accept financial help in these ways. Nor is it clear that MPs getting financial assistance from pressure groups are more vigorous in furthering the interests or causes of the groups than are other MPs who act without payment for groups with which they sympathize. As has been remarked: 'Increasingly parliamentary spokesmanship is thought of as a role all private Members may undertake more or less regularly on behalf of the interests and causes to which they are attached. No MP or peer is so characterless as to fail to have a few such attachments' (Potter 1961: 276).

However, in 1995 it emerged that some MPs had been receiving large payments to put down questions to ministers, which was deemed to be unethical as they had never acknowledged that any personal interest was involved. An independent committee under Lord Nolan was appointed to investigate the whole question of outside payments to Members, and this committee reported that a number of Members had also set themselves up as freelance consultants, who were in effect willing to hire themselves out to outside groups wanting advice or other assistance on how to promote their interests in Parliament. It was recommended, and accepted by a large majority in a parliamentary vote, that henceforth all MPs should be required to report all outside earnings, from whatever source, for publication in the Register of Member's Interests, published annually.

The ways in which MPs can help a group are many and varied. They may ask questions in Parliament on the group's behalf. They may take up particular matters with the minister concerned. They may speak on behalf of the group at party meetings, particularly at meetings of specialized groups of backbenchers. They may sign motions calling upon the government to modify its policies in this way or that; for instance, on one occasion lobbyists from the theatrical world persuaded over half the Members of Parliament to sign a motion asking the government to abolish entertainment tax on the theatre. Governments are naturally concerned to keep in favour with backbench MPs when this is possible, and these activities are not without influence on policy.

In the legislative field, MPs may introduce Private Members' Bills that have been drafted by, or in consultation with, particular pressure groups. The animal welfare groups are particularly successful in promoting legislation, partly because there are no countervailing groups arguing the opposite case. The Royal Society for the Prevention of Cruelty to Animals has a Parliamentary Department that advises friendly MPs and provides them with draft legislation. Smaller groups may employ one of the several firms of parliamentary agents to draft legislative proposals.

Moral issues provide good opportunities for MPs acting on behalf of pressure groups, because governments are reluctant to insist on party discipline in such matters. The death penalty was abolished by a Private Member's Bill promoted by the National Campaign for the Abolition of Capital Punishment. The law relating to abortion was liberalized as a result of the activities of the Abortion Law Reform Association. The Society of Authors (which is neither powerful nor wealthy) was instrumental in securing the passage of the Obscene Publications Act which makes literary merit a defence against censorship and gives literary critics the status of expert witnesses if legal cases arise. These and other reforms show that in some areas of legislation Parliament is very amenable to influence by a well-organized and determined group of reformers.

The Committee Stage of legislation provides another opportunity for pressure groups to exert influence. Sympathetic MPs get a daily briefing from groups during this stage, and it is easier to get a minor amendment accepted here, or to persuade the government to modify a clause, than it is to secure amendments on the floor of the House.

Public campaigns

It has sometimes been said that public campaigns by a pressure group are a sign of weakness, indicating that the group has failed to secure acceptance by the appropriate government department as an affected interest (or a body with useful information), and cannot achieve its aims by parliamentary action. There is clearly some truth in this generalization, which was exemplified by the activities of the Campaign for Nuclear Disarmament (CND) in the late 1950s and the 1960s. CND was not regarded by the government as representing an affected interest and it had no specialized information not possessed by the Ministry of Defence. It therefore had no direct access to the administration and it could not hope to win parliamentary votes since party discipline on this subject was strict. A public campaign was the only alternative, and CND was able to get the support of tens of thousands in massive demonstrations and marches. However, there is no evidence that this campaign advanced the cause of nuclear disarmament. It certainly increased public awareness of the issue, but polls suggested that the number of converts made by CND was smaller than the number of previously apathetic citizens who were activated into opposition to the aims of the movement.

Nevertheless, it would be wrong to conclude that public campaigns are usually a waste of time. On the one hand, they may have an educative effect on public opinion that pays dividends in the long run. On the other, they can be very successful, when waged by 'fire-brigade' groups, in preventing developments that are promoted by governmental authorities but are unpopular with citizens.

Alderman has given several examples of the educative effect, notably the success of the Homosexual Law Reform Society in liberalizing public attitudes between 1958 and 1967 and the success of the Abortion Law Reform Association in accomplishing the same task between 1963 and 1967 (Alderman 1984: 104–6). Both these campaigns led to legislative reform in the latter year. Other examples include the campaign against bad housing and the campaign to secure government aid to disabled people (ibid.: 107–8).

There are numerous examples of local campaigns to stop proposed construction projects or divert them to other locations. The most dramatic was the intense campaign waged by local citizens to overturn the government's decision in 1964 to build a third London airport at Stansted, some 30 miles to the north-east of the city. The noise and the destruction of historic buildings were the reasons for the objection, which was supported by over a hundred organizations and rapidly formed community groups. After over three years of controversy, the government agreed to appoint a commission to inquire into the costs and benefits of various alternative sites. The popular favourite was Foulness, a marshy island near the mouth of the Thames where aircraft noise would disturb relatively few people. After the most extensive cost–benefit analysis ever undertaken anywhere, the commission rejected this alternative and proposed another inland site at Cublington, to the north-west of London. There followed another dramatic campaign by local residents, which eventually led the government to capitulate and agree (in 1971) to build the airport at Foulness. Ironically, it was decided in 1974 that a new airport was not really needed in view of the move to larger (and therefore fewer) aircraft, so that popular resistance not only spared the residents of Stansted and Cublington from disturbance but also spared the taxpayer from unnecessary expense. In the 1980s the issue was re-opened, the upshot being that the small airport at Stansted is being enlarged gradually.

Other campaigns have been waged to change the planned location of new highways and power stations. If sufficient local residents object to such a plan, the government is obliged to conduct a public inquiry at which evidence can be heard. At one stage in the 1970s it was found that if objectors made so much noise at the inquiry that the witnesses could not be heard, the plan had to be deferred. Several projects were defeated, or had to be modified, as a result of this kind of tactic. The government now goes to great trouble to ensure that all critics are seen to be given a fair hearing; thus, a 1984 inquiry into a proposed nuclear power station on the east coast lasted just over twelve months.

Public campaigns of this local kind illustrate how much political influence can be exerted by groups of citizens, having very little money and no professional staff, if they feel strongly about an issue. This sort of popular influence on government has tended to increase over the past two decades, both because environmental concerns have increased and because campaigners have learned by example. It follows that public campaigns are almost as important as parliamentary campaigns as a means of securing changes in policy.

Pressure groups and democracy

It is possible to doubt whether the influence of pressure groups in the process of government is entirely compatible with the traditional democratic view that policy ought to reflect the wishes of the electorate, as expressed through their representatives in Parliament. It can be argued that sectional interests or groups of enthusiasts have shown themselves able to frustrate or distort the will of the majority, either through the use of superior resources or because they acquire a privileged position in the system.

The concern that is occasionally voiced about the resources of pressure groups seems to have little foundation in Britain. There is as much freedom to organize pressure groups as there is to contest elections or form political parties. Wealth is not necessary to success and can never guarantee it. Money is always useful, but as a resource for a pressure group it appears to be less valuable than specialized information, enthusiasm, good contacts, the ability to get favourable publicity and the power to hinder the administrative process by obstruction of one kind or another. There is no money in penal reform, but the Howard League has exercised a good deal of influence over the years. The weekend walkers who formed the Friends of the Lake District have fought successful battles against the Central Electricity Generating Board. Representatives for Welsh dinghy sailors took on the Standard Oil Company, with the result that the company modified its plans to build a harbour and oil refinery at Milford Haven so as to preserve sailing facilities in the estuary. The campaigns on moral issues mentioned above have succeeded by virtue of the intellectual arguments and convictions of their leaders.

Though there is little need for concern about the possibility that wealth might be able to buy political influence, it certainly does not follow that group pressures are perfectly balanced. The postwar period in Britain has been marked by a general tendency for producers' groups to be more influential than consumers' groups. Beer has argued persuasively that the national interest has been harmed by the 'scramble for subsidies' engaged in by industrial groups and the 'scramble for pay' engaged in by trade unions (Beer 1982: 48–76). Many of these groups, along with several professional associations, have also shown hostility to radical innovations and have thus strengthened the forces of inertia in British society. But in doing this they have, for better or worse, performed a function that most British people seem to approve of.

Further reading

The best introduction to this topic is Alderman (1984) *Pressure Groups and Government in Great Britain*; for interesting and more discursive treatments see Grant (1989) *Pressure Groups, Politics and Democracy in Britain* and Richardson and Jordan (1987) *Government and Pressure Groups in Britain*; for some useful chapters on group pressures in Parliament see Rush (1990) *Parliament and Pressure Groups*; for some excellent brief case studies of pressure see James (1997) *British Government: A Reader in Policy Making*, section 4.

8

POLITICIANS AND LEADERS

The process of government is a complex activity in which the participants fill a variety of roles, including those of elector, party worker, group spokesperson, legislator, administrator and minister of the Crown. All are engaged in political activity, but in a democratic system the term 'politician' is normally reserved for those who compete for public office: councillors and aldermen in local government and MPs and ministers in national government. This book is concerned mainly with national government, and the purpose of this chapter is to examine the recruitment and characteristics of Members of Parliament, their role in parliamentary politics, and the way in which some of them emerge as ministers and national leaders.

The recruitment of politicians

The first point to be made on this topic is a negative one. Britain does not have a locality rule of the kind that exists in the United States, and prospective Members of Parliament do not follow such a standardized route to political success as prospective Congressmen. In the United States there is a firm convention (to some extent backed by law) that candidates for political office should be residents – and usually long-standing residents – of the area in which they are nominated. A person who tries to ignore this convention is known as a 'carpet-bagger', and his or her chances of electoral success are much less than they would be if he or she were a local person. Partly because of this, aspiring politicians normally have to work their way up a well-established ladder in which they are first active in local political clubs, then run as a candidate for local or state office, and after some success in these endeavours are able to secure their party's nomination for a congressional election. It follows that the great majority of members of the US Congress serve an apprenticeship in local or state politics before going to Washington. In most European democracies there is also a strong tendency for representatives to have roots in their constituencies; in some (such as France and Belgium) it is common for people to retain a municipal office even while serving in the national legislature.

In Britain candidates for parliamentary elections are selected by local party branches, who in this matter are virtually (though not completely) autonomous. But, except in a few areas, local parties do not have any particular preference for local people. Candidates may indeed have served in municipal or county governments, but this service is as likely to have been in another locality as in the area where they secure a parliamentary nomination. Local selection committees want the best candidate they can get, and by and large they do not much mind where this candidate comes from. Most candidates have weak points as well as strong ones, and a local person labours under the disadvantage that their weaknesses may be known to the selection committee. Moreover, if there are two local contenders it may be difficult for the committee to choose between them and less divisive to pass over both in favour of an outsider (see Ranney 1965: 110). Nor as a general rule does place of origin have any perceptible effect on the support given to candidates by voters; they vote for the party, not for the person, and are rarely interested in the personal characteristics of the candidate nominated by the party they support. Very few candidates make any claims to local residence or activities in their election addresses.

The only important qualification that has to be made to these generalizations is that most candidates in Scotland are Scots, in Wales, Welsh and in Northern Ireland, Irish. But candidates are not tied to any particular area within these countries, and ethnic identity is not an essential characteristic. Thus, James Callaghan is an Englishman (albeit with an Irish name) who represented a Welsh constituency for many years, while Roy Jenkins is a Welshman who lives near London and represented a constituency in Glasgow.

How are people recruited to a career in national politics? What kind of previous experience is common among candidates? One kind of experience that is fairly common is service in municipal or county government. In recent elections something like a third of the candidates had at some time in their careers been elected to a local council. It should not be thought that all these candidates had fixed their eyes on a parliamentary career and had become active in local government as a step towards this goal. This happens in some cases, but for most people in this category recruitment to national politics is a discontinuous three-stage process. First they become active in a local party branch; then they volunteer or are persuaded to stand for the local council; and later they decide to seek a parliamentary nomination. Entering national politics by this route has always been common among Labour MPs but has only recently become common among Conservatives. In postwar Parliaments between 39 and 47 per cent of Labour MPs have had local government experience, with an average per Parliament of 45 per cent. Among Conservatives only 14 per cent had had local government experience in the Parliament of 1945–50, but the proportion rose steadily to 38 per cent in the Parliament of 1974–9 (Burch and Moran 1985).

Another established ladder to a career in national politics is through the trade unions, which, as noted in Chapter 7, have sponsored many Labour candidates. These candidates, like those from local government, are usually recruited by a three-stage process. First, they are active in union affairs in their place of work; then they often become branch officers or full-time union organizers; later they have been chosen by the union as prospective parliamentary candidates. One or two unions have chosen people when they are young and consciously attempted to prepare them for a political career, either by asking them to study the social sciences or by getting them nominated to fight elections in hopeless seats, or by a combination of these methods. But most sponsored candidates have been in their middle years when they first stood, and the union concerned has normally found them a safe seat. A union like the National Union of Mineworkers has been able to do this because it controls the constituency branches of the Labour Party in many mining areas. Other unions have got safe seats for their nominees by offering substantial contributions to local party funds and campaign expenses. Between 1950 and 1997 between 40 and 50 per cent of the Labour Members in each Parliament were sponsored in this way. Many of them had served in local government, so there is a considerable overlap between this group and the group described above.

The only other source of parliamentary candidates that can be readily identified is the small group of political families whose sons are brought up to think in terms of a political career. The Churchills and the Cecils have played leading roles in British politics for several generations. Other families that have contributed politicians over at least two generations in this century include the Chamberlains, the Hoggs and the Woods (the family name of Lord Halifax) on the Conservative side, the Bonham Carters and the Lloyd George family among the Liberals, the Greenwoods and the Wedgwood Benns on the Labour side. The actual number of MPs recruited from this source is very small, but they are important because they have so often achieved positions of leadership.

Taken together, local government, the trade unions and the political families produce between 50 and 60 per cent of British MPs. The remainder cannot easily by 'typed'. They first make their appearance on the political scene when they apply for inclusion in the parliamentary panel of one of the three main parties, or when they apply directly for selection in a constituency. It may be appropriate to describe them as 'self-starters', since they embark on a political career without the pressures that impel members of the other three groups towards this objective.

The self-starters are on average younger than the local government candidates and the trade unionists when they first enter national politics, though older than the 'political heirs'. As a group they are better educated than the local government candidates and the trade unionists, and almost as well educated as the political heirs. It is quite common for them to have made their start in politics by achieving prominence in a political or debating club while at university. Edward Heath was President of the Oxford Union while Margaret Thatcher was President of the Oxford University Conservative Association. In January 1993, four Cabinet ministers had held office as President of the

Cambridge University Conservative Association. The self-starters are more likely than recruits from any of the other three sources to give up after an unsuccessful election campaign, or to withdraw from Parliament after only a few years. But if they stay on they are sometimes very successful; most of the country's top political leaders are drawn from the self-starters, not from the other three groups. Of the twenty-two ministers in Major's Cabinet in the summer of 1992, twenty-one (all but Major himself) were self-starters.

The selection of candidates

In all three main parties the responsibility for selecting candidates rests with the local party branches. When a branch decides to adopt a prospective candidate a selection committee is appointed and applications are invited. Usually at least one person will have had their eye on the constituency and will have tried to cultivate good relations with the branch chairman. Sometimes members of the selection committee invite people to apply. If the seat is safe for the party, a hundred or more applications are likely to be received, most of them from people who have no connections with the constituency and who may never have been near it. If the seat is hopeless, on the other hand, the committee may have to search around for suitable applicants.

After the last date for applications the committee prepares a short list, usually of between two and six people. These applicants are then interviewed, the common procedure being for each to be asked to address the committee for twenty minutes or so, after which they are questioned for a rather longer period. At the end of the interviews the members of the committee are usually able to agree on a candidate.

The head offices of the parties are involved in this process in two ways. First, each has a panel of approved applicants and on request head office will suggest names from this panel to local parties. Sometimes head office has favoured applicants for whom it wishes to find safe seats, and the names of these applicants may be suggested time and time again. But the choice rests with the local parties and they cannot be forced to accept someone they do not like. This has been made abundantly clear when senior party members have failed to get themselves accepted for new constituencies after their old ones have been abolished by boundary changes. A slightly different example occurred in 1959, when the General Secretary of the Labour Party, having decided to enter Parliament, was unable to find a party branch willing to nominate him.

The head offices are also involved in that in each party, apart from the Liberal Democrats, they reserve the right to veto the selection of candidates whom they consider undesirable. This right is very rarely used but when it is the local party has little choice but to accept the decision and choose another candidate. If the local party refuses to toe the line, the normal practice is for head office to sponsor its own candidate, who is advertised as the official party candidate. Since British voters are generally loyal to the national party rather than to the local branch, the normal (though not invariable) consequence of this conflict is that the head office candidate gets the majority of the votes cast by party supporters.

When a local party has to choose a candidate, what considerations are apt to influence the selection committee? The most obvious and openly acknowledged considerations are purely personal: whether the applicant writes a good letter of application, their career outside politics, the impression they make when interviewed, whether they have any experience of electioneering and, if so, whether they did well in their previous campaigns. In the Labour Party union membership is regarded as almost essential. In the Conservative Party some preference has been given to candidates who have served as officers in the regular armed forces; between 1945 and 1975, 12 per cent of all Conservative MPs had a service background, mostly as army officers (Mellors 1978: 99). Conservative selection committees attach considerable importance to success in a career outside politics, and they also like candidates to have suitable wives or husbands, who are vetted at the time of their spouses' interviews.

All the parties now stress the desirability of recruiting women candidates, but until 1997 none of them was very successful in doing this. Relatively few women have put themselves forward for nomination, and few of those who did were accepted for winnable seats. Labour Party selection committees have always been male-dominated and their Conservative equivalents, although often having a majority of women, have always shown a marked preference for male candidates. The development of the women's liberation movement of the 1970s made no immediate difference to this, the number of women elected in 1983 (twenty-three) being no greater than the number elected in 1945 (twenty-four). Margaret Thatcher's leadership did not transform the position, as she has never been a feminist and never appointed a woman to her Cabinet. However, her position as a role model may have had some influence, as in 1987 the number of women MPs elected jumped to forty-one, but this was still only 6 per cent of the total. A much more substantial breakthrough came in 1997, as a consequence of a deliberate national policy by the Labour Party leadership, with local party branches being encouraged to adopt all-female shortlists for the nomination. In 1997 120 women MPs were elected, 101 of them Labour, and Blair emphasized the change by appointing five women to his first Cabinet, compared with the previous maximum of two under Major.

Attitudes to political doctrines and issues have not generally been stressed by the local selection committees, but they became significant in 1983 in the case of Labour and 1997 in the case of the Conservatives. In the early 1980s some local branches of the Labour Party were captured by left-wing militants, who managed to replace moderate MPs by left-wingers in twelve constituencies, all in large industrial cities, and may have influenced the selection process in a few more. This attracted nationwide attention, but it did not make much difference to the balance of influence among the 209 Labour MPs who were elected. In 1997 attitudes towards Britain's future role in the European Union were certainly on the minds of many Conservative selection committees, but it is difficult at the time of writing to say how much difference this made to the composition of the parliamentary Conservative Party.

The characteristics of MPs

In terms of the occupations from which they are drawn, most MPs are from the professional and business classes, but lawyers are not dominant in the way that they are in the US Congress. The category that has seen the greatest increase in the postwar period comprises what have been called the 'talking and writing professions' or 'the chattering classes', namely lecturers, teachers and journalists. The number of such MPs rose from 82 elected in 1950 to 151 elected in October 1974 (Mellors 1978: 62–6). The number was 149 in 1992 and rose in 1997. The detailed figures for 1992 are shown in Table 8.1. It should be noted that only a few of the 63 MPs classified as manual workers had moved straight from the factory or pit into Parliament, most of them having spent an intermediate period as trade union officials. However, the difference between the two main parties is clear.

Some figures regarding the educational background of MPs are given in Table 8.2. For simplicity, only the two main parties are included. The contrast between the parties is clear. It was not so stark in 1983 as it had been in 1945, but the degree of convergence was quite modest. In the Parliament elected in 1983, two-thirds of Conservative MPs had been educated at public schools compared with one-eighth of Labour MPs. In considering these figures it should be borne in mind that only one-fiftieth of British children go to such schools. Among Conservative university graduates, almost two-thirds had studied at Oxford or

Table 8.1 Occupational background of MPs, 1992

Type of occupation	Conservative	Labour	Liberal Democrat
Lawyer	60	17	6
Teacher	24	76	5
Journalist or publisher	28	13	3
Other professions	33	22	–
Company director	37	1	–
Business executive	75	8	2
Other business employee	16	13	–
White-collar worker	9	36	1
Farmer	10	2	–
Armed services	14	–	1
Politician or political organizer	20	24	2
Housewife	6	–	–
Manual worker	4	59	–
Total	336	271	20

Source: Criddle 1992: 226.

121

Table 8.2 Educational background of MPs (%)

Education	Elected in 1945		Elected in 1983	
	Conservative	Labour	Conservative	Labour
Public schools	83	19	64	13
Oxford or Cambridge	53	15	46	14
Other universities	12	19	26	40
All universities	65	34	72	54

Source: Burch and Moran 1985: 13–14.

Cambridge, while only a quarter of Labour graduates had done so. The contrast has diminished further since 1983, but it remains substantial.

The work of MPs

The basic duties of MPs are easily enumerated. First, they are expected to look after the interests of their constituents, taking up their grievances with the relevant minister when they think this appropriate. The best approach is by a personal letter to the minister, but if this does not get results the MP can raise the matter in Parliament. If this still fails, and the MP believes that officials in the ministry have been guilty of maladministration, the matter can be referred by the MP to the Parliamentary Commissioner for Administration, who can conduct a detailed inquiry. Work of this kind takes up a good deal of time, and the majority of Members not only correspond with constituents but also make themselves available for consultation in the constituency on a regular basis.

The second main task of MPs is to conduct debates on public policy and to hold the government of the day accountable for its decisions and behaviour. This will be discussed in Chapter 12. The third main task, to be discussed in Chapter 13, is to consider legislative proposals brought before Parliament by ministers or, with less chance of success, by backbench Members.

According to the British understanding of parliamentary democracy, MPs should act as trustees for the national interest when they carry out the second and third types of duty, not as delegates from the area in which they were elected. Since the last third of the nineteenth century, it has become normal for Members to assume that the nature of the national interest is best interpreted by their party. They naturally have some say in the determination of party policy; but as the political process has become essentially one of party government, individual MPs are expected to conform to the party line in parliamentary votes and they rarely depart from it unless they have strong beliefs or commitments regarding the issue in question.

Party management in the House of Commons is the responsibility of a small group of Members known as Whips. The Chief Whip in each party draws the attention of his or her colleagues to forthcoming debates by circulating notes, also (rather confusingly) known as whips, which indicate the importance of the occasion by variations in the degree of underlining. A debate underlined once is one in which no division is expected; one underlined twice is one in which there will be a division, and which MPs are expected to attend unless they have arranged to 'pair' with a Member of the other main party; a three-line whip means that the division is deemed to be of vital importance and all Members are required to attend unless the Whips have arranged a pair for them, which they will do only in cases of serious illness or absence overseas on official business.

In addition, the Whips have other important functions. They make themselves responsible for lining up speakers so as to keep each debate running smoothly, and they act as a channel of communication between backbenchers and party leaders. The Chief Whip of the governing party normally attends Cabinet meetings so that they can inform the Cabinet of the state of feeling of backbench Members.

The arrangements for party management are therefore rather elaborate. On most occasions they operate effectively, and the first seven decades of the twentieth century were marked by a very high degree of party discipline in the House of Commons. Since 1970, however, there have been numerous issues on which backbench MPs have broken with the official party line. One reason for this development is the emergence of important issues that cut across the left–right division of view that separates the two main parties.

The British application to join the European Community was one such issue, on which backbenchers on both sides of the House were willing to defy their Whips because they could not accept their party's interpretation of the national interest. When the Parliamentary Labour Party issued a three-line whip instructing Labour MPs to oppose British entry into the Community, sixty-nine Labour MPs voted in favour of entry and another twenty abstained. Another constitutional issue that produced dissidents on both sides was the proposal to create national assemblies for Scotland and Wales; the first government Bill on this subject had to be withdrawn for lack of support and subsequent Bills were amended in important ways by amendments passed in opposition to government wishes. As noted in Chapter 5, in the 1992–7 Parliament the Conservative government was troubled by backbench dissent over Britain's future relations with the European Union, which harassed the Prime Minister and led to the party's massive defeat in 1997. Backbenchers do not behave like sheep when great issues of principle are at stake.

A second reason for the increase in dissent is the growth of ideological discord within the two main parties. And on top of these specific causal factors, there has been a general change of attitude among younger MPs, who are just not so willing to toe the party line as their predecessors were. Moreover, defying the Whips tends to be a progressive process. A backbencher who has done so once finds it easier to do so a second time. Other backbenchers take note of the trend and assert their own independence. In the Parliament of 1974–9, 89 per cent of Conservative MPs and 81 per cent of Labour MPs voted against the Whips' instructions at least once, while 33 per cent of Labour MPs did so twenty times or more (Rose 1983: 289). In the 1987–8 session, 121 Conservative MPs defied the Conservative whip on legislative issues. As about 100 of the 373 Conservative MPs had government posts of one kind or another, this means that about 44 per cent of government backbenchers voted to amend or reject a government Bill at least once, while 31 of them, or 11 per cent, did so five times or more. It is still the case that a government with a majority in the House of Commons can be sure of avoiding defeat on a vote of confidence, and can expect to get most of its legislation passed without critical amendment. But defeats on legislative matters have become more common than they were, and party managers now have to accept that a proportion of government Bills will be revised against the wishes of the government, with outright rejection also being a possibility.

The way to the top

It is impossible to give an exact figure for the proportion of MPs who hope to acquire ministerial office, but it seems reasonable to assume that more than half harbour this ambition. Most of these are disappointed. Of over 2,000 MPs who served in Parliament between 1918 and 1955, 74 per cent failed to get any kind of ministerial appointment. A further 10 per cent achieved only the humble and unpaid office of Parliamentary Private Secretary (PPS), 9 per cent became junior ministers and only 7 per cent became full ministers (Buck 1963: 47). Members may reach Parliament without having served in any other political post, but they then face a hard struggle to secure further advancement. With very few exceptions, the way to the top in British politics is through a successful performance in Parliament, first as a backbencher attracting favourable comment by speeches and questions, then as a PPS or junior minister and finally, for the few, as a minister.

Since recommendations for ministerial posts are made to the Prime Minister by the Chief Whip, party loyalty is generally an advantage in gaining such a recommendation. Knowledge of this is one of the factors that keeps party discipline as effective as it is. However, it should not be thought that disloyalty always acts as a disqualification. Prime Ministers are looking for talent when they make appointments; evidence of independence raises questions but is not necessarily a bar. Of the eleven postwar Prime Ministers, four (Churchill, Eden, Macmillan and Wilson) had been rebels at some stage in their careers. And with the recent growth of independence, it would be unrealistic for Whips or party leaders to insist upon complete loyalty as a condition of promotion. Only 93 of the 596 Labour and Conservative MPs in the Parliament of 1974–9 failed to vote against the instructions of the Whips at least once (Rose 1983: 289).

A study has been made of the careers of the 282 ministers first appointed to Cabinet posts in the ninety years following 1868, the best date to mark the beginning of the modern system of disciplined parties (Wilson 1959). This shows that 214 were drawn from the House of Commons, 24 were former MPs who had gone to the Lords, 15 had acquired their parliamentary experience entirely in the Lords and the other 29 were unorthodox appointments in the sense that they could not be described as career politicians. Most of the unorthodox appointments were made as a direct result of one or other of the two world wars. The 238 who had come up in the normal way through the House of Commons had on average spent fourteen years in that House before reaching the Cabinet. A check on the careers of members of Thatcher's Cabinet after the 1983 election shows that – apart from two peers – they had on average spent thirteen years in the House of Commons before achieving Cabinet office. It follows that Cabinet ministers are experienced parliamentarians holding positions in the government that are certain to be temporary, and they are likely to be struggling again in the Commons when their term of office comes to an end. It is important to remember this when considering the view that the Cabinet has 'usurped' Parliament's position as the centre of political power.

A small minority of ministers reach one of the top posts, to become Foreign Secretary, Chancellor of the Exchequer or Prime Minister. Since the last war, forty-five politicians have filled these posts. An examination of their careers reveals only one way (apart from their success) in which they have differed from MPs as a whole. This is that more of them were 'self-starters', as defined above: 80 per cent compared with between 40 and 50 per cent of all MPs. Of the others, Churchill came from a political family, Bevin and Brown were trade unionists, and Attlee, Morrison, Amory, Pym, Major and Cook reached Parliament after serving in local government.

It is difficult to make any generalizations about what distinguishes those among the top leaders who reach the office of Prime Minister, as luck plays such a large part in this. Of the eleven postwar Prime Ministers, Churchill would never have made it had it not been for the war, Douglas-Home's appointment was a surprise to all commentators, and Wilson and Blair both got there because of the premature deaths of their predecessors as party leaders. Thatcher and Major got to the top by seizing sudden opportunities. In 1975 Heath put himself up for re-election as party leader to quell criticism after he had lost office as Prime Minister, but lost to Thatcher. In 1990 Major became Prime Minister when Thatcher lost the support of her parliamentary colleagues.

It may also be observed that party leaders often have to face attacks from critics within their own party. An American President is secure in office for four years and can be sure of re-nomination if he wants a second term. A British Prime Minister is apt to be less secure. Eden would have faced an attack on his leadership had bad health not forced him to resign after only twenty months in office. Macmillan faced mounting criticism during his last year as Prime Minister. Douglas-Home would have had to cope with pressures to resign had he not stepped down after only twenty-one months as party leader. Heath was defeated by the votes of backbenchers from whom he had expected support. Thatcher had to cope with constant criticism from Heath and a group of Conservative MPs, until she was forced to resign. Major was given a very hard time by dissenters within his Cabinet as well as outside. These examples are all from the Conservative side of the House because Labour critics are apt to focus on ideological issues rather than on the personal position of their leader, but Wilson is an example of a Labour leader who had to spend much of his energy holding the party together. The lesson is that political leadership is a challenging and difficult activity, which requires both dedication and courage from those who practise it.

Further reading

For a general account of the recruitment and selection of parliamentary candidates see Ranney (1965) *Pathways to Parliament*; for a short but lively picture of how one candidate was selected see Lees and Kimber (1972) *Political Parties in Modern Britain*; for an account of the activities of backbench MPs see Richards (1972) *The Backbenchers*, and Radice, Vallance and Willis (1990) *Member of Parliament: The Job of a Backbencher*.

9

GOVERNMENT AND OPPOSITION

As we have seen, the leaders of the two main parties are now chosen by elections within their parties. Each can claim, in Disraeli's celebrated phrase, that he has 'reached the top of the greasy pole'. But which of them becomes Prime Minister depends on the electorate, and in a closely fought election it is not until nearly all the returns are in that one leader knows he or she will spend the duration of the next Parliament in 10 Downing Street and the other knows that his or her role is to be Leader of the Opposition. For one, the following days will be crowded with activity, picking the members of the government; the other will be faced with the less rewarding task of conducting a post-mortem on the party's defeat.

The choice of ministers

Commentators have vacillated in their accounts of the relations between the Prime Minister and his or her senior colleagues. It used to be fashionable to describe him or her as 'first among equals', a description that is clearly inaccurate in view of the fact that he or she, alone, has the power to appoint them to and dismiss them from ministerial office. Recently the pendulum has swung to the other extreme and it has become fashionable to liken the powers of the Prime Minister to those of the United States President. That this is also misleading can be demonstrated by citing one simple example. When John F. Kennedy was elected to the presidency in 1960 he did not give one of the three top posts in his Cabinet to leading members of his party: the Republican Secretary of the Treasury was kept on in that office; the chief executive of the Ford Motor Company (also a Republican) was appointed Secretary of Defense; and the post of Secretary of State went to a man active in the management of a charitable foundation who had not previously held political office. No British Prime Minister has anything like this degree of freedom; in peacetime the choice is almost entirely limited to leading members of his party whose parliamentary careers have put them in the running for ministerial appointments.

Some members of the party have such status that their inclusion is almost automatic. Thus, Harold Wilson had to appoint George Brown and James

Callaghan; Margaret Thatcher had to appoint William Whitelaw, Geoffrey Howe, James Prior and Peter Walker; John Major had to appoint Michael Heseltine and Douglas Hurd; Tony Blair had to appoint John Prescott, Gordon Brown, Robin Cook, Jack Straw, David Blunkett and Margaret Beckett. On the other hand, even the most senior people cannot choose which posts they will have, for getting the right balance of people and posts in the Cabinet is a tricky matter that must be left to the Prime Minister.

Prime Ministers have to bear various considerations in mind when making appointments. They must get a team who will work together in the senior posts. They must consider the balance of power in the party and appoint people who represent the various viewpoints within it. They must get a balance of ages in the administration and encourage young colleagues of ability. They may have to consider sectional interests; every Cabinet must now contain at least one Scottish and, if possible, one Welsh member, while a Labour Prime Minister will also have to appoint an appropriate number of trade unionists. They have a large number of posts to distribute and can find room to take account of all these factors, but much energy and thought must be spent in getting the right combination for effective government.

One of the problems that most Prime Ministers have to face is the existence of senior colleagues whose views on policy differ from their own. Experience shows that it is much wiser for a Prime Minister to include such critics in the government than to leave them out, for if they are included they will be forced to support government policy in public, no matter how many private reservations they may have. In extreme cases their reservations may be obvious, as exemplified by the *Guardian*'s comment on Tony Benn's position between 1974 and 1979: 'For much of the last Parliament, Mr Tony Benn occupied a position of almost total isolation within the Cabinet, acquiescing in its collective decisions while frantically signalling to the party outside that it hurt him grievously to do so' (*Manchester Guardian Weekly*, 20 May 1979). But, even so, it was safer for Wilson and Callaghan to have the party's leading radical partially muzzled than to have him leading an open revolt against their policies. Heath's decision to exclude Enoch Powell from his government confirms this general rule, for although it may have been almost inevitable in the circumstances it is nevertheless the case that Powell's subsequent attacks on the government weakened it and may have contributed to its defeat in 1974.

Normally ministers are drawn from the two Houses of Parliament, the great majority being MPs who have climbed the political ladder rung by rung in the way described in the previous chapter. As noted there, outsiders are occasionally brought in to strengthen the team, and two at least of these unorthodox appointees proved to be superb politicans who have left their mark on British history and British government. One was Ernest Bevin, who as General Secretary of the Transport and General Workers' Union was invited to become Minister of Labour and National Service in 1940, largely because it was thought desirable to have a leading trade unionist to deal with the delicate problems posed by conscription and direction of labour. He subsequently became a Foreign Secretary of great distinction. The other was Lord Woolton, who as a chairman of a chain of department stores was asked to become Minister of Food during the war, and who played a leading role in the reform and revitalization of the Conservative Party after its defeat in 1945.

Unorthodox appointments of this kind are exceptions to the general rule that Prime Ministers must select their ministers from the two Houses of Parliament. In peacetime it remains true that nine out of ten senior ministers (as well as all junior ministers) are parliamentarians before they are appointed. It should be added that when non-parliamentarians are appointed they must (by convention) be either given a peerage or found a seat in the Commons within a matter of weeks, but there is rarely any problem about this as it is not difficult to persuade a backbencher of long service to retire to the Lords so as to enable the new minister to compete for the seat in the ensuing by-election.

The ministerial hierarchy

At the beginning of this century there were no more than fifteen departments of state, each one of them headed by a minister who was automatically a member of the Cabinet. The great expansion of governmental activities since that time has changed the picture. There are more departments and since 1964 at least nine of them have had a second full minister (usually known as a minister of state) while one or two have had three, four or even five ministers. As there are also the Law Officers and the holders of non-departmental appointments like the Lord Privy Seal, the result is that in recent years there have been at least forty ministerial appointments. Not all of their holders can be in the Cabinet, since by general agreement a Cabinet of more than about twenty members would be too large for effective discussion. It follows that the ministerial hierarchy is more complex than it used to be. There are now: (1) Cabinet ministers; (2) ministers holding offices that might but do not at the moment entitle them to a place in the Cabinet; (3) other full ministers (e.g. ministers of state); and (4) junior ministers (i.e. under-secretaries and parliamentary secretaries).

In times of peace the Cabinet normally has about twenty members; since 1946 the minimum has been sixteen and the maximum twenty-three. By convention, the holders of the following offices are always members of the Cabinet:

Lord Chancellor
Lord Privy Seal
Home Secretary
Foreign Secretary
Chancellor of the Exchequer

Secretary of State for Defence
Secretary of State for Trade and Industry
Secretary of State for Employment (now Education and Employment)
Secretary of State for Social Security
Secretary of State for the Environment
Secretary of State for Scotland
Secretary of State for Wales
Secretary of State for Northern Ireland

The other departments represented in the Cabinet vary from year to year, depending partly on the personal status of the ministers concerned and partly on which issues are thought likely to cause most controversy. Thus, the ministers in charge of education and transport were included in the Cabinet formed after the 1983 election, but are not automatically given that position.

Resignation and dismissal of ministers

As a class, ministers have less security of tenure than members of any other profession, with the possible exception of football managers. Their appointments are the fruits of a long struggle and confer high status upon them, yet within a year or two they may be wondering how long they will survive. Junior ministers – that is, parliamentary secretaries and under secretaries – know they are on probation and that if they are not promoted within four or five years they will soon find themselves backbenchers again. They also know that the odds are against them. The minority who are promoted can look forward to only a few years as full ministers, unless they are exceptionally talented and also blessed with a modicum of good fortune. Thus, when the Conservative government took office in 1951, thirty-eight ministers and thirty-six junior ministers were appointed. Ten years later only ten of the ministers and six of the junior ministers were still in office (Blondel 1963: 157–9). Many of the others had retired or abandoned political life for a career that offered them greater security; some had been asked to resign or openly dismissed from office.

It cannot be easy for a Prime Minister to dismiss one of his colleagues but all Prime Ministers who hold office for any time find that it is an inescapable duty. Sometimes it becomes clear that a minister is unsuited to his post; sometimes there are disagreements over policy; and sometimes a Prime Minister finds it necessary to rejuvenate a government that is beginning to look (or to get) a little stale. Prime Ministers are quite frank about this. Churchill has said that a Prime Minister must be 'a good butcher'. Attlee has stated that a Prime Minister should always warn his ministers that 'if you don't turn out all right I shall sack you', adding: 'It's awkward to have to sack a man and tell him he doesn't make the grade. But I always think it's best to tell him so frankly' (Williams 1961: 84–6). Macmillan dismissed seven of his senior colleagues in one fell swoop in 1962. Wilson announced within a few days of accepting office that he would not hesitate to reshuffle his administration when this proved necessary. Thatcher was more ruthless than any of them, dismissing twenty-one Cabinet ministers in her first ten years. Major, in contrast, was not ruthless enough.

When ministers resign or are dismissed, they may be offered a seat in the House of Lords, which is a gracious way of compensating a politician who has given many years of life to public service. They may return to business or the Bar, where the financial rewards are higher than they are in politics. Or they may simply return to the backbenches in the hope that hard work or good fortune will carry them into office again a year or so later, as sometimes happens.

The Prime Minister and the Cabinet

Prime Ministers are chairpersons of the Cabinet and wield a good deal of authority over it. They determine the agenda, guide discussion and declare the sense of the meeting. They derive a great deal of power from the fact that ministers owe their appointments to them and know that they can without notice either dismiss them or promote them to posts that are higher in the ministerial hierarchy. And since the Cabinet is not only an administrative body but also a committee of party politicians, the position of the Prime Minister is further strengthened by the fact that he or she is the chosen leader of the governing party, bearing more responsibility than anyone else for its success in the previous election and its fortunes in the next.

This does not mean that he or she can act as a dictator. The tradition is that the Cabinet reaches agreement on matters of policy, not that the Cabinet acts as a rubber stamp to policies enunciated by its chair. The convention of collective responsibility means that Cabinet members have to be prepared to defend Cabinet decisions in public once they are reached, and if a minister is not prepared to do this the alternative is for him or her to resign. Naturally ministers do not want to resign, and this strengthens the hand of a Prime Minister who is trying to get colleagues to agree to proposals. But it is equally true that a series of resignations would weaken the position of the Prime Minister, and this strengthens the hand of their critics. Moreover, politicians will never forget that in 1917 Asquith was forced to resign as Prime Minister because his Cabinet colleagues were dissatisfied with his conduct of affairs, while in 1990 Margaret Thatcher's defeat was precipitated by an attack on her policies by her former Foreign Secretary, whom she had dismissed, and a leadership challenge by her former Minister of Defence.

Relationships within the Cabinet depend on a variety of personal and political factors and vary from one Prime Minister to another. Wilson was a very different leader from Heath, and Thatcher was different from them both. Moreover, in all governments there is a handful of senior ministers whose support is much more crucial for the Prime Minister than that of the lesser ministers. The formal meetings of the Cabinet are supplemented by informal discussions between the

Prime Minister and these senior colleagues (sometimes known as the 'inner Cabinet') and if they all agree on a policy it is pretty certain to be accepted by other ministers.

In Cabinet meetings Prime Ministers have to ensure that disagreements between ministers are resolved and to see that policies advocated by particular ministers for their departments are understood and supported by their colleagues. They also have to guide the Cabinet in its discussions of broad issues of policy and to persuade them into supporting their own views on questions of political strategy. On occasion they may find that the weight of opinion is against them and yield to the majority view. In exceptional circumstances they may act in a more authoritative way, two outstanding postwar examples being the Suez crisis of 1956, when the Cabinet was not told of the ultimatum to Egypt until after it had been sent, and the decision to manufacture a British atomic bomb, which Attlee took after consulting only a small group of colleagues. In normal circumstances Prime Ministers would not act without Cabinet authorization, but their ability to control the agenda gives them a great deal of power provided they have the support of the departmental minister or ministers most involved. Margaret Thatcher used her power to control the agenda and her power to create Cabinet committees in a fashion that enabled her to dominate her Cabinet more than any other peacetime Prime Minister has done in the twentieth century. In her first two years, knowing that she could not get the majority of Cabinet ministers to support her chosen economic policies, she put economic affairs under the control of a small committee of supporters, with herself as chairman. The committee took decisions and economic policy was kept off the agenda of the Cabinet itself for twenty-five months. In 1981 she encouraged her Chancellor to prepare a very harsh budget which she knew would be opposed by several Cabinet ministers. The budget was presented to the Cabinet on the day it was also presented to Parliament, with no advance leaks or discussions, thus giving the dissenting ministers only a few hours in which to decide whether to accept the budget or resign. They all decided to stay.

A further power that can be exercised by the Prime Minister is that of controlling the information that goes to Cabinet. During discussions on Britain's application to join the European Community the President of the Board of Trade (Douglas Jay) produced a paper prepared by his department on the industrial and commercial consequences of entry that was much more pessimistic than the view taken by Harold Wilson and the other ministers. To deal with this, 'The Prime Minister evoked the rule that the Cabinet will consider only opinions and not disagreements on matters of fact and Mr Jay's paper therefore was not circulated, though his continual efforts to reopen the issue finally led to his dismissal in August 1967' (Mackintosh 1977b: 70). In recent years, and particularly in the 1980s, the number of papers circulated to the Cabinet has sharply declined, as more and more of the detailed work is done, and many decisions are now taken, in Cabinet committees. However, there is now more opportunity than there was in the past for ministers to raise questions orally and without notice at Cabinet meetings, so this is a partial compensation for the loss of decision-making power to committees. (On this, see James 1992: 79–82.)

The style that a Prime Minister adopts naturally affects the character of Cabinet meetings. In this respect, Prime Ministers can be divided into three broad categories, which can be labelled brokers, helmsmen and programme setters respectively. Prime Ministers who are primarily brokers see their role as that of keeping the party together, minimizing damage from crises and building support for the next election. Their own policy objectives will be defined, if at all, only in very vague terms. Of Britain's twelve postwar Prime Ministers, Douglas-Home, Wilson and Callaghan may be placed in this category. It is true that Wilson had ambitions to be more than a broker, particularly in his first years of power when his self-proclaimed objective was to modernize the British economy. But he was not able to pursue this objective for long; he had to abandon his plan to reform the system of industrial relations because of opposition from within his party; and he was forced to make repeated somersaults in regard to British membership of the European Community. In 1962 he was against Macmillan's plan to join; in 1967 he supported a British application; in 1972 he opposed Heath's bid for membership; and in 1975, while back in power and in favour of membership, he was forced to permit Cabinet members to speak publicly against his own policy. These are the actions of a leader acting as broker.

Prime Ministers who adopt the role of helmsmen play a more positive part in the proceedings of the government. They will be steering the ship of state towards some objective, as generally agreed by the top leaders of the party. They will assume leadership of the crew and will not hesitate to throw weak crew members overboard. Among postwar leaders, Attlee, Churchill, Eden and Macmillan all fall into this category. Major started off in this way, apart from the fact that he did not dismiss failing ministers promptly. In his latter years in office, internal party divisions pushed him towards the role of a broker, but, unlike Wilson, he stuck doggedly to his favoured policies, so he does not fall clearly into either category.

The third category, that of programme setters, is reserved for Prime Ministers who set their own objectives for the government and inspire their colleagues to pursue these objectives. Churchill filled this role superbly during the war, but when he came back to power in 1951 he did not have any over-riding objective equivalent to beating the Germans. Heath was a programme setter, coming to power as he did with the three objectives of taking Britain into the European Community, transforming the system of industrial relations and pursuing a policy of economic expansion notwithstanding the risk of inflation. He succeeded in only the first of these aims, but he was resolute regarding the others and was unlucky in that the quadrupling of oil prices in 1973 sabotaged his plans for economic expansion. Thatcher was clearly the most successful member of the category, achieving all her original aims of controlling inflation, breaking the power of trade unions and increasing productivity in British industry. Tony Blair seems all set to follow her example of determined leadership, though it is too soon to know whether he will emulate her success.

Further reference to the role of the Cabinet in administration will be made in Chapter 11. But before we turn to the role of the Opposition, it is worth stressing that the Cabinet is as much a political as an administrative institution. It is a committee of party leaders, and as such its concerns are to plan the strategy of the ruling party in Parliament, to keep the public image of the governments as favourable as possible and to conduct its affairs in such a way that the party will keep or increase its majority in the next election.

The role of the Opposition

Throughout this century Parliament has normally been dominated by the conflict between two main parties, and the smaller of these parties is officially recognized as Her Majesty's Opposition. There is no parallel to this situation in the United States, where party discipline is weak and the support given to the President in Congress may cut across party lines and may vary from one issue to another. No American politician could be given the official status and salary that are now enjoyed by the Leader of Her Majesty's Opposition.

Although in this sense the Opposition has a privileged position in Britain, the very fact of party discipline that gives it that position also denies it much influence over the activities of the government. In normal circumstances the government has a clear majority; party loyalty and party discipline ensure that this is reflected in parliamentary divisions, and the Opposition has little chance of defeating the government on an issue of substantial importance. This means that the Opposition has little hope of coming to power until the next general election is called, at a time chosen by the Prime Minister. The Opposition is almost as impotent in respect of legislation. There is no filibuster in Britain, and the government has complete control over the parliamentary timetable, subject to various conventions that are respected by the leaders of both parties. The result is that the Opposition cannot prevent the passage of government Bills and cannot even insist on revisions to them if the government is determined to keep them in their original form and its supporters do not waver.

The main function of the Opposition, it has often been said, is to oppose. There is a good deal of truth in this. The British devotion to parliamentary democracy is based partly on the belief that no one party or group ever has a monopoly of political wisdom. Every policy has some drawbacks, and it is thought to be a good thing that the Opposition should point them out. The need to defend their policies in Parliament may well lead ministers to think more carefully about the advantages and disadvantages of each policy before it is adopted. Apart from this, the exposure of government actions and plans to continuous criticism in Parliament is a reasonably effective way of keeping the public informed about what their government is doing. Press conferences and television interviews are often more lively and searching, but ministers are under no obligation to take part if they do not wish to do so. And it should perhaps be stressed that public information about government is valuable not only in the very general sense of contributing to an education in citizenship but also in two very specific senses. First, it alerts groups within the community to the prospect of government actions that may affect their interests. Secondly, it helps electors to form some kind of judgement on the efficiency and equity of government policies.

This activity of criticism and verbal opposition is carried on within limits that are fairly well defined and understood. The parliamentary game has rules that everyone normally observes, and these rules maintain a delicate line between what is regarded as legitimate criticism and what would be regarded as obstruction. Indeed, to some extent the Opposition co-operates with the government in arrangements that contribute to the orderly progress of parliamentary and government business. Thus, a minister going abroad for a conference may pair with an Opposition Member who is going on business in the provinces. These pairing arrangements are always strictly observed. They are often arranged by the Whips, who in both parties are responsible for the smooth running of parliamentary business and for a certain amount of stage management in debates. Other courtesies of parliamentary life ensure that snap votes are not taken at unexpected times, that all-night sittings are rarely held and that Members refrain from abusing one another in debate.

The weekly programme of parliamentary business is arranged by the government Chief Whip in consultation with his opposite number. By convention, the subjects of debate of twenty-six days of each session are chosen by the Opposition. By convention also, the government will allow the Opposition to interrupt the planned programme (provided a request is made through 'the usual channels') in order to move a vote of censure on the government in connection with a new development of government policy. By convention again, the Opposition normally refrains from harassing the government in ways that would impose a physical burden on ministers or otherwise hinder the business of governing the country.

In a more general sense, too, the Opposition refrains from attempts to obstruct the government. In many democratic countries the debates on financial Bills are the occasion for a vigorous attempt by the Opposition party or parties to reduce taxation or to cut the expenditures authorized for government departments. In modern Britain this does not happen. Technical revisions of Bills levying taxation are often urged, but there is no general attempt by the Opposition to reduce taxes and no attempt at all to cut government expenditure. The principle adopted is that it is better to give the government enough rope to hang itself with, and Oppositions hope that an extravagant administration will be punished by loss of popularity with the electors.

This brings us to the other main function and aim of the Opposition. Not only must it criticize the government of the day, it must also present the image of a credible alternative government. If it is to win the next general election, it must look like a united body of people who would be competent to govern the country, and if possible it must develop a theme with which to capture the attention of electors and the support of a majority of them. The government of the day is in such a strong position in Britain, and has such a near-monopoly of information and initiative, that no Opposition can hope to win power by its own efforts alone. What it can do is to look like an alternative government, to exploit every weakness of the administration and to put itself in a position to win support when the government loses momentum or popularity.

Further reading

The best book on the Cabinet system is James (1992) *British Cabinet Government*; for good illustrative material see Madgwick (1991) *British Government: The Central Executive Territory* and James (1997) *British Government: A Reader in Policy Making*, sections 1–3; for a focus on the Prime Minister see King (1985) *The British Prime Minister* and Barber (1991) *The Prime Minister Since 1945*.

10

CIVIL SERVANTS

Over 5 million people are now employed by public authorities in Britain. They are engaged in all kinds of activities that range from nursing to diplomacy and include teaching, scientific research and printing. They are employed by government departments, by local authorities and by a variety of other agencies. In view of this, it may seem a little arbitrary to concentrate all our attention in this chapter on the 500,000 or so people who staff the central departments of Whitehall.

There are two justifications for doing so. One is that the Whitehall departments control finance and therefore, in the last resort, determine what all the other public authorities can do. The other is that the civil servants in Whitehall provide the link with the minister and with Parliament; if this vast system of public administration and public enterprise is democratically controlled, it is done through Whitehall. In this chapter, therefore, we are concerned not with all those who are engaged in public administration, but simply with those who staff the central departments of state.

The role of civil servants

There are four aspects of the role of British civil servants that deserve brief comment: the tradition that they should be anonymous; the principle that they should be impartial; the principle that the task of the civil servant is to carry out the policies decided upon by ministers; and the traditional assumption that it is not the task of the civil service to initiate change or to take responsibility for planning future lines of social or economic development.

The tradition of anonymity follows from the convention that the minister and the minister alone is responsible for the work of a department. He or she gets the credit for all that goes well and the censure for all that is criticized. He or she answers to Parliament for the activities of the department and is not expected to evade this responsibility by naming or blaming their permanent officials. The principle is that they are ministers' servants carrying out their instructions.

There is of course an element of unreality about this principle. Ministers cannot have direct knowledge of all the multifarious activities of their departments

137

and often find themselves defending actions taken by civil servants in terms drafted by civil servants, the minister's role being that of spokesperson. A new minister in a department may have to accept responsibility for decisions taken before he or she assumed the appointment, and is expected to defend them even if they do not have his or her entire approval. Nevertheless, the principle is operative. The tradition of civil service anonymity is deeply rooted and is generally respected by ministers, by backbenchers and by others concerned with government. Many journalists, for instance, know the names of leading officials, but they rarely publish them. Group spokespersons are in a similar position; when they are disappointed with the outcome of negotiations, they can easily identify the responsible officials, but they do not criticize them in public; instead they criticize the minister. If things go conspicuously wrong, civil servants may be criticized publicly by a special inquiry or by the minister concerned, but this is by no means a common occurrence.

The principle of civil service impartiality is bound up with the tradition of anonymity. The idea is that civil servants are servants of the Crown, serving with complete impartiality whichever ministers happen to be in office. This principle was questioned between the wars by a number of left-wing writers, who argued that the middle-class backgrounds of senior officials would make it difficult for them to sympathize with Labour aims and to co-operate fully with Labour ministers. But the Labour government of 1945–51 carried through a series of reforms with complete co-operation from the civil service, and after that no more was heard of these criticisms; as Lord Attlee said, 'all doubts disappeared with experience' (quoted in Robson 1956: 16). In point of fact, there is no evidence that civil servants are right of centre in their sympathies, let alone in their actions; a study made of the higher civil service reached the conclusion that higher civil servants as a group are somewhat to the left of centre in their political sympathies (see R. Chapman 1970: 115–17).

The principle of impartiality carries with it certain restrictions on the political activities of civil servants. The present position is that staff in the higher grades of the service may not take any part in national politics apart from voting and may take part in local politics only if prior personal permission to do so is given by their department. Staff in the various clerical grades may not stand for Parliament but may engage in other political activities in so far as the regulations of their department permit this. Departments were advised by the Treasury to 'grant permission or refuse it mainly according to the degree and nature of the contact with the public involved by the duties of the officer concerned, and the extent to which his political activities are likely to be known ... as those of a civil servant whose official duties involve his taking decisions ... affecting the personal well-being of the department's clients' (see Mackenzie and Grove 1957: 157–8). This means, for example, that clerks in local employment offices may be excluded from participation in national politics, and clerks in departments dealing with local authorities may not be able to take part in local politics.

The third principle, that ministers make policy and officials carry it out, is a very simple statement about a very complex situation. Most questions of policy emerge from the normal process of administration and are brought up from within the department for the attention of the leading officials and, if they are important enough, for the decision of the minister. When the file is given to the minister it does not end with a question mark, it ends with a recommendation, supported by reasons. The minister may accept this recommendation or may query it. In the latter case he or she will normally discuss the matter with the permanent secretary and may suggest that an alternative policy would be preferable. If he or she does this, it would be the duty of the permanent secretary to draw the minister's attention to difficulties that might be created, and other officials might be asked to join in a frank discussion of the merits and problems of the alternative courses of action. In the end it is the minister's responsibility to reach a decision, knowing that if things go wrong they will have to justify it to colleagues in the government and to defend it in Parliament.

Civil servants are not supposed to obstruct their ministers, and it is often said that the duty of the most senior officials is to 'know the minister's mind', so that they give him or her the kind of information they need and make recommendations that accord with the general line of policy he or she wishes to pursue. As Ridley has said, top officials are expected to have 'a chameleon-like ability to identify with successive governments of quite different political complexion' (Ridley 1983: 29). However, ministers vary greatly in their personalities, their experience and the extent of their knowledge about the work of the department. Some ministers move quickly from one department to another and in a short stay they may find it difficult not to accept the recommendations that are made to them, particularly when the problems are technical or involved. In these circumstances there may develop a 'departmental policy' that is made by civil servants and accepted by successive ministers. Readers who have seen the television programme 'Yes, Minister' will have a good idea of the relationships between top civil servants and ministers, though it should be added that a really determined minister, if backed by the Cabinet, can insist on reforms whether their officials approve of them or not.

A fourth aspect of the role of the civil service can be seen most clearly if a comparison is drawn with the situation in France. In that country it is taken for granted that the state, which in practice means the permanent departments of state, has a general responsibility for watching developments in the country and for providing such public services as are necessary. In recent years French ministries and commissions have compiled and published a number of reports on matters such as the expected size and location of the future population of the country, the transport needs of the country, the demand for technical and university education and – best known of all – the five-yearly national plans for economic development. The recommendations are not always translated into practice, for they are subject to scrutiny and often to substantial revision by the National Assembly. But the ministries accept a responsibility for making recommendations and their reports provide factual information on which politicians can draw.

In Britain the departments do not normally accept this kind of responsibility. They see their role as that of dealing with routine administration, of arbitrating between conflicting interests and of advising their ministers about matters of policy. They do not conceive it to be their duty to make predictions about the future, except in so far as these are necessary for particular decisions that have to be taken at the present time; and even when predictions are made it is not usually thought appropriate to publish them, lest they provide ammunition for critics. The 'national plan' published by the Department of Economic Affairs in 1965 was a break with tradition, and its total failure must have provided an additional argument for those who uphold the traditional approach.

In 1963 the limited nature of the role of the civil service was vigorously criticized by Brian Chapman, who argued that things were done better in France and that widespread reforms were needed if the British administrative system was to cope effectively with the increased responsibilities of government in the second half of the twentieth century (Chapman 1963). The merits of the French system are not our concern. The relevance of this criticism is that it draws attention to one of the most important features of British administration. In Britain, as in most advanced countries, the first half of the twentieth century was marked by a transformation in the extent of governmental activities. But while in France and many other European countries this was paralleled by developments in the role of the civil service, in Britain this did not occur. Here the structure and the role of the civil service in the 1960s were in most respects the same as they were at the end of the nineteenth century, and it is only since then that small reforms have been made.

This relative lack of change has been possible partly because of the habit of consultation with affected interests, partly because of the habit of appointing committees of eminent outsiders to advise on delicate problems, and partly because of the creation of a rich variety of autonomous and semi-autonomous institutions to deal with many of the responsibilities of the state. No attempt will be made in this book to delineate the powers and duties of the BBC, the Monopolies Commission, the Racecourse Betting Control Board, the National Insurance Advisory Committee, the Local Government Commission for England, the Bank of England, the Regional Hospital Boards or the numerous other bodies that are engaged in public administration but cannot be regarded as government departments. But the student should realize that it is partly because of this tendency to proliferate administrative institutions that the civil service as such, sitting at the centre of the web, has been able to retain for so long the main features that characterized it at the end of the nineteenth century: an impartial and anonymous service, composed largely of non-specialists, enjoying remarkable freedom from public scrutiny.

140

Staffing policies

The modern British civil service is essentially a career service of professional bureaucrats and there have been two marked turning-points in its development. The first of these was the publication in 1854 of the Northcote–Trevelyan Report, which outlined a set of principles about the organization of the civil service that were adopted by the government of the day and were not seriously challenged until very recently. The second turning-point was the publication in 1968 of the Fulton Report, which consciously questioned or rejected several of these principles and recommended a number of reforms. The changes in the size and composition of the service between these dates were very extensive and there were a number of intermediate inquiries and reports. Nevertheless the basic principles enunciated in 1854 remained virtually intact until 1968, and this gives the period a certain unity.

The first of these principles is that civil servants should be recruited immediately or very shortly after the end of their full-time education, by open competitive examinations directly related to the candidates' studies at school or university. The argument for this procedure was put in the following terms by Lord Macaulay (Trevelyan's brother-in-law) in a parliamentary speech on 23 June 1853: 'It seems to me that there never was a fact proved by a larger mass of evidence, or a more unvaried experience, than this; that men who distinguish themselves in their youth above their contemporaries almost always keep to the end of their lives the start which they have gained.'

The long-standing belief in the merits of competitive examination reflects the desire to select civil servants from among the most gifted members of each age-group. The dominant official view for over a hundred years has been that intelligent recruits could be trained (by apprenticeship rather than formal instruction) to do whatever is required, leaving no need, save in exceptional circumstances, to recruit people of more mature years who had experience in other occupations. Exceptional circumstances obtained during the Second World War, when the civil service almost doubled in size, and many of the temporary recruits were given permanent appointments after 1945. But the general principle of recruitment immediately after the completion of full-time education was made operative again after the war.

A second principle is that recruits should be given jobs for life, with complete security of tenure unless the official behaves in a scandalous way. The great majority of civil servants at the present time – meaning about four-fifths of them – have held no other job.

The third principle is that staff should be recruited for general classes of work rather than for specific posts or even specific departments. There are numerous classes, each with its own career structure, and with somewhat rigid divisions between them. Some of the divisions are horizontal, such as those between what used to be called the clerical class, the executive class and the administrative class. Others are vertical, dividing these general classes from the specialized classes of lawyers, accountants, statisticians, engineers, scientists, medical officers and so forth. Once appointed to a class, it is difficult to move to another class, though relatively easy to move from one government department to another or one location to another.

The officials who enjoy most power in all departments, and have sole responsibility for determining policy and advising ministers, are those filling the ranks of permanent secretary, deputy secretary, assistant secretary and principal. These are the grades that, with assistant principals, were collectively known as the administrative class until the reforms of 1969. They comprise only 4 per cent of the total staff, with about 20,000 officials out of the current total of around 500,000. Most of the staff in these positions were recruited to the administrative stream directly after graduating from university. Staff in the specialized classes have virtually no opportunity to get into these policy-making ranks.

Applicants for the administrative stream have to have a degree with first- or second-class honours and must take a written qualifying examination. The subject of the degree is not thought important. Those who pass the qualifying examination then go through a selection process involving two days of verbal presentations, group discussions and interviews. The successful few join the élite and are involved with policy questions from their first years of service onwards.

The principle underlying this recruitment policy is that the top people in the civil service should be 'generalists' rather than specialists. It is in sharp contrast to the principles adopted in most other advanced societies. In the United States, for instance, top officials are in most cases picked for their special skills, with agricultural economists taking jobs in the Department of Agriculture and specialists in strategic studies being appointed to the Department of Defense. In France, all recruits for the equivalent of the administrative class first study the social sciences and then spend two-and-a-half years in the Ecole Nationale d'Administration, which provides them with the specialized training that the French consider necessary for high administrative office. The British tradition has been one of suspicion towards the specialist and a preference for giving individuals of broad general education the responsibility for assessing specialized advice in terms of the public interest.

Criticisms and attempted reforms

These principles of civil service recruitment, accepted without serious question for over a hundred years, were the object of mounting criticism during the 1960s. It was in this decade that the British realized that most of the other industrial states of western Europe had grappled with their economic problems more successfully than Britain, and to some extent the blame for this was laid at the door of the civil service. A series of writers alleged that higher civil servants were 'amateurs', lacking the training in the social or natural sciences that they were thought to need. It was suggested that an education in the humanities may have been appropriate when the domestic role of government was simply to hold the ring, but was inadequate in an age when the government had direct responsibility for a public sector employing 20 per cent of the country's workers, and indirect responsibility for the level of economic activity in the private sector employing the other 80 per cent.

This criticism of the education of senior civil servants was supplemented by other criticisms, also directed mainly at the administrative class. It was said that the fact that four-fiths of the entrants to this class were graduates of Oxford or Cambridge indicated class bias in the recruitment system, which was not only unfair to applicants from other universities but also deprived the administrative class of a broader range of experience that would probably have been beneficial. Critics also regretted that in peacetime the great majority of senior civil servants spend their entire careers in the civil service, without acquiring any direct knowledge of the world outside Whitehall. Whereas senior civil servants in France have all spent part of their training period in a government office outside Paris and part in an industrial enterprise, most senior civil servants in Britain spend their whole working lives, from the age of 21 to the age of 60, in the closed world of government head offices in central London. It was asserted that senior administrators lacked managerial skills and displayed no wish to acquire them.

In 1966, in response to these criticisms, the government appointed a Committee on the civil service, commonly known as the Fulton Committee, with very wide terms of reference and the clear expectation that radical changes would be proposed. This committee set out deliberately, and perhaps a little self-consciously, to remodel the civil service. The opening paragraph of its report stated bluntly: 'The Home civil service today is still fundamentally the product of the nineteenth-century philosophy of the Northcote–Trevelyan Report. The tasks it faces are those of the second half of the twentieth century. This is what we have found; it is what we seek to remedy' (Fulton Committee 1968:69).

The main concern of the committee was with the non-specialized character of the members of the administrative class. The committee regretted that most members of this class had degrees in classics or history, that they had no post-entry training in management or the social sciences and that they rarely stayed long enough in any one job to become an expert in that job. To preserve the principle that policy-makers should not be specialists, they were moved with great rapidity from one task to another, lasting on average only 2.8 years in any one position. The committee called this 'the cult of the generalist' and referred to members of the administrative class as amateurs. This last term infuriated top civil servants, who were proud of the fact that they were generalists but regarded themselves as professionals – not, to be sure, in any particular subject, but professional governors of Britain.

The most significant recommendations of the Fulton Committee were as follows:

1   All classes should be abolished and replaced by a single unified grading structure. The correct grading of each post should be determined by job evaluation.

2   The service should encourage greater professionalism among its staff, with post-entry training in management and encouragement for administrators to become specialists in particular areas.

3   When recruiting university graduates, preference should be given to graduates in relevant disciplines, such as the social sciences and the natural sciences.

4   A civil service college should be established to provide post-entry training for recruits, giving courses in administration, management, economics and allied subjects.

5   Each government department should establish a planning unit, whose director would have direct access to the minister.

6   There should be expanded opportunities for late entry, for short-term appointments and for exchange between the service, the universities and the private sector.

7   A new department, to be called the Civil Service Department, should be created to manage the service.

8   The rules regarding secrecy should be relaxed and the administrative process made more open to public knowledge and consultation.

Not surprisingly, these recommendations were received with hostility by top civil servants, who regarded the proposals (quite correctly) as an attempt to change the whole character of the senior civil service. Officials persuaded ministers that the proposal to give preference to graduates in relevant disciplines would deprive the service of some of their best recruits, and this recommendation was rejected by the government. The other recommendations were accepted by the Cabinet, given strong personal backing by the Prime Minister (Harold Wilson) and supported by the Leader of the Opposition (Edward Heath). However, the proposals had to be implemented by the civil service, and there followed a protracted defensive action by top civil servants to minimize the changes.

In November 1968 the Civil Service Department was established, and its first head was appointed with a mandate to see that the Fulton recommendations were translated into practice. Eight years later, when asked by a House of Commons committee to explain why the recommendation that classes should be abolished had not been implemented, he replied that he had been 'quite prepared to examine this, though I was not particularly impressed' (quoted in Garrett 1980: 44). In fact, the record suggests that he was determined not to implement any more of this proposal than was absolutely unavoidable. The distinction between the administrative and executive classes has been blurred and the nomenclature changed, which adds a little flexibility to the recruitment process. However, the vertical divisions have not been abolished, specialists still have their own career structures within the specialized classes, and policy-making is still the prerogative of non-specialists in the general administrative grades.

The second and fourth of the proposals listed above have been implemented only in a half-hearted way. The Civil Service College was established by the government in 1969, but it was put under the control of the Civil Service Department. The academics on its staff were frustrated by bureaucratic control and its first director, a social scientist, took early retirement after a few years – to be replaced by a civil servant. The courses do not compare with those given by the Ecole Nationale d'Administration, lasting for only twenty-two weeks instead of for two-and-a-half years. The course on economics lasts for only four weeks. The college provides a useful introduction to existing civil service practice, but does very little indeed to give future administrators the social science training that the Fulton Committee had thought necessary.

The recommendation about the establishment of planning units within departments has been ignored. More civil servants are recruited after a period in other occupations, but they form only a very small proportion of all recruits. The Official Secrets Act was not modified until 1989, and was then only slightly liberalized. All in all, the story of the Fulton Committee and its aftermath is a story of bureaucratic resistance to reform, with the bureaucrats winning partly because of their tenacity and skill in administrative manoeuvres, and partly because they have permanent posts whereas ministers (even Prime Ministers) come and go.

A parallel story with the same conclusion is the story of the various efforts made to reduce the dominance of Oxford and Cambridge (Oxbridge) graduates among recruits to the administrative class. The number of applicants from the other universities has risen greatly. The only snag is that they rarely get through the civil service selection tests. In 1968 it was reported that Oxbridge candidates provided 35 per cent of the candidates but 59 per cent of the successful ones (Kellner and Crowther Hunt 1980: 119). In 1987 Oxbridge provided only 13 per cent of the applicants but 54 per cent of those appointed (*Civil Service Commission Annual Report, 1987*: 46). An Oxbridge candidate in 1987 was nine times as likely to be appointed as a candidate from another university. Of those appointed, 60 per cent had degrees in the humanities compared with 23 per cent in the social sciences and 17 per cent in science and technology.

How should this bias be interpreted? Marxists would say that it reveals a determination to ensure that positions of power within the state are occupied only by defenders of the existing social order. Statistics published in the 1970s showed that most of the successful Oxbridge candidates had been educated at fee-paying schools and were therefore members of the upper and upper-middle classes. The whole selection process, it could be said, makes certain that radicals are excluded from the higher civil service.

This interpretation cannot be denied, but it is not the whole story. There is also a cultural bias in the selection process that favours arts graduates over others, and there is a degree of complacency in the higher ranks of the service, which is reflected in the whole system of recruitment. Broadly speaking, higher civil servants are proud of the service, believe it to govern the country well and are quietly determined to ensure that the top civil servants of the future shall be similar in character and training to the top civil servants of the present. This is entirely understandable in view of the emphasis that is placed on informal relationships and personal trust in the higher civil service. As a senior Treasury official told two American scholars: 'The civil service is run by a small group of people who grew up together' (Heclo and Wildavsky 1974: 76). For better or worse, the system has been somewhat self-perpetuating.

Developments since 1979

Margaret Thatcher's arrival at 10 Downing Street in 1979 brought to office a Prime Minister of radical disposition who was determined to arrest British economic decline. In her words, she wanted 'to turn Britain around'. Among her early actions was the appointment of policy advisers with a mandate to investigate the efficiency of the civil service machine, and to report personally on this to the Prime Minister.

One of the advisers was Sir John Hoskyns, a former entrepreneur in the computer business and, from 1975 to 1979, a policy adviser to Thatcher and her colleagues in opposition. Hoskyns focused on the attitudes of senior civil servants to British economic affairs, which he found deplorable. In 1980 a former head of the civil service stated publicly that in his view 'the task of the British civil service is the orderly management of decline' (quoted in Fry 1984: 353). Hoskyns discovered that this view was widely shared. Senior civil servants were resigned to the relative decline of the British economy and deeply sceptical of any radical attempt to reverse it, whether the radicalism was of the left or of the right. Most top administrators had entered the service in the years immediately following 1945, and in Hoskyns's view joining the service in that period was 'like joining Napoleon's army just in time for the retreat from Moscow' (Hoskyns 1983: 142). He recommended that a fairly high proportion of senior officials over the age of fifty should be removed from their posts and replaced by outsiders, brought in on contract.

This recommendation was too radical even for Thatcher. A number of top people were pushed into early retirement, which they and many of their colleagues resented, but they were replaced by other officials given rapid promotion rather than by outsiders. However, Thatcher broke with precedent by controlling these promotions herself. She did not do so on a party-political basis, as civil servants do not make their partisan sympathies known, but she had strong preferences in terms of policy attitudes, style and personal qualities. As has been said, 'she is not attracted to the qualities of detachment, versatility, caution ... traditionally prized among British senior civil servants' (Drewry and Butcher 1988: 164). She favoured officials who were dynamic and prepared to be ruthless, at the expense of those who valued consensus and continuity. There are about forty permanent secretaries and 135 deputy secretaries in Whitehall, and by the end of her second term of office in 1987 she had made appointments to the great majority of these posts.

The impact of Thatcher's influence has been very considerable. Top civil servants have become less tied to tradition and quicker to advance and implement fresh policy developments. A new emphasis on managerial approaches and methods has both changed the structure and modified the style of the Whitehall machine. Thatcher set up an Efficiency Unit, guided by Sir Robin Ibbs, and in the spring of 1987 the first substantial report by this unit showed that, despite Thatcher's reforms and pressures, 'how meddlesome the Treasury and Cabinet Office remained; how dominant was the Whitehall culture of caution; how great was the premium placed on a safe pair of hands; and how rarely were proven managerial skills perceived as the way to reach the top of the bureaucratic tree' (Hennessy 1990: 620). To remedy this, Thatcher and her fellow reformers decided to transfer many responsibilities and staff from the large core departments to new executive agencies, still under the political control of ministers in the core departments but one step removed from the cautious attitudes of the traditional mandarins. By the time of her resignation thirty-four such agencies were in operation and, with powerful encouragement from Major, the number had grown to ninety-six by 1994. By that date 65 per cent of civil servants were working in executive agencies, compared with only 25 per cent in the main departments and 10 per cent in small departments (Theakston 1995: 135).

These reforms have involved some rather brutal dismissals of senior officials and some loss of institutional memory, but their overall effect has been to make the civil service more flexible and more efficient. It would now be unfair to complain that it acts as a serious brake on the plans of innovating ministers, though it can still be slow in dealing with matters that do not have high priority.

At the same time, the civil service has retained its traditional virtues. It is, for example, entirely honest. In the entire postwar period only one civil servant has been found guilty of corruption. That is one out of half a million, over nearly fifty years. Moreover, there are no rumours of bribes or graft. Secondly, its political neutrality is in general terms undoubtedly an advantage. Thirdly, it is singularly lacking in the addiction to red tape and formality that plagues the bureaucratic process in many countries. Civil servants write in plain English rather than in legal or bureaucratic jargon. It is easy to get an interview with civil servants and they are invariably courteous in their dealings with members of the public. Tax inspectors and customs officers are rarely disagreeable. Citizens are not penalized, as they are in Canada and some other countries, if they are a few weeks (or even months) late with their tax returns. There is some tension between the long-term unemployed and the officials responsible for assessing their financial needs, but relations between civil servants and the public remain generally good. These virtues are important and should never be overlooked.

Further reading

The best books on the civil service are Drewry and Butcher (1988) *The Civil Service Today* and Theakston (1995) *The Civil Service Since 1945*; for the official statement of the role and duties of civil servants see *The Civil Service Code* (1995); for a very detailed analysis of the whole Whitehall machine see Hennessy (1990) *Whitehall*; and for an excellent study of the relations between senior civil servants and ministers see Barker and Wilson (1997) 'Whitehall's disobedient servants? Senior officials' potential resistance to ministers in British government departments', *British Journal of Political Science*, 27, 223–46.

IV

THE PROCESS OF
GOVERNMENT

11

ADMINISTRATION AND POLICY-MAKING

Co-ordination and control

The administrator lives by the pen, and the administrative process is largely a process of communication. An administrative system is essentially a network of communication channels, and it is effective if it ensures that messages are speedily transmitted, information and advice are readily available, and the activities of those on the periphery are co-ordinated and controlled by those at the centre. In the British system, which is highly centralized, co-ordination and control are the responsibilities of the central departments of the government and the Cabinet.

Although the central departments employ only about a tenth of the people engaged in the public sector, they maintain effective control over activities within the sector. Municipal authorities, public corporations and other public bodies enjoy legal and formal independence of government departments but they do not enjoy a great deal of administrative independence. Thus, education is the responsibility of local authorities, and the government does not employ a single teacher or own a single school. But the administration of education is shaped by ministry circulars, and teaching methods are kept in line by government inspectors, who visit schools and watch teachers at work in their classrooms. Again, public corporations enjoyed a good deal of independence in their day-to-day activities, but they were not allowed to do anything that conflicted with government policy and were sometimes made to do things that were directly contrary to their own interests. Thus, the railways were told to keep open numerous uneconomic branch lines; a nationalized steel firm was refused permission to import American coal, which was cheaper than any it could buy in Britain; the Central Electricity Generating Board was told by the Department of Energy whether its power stations should be fuelled by coal, oil or nuclear power.

There is no question about the power of Whitehall in its relationships with all these other administrative authorities. A local authority that refuses to obey a ministry directive can be brought to heel by the immediate suspension of its grant, without which it cannot finance its activities. A public corporation that declined to co-operate found that its capital projects were not approved and its chairman was subject to abrupt dismissal, a fate that has befallen two of the chairmen of British Airways.

The Whitehall departments, staffed in the way described in the previous chapter, thus sit at the centre of the administrative system. Considered in historical terms, one of the most remarkable features of this system is how little the process of central decision-making has changed in the past century. The size of the civil service has grown by a multiple of about twenty and it is supplemented by a vast and complex array of semi-autonomous agencies, but the crucial decisions are still made by two or three hundred top officials in Whitehall who know each other personally and are in constant communication with one another. Heclo and Wildavsky have described the world of these top administrators as a village, whose inhabitants are linked by networks of gossip as well as business relationships, and where everyone has a good idea of what everyone else is doing (Heclo and Wildavsky 1974: chs. 1, 3). It is quite different from the divided world of federal administration in the United States. There is no danger in Britain of departments working at cross-purposes, either through ignorance or because of rivalry. Differences of opinion and interest naturally occur, but they are resolved at the top rather than reflected in the pursuit of inconsistent policies.

A vitally important role in the process of central co-ordination is played by the Treasury. The power of the Treasury depends on its control of expenditure. Government departments cannot do much without spending money, and all expenditures are subject to the prior approval of the Treasury. Each year each department prepares detailed estimates of proposed expenditure for the following year, and these are discussed in detail with Treasury officials and are rarely approved without reductions being made. Moreover, no provision for a new service or new development may even be included in the estimates unless the department has secured the prior approval of the Treasury for it in writing.

Once the estimates are accepted the department is tied to them, and cannot transfer money saved under one subhead for use elsewhere unless the Treasury agrees. If there is a prospect of overspending on any subhead, the department must immediately inform the Treasury, when a decision will be taken as to whether the department should cut expenditure, should transfer money from some other subhead, or should apply for a supplementary estimate. To emphasize its control of the purse-strings, the Treasury doles out money to each department in a monthly allowance that is carefully calculated to ensure that the departments never have very much in hand.

The departments do not always accept Treasury rulings without argument, and if officials feel that Treasury decisions are not in the interest of good government they will put the matter to their minister. The latter may then raise it with the Chancellor of the Exchequer, and if agreement cannot be reached between them they may take the whole problem to the Cabinet. Cabinet discussions of this kind are not uncommon, and the outcome may depend on the relative political strengths of the ministers involved as well as on the merits of the issue. But Cabinet decisions are binding and are invariably accepted by all parties. A minister has no choice but to accept or resign; civil servants have no further discretion in the matter, and stoically accept what has been decided.

The Cabinet settles differences between ministers not only over finance but also over the application of government policy and the situations that arise when the policies of one department affect the interests of another. The Cabinet is the highest agency of co-ordination and must be prepared to discuss conflict until agreement is reached – not always unanimous agreement, but agreement that can be accepted by the minority as 'the sense of the meeting'.

Consultation and advice

As explained in Chapter 7, it is the normal practice of government departments to consult representatives of affected interests before taking decisions. One reason for this is that civil servants need specialized information about the practices and problems of the group involved. A representative association is the most convenient source of such information, and even if a government department decides to collect its own data, for instance by requiring firms to make regular returns of production, the officials will need to consult the appropriate trade association about how to draw up the questionnaire. Another reason is that consultation often helps to ensure that the decisions of the department will be accepted by members of the trade or profession concerned, and that their co-operation will be forthcoming. A third point is that organized groups often act as a buffer or filter between Whitehall and the various interests, firms and individuals represented by the group, who might otherwise inundate the department concerned with letters of protest and contradictory expressions of view about what should be done. For all those reasons regular consultation with group spokespersons is now regarded as a principle of good government.

The advantages of this practice to the group spokespersons are obvious. It enables them to press the claims of their groups before decisions are taken, which is much more useful than the ability to protest after the event. It also establishes their status in the eyes of members of the group, so that their position as an organization is made secure. Of course, the privileges such spokespersons enjoy in Whitehall imply certain unwritten obligations. They are expected to maintain the confidential nature of some discussions and to respect the anonymity of civil servants; they may feel that if they fail to gain their point they ought to accept failure gracefully rather than launch a public attack on the ministry; they often slide into the role of an intermediary between the ministry and the more demanding members of the group they represent. It is natural for an organization that becomes an established channel of communication to transmit messages in both directions, and occasionally this leads the more impatient or radical members of a group to feel that their spokespersons have become excessively responsible and moderate. Some motorists feel that the AA and the RAC have moved in this direction; some animal-lovers feel the same about the RSPCA.

One of the features of this system of consultation is that each department has its own set of client organizations, mainly representing groups with common interests but sometimes representing groups with shared attitudes. Thus, the Department of Trade and Industry deals mainly with trade associations; the Ministry of Transport deals with the Road Haulage Association, the AA and the RAC, the Traders' Road Transport Association, the Transport Workers' Union and the three unions of railway workers; the Ministry of Agriculture and Fisheries deals with the National Farmers' Union, the British Trawlers' Federation and the Country Landowners' Association; the Home Office deals with the Howard League for Penal Reform, the National Council for Civil Liberties and organizations representing immigrants; the Department responsible for education deals with the National Union of Teachers, the Association of Municipal Corporations and the Association of Education Committees. If no organization exists to represent an interest, the government department concerned may sponsor one. Thus in 1956 the Forestry Commission stated that it was prepared to give a substantial sum to assist the establishment of a Woodland Owners' Association to represent the interests of private owners; in 1959 a grant of £30,000 was included in the Commission's estimates for this purpose (with the approval of the Treasury); and a few months later the new association was reported to be urging the government not to accept any large increase in timber imports from the Soviet Union (Potter 1961: 32). Equally, the government may take action to reduce the number of organizations representing an interest if they are inconveniently numerous; in 1945 'the Ministry of Works took the initiative in setting up a National Council of Building Producers, bringing together forty-one separate trade associations for common action in dealing with the Department' (Grove 1962: 146).

This feature of British government is of constitutional as well as administrative importance. There is no theory or model of the constitution that takes account of the practice of consultation between government departments and the spokesmen for organized groups. Traditional theories of the constitution suggest that the influence of the citizen on the process of government is secured solely through the House of Commons, either by the general impact of elections or by the specific means of an approach to an MP, who then approaches or questions the relevant minister. In practice citizens who want action from the government do not normally go to their MP. They may do this, but they are more likely to raise the matter through an organized group whose spokespersons will deal directly with Whitehall. Such groups cover all activities and all categories of the population. Newly born babies cannot organize themselves, but their mothers or prospective mothers can join the Association for the Improvement of Maternity Services; parents who are dissatisfied with the provision of playing-fields for children can approach the Central Council of Physical Recreation; students discontented with their grants can ask the

154

National Union of Students to make further representations; workers unhappy about safety precautions at the factory can approach their trade union; shop-keepers' interests are defended by the Association of British Chambers of Commerce; consumers' interests are protected by the British Standards Institute and the Consumer's Association; old people, disabled people, ex-servicemen and other groups all have spokespersons who enjoy access to government departments. This is clearly one of the central features of the modern British constitution.

Having said this, it should be added that the constitutional status of officials (i.e. their position as servants of the Crown and the minister) affects the form taken by the discussions, which are usually described as a process of consultation even when they are in reality a process of bargaining. One former civil servant has written about them in the following terms.

> The conversation will preserve all proper forms. The unofficials will inquire of the official, not 'Will you agree to this?' but 'Do you think the minister will agree?' The official replies: 'No, I feel sure he won't go as far as that; but I think he will probably consent to do so much, on the understanding that the rest is left over until next year.' The unofficials answer: 'Well, we think we can persuade our people to be content with that for the present.' And they part with mutual expressions of affection and esteem, each side understanding perfectly that pledges have been given and received to the effect that the department will go some way to meet its unofficial critics, and that the critics will make no trouble in the House of Commons or elsewhere because it does not at once go the whole way.
>
> (Dale 1941: 182–3)

Apart from consultation with group spokesmen, government departments also rely heavily on advisory committees. At the last count there were almost 1,000 permanent (but unpaid) committees advising the departments in London, together with an almost uncountable number of local committees. Many of the members of these committees are drawn from the ranks of group spokespersons, who thus get a further opportunity to advance their views. Other members are technical experts, civil servants and independent lay people. Thus, when the Cinematograph Films Council was set up to advise the President of the Board of Trade, its twenty-two members comprised four representatives of film producers, two of film renters, five of exhibitors, four of employees in the industry and seven independent members (including the chairman) of whom some were experts and some were lay people (Wheare 1955: 57). In this case only the secretary was a civil servant, though often one or two officials are included in the committee. The reports of these advisory committees are not normally published; their function is simply to make specialized information and informed recommendations available to the departments.

In addition, special committees to inquire and to advise are frequently appointed, sometimes being known simply as committees and sometimes being given the status of Royal Commissions. These committees differ from the permanent advisory committees in that they are much more likely to contain a preponderance of independent members, who may have experience in the field of activity under consideration but are not appointed as representatives of groups. Committees of this kind hear evidence from interested parties and sometimes commission specialists to conduct studies on their behalf. Thus, the Royal Commission on Population commissioned economists and demographers to make predictions about population trends, and the Robbins Committee on Higher Education had studies made of several problems. The reports of committees of inquiry are normally published.

Committees of this kind are appointed for a variety of reasons. Sometimes a department realizes that something has to be done and appoints a committee as the best way of getting informed advice about what is needed. Sometimes a department has a delicate problem on its hands and wants a committee, for whose work the government takes no responsibility, to examine the alternatives and make recommendations. An example is the Committee on Homosexual Offences and Prostitution, which interviewed homosexuals and whose report caused a great deal of controversy. Sometimes a department wants to prepare Parliament and public opinion for a reform that officials and the minister consider desirable and appoints a committee partly so that the evidence in favour of the reform can be mustered and the need for the reform can be endorsed by an independent body. As Enoch Powell said, a minister may feel: 'There is a big change to be made here, quite clearly, or a big advance. It will be much easier to commend it to Parliament and the country if I have set up a group of reasonable beings, well experienced and so on, and they have come to that conclusion' (Hunt 1964: 48). An example is the Royal Commission on Betting, Lotteries and Gaming, whose recommendations led to the legalization of off-the-course betting in cash and the establishment of betting shops all over the country.

Sometimes committees of inquiry are appointed without any serious expectation that their reports will be acted upon. They are appointed to pacify critics, examples being the Royal Commission on the Press of 1947 and the Royal Commission on Equal Pay for Men and Women in 1948. They are appointed to buy time, a possible example being the Royal Commission on Marriage and Divorce of 1951. Finally, they may be appointed to kill a proposal by demonstrating its disadvantages or by taking it out of the public eye: a possible example of this being the Palestine Partition Committee of 1938, whose report helped to kill the plan of partition that a former committee had proposed. But it is probably fair to say that most committees of inquiry lead to some kind of action sooner or later, even though it is unusual for a committee's recommendations to be adopted *in toto*.

It should be clear by now that, although leading civil servants are rarely specialists, neither they nor their ministers need lack specialized advice. It is pressed on them from all sides, and the custom is for government departments to welcome this. Quite apart from their need for information, it is in accordance with the traditional role of the British civil service that other people should come forward with controversial proposals, leaving officials with the task of giving their ministers discreet and anonymous advice on the merits of the alternative courses of action that are open.

Decision-making and policy

It is part of the familiar theory of British government that ministers take decisions and officials simply give advice. While this was never entirely true, it was much nearer the truth in the latter part of the nineteenth century than it is today. When departments were small, ministers could be personally acquainted with all issues of any importance. But this is no longer the case; the civil service is about twenty times as big as it was a hundred years ago and there are only about three times as many ministers. Now about forty ministers, helped by about fifty junior ministers, control the work of about 500,000 officials. The great majority of decisions are clearly taken without reference to a minister.

Within the civil service there is a well-established hierarchy of decision-making, so that a principal knows what he or she can decide on his own account and what must be referred up to an assistant secretary. In Whitehall one of the basic techniques of administration is the rotating file, which is carried from out-tray to in-tray by a small army of uniformed messengers. When a file reaches the official who is empowered to decide on the case he or she does so unless it poses a special problem of one kind or another, which is quite rare in some departments (e.g. the Department of Social Security) but quite common in others (e.g. the Foreign Office). The special problems that arise out of day-to-day administration are the seeds from which many changes of policy develop.

One kind of problem is the possibility of conflict with another department. Questions about the school dental service raise the possibility of conflict, or at any rate differences of opinion, between the Department of Health and the Department of Education and Science. Questions about regional unemployment involve both the Department of Trade and Industry and the Department of Employment. In these and similar cases the civil servant must consult his opposite number in the other department before taking action. They may be able to settle the matter between them. But, if it is not as easy as that, each must refer the matter to his departmental superior. Sometimes issues between departments can then be settled by an informal conference or a committee; in other cases this is not possible and the files go right up the hierarchy to the permanent secretaries and perhaps the ministers, with each official on the way adding his comments in the form of a minute.

Another kind of problem arises when the implementation of a routine decision seems likely to create political controversy. Thus, the decision to construct concrete lamp standards in front of a row of country houses took on a special significance when it was realized that one of the houses was owned by the President of the Royal Academy, an outspoken opponent of modern street furniture. In cases like this the department is likely to be mentioned in the press and questions may be asked in Parliament. The wise official will draw the attention of his or her superiors to such cases (an activity known in Whitehall as 'putting up an umbrella') so that they can be sure of their ground and be prepared to defend themselves against a possible storm of criticism.

Important questions arising from the administrative process reach the permanent secretary, who must decide whether or not to put them before the minister. This decision again depends on how far it impinges on other questions of policy with which the minister is grappling. A permanent secretary will not want to worry the minister unnecessarily, but will try to keep the latter in touch with the questions that may lead to criticism. The minister, unlike the officials, has to deal with questions in Parliament, in press conferences and in public meetings, and will not want to be caught off guard because of ignorance of one of the problems of the department.

Ministers, in turn, have to decide whether to take matters to the Cabinet. Clearly they will have to do so if they cannot reach agreement with another minister, for the Cabinet is the only place in which differences of this kind can be resolved. Apart from this, they will take matters to the Cabinet if they are intrinsically important or if they are likely to cause a major political row. All proposals for legislation are normally referred to the Cabinet, for even if they are not controversial in themselves they will take up parliamentary time and a case must be made for their priority. Developments that will affect the reputation of the government should be brought to the attention of the Cabinet, which is a meeting of party leaders as well as a meeting of departmental heads. Thus, when a new government takes office a minister may find that for administrative reasons it is impossible to achieve something to which his or her party had committed itself in the election, and this must be reported to the minister's colleagues. Topics that arouse great public interest will tend to appear on the Cabinet agenda for a similar reason, though they may be disposed of quickly. Finally, ministers will take to the Cabinet all those knotty problems that are virtually insoluble but are likely to be used as a stick with which to belabour the government. One former Cabinet minister has said that 'most of the Cabinet's time is spent in dealing with matters which are insoluble, in the sense that there are serious disadvantages attaching to any possible course of action' (Hunt 1964: 56). Notable examples in recent years include the position of Rhodesia between 1965 and 1979 and the crisis in Northern Ireland from 1969 onwards.

The agenda of Cabinet meetings is controlled by the Prime Minister. The Cabinet secretariat is responsible for circulating papers, and when an item is reached the minister concerned speaks to it. The other members then speak and the Prime Minister eventually declares the sense of the meeting, no vote being taken. The style and character of Cabinet meetings depend partly on the personality of the Prime Minister. We learn from memoirs that Churchill was loquacious and sometimes rather arbitrary, allowing lengthy discussions on some items but dismissing others very briefly. We learn that Attlee, in contrast, was quiet, concise, methodical and sometimes extremely curt. We know that Thatcher was rather domineering. But these are variations within limits that are set by the pressure of business, by the influence of the secretary of the Cabinet (who is a senior civil servant) and by the traditions that all Prime Ministers respect.

The strength of the Cabinet *vis-à-vis* the Prime Minister was illustrated in the 1980s by a series of important issues on which Thatcher's views were repudiated by her colleagues. These included her wish to push through drastic legislation to curb the power of trade unions, her wish to curtail spending on social welfare, her view that rent restriction should be abolished, and her wish to accept the Ford Motor Company's bid to take over Austin Rover. (For these and other examples, see James 1992: 131–2.)

So far policy-making has been discussed as if all policy questions arose out of the ordinary business of administration. In fact the majority of policy questions arise in this way. Even when a team of new ministers take office after defeating the previous government what they normally do is deal with existing departmental problems with a rather different emphasis, not come into their departments with a sheaf of new policies under their arms. Harold Laski once said that the task of a minister is to 'inject a stream of tendency' into the decisions of the department, and although the phrase is inelegant it is quite appropriate.

Other policy decisions have their origins in the ideas of ministers or the Cabinet. Some examples are the decisions to nationalize certain industries after 1945, to create a completely free National Health Service in 1946, to develop commercial television in 1954, to abolish resale price maintenance in 1963, to compel local authorities to offer council housing for sale to tenants in 1979 and to privatize numerous publicly owned undertakings in the 1980s and 1990s. In cases like these the minister will get the authority of the Cabinet to draw up detailed proposals; he or she will discuss the idea with senior officials, who may already have thought about alternative methods of achieving the objective; and a specific set of plans will be worked out in the department. The minister will then ask the Cabinet for approval of these plans, which he or she must be prepared to defend against probing questions from colleagues, who may seek to anticipate the criticisms that will be made in Parliament and in the country. If approval is given, it is then a matter for more detailed work in the department and for the preparation of legislation if that is required. If the Cabinet does not approve, the minister will have to think again, or may have to abandon the proposals for the time being. Occasionally a minister resigns when his or her proposals are rejected, but politicians acquire thick skins in the course of their careers, and resignations on this ground are infrequent.

Problems and controversies

The British central administration is well organized and thoroughly co-ordinated. It operates with impressive smoothness. However, this does not mean that it is free from problems and criticisms. It is rarely attacked in the mass media, but it has often been criticized by politicians. Moreover, such criticisms have come from politicians whose ideological commitments have varied widely. Tony Benn, of the left wing of the Labour Party, said repeatedly that civil servants tended to distrust radical initiatives. Lord Boyle, a former Conservative minister, told this author in 1974 that 'Being political head of a department is like making a journey in a Rolls-Royce; it's a remarkable machine, but you are not allowed to drive it yourself.' The general tenor of many criticisms in the 1960s and 1970s was that senior servants were unduly cautious, aloof and slow to implement change. As indicated in Chapter 10, the tendency of more recent years has been for their style to become brisker, but it is nevertheless relevant to consider the postwar record with these criticisms in mind.

If this is done, four points emerge fairly clearly. The first is that there have been no problems about the implementation of policies that have been included in the governing party's election manifesto and are central to the government's ambitions. Between 1945 and 1951, the nationalization of six major industries was carried out swiftly and efficiently. During the 1980s, the privatization of numerous public enterprises was carried out with equal speed and efficiency. Major changes like the introduction of the national health service, the deci-malization of the currency, and the introduction of value added tax were also carried through with impressive smoothness. The record provides no support for Benn's accusation of ideological bias in the administration.

On the other hand, government policies towards industry have been hampered by the excessive centralization of the administrative system and the deep reluctance of civil servants to be concerned with the way that industry and commerce are conducted on the ground. Budge and his colleagues have said that governments and administrators have displayed a consistent 'distaste for detailed intervention' (Budge et al. 1983: 214). This is an appropriate comment, and perhaps 'distaste' is too weak a word. Higher civil servants have a concept of their role that appears to preclude discrimination between firms or between areas except on the basis of some generalized national rule that can be universally applied.

Two examples may suffice to illustrate this point. First, when grants were made in the 1970s to help firms in the woollen textile industry that had promising schemes of modernization, 370 of the 400 or so firms in the industry made applications that were accepted (see Beer 1982: 72). The grants thus gave general assistance to a declining industry, which helped to postpone bank-ruptcies but did very little to help the more efficient firms to modernize in a way that would make them competitive in international markets, as discrimi-nation based on local inquiries might have done.

160

A second example is provided by the administration of regional policy, designed by politicians to stimulate economic growth in stagnant industrial areas. For some years the benefits of this policy were bestowed upon all areas that had an unemployment rate of 4.5 per cent or more, without any attempt to distinguish between areas that were doomed to decline and areas that might, with government help, become centres of growth. A great attraction of this mode of implementing regional policy, in the eyes of civil servants, was that it provided a simple rule that could be applied from London without any necessity for officials to get to know the problems and potentialities of particular cities. Further attractions were that it insulated the government department concerned from lobbying and special pleading by representatives of local areas, and made the department invulnerable to allegations of bias, unfairness or corruption in connection with the implementation of the policy. This particular policy was changed after a few years, but it illustrates the way in which government departments like to run the country's affairs.

Budge *et al.* have suggested that this kind of preference – which has been built, it may be said, into a tradition of behaviour – helps to account for the reliance of successive postwar governments on central financial policies for the management of the British economy. Such policies, whether Keynesian or monetarist, can be applied across the board by pulling levers in Whitehall. They do not involve central administrators in making discriminatory judgements, as micro-economic policies would (see Budge *et al.* 1983: 213–16). As the basic problems of the British economy have been at the micro-economic level, in low productivity in manufacturing industry above all else, it can well be argued that this administrative tradition has been a handicap in Britain's postwar economic development.

A third general comment that can be made about the British administrative system is that it tends to a certain degree of inertia when dealing with problems that are not central to the policies of the government. If ministers insist on urgency, the machine can move quickly, but, if matters are left to the administration, a snail's progress is more common. The tradition is that all interests likely to be affected by a proposed innovation should be consulted, and all their concerns dealt with, before any action is taken.

An interesting example was the move, common to all advanced western societies, to enact regulations that would protect personal privacy from violation by the exchange of computerized data, collected for one purpose but then used in connection with other matters. In Britain, a Private Member's Bill on the matter was first introduced in late 1969, but was withdrawn in exchange for a government promise to establish an interdepartmental committee to report on the question. This committee did not report until July 1972; the government then announced its intention to consult all interested parties before reaching any decision; and legislation to protect privacy was not passed until 1984. Bennett has compared sixteen western democracies in respect of their speed in policy-making in this area, showing that Britain came fifteenth in the resulting league table (see Bennett 1992: 59). In the United States 34 months elapsed between the establishment of the first official committee to inquire into the need for legislation on data protection and the date of the legislation. In France the delay was 37 months, in West Germany 39 months, in Sweden and Ireland 49 months, in Britain 170 months (ibid.). Bennett alleges that the legislation might have been put off indefinitely had other countries not threatened to withhold data from British enterprises if nothing was done (ibid.: 236).

A fourth general comment is that the style of British administration is somewhat secretive. There is no commitment to open government, as in Sweden or the United States. The Official Secrets Act is more restrictive than similar legislation in other democracies. When administrators are interviewed, whether by journalists or scholars, they are invariably polite, articulate, extremely helpful up to a point, but blandly uninformative beyond that point. The very rare official who gives away too much is apt to suffer loss of promotion, dismissal or even prosecution.

A defender of the British administrative tradition would say that it is highly democratic in that affected interests are always consulted, it protects confidential discussions or communications, it maximizes consensus, it minimizes difficulties in implementation, and it ensures stability in government. A critic might acknowledge that all these points are broadly true, but still prefer a style that would be more open and more willing to see chances being taken.

Further reading

For a general account of the administrative system see Brown and Steel (1979) *The Administrative Process in Britain*; for the role of the Treasury see Heclo and Wildavsky (1974) *The Private Government of Public Money*; for some illustrative material see Madgwick (1991) *British Government: The Central Executive Territory*; for numerous short case studies of policy-making see James (1997) *British Government: A Reader in Policy Making*; and for a fascinating account of a dramatic policy failure see Butler, Adonis and Travers (1994) *Failure in British Government: The Politics of the Poll Tax*.

12

PARLIAMENT AND THE ADMINISTRATION

Constitutional theory

It is a basic principle of the British constitution that the function of Parliament is not to govern the country, but to control the government. As noted in Chapter 2, the responsibility for government and administration rests with the monarch's ministers, but developments in the past three centuries have rendered them accountable to Parliament (and in particular to the House of Commons) for their actions. Parliament is, in fact, the only institution that has power to control the actions of government departments, provided their officials do not break the law. There is no equivalent in Britain of the United States Supreme Court or the German Constitutional Court, both of which have power to declare executive actions contrary to constitutional principles. Nor does Britain have a system of administrative courts, like the French Conseil d'Etat or the Italian Consiglio di Stato, which can review administrative decisions and decide whether or not they were justified. In Britain government departments can do largely as they like, provided they have parliamentary approval and keep within the letter of the law. In constitutional theory there is a division, not of powers, but of functions, ministers being responsible for governing the country and Parliament being responsible for calling ministers to account as well as for legislation (which will be dealt with separately in the following chapter). The accountability of the government is said to be ensured by two constitutional conventions: the convention that ministers are collectively responsible to Parliament for the policy of the government as a whole, and the convention that each minister is individually responsible to Parliament for the work of his or her department.

There is a degree of unreality about this constitutional theory, which assumes a dichotomy between the government on one hand and Parliament on the other. In fact nearly a hundred Members of Parliament at the present time are members of the government and more than two hundred other MPs are loyal supporters of the government. The real dichotomy in British politics is between the government and the Opposition, not between the government and Parliament. But this is not yet reflected in constitutional theory and it will be convenient in this chapter to begin by examining the established principles and conventions.

Collective responsibility

The essence of this convention is first, that members of the government should present a united front to Parliament in defence of their policies; and secondly, that if the House of Commons defeats the government on a vote of confidence the Prime Minister should either ask the monarch for an immediate dissolution of Parliament or should resign, together with all his or her ministers. The convention was developed in the years between 1780 and 1832, and in the middle decades of the nineteenth century it led to the resignation of a series of governments. Between the first Reform Act of 1832 and the second Reform Act of 1867 no government survived for what is now regarded as a government's normal life, from a general election until the Prime Minister asks for a dissolution, at a time of his or her own choice, towards the end of that Parliament's allotted span. In this period the convention of collective responsibility was an effective weapon that ensured parliamentary control of the executive, and ten governments in thirty-five years were brought to an end by adverse votes in the House of Commons. It was largely on the evidence of this period that commentators and politicians based their claims, in the latter part of the century, that the British system of government was one in which the actions of the government were effectively controlled by Parliament.

In fact, even as these claims were gaining general acceptance, the development of party discipline was changing the situation. Between 1900 and 1997 only three governments were forced out of office as the result of parliamentary defeats. In January 1924 Liberal and Labour MPs joined forces to defeat the Conservative government (which had lost seats in a general election a few weeks earlier). The Conservative Prime Minister resigned and a minority Labour government was formed with Liberal support. In October 1924 the Liberals combined with the Conservatives to defeat the Labour government. The Prime Minister dissolved Parliament and the Conservatives won the ensuing election. In March 1979 the Labour government was defeated by the combined votes of Conservatives, Liberals, Scottish Nationalists and Ulster Unionists. This was followed by a dissolution and a Conservative victory in the election.

On these three occasions no single party commanded a majority in the House of Commons, so that the government of the day was at the mercy of the smaller parties, which held the balance of power. However, throughout the greater part of the twentieth century the leading party has had an overall majority in the House of Commons, and party discipline has been so effective that no ruling party in that situation has been brought down by a vote of no confidence. This has held good even when the governing party has commanded only a tiny majority. The Labour government of 1950–1 survived with a majority of only six, and the Labour government of 1964–6 got by with a majority that varied between four and one. The maintenance of a majority in the division lobbies in this kind of situation puts a severe strain on government supporters, who have to be prepared to attend no matter how inconvenient it is to them, even to the extreme of being brought into the precincts of Parliament by ambulance and being counted by the tellers while lying on a stretcher. But so far they have always measured up to these demands.

This does not mean that the convention of collective responsibility is obsolete, for clearly it still exists; a government that is defeated on a vote of confidence has no choice but to resign or to dissolve Parliament. But, as a general rule, governments in the twentieth century are defeated not by Parliament but by the electorate, and this affects the significance of the convention of collective responsibility. A government that faced the constant possibility of defeat in Parliament would be more likely to have to resign or ask for a dissolution when things were going badly for it than when things were going well; in this sense responsibility to Parliament would provide an immediate sanction for a failure of government policy. In the modern British political system this sanction is absent. As a general rule a government is not more likely to resign or dissolve Parliament when its policies meet with a major reversal than when it is prospering, but less likely to do so. The public has a short memory, and a government's best strategy in times of crisis is to ride the storm and hope that it will be able to recapture public support before the next general election is held. The Labour government of 1945–50 survived through the fuel crisis of 1947, the devaluation of the pound in 1948, the collapse of its Palestine policy in the same year and the fiasco of the groundnuts scheme in 1949. In 1950 it was returned to power, though with a reduced majority. The Conservative government of 1955–9 succeeded not only in surviving after the débâcle of Suez, but in winning an increased majority at the next general election. James Callaghan's government of 1976–9 tried desperately to stay in office until the parliamentary term came to an end in October 1979, in the hope that a good summer would induce the electorate to forget the hardships caused by industrial disruption during the previous winter.

The role of the convention of collective responsibility in British government may perhaps be summarized in the following terms. It does not provide a continuous sanction for the blunders and failures of government, as it did in the middle decades of the nineteenth century. On the other hand, it continues to play a vital role in the British political system, ensuring that governments resign immediately they lose their parliamentary majority in an election. On these admittedly rare occasions when the governing party leads the others by only a hair's breadth the convention may prompt the government to modify its plans, as in 1965 when the Labour government decided not to go ahead at that time with its declared policy of renationalizing the steel industry. At all times the convention gives some procedural advantage to the Opposition; if it puts down a motion of censure on the government, this has precedence over other parliamentary business, and the government will be obliged to rearrange the timetable to find time for it.

Finally, the convention compels ministers to maintain the appearance of unity; they are expected to resign from the government if they are not prepared to defend its policies in public. Instances are fairly rare, but the principle is undoubtedly effective; in 1985 Michael Heseltine resigned from his post as Minister of Defence because he could not accept the Cabinet view that a British firm making military helicopters should be taken over by an American firm, and did not believe that his contrary view had been given a fair hearing. There have been one or two obvious instances of ministers disagreeing in public, as in 1975 when Cabinet ministers opposed to British membership of the European Community were permitted to campaign for a negative vote in the referendum on that issue. But there is no general tendency for Prime Ministers to relax their insistence on unity.

Individual responsibility

This convention has two strands, one of which is in full operation, the other of which is something of a myth. The first strand is that the minister in charge of a department is answerable to Parliament for all the actions of that department. As Gladstone said: 'In every free state, for every public act, some one must be responsible, and the question is, who shall it be? The British constitution answers: "the minister, and the minister exclusively" ' (Gladstone 1879: vol. 1, p. 233). The positive aspect of this is that Members of Parliament wishing to query the actions of a department, either privately or publicly, know that there is one person who cannot evade the duty of answering their questions. The negative aspect of it is that it protects the anonymity of civil servants and shields them from political controversy. This strand of the convention can be seen on four days a week when Parliament is in session, for the first hour of each sitting is devoted to Question Time, at which ministers answer questions put to them in advance by MPs and have also to deal with supplementary questions that arise out of their answers.

According to the second strand of the convention, ministers must accept responsibility for the actions of their department not only in the sense that they must be ready to explain and defend them but also in the sense that they must resign their appointments if serious blunders or failures are exposed. This, at any rate, is what is implied by many commentators and what is widely thought to be part of the practice of British government.

In fact, resignations of this kind are extremely rare. Mistakes are constantly being made, and from time to time they are exposed or admitted, but it is exceptional for a minister to resign on this account. The most conspicuous failures of postwar British governments have led to stormy debates in Parliament and to scathing comments in the press, but they have not led to the resignation of the ministers concerned. The total failure of British policy in Palestine between 1945 and 1948 did not lead the Foreign Secretary to think of resigning, even though he had said in a rash moment that he would stake his political future on his ability to deal with the problem. The humiliating collapse of British policy towards Egypt at the time of the Suez expedition was not followed by the resignation on political grounds of any of the ministers concerned, though ill-health forced the Prime Minister to resign a few weeks later. The waste of vast sums of public money on the design of missiles and aircraft that have never been produced has not led to the resignation of any of the Ministers of Aviation and Defence who were responsible for it. The list could be extended to include the various failures of economic policy in the past forty years, the slaughter of eleven prisoners in a Mau Mau detention camp in Kenya, the gross errors made in estimating the development costs of Concorde and many other examples.

Looking at the matter another way, S. E. Finer traced only sixteen cases of a minister resigning as the result of parliamentary criticism of his department between 1855 (when the first case occurred) and 1955 (Finer 1956). Since there were no cases between 1955 and 1980, this makes sixteen cases in 125 years. The smallness of the number indicates that it is only in exceptional circumstances that failure leads to loss of office, and Finer suggested that what made these cases exceptional was not the gravity of the failures but, in general, the fact that the ministers had lost popularity or respect within their own party. However, in 1982 the Foreign Secretary, Lord Carrington, resigned because he and his advisers had failed to predict that Argentine forces would invade the Falkland Islands. Carrington's action was emphatically not an example of Finer's rule, as he was held in very high regard by his colleagues and he resigned in spite of personal requests from the Prime Minister that he should stay in office. Two more junior ministers at the Foreign Office resigned with him. There were no examples in the following fifteen years.

Of course, the exposure of departmental failings may affect ministers' careers even though it does not lead to resignation. In the next ministerial reshuffle they may find that they are transferred to a less attractive ministry or even relegated to the backbenches. The point is that most failures do not have any such consequence, and whether they do or not is apt to depend more on the general standing of the minister with the party and Prime Minister than on the extent of parliamentary criticism. In view of this, it cannot be said that the convention of individual ministerial responsibility to Parliament renders the minister liable to loss of office if the work of his or her department comes under fire.

The first part of the convention, however, is of considerable importance. The fact that ministers have to answer for their departments gives MPs the right to demand information about administrative decisions, whether these be related to large issues of policy or to dealings with individual citizens. MPs frequently exercise this right, sometimes by questions in Parliament, more often by private correspondence. It enables MPs to investigate the grievances and press the claims of their constituents at the highest level, and the knowledge that this has been done is a comfort to constituents even if the decision cannot be changed.

In the second place, the ability to hold ministers to account for their actions in Parliament facilitates the work of opposition MPs. They can use parliamentary questions to expose weaknesses in the government's policies and lack of efficiency in the administration. If the matter that is brought to light is both serious and urgent, the Opposition may be able to secure the adjournment of the House and hold a full debate on the same day. Failing this, the Opposition can move a vote of censure or debate the issue on one of the twenty-six days on which Opposition motions have priority. If the matter is potentially damaging to the government's reputation, members of the Opposition can return to it time and time again by asking questions on its different aspects. In this way the Opposition can bring the government's weaknesses to the attention of press and public and so hope to win votes in the next election.

If these three points about individual responsibility are considered in conjunction with the earlier points made about collective responsibility, it is clear that ministerial responsibility to Parliament is one of the central features of the British political system. It does not normally lead to the resignation or dismissal of ministers, but it does mean that they have constantly to explain and justify the work and plans of the administration to a critical assembly, and it provides an important channel of communication between those who govern and those who are governed.

The MP and the administration

Ordinary Members of Parliament, whether they be government backbenchers or members of one of the opposition parties, have various methods open to them by which they can check or criticize the work of the government. The most straightforward method is to put down a parliamentary question. The questions have to be submitted in advance, in writing, but Members are given the opportunity to follow them up by supplementary questions.

This procedure is significant in two different ways, beyond its utility in providing MPs with an opportunity to extract information about the implementation of government policies. It has an impact on the civil service and it gives MPs an additional channel through which they can hope to embarrass and criticize ministers. There is no doubt that the behaviour of civil servants is affected by the knowledge that, if they make a mistake or offend a member of the public, the matter may subsequently be raised in Parliament. The name of the civil servant will not be publicly disclosed, but no official likes the prospect of having to justify his or her actions to his superiors in response to an urgent demand by the minister, knowing that the reputation of the department rests, for the moment, on his or her shoulders. It is not without significance that every draft answer to a parliamentary question is normally scrutinized and checked by the permanent secretary of the department. It is true that, since the size of the civil service has increased far more rapidly in the past fifty years than the number of questions asked, the chances of any individual decision leading to a parliamentary question must have diminished. But there is no evidence that this has led civil servants to stop worrying about the possibility of a question, and no serious reason to doubt the truth of the following comment by a senior official of the Department of Employment.

> One may say of the British official that, if he is engaged on a job with no immediate outlet to minister and Parliament, he will still be working tacitly with the sort of notions of relevance that would mean something to them; he must try to so order things that, of all that can happen, only those things happen which are susceptible of explanation in the parliamentary context.
>
> (Sisson 1959: 123)

The opportunity to embarrass ministers is afforded more by the supplementary questions than by the original written questions. Civil servants are experts in drafting answers to written questions that protect the department and the minister, but they cannot always predict the supplementaries, which the minister will have to answer off the cuff. In recent decades, as parliamentary conflicts have tended to become sharper, supplementary questions have become more numerous. In the early years of the twentieth century there was one supplementary for every two or three main questions, but by the 1970s there were on average two supplementaries for every question – a fivefold increase in the proportion of supplementaries (Borthwick 1979: 488). The supplementary questions have become a means of harassing ministers and scoring partisan points. While they have to take the form of questions to be within the rules of order, there has been a tendency for them to become longer so as to contain assertions and implicit accusations as well as questions. By 1974 the average supplementary occupied ten lines in the official reports (ibid.: 488).

In recent years there have been three other developments of note. One is a sharp rise in the number of questions put down for oral answer. In consequence, the proportion of these for which time has actually been found for oral answers fell from about half in the period 1945–67 to only about a tenth in the years 1988–90 (Irwin *et al.* 'Evolving Rules', in Franklin and Norton 1993: 27). The others get written answers. The second is that, as questions have become less and less information-seeking and more and more a part of the partisan conflict in the House, there has been a tendency for groups of like-minded MPs to get together to organize them. The third is that the introduction of radio coverage and then (in 1989) of television coverage has tended to turn Question Time into more and more of a shouting match between government and opposition Members.

This has been particularly true of Prime Minister's Question Time, which until 1977 occurred twice a week. Questions in this period range over a wide selection of topics and are sometimes used as an attempt to ambush the Prime Minister, following seemingly innocuous questions with unpredictable supplementaries on delicate issues. For instance, on one occasion a question about whether the Prime Minister had any plans to visit Derbyshire was followed by a supplementary asking whether she realized that job opportunities for Derbyshire workers employed by Rolls-Royce were being jeopardized by her government's refusal to sell certain types of arms to Chile. Prime Minister's Question Time is in consequence a test of wits that may become an ordeal. It does little or nothing to improve the quality of policy-making but it is a remarkable aspect of British democracy that Prime Ministers should be willing (or feel compelled, as the case may be) to expose themselves in this way.

One of Blair's first decisions, announced only seven days after his appointment, was to modify the timetable with the hope of improving the quality of the interchanges in Prime Minister's Question Time. Instead of meeting the House twice a week, for fifteen minutes each time, he proposed to meet it only once a week, for thirty minutes. The two short periods, he said, had become fun for television viewers but not so good for the democratic process, with the Prime Minister struggling to make himself heard above the bawling of a couple of hundred Opposition backbenchers. He hoped that a longer period would encourage a more calm and reasoned interchange, and would also allow for more questions to be put by Members other than the Leader of the Opposition.

In addition to asking questions MPs have various opportunities to debate the wisdom of governmental policies. They do so at the beginning of each session, when there is a debate lasting five or six days on the government's legislative programme for the year. They do so during debates initiated by the Opposition on twenty-six days each year, these days formerly being called Supply Days and now known simply as Opposition Days. They do so when the government finds time to discuss an important and urgent current issue, sometimes on its own initiative and sometimes on the request of Opposition parties. All these debates are normally adversarial in character, though debates on urgent current issues sometimes find the main parties in substantial agreement. This is particularly likely to be the case when the issue is one of foreign affairs.

In addition, there is an adjournment debate of thirty minutes at the close of each day's business, with MPs balloting for the right to choose issues and open the debate, except that on one day a week the Speaker of the House chooses the opening speaker. The matters raised in these short debates tend to be local issues, or specific questions about the implementation of national policies. Attendance tends to be small, as most Members leave at the conclusion of the main business of the day around 10 p.m. The discussions are not usually adversarial in character.

Finally, there is a procedure by which Members can secure the adjournment of normal business in order to obtain an immediate debate on an urgent issue of national importance. Under Standing Order 9, the Speaker will allow a motion for the adjournment of the House if he or she is persuaded that the issue is of public importance, is within the competence of a minister, could not reasonably have been debated earlier and could not reasonably be left until time could be found for it in the normal timetable of the House. These are stringent conditions, which are met only once or twice a year. But occasionally there is a sudden development that arouses the concern of Parliament – a crisis in foreign affairs, a breakdown of public order, a decision to deport an alien at short notice – and in these circumstances the motion may be put. If forty Members support the motion, no matter how many Members oppose it (they are not counted), the motion succeeds and is the subject of a three-hour debate the same evening or the following afternoon.

Specialized committees of investigation

The main factor that limits the influence MPs can exert through the channels so far mentioned is the average Member's lack of specialized knowledge of governmental affairs. Ministers have all the resources of their departments behind them and can often fend off attacks by being armed with more detailed facts and figures than their opponents can possibly muster.

To remedy this weakness, reformers in the postwar period have repeatedly urged that the House of Commons should develop a set of specialized committees, aided by professional staff, with the power to call for papers and cross-examine civil servants. There can be no doubt that committees of this kind, which have flourished over many decades in the United States, are the only channel through which a large representative assembly can exercise effective and continuous control over the work of government departments. Without this opportunity to find out for themselves what is being done in departments, members of the assembly are in a poor position to offer detailed and constructive criticism.

Until the late 1960s, the House of Commons had only three specialized committees of investigation, none of which corresponded in scope to the activities of a department. These were the committees on Public Accounts, Estimates and Nationalized Industries. Of these, the Public Accounts Committee has the most precise function. Its task is to consider the annual report of the Comptroller and Auditor-General on departmental expenditures. If this report criticizes particular departments for transgressing the very detailed rules that govern administrative expenditures, the Public Accounts Committee is likely to issue a kind of public reprimand to the senior civil servants responsible. This procedure serves as a way of confirming the principle that Parliament has ultimate control over the budget, even though this control is exercised retrospectively.

The function of what used to be called the Estimates Committee, but now has the much more logical title of the Committee on Expenditure, is to scrutinize government expenditures with a view to assessing whether or not the taxpayer has got good value for money. Until 1965 the committee had only a small staff of clerks and could do no more each year than to pick out a few examples of government expenditure for examination. In 1965 the committee's membership and staff were increased, and five specialized subcommittees were established. This move was in line with Whitehall's new emphasis on managerial efficiency in the public services, and in recent years the committee has produced a stream of useful reports.

The Select Committee on Nationalized Industries was set up in 1956 to examine the reports and accounts of public corporations in charge of the nationalized industries, and it interpreted its terms of reference in a broad way. Taking one industry at a time, it conducted fairly thorough inquiries into matters of administration and policy, and felt free to examine officials of the relevant government departments as well as officials of the public corporations. The committee rarely divided on party lines or approached issues in a partisan way, and this helped it both to secure the co-operation of civil servants and to command respect in Parliament for its reports.

The undoubted success of this committee lent support to those reformers who wished to see the establishment of specialized committees of Parliament covering a wide range of government activities. It was argued that this reform would make Parliament's influence over administration more effective as well as increasing the knowledge and extending the experience of backbench MPs. However, the extension of the committee system had to wait for the support of a sympathetic administration.

This support was forthcoming in 1966, when it was announced that several new committees were to be established on an experimental basis, the experiment to be reviewed after a few years. The first two committees dealt respectively with agriculture and with science and technology. These were followed in 1968 and 1969 by new committees on education, on race relations and immigration, on Scottish affairs and on overseas development.

Of these committees, three were devoted to the affairs of particular government departments, while the other three dealt with a broader range of topics. Committees in the first category – those dealing with agriculture, education and overseas developments – made less impact than the others. Having terms of reference that coincided with the responsibilities of departments, they were viewed with suspicion by senior civil servants in those departments. The latter were simply not happy to see a group of MPs acquire specialized knowledge about departmental affairs, which might serve as a basis for penetrating criticisms of departmental policies. Relations between the Committee on Agriculture and the Department of Agriculture, Fisheries and Food were particularly strained, and this committee was abolished after just over two years, early in 1969. The Committee on Education was also limited to two years, from 1968 to 1970. The Committee on Overseas Development had a smoother passage and continued until 1979.

The other committees were more successful. The Committee on Science and Technology dealt with matters that are not normally subject to partisan controversy, and some of its members had scientific expertise that could be used more effectively in committee than on the floor of the House. The committee's investigations of alternative designs for nuclear power stations were widely welcomed as a useful contribution. The Committee on Race Relations and Immigration was successful for a rather different reason, namely that the topics with which it dealt were politically sensitive issues for which the ministers and civil servants concerned were happy to share responsibility. This committee made a number of valuable studies.

The result of this experiment with specialized committees of inquiry was therefore mixed. The committees themselves functioned well, with members taking a constructive interest in the issues involved and with hardly any divisions on party lines. However, one would be hard pressed to identify their impact on policy-making and administration. The committees on agriculture and on education were somewhat resented by the departments, and their recommendations were ignored. The reports of the other committees contributed to the general pool of ideas about their respective subjects, but it is almost impossible to trace a causal relationship between recommendations and action. The reports contributed to the education of Members of Parliament, but there was rarely time for them to be debated on the floor of the House. Those who wanted further reforms of Parliament could point to useful work done, whereas sceptics could and did say that the results were hardly worth the effort.

The next stage in the story opened in 1978, when a report of the Select Committee on Procedure recommended a completely new committee structure in the House of Commons, giving committees a comprehensive coverage of government departments and also enlarging their powers. The then Leader of the House, Michael Foot, was opposed to these recommendations, but they were supported by backbenchers of all parties and also by Conservative frontbenchers. In the 1979 general election the Conservative Party committed itself to the proposed new structure and one of the first decisions taken by the new Parliament was to endorse the majority of the recommendations.

Under the new system, there are fourteen specialized committees, covering the subjects listed in Table 12.1. The long-standing Public Accounts Committee

Table 12.1 Specialized committees of Parliament established in 1979

Topic	Numbers of members	Number of professional advisers
Agriculture	9	4
Defence	11	4
Education, Science and Arts	9	4
Employment	9	4
Energy	11	9
Environment	11	7
Foreign Affairs	11	4
Home Affairs	11	2
Industry and Trade	11	2
Social Services	9	5
Transport	11	2
Treasury and Civil Service	11	7
Scottish Affairs	13	1
Welsh Affairs	11	3

continues unchanged, but the other committees mentioned above have had their work taken over by one or other of the new committees. These committees are small in size, having either nine or eleven members each (apart from the Committee on Scottish Affairs, which has thirteen members). They appoint their own chairperson, and in the first session seven appointed Conservative Members to that position while the other seven appointed Labour Members. They each have several professional advisers, who are paid on a daily basis. There is also a Liaison Committee, consisting of the fourteen chairpersons. Their terms of reference enable the committees to discuss the activities of nationalized industries and of the whole range of semi-autonomous public authorities that come under the ultimate control of government departments.

With the establishment of these committees, the House of Commons has gone a considerable way towards accepting responsibility for the continuous scrutiny of the work of government departments. It is a step away from the Whitehall view of the constitution and towards the liberal view. Several positive things can be said about the work of the new committees. They have proceeded in a businesslike way, getting advice from professional staff and consultants, taking evidence from spokespersons for pressure groups and cross-examining civil servants. They have rarely divided on party lines, so that they have escaped from the adversarial conflict that marks most debates on the floor of the House. They have worked hard, meeting frequently and each producing several reports a year.

The limitation of the new committees is that they have no powers of action except to submit reports to the House. They have no powers over legislation, which are the prerogative of a quite different set of committees, to be discussed in the following chapter. Parliament may or may not find time to hold debates on committee reports, and in the majority of cases is not able to do so. It is clear that the committees add considerably to the amount and (more important) the quality of specialized information about policy-making and policy implementation that is available to Parliament, but it is not clear how much practical difference this makes to the conduct of British government and administration.

Further reading

Norton (1981) *The Commons in Perspective*, is the most accessible general account of Parliament at work; Marshall (1989) *Ministerial Responsibility*, is an excellent guide to conventions and practice; for some essays on parliamentary reform see Judge (1983) *The Politics of Parliamentary Reform*; for detailed accounts of the specialized committees see Drewry (1985) *The New Select Committees*; for a good guide to parliamentary questions see Franklin and Norton (1993) *Parliamentary Questions*.

13

CHANGING THE LAW

Legislative procedure

The law of Britain consists of Common Law, as interpreted by judges over the centuries, and Statute Law, as enacted by Parliament. In this context the word 'Parliament' signifies the two Houses together with the monarch, for all three must agree to a new law before it can be placed on the Statute Book. The procedure is for a Bill to be introduced in one of the Houses, where it must pass three readings and a Committee Stage, for it to be sent to the other House for the same treatment, and for it then to be presented to the monarch for assent. In constitutional law the monarch retains the right to refuse assent but in practice he or she has no choice in the matter. After the Royal Assent the Act is entered in the Statute Book and immediately becomes part of the law of the land.

Parliamentary Bills are of two kinds. The great majority in the present century are 'public Bills', which affect the community generally. The others are 'private Bills', which relate to a matter of purely private or local interest; for instance, an individual may promote a private Bill to free his property from some legal restriction as to its disposal, or a local authority may do so to acquire the powers necessary for the damming of a river or the conversion of a burial ground into a park. There is a special procedure for private Bills that is quasi-judicial in nature. First, the promoters of the Bill must notify all persons and organizations whose interests may be affected by the Bill. After a formal first reading there is a second reading that is also formal unless someone objects to the Bill in principle, as might happen, for example, in the case of a Bill that would extend the power of a municipal authority to engage in trade. If the Bill passes the second reading, it is then referred to a special committee of four or five Members, before which the proponents and opponents of the measure argue their case with the assistance of counsel. This is the important stage, and if the Bill gets through this committee it is usually passed without further amendment.

In the case of public Bills the second reading in the House of Commons is the most important stage. The first reading is a pure formality. On the second reading there is a debate on the principles and purpose of the Bill, which may last for several days. The Bill is then referred to a committee, which considers it clause by clause. Finance Bills and some other Bills of exceptional importance are heard in committee of the whole House. Bills relating only to Scotland are referred to the Scottish Committee and other public Bills are normally referred to one of the six standing committees of the House, which are not specialized in function or title and are known simply as Standing Committees A, B and so on through to F.

Each standing committee deals with Bills on a wide variety of topics, and for this reason it is commonly thought that there is only a random relationship between the subject of a Bill and the interests and expertise of the members of the committee that considers the Bill. The truth is very different. Each committee is composed of a nucleus of twenty members, chosen by the Committee of Selection in proportion to the strength of the parties in the House, together with up to thirty members who are appointed for the consideration of one Bill only and are chosen for their interests and qualifications. Given the nature of party management in Parliament, these additional members are also chosen in rough proportion to party strengths, but they are people who have an active interest in the Bill to be discussed. Furthermore, the Committee of Selection does not appoint the twenty nuclear members of a standing committee until after it is known what Bill will first be discussed by that committee, and the choice is usually influenced by that knowledge. If the subject of the second Bill is markedly different, several of the nuclear members may resign from the committee and be replaced by others who are better qualified to discuss the second Bill, and so on through the session. It follows that the standing committees of the House of Commons are much more specialized in composition than appears at first sight. The minister responsible for the Bill in the House always sits on the committee, advised by his or her officials, while the Attorney-General and Solicitor-General are entitled to take part in the proceedings of all standing committees so as to advise on legal points. The standing committees are therefore well-informed bodies. They consider each Bill clause by clause, though they are sometimes limited by shortage of time. In order to keep up the pace of legislation that is required in modern Britain, the government has occasionally to use the closure in committee, together with other procedural devices known as the guillotine (which stops debate on a clause after a predetermined time) and the kangaroo (which takes the committee in jumps from one important clause to another).

When a Bill comes out of committee it is reported to the House, at which stage the House discusses and occasionally reverses the amendments made in committee, as well as having the chance to add detailed changes of its own. There quickly follows the third reading, at which only changes in wording are permitted, and the Bill is then sent to the House of Lords for similar (though briefer) treatment, unless it is one of those non-controversial Bills that go through the Lords before they are presented to the Commons.

The origins of legislation

Before 1867 most Bills were initiated by Private Members. However, since that date governments have progressively increased their control over the legislative process so that Private Members are now given only the most limited opportunities to introduce Bills. Every alternate Friday in the first twenty weeks of each session is reserved for Private Members' Bills, and as the House rises early on Fridays this means that in practice Private Members have no more than 10 per cent of parliamentary time at their disposal for legislation. This is often regarded as an inevitable consequence of the great extension of government activities that the past century has seen, but in fact the British Parliament is dominated much more completely by the government than are the legislatures of most other liberal democracies. In the United States Congress all Bills are technically introduced by Private Members and most Bills are actually initiated by them; in Sweden Private Members' Bills usually outnumber government Bills (though they do not deal with such important subjects); in the Fourth French Republic the ordinary deputy had a good deal of room for initiative; and even in the Fifth Republic the members of the National Assembly enjoy somewhat more scope for legislative enterprise than do their British counterparts.

The present practice in Britain is for backbenchers to ballot for the opportunity to introduce Bills. Only twenty of the 650 MPs win a place in the ballot each session, and members do not have much chance of getting their Bills a decent hearing unless they are in the top half of this twenty. Some MPs have draft Bills in their pockets to introduce if they win, while others use the opportunity to sponsor a Bill drafted by a pressure group or by one of their colleagues. Success in the ballot entitles a Member to introduce a Bill for its first and second readings, but progress beyond this stage depends upon the goodwill of the government. In an average session only about eight or nine Private Members' Bills pass into law. To get a Bill enacted requires skill, patience, determination, a measure of support from more than one party and the sympathy of the ministers most directly affected. An interesting example is the Obscene Publications Bill, which was originally drafted by Roy Jenkins in the autumn of 1954. In the spring of 1955 this got a brief first hearing in the House but lapsed at the end of the session. In the following winter it was reintroduced by a friendly MP who had won a place by ballot, but was 'talked out' by the Under Secretary for Home Affairs, who spoke for so long that the House passed to other business without there being time for a vote. A year later a third Member sponsored it and it was passed on second reading, after which it would normally have been referred to a standing committee that was so choked with other Bills that it would never have got round to discussing this one. The Bill was saved from this fate by R. A. Butler, the new Home Secretary, who arranged for a select committee to be established to discuss the Bill in detail. This took time, and the committee did not produce its report until the spring of 1958, by which time the Bill had once again lapsed, as all uncompleted legislation does at

177

the end of each session. In the ballot the following autumn none of the twenty successful Members proved willing to sponsor the Bill and the whole operation was back to square one, from which it was rescued a few months later by the Home Secretary, who offered government time for a new second reading, on the understanding that the principles as well as the details of the Bill would be open to debate. What emerged from this was a compromise Bill that was not unacceptable to the government and eventually passed into law, after a good deal of hard bargaining in the committee and report stages, in July 1959. The whole process has been likened to a game of snakes and ladders lasting five years (Jenkins 1959).

Although Private Members' Bills are not numerous, some of them are very important. Postwar examples include the 1967 Sexual Offences Act, which legalized homosexual practices between consenting adults, the Act that authorized abortion more or less on demand and the Act that abolished censorship in the theatre.

Government Bills are much more numerous, and their passage through Parliament is more certain. In an average session about seventy are introduced and nearly as many are enacted. Their origins are various, and may be discussed under the headings of: (1) party policy; (2) Cabinet decisions; (3) committee reports; (4) outside pressures; and (5) administrative needs.

(1) Legislation based directly on policy statements put out by the parties tends to be at the head of the programme after a general election has led to a change of government. The 1945 election brought a government into office that was committed to a set of reforms that had been under discussion for many years. In the following five sessions Parliament passed more major Acts than it has ever passed in a period of comparable length. The coal, gas, electricity and transport industries were nationalized, the civil airlines were established, the National Health Service was set up, national insurance was reorganized, and an elaborate Act regarding town and country planning was passed. But this was altogether exceptional. When the Conservatives regained power in 1951 the only major Acts that followed from their party programme were those to denationalize road transport and the iron and steel industry. Some other important changes were made, such as the abolition of petrol rationing, but these did not require legislation apart from the making of orders under powers already granted to ministers.

The Labour victory of 1964 produced a Bill to extend rent control and a number of financial measures to deal with the balance-of-payments crisis, but Labour's electoral programme was reflected more in administrative changes and the appointment of committees than in the passage of legislation. The Conservative victory of 1970 led to the Industrial Relations Act, the Housing Finance Act and the enabling legislation consequent upon Britain's entry to the European Community. When Labour returned to power in 1974 the main immediate legislative consequences of its election manifesto were the repeal of Conservative laws regarding industrial relations and housing, but in the following two years several new measures were introduced that had their origins in party promises. These included measures to increase security of employment and to extend the compensation payable to workers who were made redundant. The Thatcher victories of 1979, 1983 and 1987 were followed by a stream of legislative changes introduced to give effect to party policy, notably measures to restore nationalized undertakings to private ownership, to compel local authorities to offer municipal housing for sale to tenants, to place ceilings on the expenditure of local authorities, to abolish the authorities governing the seven largest cities and to reform the education system. Statistically, only a small proportion of government Bills have their immediate origins in party policy statements. An analysis of legislation between 1970 and 1979 has shown that only 8 per cent of Bills in 1970–4 followed directly from the Conservative election manifesto, while only 13 per cent of Bills in 1974–9 followed from the Labour election manifesto (Rose 1980b: 72). However, some of the most important Bills begin life in this way.

(2) Many other Bills are party-political in origin in the sense that they are sponsored by ministers or by Cabinet committees who become convinced that changes are needed. For instance, Conservative Cabinets between 1951 and 1964 decided to grant independence to a large number of British colonies, to disband the Central African Federation, to abolish resale price maintenance, to establish machinery for economic planning and to extend the control of restrictive practices in trade. The annual Finance Act is also a highly political measure, as are the various legislative attempts to control prices and incomes.

(3) Other Bills are based on the reports of committees of inquiry. Examples are the Clean Air Act, which followed the Beaver Committee on Air Pollution, the Act to reorganize the government of Greater London, which followed the report of the Herbert Commission, the Act to liberalize the laws regarding gambling, which followed the report of the Royal Commission on Betting, Lotteries and Gaming, the Act designed to drive prostitutes off the streets, which followed the report of the Wolfenden Committee, and the Local Government Act of 1972, which drew on the analysis (though not the conclusions) of the Redcliff–Maud Commission. None of these Bills was partisan in character, and in each case the government would have welcomed the support of the Opposition for a measure that an impartial committee had recommended. In most cases, though not in the case of London government, Opposition support was secured for the principle of the Bill even if not for its details.

(4) Some Bills result from outside pressures, usually overt but occasionally covert. The Act that led to the establishment of commercial television is an outstanding example of a piece of legislation promoted largely as the result of the activities of a well-organized pressure group that acquired influence through friends and contacts in the governing party and the Cabinet. The parliamentary debates on this Bill were frank, lively and well publicized, but the previous negotiations had been devious and fairly secret. However, this example is exceptional. Most legislation that has its origin in outside pressures results either

179

from open campaigns by promotional groups, such as the RSPCA or the Abortion Law Reform Society, or from frank discussions between government departments and spokespersons for economic interests.

The RSPCA is without question the most successful promotional group in Britain. It has keen supporters in both main parties and enjoys the great advantage that animal welfare is not a cause to which anyone objects, so long as it is not taken to the length of interfering with a traditional sport like hunting. Other promotional (as opposed to interest) groups that have attempted, successfully or not, to promote legislation since 1949 are the National Campaign for the Abolition of Capital Punishment, the Marriage Law Reform Society, the League Against Cruel Sports, the Abortion Law Reform Association and the National Temperance Federation.

Interest groups also propose legislation from time to time on behalf of their members, sometimes by drafting a Bill for introduction as a Private Member's Bill, sometimes by approaching the government department most directly concerned. In 1951 the British Veterinary Association drafted a Bill to make the use of anaesthetics compulsory for operations on domestic animals, which was eventually passed as a Private Member's Bill in 1953. In 1954 the Society of Authors was partly responsible for the first draft of the Obscene Publications Bill, discussed above. An initiative taken by the Joint Committee of Ophthalmic Opticians resulted in the passage of a Bill requiring opticians to be registered. A similar initiative taken by a society representing estate agents has led to a good deal of debate but has not so far resulted in legislation, because there are differences of view within the profession, and the government, while willing to find time for a Bill that meets the wishes of the profession, has not been willing to impose its own view on the profession. A good deal of legislation, over the years, has resulted directly or indirectly from proposals made by trade unions. The Catering Wages Act of 1948 was introduced by the government to meet long-standing complaints by unions about the treatment of workers in the catering trades. The Offices Act of 1960 was designed to meet some of the complaints by white-collar unions about the conditions of work in offices. The Trade Disputes Act of 1965 was passed at the request of the unions to remove the possibility that a union might be sued for damages if it broke a contractual agreement for the purpose of injuring a third party.

(5) A good deal of legislation has its origins within the administration. Government departments find that problems arise that cannot be solved without a change in the law, and the officials persuade their minister that a Bill must be drafted. Each year there is a substantial body of legislation about fairly technical matters that is essentially 'administrative legislation', drafted by government departments after consultation with the affected interests, and controversial only in so far as spokespersons for groups that are not entirely happy with it try to get it amended in Parliament. Examples are Bills dealing with wage negotiations, with weights and measures, with national insurance and with public health.

From a proposal to the law

After a government department has decided to sponsor a piece of legislation, there is much work to be done. The minister and the senior officials concerned with the Bill will have agreed upon its general principles and the latter should 'know the minister's mind' sufficiently well to be able to negotiate with affected groups without having constantly to refer back to their chief. Consultation with all the groups likely to be affected by the Bill is essential, and is recognized as an integral part of the British system of government. A minister whose department omitted to consult a significant group would undoubtedly be criticized in Parliament for this omission, for the group would not fail to find a backbencher willing to express its objections.

Of course, consultation with groups does not imply acceptance of all their suggestions and criticisms. The government's task is to balance group claims against one another and to assess them in terms of the national interest. But a wise minister will give group spokespersons every chance to press their claims, for three reasons. First, he or she needs to know all the practical difficulties involved in the proposal so as to get the details right, to avoid ambiguity and to reduce the opportunities for evasion of the law. Secondly, he or she will want to get as much support as possible for the Bill from those directly affected by it and to assess the arguments and strength of any probable opposition. Even when groups dislike the proposal in principle, it will pay the minister to put the case to them, if they are influential, and perhaps to moderate their opposition by offering them concessions on points of detail. If he or she does not do so, the Bill will have a more difficult passage through Parliament and the party may lose a certain amount of public support. Thirdly, the minister will be concerned about future relations between his or her department and the groups. For better or worse, government departments and interest-group spokespersons have to live with one another, and both sides normally do everything they can to keep the relationship harmonious.

It is an established convention that a Bill is not published in advance of its presentation to Parliament. These consultations and negotiations therefore normally take place on the basis of either a report of an official committee or a White Paper explaining the government's intentions. In the case of Bills that are unlikely to arouse party controversy the whole process may be based on discussions and departmental papers, without anything being published in advance of the Bill. The following quotation from the 1948 *Year Book* of the National Farmers' Union illustrates the kind of detailed discussion that often takes place before a Bill sees the light of day, though (as noted earlier) the NFU is more fortunate than most interest groups in that it does not have to contend with rival or hostile groups of any significance. The degree of influence claimed may therefore be untypical, but the extent of discussion is not unusual.

> The Agriculture Bill was introduced ... in December 1946. For as long as two years before this date discussions had been going on

between the Union and the Minister of Agriculture as to the form which this Bill was to take. . . . When the Bill was introduced it represented, in substance, the result of discussion and a large measure of agreement. . . . There were, however, still many points upon which the Union wished to see the Bill amended, and during the first six months of the year an intensive campaign was conducted inside and outside Parliament to persuade the government to adopt these amendments. On three points only were we unsuccessful.

(Potter 1961: 207)

When the draft Bill is in shape the minister must get Cabinet approval for it, together with a firm place in the parliamentary timetable. He or she will previously have secured provisional support for the Bill and some promise of parliamentary time, but the timetable is crowded and draft Bills are sometimes delayed from one session to the next for this reason. The political climate also changes, and Bills may be deferred if the government is going through an anxious period or if the Bills seem likely to provoke more controversy than had previously been anticipated. Occasionally a measure that has been given provisional approval by the Cabinet alarms government backbenchers, who communicate their feelings through the Whips and at meetings of the specialized party committees. Many Conservative backbenchers disliked a 1957 proposal to liberalize the law regarding shop closing hours and substantially the same group were opposed to a later proposal to abolish resale price maintenance. In the former case the government dropped the Bill; in the latter case the minister concerned defended his policies before the party committee and then before the whole committee of backbenchers, known as the 1922 Committee, gaining enough support to let him continue with the Bill, which was subsequently passed.

Bills that are deferred by a government or left stranded by a change of government are consigned to the pigeon-holes of Whitehall. But the majority avoid this fate and, after Cabinet approval, are put into legal shape by the parliamentary draftspersons and duly presented to Parliament.

Party discipline and legislation

Ever since the development of effective party discipline in the 1860s, the great majority of government Bills have been enacted without substantial change. As early as 1908, the American scholar A. L. Lowell commented that 'to say that at present the Cabinet legislates with the advice and consent of Parliament would hardly be an exaggeration' (quoted in Walkland 1979: 251). Richards reports that in the first twelve years after the Second World War governments introduced 732 Bills in Parliament and secured the passage of 703 of them (Richards 1959: 110). This is a success rate of 96 per cent. Statistics of this kind have led some commentators to conclude that the House of Commons

Table 13.1 Government Bills checked or wrecked by the House of Commons since 1970

Year	Bill	Result
1972	Industry Bill	Significant amendment
1975	Housing Finance (Special Provisions) Bill	Emasculation
1976	Dock Work Regulation Bill	Emasculation
1977	Scotland and Wales Bill	Forced withdrawal
1977/8	Scotland Bill	Three vital amendments
1978	Wales Bill	Vital amendments
1978	Budget	Two important amendments
1981	Local Government Finance Bill	Forced withdrawal
1982	Local Government Finance (No. 2) Bill	Significant amendment
1984	Rates Bill	Significant amendment
1986	Shops Bill	Defeat of Bill

acts as little more than a rubber stamp in the legislative process, using the debates as yet another opportunity to appeal to the electorate rather than as an occasion for legislative revision.

This kind of conclusion is understandable but is less than the whole truth. If Richards's figures are viewed from another perspective, they show that in those twelve years of maximum party discipline, governments had to abandon twenty-nine legislative measures in the face of parliamentary opposition. Other Bills were amended in significant ways. Since the late 1960s party discipline has become somewhat less effective, and governments have had repeatedly to accept unwelcome amendments, to introduce ministerial amendments to ward off criticism, or even to withdraw a Bill altogether. Between 1970 and 1979 the government of the day suffered forty-eight defeats on legislative issues on the floor of the House of Commons, together with more defeats in committee.

Table 13.1 lists some of the more important defeats on legislative issues that governments have experienced since 1970. Some of these defeats were remarkable. Thus, in 1977 the House of Commons forced the government to abandon its first attempt to establish national assemblies in Scotland and Wales. When a second attempt was made, this time with provision for referendums on the issue, the insertion by backbenchers of the requirement that a majority in the referendum must include 40 per cent of all electors to count as a positive endorsement effectively wrecked the chances of establishing these assemblies. In 1978 a Commons revolt on the budget lowered the standard rate of income tax. In 1986 a government with a majority of over a hundred was defeated in its attempt to liberalize the shop closing laws so as to permit Sunday trading.

The House of Commons therefore plays a crucial role in the legislative process, even though, as a consequence of party loyalty and governmental control of parliamentary time, it exercises less power than the Cabinet. Since 1974 the House of Lords has also played a significant role, making itself awkward to Labour governments between 1974 and 1979 and to Conservative govern-ments since 1979. The government still dominates the scene, but Parliament cannot be written off as a rubber stamp.

Delegated legislation and European legislation

For various reasons there has been a considerable increase in postwar years in the volume of legislative orders and regulations that are drafted by government departments and pass into law unless Parliament disagrees within a certain stip-ulated period. The main reasons are the increased complexity of the regulations needed, the need to change them from time to time and the shortage of parliamentary time. The House of Commons now passes between sixty and seventy-five public Acts each session, for which it has about eighty days of debate available. It would clearly be counter-productive to overwhelm Parliament with all the details that are necessary for modern legislation in the economic and social fields, and it is much more sensible to have the details added by the departments concerned after Parliament has agreed on the principles. Equally, it would be a waste of time for the full legislative proce-dure to be employed whenever national insurance contributions or benefits are increased, to take only the simplest example.

In consequence increasing use has been made of the device of authorizing the minister concerned to add (and when necessary change) the details after the main Act has been placed on the Statute Book. To give an idea of the volume of legislation involved, in 1900 there were 202 pages of new statute law and only a little delegated legislation, whereas in 1965 there were 1,817 pages of new statute law and 6,435 pages of delegated legislation.

The rules and orders thus made are known collectively by the rather odd title of 'statutory instruments', and the general procedure is for them to be laid on the table of the two Houses of Parliament and to become law after so many days unless either of the Houses passes a motion to reject them. Amendment is not a possible option. From 1944 to 1973 the responsibility for scrutinizing all these orders rested with a committee known as the Select Committee on Statutory Instruments, which would draw the attention of the House (at certain specified times) to any orders that it considered inappropriate or improper. In 1973 this committee was replaced by a Joint Committee on Statutory Instru-ments, composed of seven members from each House. In 1973 also a Standing Committee on Statutory Instruments was established, with the main function of considering the merits of orders referred to it by the Joint Committee. It is clear, however, that the scrutiny provided by these committees falls short of what would be desirable in terms of liberal principles of representative govern-ment. The volume of delegated legislation is just too great for Parliament to be able to give it thorough attention, and there is no prospect of any change in this situation. It can only be said that the members of the committees do their best.

The question of European legislation is more complex. Within the European Community, the European Commission has power to draft legislation that is binding on member-states, though it is subject to ratification by the European Council of Ministers. The various national parliaments have no legal powers or functions at all in this process. What has been done in Britain is to establish a Select Committee on European Legislation, which has the function of considering draft legislation proposed by the European Commission and reporting to the House of Commons. The House of Lords has a similar committee, together with several subcommittees, and as the Lords' committees have more time available than the Commons' committee the scrutiny of proposed European legislation has generally been more effective in the Lords. The Houses of Parliament can then, separately or jointly, ask the minister concerned to oppose measures that they consider harmful to British interests when these measures come up for ratification in the European Council of Ministers. The minister is not obliged to act on such requests and might find it difficult to do so if he or she were involved in a bargaining procedure within the Council. However, the minister will in most cases abide by the wishes of Parliament and, in so far as he or she has a veto in the Council of Ministers, he or she can then be expected to block the proposed measure.

European legislation increases in scope and importance all the time. Moreover, since 1987 the Council of Ministers has taken decisions by majority vote in a weighted system of voting that takes account of the population of each member state, so that British ministers have lost their veto power on a whole range of issues. It follows that the British Parliament's ability to influence European legislation has been diminished, and will be further diminished in so far as Britain participates in further moves towards European integration. This is inevitably one of the costs of European unity.

Further reading

The best introductions to this topic are Walkland (1968) *The Legislative Process in Great Britain*, and Norton (1981) *The Commons in Perspective*, ch. 5; Private Members' Bills are discussed in Richards (1970) *Parliament and Conscience*; some valuable essays on the topic will be found in Walkland (1979) *The House of Commons in the Twentieth Century*.

14

GOVERNMENT AT THE LOCAL LEVEL

Although the British system of government is highly centralized, it is not feasible for environmental and social services to be provided in a country of 57 million people except through the medium of local agencies. In Britain these agencies have varied and still vary considerably in their character. When water, sanitation and educational services were developed in the nineteenth century, this was at first done through specially constituted authorities with overlapping areas. The system was then rationalized and democratized in 1888 and 1894. The whole country was divided into counties and county boroughs, each of which was a multipurpose authority controlled by an elected council. Within the counties there was established a second tier of district authorities providing local services like street lighting, and these were also controlled by elected councils.

This system was not without problems, but it was tidy in the sense that there were no overlapping areas and it was democratic in the sense that the authorities were under the immediate control of elected representatives. However, from the 1930s onwards national governments have followed a pattern of removing services from the control of the counties and county boroughs and placing them under new specially constituted agencies, directed by people who are appointed rather than elected. The relief of poverty was placed into the hands of the National Assistance Board, replaced later by the Supplementary Benefits Commission. Hospitals were transferred from elected authorities to the National Health Service, administered through twelve Regional Hospital Boards. The distribution of electricity was made the responsibility of regional electricity boards and the distribution of gas made that of regional gas boards, the areas of those regions being coterminous neither with each other nor with the areas of the hospital boards. Some years later, regional water boards were established, with different areas again.

It follows that the British system of government at the local level has a marked lack of uniformity. First, there are branch offices of national government departments, such as the Inland Revenue and the Department of Social Security. The ministerial head of each department is ultimately responsible to Parliament for the work of these branch offices, and the Parliamentary

Commissioner for Administration can investigate their actions if accusations of maladministration are levelled against them.

Secondly, there have been (before privatization) the regional organizations of the public utilities mentioned above. They were directed by boards whose members were nominated rather than elected. Ministers were not responsible to Parliament for the work of the boards and there were no other democratic checks on their activities except for some rather ineffectual local advisory committees. Complaints about maladministration within these organizations could not be investigated by a government official or parliamentary committee. They operated like private monopolies, whose discontented customers could sometimes take them to court but did not have any public machinery for the redress of their grievances.

Thirdly, there are county councils and district councils, each controlled by elected councillors who play a much more direct role in local administration than MPs play in national administration. The councillors are part-time politicians, unpaid except for a very small allowance, who have important administrative functions in regard to education, housing, town planning and a range of other services.

Fourthly, there are the local and regional organizations of the National Health Service, which have to be put into a category of their own. The service is an enormous undertaking, being the largest employer in western Europe, and its organizational structure is elaborate. The Secretary of State for Health is ultimately responsible for its work, though he or she is not accountable to Parliament for its day-to-day activities. It has a Health Service Commissioner with the power to investigate accusations of maladministration, and it is possible (though not at all common) for patients to sue doctors or hospitals in cases of inappropriate treatment that caused harm.

It has become fashionable to give all these local and regional agencies the collective title of 'the local state', while maintaining the traditional terms 'local authorities' and 'local government' for the elected councils, their staff and their activities. In this book there is space to deal only with the local authorities, and to deal with these only in a general way, emphasizing their distinctive characteristics and their relations with the national government. The generality and relative brevity of this treatment should not be thought to imply that local government is unimportant. British local authorities employ over 2.5 million staff, compared with only about 500,000 civil servants, and they provide many services that are essential to the citizen. The nature of the treatment is determined by the fact that local government is a complex topic in its own right, which cannot be dealt with fully here without unbalancing the book. Readers who want fuller information about it, or about the other agencies of the local state, are referred to texts on public administration and local government.

The character of the local government system

The British system of local government cannot be characterized as easily as can either the centralized system that exists in France or the decentralized system of the United States. France has a system of local administration. The country is divided into ninety *départements* and in each of these administration is controlled by a prefect, who is an official of the Ministry of the Interior and is moved from one area to another in the course of his or her career. The prefects and their staff are responsible not only for the administration of local services, which vary only a little from one *département* to another, but also for the enforcement of the law, the collection of taxes and the administration of a number of national services in the area. They are influenced by local politics and local pressures, made stronger since regional councils were established in 1982, but they are part of the government of France.

The United States, on the other hand, has a system of genuine local self-government. The government of an American city is not a part of either the state government or the federal government. In most states a city government has a considerable measure of independence, with power to levy taxes, to raise loans, to decide on the level of services it will provide and to change its own form of organization, provided the electors agree (and within limits set by the state constitution). The result is that American local authorities vary a great deal in their mode of organization and their policies in regard to housing, town planning and other matters.

British local government does not fit neatly into either of these categories. It has the appearance and trappings of a system of local self-government but not much of the reality. The Corporation of the City of Hull, for instance, cannot be said to be part of the British government; it is an independent corporation that was established in the fifteenth century, which owns a great deal of property and appoints its own Sheriff and Lord Mayor; it does not administer national services and it has, indeed, very little contact with the various branch offices of government departments that are established in the city. On the other hand, the Hull Corporation cannot change its own constitution, which is regulated by Act of Parliament; it cannot exercise any powers other than those delegated to it by Parliament; and it is subject to constant regulation and inspection by government departments.

The system is idiosyncratic and has not been based on any clear principles. The reader seeking a guide to the theory of British local government will search the libraries in vain, for no such book exists. What can be found instead is a plethora of volumes on the history and structure of local government. These are replete with analyses of recent reforms and discussions of the case for further reforms, for one of the characteristics of the system is that it is constantly thought to be in need of change. Between 1945 and 1980 the debates about local government revolved upon three distinct issues: the conflict between the case for financial independence and the case for financial equality; the conflict of interests between the cities and the surrounding rural and outer suburban areas; and the conflict between the case for greater efficiency (which is believed to require large units of administration) and the case for local democracy (which is believed to require small units). Since 1980 the debates have centred on a new and more politicized kind of conflict between a national government determined to impose financial restraint on local authorities and a number of urban authorities determined to resist this policy.

The arguments about financial independence have been firmly resolved in favour of dependence on grants from the national government. The main problem about giving local authorities control over taxes that would yield enough income to finance their activities, such as taxes on income or retail sales, is that this would result in large inequalities of income between poorer and richer areas. There are other problems too, notably the deep reluctance of the Treasury to surrender its monopoly of such taxes, but the problem of inequality is the crux of the issue. The position in recent years has been that local authorities derive between half and two-thirds of their net income from a block grant paid by the national government. This grant is determined by a complex formula that has been changed from time to time, but which has as its constant feature a large equalizing element. The result is that the money available for local government services enables authorities all over the country to provide services of roughly equal standard. Citizens living in poorer areas may have to accept a poorer environment, but they do not suffer appreciably in the quality of their schools, housing, road maintenance and other basic services. Most people in Britain regard the sacrifice of financial independence by local authorities as a small price to pay for this kind of equality.

The conflict of interests between the cities and the rural areas is inevitable in a crowded country like Britain. If cities have no room for new housing estates within their boundaries, they can only rehouse people from overcrowded slums by building in the surrounding county – which will usually be resented by residents of the county area affected. The conflict between groups exists no matter where the boundary is, but the location of the boundary is apt to determine the outcome. There are other issues too, and they have dogged the debates about structure and boundaries for many decades. In 1972–3 the Heath government cut through these debates by imposing a new structure, in which enlarged county councils acquired power over numerous urban areas that had previously been independent of them. From the political point of view this reform can be viewed as offering a compromise, whereby county residents could no longer wash their hands of urban problems but might (depending on the balance of populations) be able to dominate the newly enlarged county council.

The new structure also dealt with the problem of governing conurbations by creating six entirely new counties, known as metropolitan counties, to cover the contiguous urban areas surrounding Birmingham, Liverpool, Manchester, Sheffield, Leeds and Newcastle-upon-Tyne. The changes were promoted by the government not only as a way of solving boundary problems but also as a way

of creating larger units of local government that could develop planning departments and make use of modern technology to raise the level of administrative
efficiency.

Whether these structural changes were worthwhile is a question on which
most specialists have returned an unfavourable verdict (see, for example,
Alexander 1982: ch. 3). The larger counties may be in some technical respects
more efficient as administrative units, but relations between the upper and
lower tiers of local government have produced conflict and the system as a
whole is more cumbersome and more expensive to operate than the system it
replaced. Moreover, popular participation in local government was reduced by
the reform, partly because one of the overall consequences of the change was
greatly to reduce the number of elected councillors, partly because there is less
public interest in larger units of local government than in smaller units.
Controversies about structure were therefore not ended by the 1972–3 changes,
and they came to the fore again in 1985 when the Thatcher government introduced legislation to abolish the six metropolitan counties along with the Greater
London Council. The powers enjoyed by these seven authorities were mostly
transferred to the smaller district councils covering the same area.

The character of central–local relations

National control of local government determines how local authorities are organized, what services they must provide, what other services they may provide
if they choose to do so and how most of their services must be administered.
The services they must provide include education, police, sanitation and public
health. If an authority fails to provide one of these services at a level that
meets the minimum standards set by the relevant ministry, the ministry may
take powers to act in default, at the expense of the local authority. In 1954,
for instance, the Coventry City Council refused to organize a civil defence
service on the ground that civil defence, as understood in Britain, would be
irrelevant to the problems of nuclear warfare. The Home Office thereupon took
powers to organize a civil defence force in Coventry and send the bill to the
City Council, a move that eventually persuaded the council to fall into line.
In 1957 the St Pancras Borough Council decided to abandon its civil defence
department for the same reason that had motivated Coventry, and with exactly
the same result.

Some other services are optional, but the limits of a council's activities are
set by the doctrine of *ultra vires*, according to which no authority is entitled
to engage in any activity unless it has been specifically empowered to do so
by Parliament. An authority that tries to exceed its legal powers may be stopped
from doing so by a court order, as happened in 1921 when the Fulham Borough
Council proposed to establish a municipal laundry under its power to provide
public washhouses. Local laundry firms objected and the council had to abandon
the project. If an authority proceeds unheeded in an activity that is *ultra vires*,

the sanction is applied at the end of the financial year when the authority's accounts are audited by an official of the central government known as a District Auditor. If he or she finds that certain expenditures were unjustified, his or her duty is to disallow their payment from public funds, in which case those members of the authority who voted for the expenditures have to pay for them out of their own pockets. To avoid this fate, local authorities that are in doubt about the legality of a proposed measure often ask the relevant government department for a ruling before a final decision is taken.

The best-known example of disallowance occurred in 1921–2 when the Poplar Borough Council paid some of its workmen a wage considerably higher than the standard wage, on the ground that the council wished to be a 'model employer'. The District Auditor's view was that councillors had no right to be generous at the ratepayers' expense and the councillors had to pay the difference between the standard wage and the actual wage paid. Another interesting example occurred in the 1950s in Manchester. It was the custom for one of the local theatres to present a performance of the Shakespearian play that was included in the school examination syllabus each year and for the Manchester City Council to send schoolchildren of the appropriate age-group to see this. One year no performance was offered. The council thereupon decided to commission a performance for the special benefit of their pupils, thinking that this expenditure would be covered by their two powers: (1) to commission and subsidize theatrical performances; and (2) to pay for schoolchildren to see educational plays. When they asked for a ruling, however, they were told that this plan would be *ultra vires*, as the first power could be invoked only if the performances were open to all members of the public, and the second power covered only the purchase of tickets for a play that was in any case being given. A more trivial example occurred in 1963, when the District Auditor forced members of the Castle Donnington District Council to pay the cost of two telegrams they sent during the Cuban crisis, one to Kennedy and one to Khrushchev, appealing for peace. A much more serious and controversial example occurred in 1972, when the majority of councillors in the Derbyshire town of Clay Cross refused to raise the rents of council-house tenants in accordance with the requirements of the Housing Finance Act. They were subsequently ordered to pay the difference between the two levels of rent themselves; refused to do so; were disqualified by a court from holding political office; refused to take notice of the court's decision; and remained in *de facto* control of the town until the Clay Cross Council was abolished completely a few months later.

Control over the way in which services are administered is backed by the readiness of the national government to reduce or cut its grant to an authority that ignores orders. As an example, one of the rules about local police forces is that appointments to the post of Chief Constable should be approved by the Home Office. In 1947 this post fell vacant in Salford and the City Council decided to promote its Deputy Chief Constable to the vacancy. The Home Office refused to approve the appointment because it was a matter of Home

Office policy that Chief Constables should always be appointed from some other police force. When Salford confirmed the appointment in spite of this its grant was immediately cut off and after a few weeks financial pressure forced it to give in.

Needless to say, things rarely come to this pass. Local authorities accept control by Whitehall as a condition of life and their conduct of local affairs is shaped by ministry regulations, by a constant stream of ministry circulars and by the reports of ministry inspectors. Their schools are inspected by the Department of Education; their housing plans are subject to the approval of the Department of the Environment; their police forces are inspected by the Home Office. In so far as there is variety and experiment in local government, it can be said to be by permission of Whitehall. Nevertheless, there is in practice a fair amount of variety. Government departments vary considerably in the extent to which they use their powers to foster national uniformity. The Department of Health, for instance, is said to have a *laissez-faire* attitude to local authorities, believing that, provided they meet the requirements of the law, they should be allowed to enjoy a good deal of freedom in the way they develop local health services (Griffith 1966: 515–18). An example is the department's attitude to the fluoridation of water supplies; the department has long believed this to be a desirable development and has sent a number of circulars to local authorities advising them to undertake it; but though some councils have not accepted this advice the department has taken no steps to make them do so. On the other hand, the Department of the Environment exercises a great deal of control over local authorities, and the Department of Education uses its powers to minimize differences in the standards of educational provision. To this end, the department controls the output of teachers from colleges of education, the number of teachers each authority may employ, teachers' salaries, investment in school buildings and the provision of ancillary services. It also has a large staff of inspectors who visit schools and advise local authorities on teaching methods.

Local authorities naturally differ in the use they make of their discretionary powers. Authorities vary in the services they provide for old people, for mentally defective people and for the deaf and the blind. Authorities also differ in their policies for the provision of council houses or flats to be let at subsidized rents. A great deal of argument takes place about the rate and method of building, the location and the rents of council housing. In many areas housing is the most controversial service provided by local government.

Another area in which there is scope for local initiative is in the provision of recreational and cultural facilities. Some authorities spend a lot on parks and recreation grounds; some run repertory theatres and subsidize symphony concerts; some have splendid art collections; some have libraries of gramophone records as well as books and a few have loan collections of lithographs and artists' prints. There is ample opportunity here for councillors who want to improve the amenities of their town. The short answer to questions about the character of central–local relations, therefore, is that local authorities have the appearance and to some extent the legal status of independent authorities; despite this the degree of practical independence they enjoy at any time depends almost entirely on the policies of central government departments; and at the time of writing, although their activities are much more tightly restricted than they were fifty years ago, they nevertheless retain a substantial degree of initiative in fields that can make a real difference to the lives of their citizens.

The control of local expenditure

Since 1979 the relations between central and local government have been given a new twist by the commitment of the Conservative governments to controlling and if possible reducing the overall level of public expenditure. From the beginning, the Thatcher government imposed tight restraint on capital expenditure by local authorities, and in particular imposed a sharp reduction on the number of new dwellings constructed for municipal tenants. As capital projects by local authorities have been subject to governmental permission throughout the postwar period, this policy of restraint did not require any new legislation.

By 1980, however, the government had become concerned about the level of local authority spending on current account, and the Local Government Act of that year authorized the Department of the Environment to penalize authorities by cutting their grant (which then comprised approximately 60 per cent of their revenue) if they exceeded spending limits set by the department. The sanction was severe, in that the reduction in the central grant was larger than the amount by which expenditure exceeded the target, compelling the local authority concerned to raise property taxes (commonly known as rates) disproportionately. This provision had the desired effect of checking local government expenditures in areas controlled by Conservative councils, but was less successful in areas controlled by Labour councils. Many of the latter, particularly in the larger cities and the metropolitan counties, followed a deliberate policy of exceeding the government's expenditure limits and raising taxes to cover the ensuing deficit. It was reported in the autumn of 1981 that over half the local authorities in England had exceeded the specified limits.

From the point of view of countering inflation, this did not matter, as the extra sums involved were both raised and spent locally. However, the government's macro-economic policies were designed not only to counter inflation but also to stimulate business enterprise by reducing the overall burden of taxation. In terms of this objective, sharp increases in local property taxes mattered a good deal. The proportion of property taxes paid by business firms has increased in the postwar period, rising from 43 per cent in 1938 to 61 per cent in 1975 (Dearlove 1979: 240–1). In 1980–1 the Confederation of British Industry responded to widespread rate increases in urban areas by launching a nationwide campaign to reduce the burden on business, applying pressure to both local authorities and the national government (for details see May 1984). In November 1981 the Secretary of State for the Environment delivered himself of the following comment in Parliament: 'The fact is that a £1 billion over-spend is not the marginal excess of legitimate freedom. It is the extravagant consequence of political licence. It is too large, too persistent and too flagrant' (quoted in Bulpitt 1983: 213).

The government then introduced new measures in the Local Government Finance Bill, one section of which contained the following provisions: (1) that the government would set a limit for the level of property taxes in each area; (2) that any authority wishing to raise taxes beyond this limit would have to hold a referendum on the question; and (3) that the extra taxes above the limit would fall mainly on householders rather than on business.

This attempt to activate the ordinary citizen in the struggle against institutional power was entirely in line with the liberal and populist attitudes of the Thatcher government, reflected later in its attempt to limit the power of trade union leaders by requiring them to be subject to regular election by members. However, the Local Government Finance Bill ran into trouble. It met with fierce opposition from the Association of County Councils and the Association of Metropolitan Authorities, two powerful interest groups that had been fully consulted on local government matters by previous national governments but largely ignored since 1979. They were supported by many Conservative back-benchers, who disliked the provision for referendums. Within a month it became clear that the Bill was unlikely to get through the House of Commons and the government withdrew it. A modified version of the legislation, omitting the provision for referendums, was then introduced, but this also ran into opposition from Conservative backbenchers and was reduced in scope before it was enacted.

By this time the whole issue of central–local relationships had become thoroughly politicized. In London, for instance, the Labour Chairman of the Greater London Council (GLC) made it clear that he regarded it as the task of the GLC to act as a centre of opposition to Conservative rule. One issue was the subsidy for public transport services paid by the GLC, which was raised to a level that the government thought unreasonable. The GLC was taken to court on this issue by one of the district councils in London, representing a part of the city that was served by British Rail rather than the London Underground, so that its residents gained relatively little from the reduced fares made possible by the subsidy. In a highly controversial judgment, it was ruled that the GLC's subsidies were extravagant to the point of being illegal. Amid a storm of argument, the GLC then found a legal loophole that allowed it to continue sizeable subsidies, albeit on a somewhat smaller scale than those that had been disallowed. Other urban authorities, including the six metropolitan counties, also gave large subsidies to public transport services out of the receipts of property taxes.

In 1983 the Conservative Party included a provision in its election manifesto declaring that, if returned to power, it would abolish the Greater London

Council and the six metropolitan county councils, a move seen by most commentators as overtly partisan. In 1984 the government extended the battle by taking powers to set legal limits to the budgets of local authorities with a record of overspending, it being provided that any councils refusing to comply with the limits would be in violation of the law.

This produced agonized debates in several of the councils affected, including the GLC. It so happened that several Labour members of the GLC were attempting to secure selection as parliamentary candidates at the time the dead-line for the budget was reached in April 1985. These councillors faced the predicament of wanting to vote against a legal budget for ideological reasons (a step which could be expected to find favour in the eyes of constituency selection committees), while also knowing that if a legal budget were not passed they would be liable to disqualification from holding any political office. After an all-night debate, a legal budget was finally agreed with minutes to spare.

In Liverpool, an even more militant council refused to endorse a legal budget at the required time, which posed a dilemma of political authority in a partic-ularly sharp way. A government can give orders and pass laws, but it needs the co-operation of other authorities and the compliance of citizens if these orders and laws are to be translated into effective administration. The Liverpool City Council, providing public services for over half a million people, is too important a body to be ignored or abolished. The government had the option of dismissing the councillors and appointing commissioners to run the city, but this would involve several disadvantages; it would alienate people attached to the principle of local democracy, would burden the government with the respon-sibility for direct administration of the city with the highest unemployment rate in the country, and would raise the difficult future question of when it would be safe (from the government's point of view) to hold fresh elections for the council. After much controversy, the Liverpool City Council overspent its legal budget and covered the gap by securing a loan from a consortium of Swiss banks.

In consequence of these developments, relations between the national government and many local authorities have acquired an adversarial and ideo-logical character that is completely new to Britain. This raises questions about the whole future of local government, which require some discussion of the merits and value of local democracy and self-government, as hitherto practised in Britain.

The merits of local self-government

If the issue is considered in terms of democratic principles, it can be said that the idea of local democracy implies three things. First, it implies that elected representatives should have effective control of decision-making in local govern-ment. Secondly, it implies that these representatives should be fully accountable to the electorate and responsive to public opinion, through competitive elections and a fairly high level of communication between councillors on one hand and electors and pressure groups on the other. Thirdly, it implies what J. S. Mill called civic education, meaning widespread knowledge of local government activities and a reasonably high degree of popular participation in community affairs.

The first of these conditions has clearly been achieved in Britain. Control of policy rests with the council, in which the members are elected for three-year terms of office. Councils operate through a set of specialized committees such as the Education Committee, the Housing Committee and the Parks Committee, each of which keeps a continuing watch on its branch of local administration and reports to council each month. The chief officers of the authority act as secretaries of the respective committees and can expect to have a good deal of influence on what is decided, but they are not entitled to vote. The council as a whole is limited in its freedom of choice by the requirements of the central government, but within these limits the power to make decisions rests clearly in the hands of the elected representatives.

There is much more doubt about the second condition. In rural areas there is little competition to serve on local councils and most elections are uncontested. A rough check indicated that in the mid-1970s about 40 per cent of all local councillors in England and Wales had been returned unopposed at their last election. When the author lived in the East Riding of Yorkshire he went for years without a chance to vote in county elections. When there was a contested election he did not actually use his vote, as minimal campaigning and the poverty of the local press left him without any useful information about the candidates, all of whom were standing as independents.

In urban areas elections are usually contested and fought on party lines. However, in most cities voting in local elections is determined on the basis of national party loyalties and the swing of votes between one election and the next is determined by the relative popularity of the national parties. There are exceptions, but as a normal rule local issues play very little part in local elections. The turn-out in local elections is much lower than in national elections, averaging about 40 per cent instead of about 75 per cent. In view of all these circumstances, it cannot be said that local accountability is very effective in Britain. Jones and Stewart make much of it in their defence of local self-government (Jones and Stewart 1983), and it is certainly true that (when elections are contested) electors have the opportunity to return a verdict on the performance of their councillors if they wish to do so. But the argument is weakened by the fact that in practice electors rarely behave in this way.

The third argument for local democracy is that it contributes to civic education. The evidence about this is mixed. Local government provides an opportunity for people to participate in the political system, either by standing for election or by working for pressure groups that operate at the local level. Pressure groups of this kind have become increasingly influential in the last two decades, though they are not yet as active as their American equivalents.

There are certainly opportunities for the civic education of the active minority.

General public knowledge about local government is limited. It has been hindered in the past by the secrecy in which many local authorities have wrapped their activities and it is still hindered by the nature of the mass media. As noted in Chapter 1, local newspapers are less important in Britain than in most other countries because almost everyone reads one of the national papers. Local papers are read partly for their advertisements and partly as evening papers, in which case they tend to give prominence to national news because what people want is a follow-up to the news items they have read in the morning. Relatively few local papers try to make a story out of the activities of their local council. Television programmes are to some extent regionalized, but they rarely focus on municipal news.

In this situation local government cannot be said to contribute much to the civic education of the masses. Most people show less knowledge of, and less interest in, local issues than national issues. Local politics simply do not have the vitality that they have in the United States, where elections are more keenly contested, electors are often given the opportunity to vote in referendums on local issues, and the press and other mass media feature local news. For all these reasons, only limited importance can be attached to arguments about local democracy in Britain.

It does not follow, however, that the country would be equally well governed if the functions of local authorities were henceforth taken over by civil servants. 'Democracy' and 'self-government' are not synonymous terms, as the recent history of Africa makes clear. Several other arguments can be put forward in support of the rather muddled British system of local self-government.

First, it would seem to be undesirable if political power throughout Britain were completely monopolized by the party that enjoys a temporary majority in the House of Commons. In a period of Conservative rule at Westminster, it must be a good thing that there are some positions of authority controlled by the Labour Party and some opportunity for Labour politicians to translate their ideas into practice. From the point of view of the citizen, it must be desirable that Labour supporters in industrial cities should be able to feel that the city council is on their side, even though the national government is controlled by their political opponents. The same argument would apply to Conservative supporters in the southern counties during periods of Labour government at the national level.

Secondly, local self-government provides opportunities for diversity and experimentation. There are significant differences between school systems in different counties, even though these are limited by the activities of government inspectors and the fact that all children have to be prepared for national examinations. There are differences in the administration of libraries, the collection of rubbish, the planning of housing estates and many other matters. Local authorities learn from one another, and this is a real benefit even though it is impossible to quantify.

Thirdly, there is a considerable advantage in what, for want of a better name, can just be called 'localism'. Communities vary in their needs and their atmosphere, and it must be desirable for personal services at the local level to be controlled by people who are familiar with the area and can tailor the delivery of services to fit local circumstances.

For these reasons, a strong case can be made for the continuance of local self-government. If it is to continue, it seems evident that local authorities should have enough autonomy to make the work of local councillors sufficiently satisfying for talented people to be attracted to this kind of unpaid public service. Moreover, local authorities need more stability of expectations than they have been granted in recent years. If they prepare a budget that conforms to governmental guidelines, they have a right to expect that the rules of the game will not be changed during the course of the financial year, which has happened on several occasions since 1979.

Since 1989, it has seemed that the local government system might indeed be moving towards greater stability, but under a new set of rules framed by the central government. On the one hand, the Local Government and Housing Act of 1989 imposes new rules about the internal workings of local authorities. There are rules about the partisan make-up of local government committees, designed to ensure a fair balance between the parties represented on the whole council. There is a ban on the practice that some local authorities have adopted of giving voting rights to co-opted members of committees. There is a ban on people employed in a range of executive or professional positions in local government seeking election as local councillors, to terminate what the government regards as an abuse that has become more common in recent years.

On the other hand, the government has insisted that local authorities become more open and competitive in the provision of services. Council tenants have not only been given the option of buying council houses but, if they live in blocks of flats, of deciding by majority vote to switch from the municipal landlord to a private landlord if one approved by the central government comes forward with a suitable offer. Council schools have been given the chance to opt out of local government control if a majority of parents wish their school to become independent, with direct grants from the central government. Local authorities are being required to engage in competitive tendering for the provision of certain local services, including school meals, street cleaning and refuse collection. In these ways local authorities are being transformed, whether they like it or not, from being monopolistic providers of public services in their area to being 'enabling authorities' (N. Ridley 1988), with an overall responsibility for ensuring that the services are provided, by themselves or by others, in ways that are cost-efficient and popular with the consumers.

Critics of the Thatcher government's approach have alleged that the new rules add up to a serious reduction in local autonomy, while supporters have claimed that the changes have liberalized and opened up the local government system. Both arguments are largely valid, which probably explains why the

1997 Labour manifesto was somewhat ambivalent in its proposals for reform. It stated that 'although crude and universal council tax capping should go, we will retain reserve powers to control excessive council tax rises'. Although 'local decision-making should be less constrained by central government', the central government will in fact be given a powerful new tool of control, because 'The Audit Commission will be given additional powers to monitor performance and promote efficiency. On its advice, government will where necessary send in a management team with full powers to remedy failure.' It is said that 'councils should not be forced to put their services out to tender', but it is also said that they 'will be required to obtain best value' and 'we see no reason why a service should be delivered directly if other more efficient means are available'. Municipal elections will be held more frequently and the government will experiment with directly elected mayors in some cities, but there is no mention of what powers these mayors might be given.

The overall impression left by the manifesto is that the new government will introduce reforms with considerable caution, and that they are unlikely to give local authorities anything like the degree of independence that they enjoyed before 1979.

Further reading

An account of the structure of local government is given in Alexander (1982) *Local Government in Britain since Reorganization*; a discussion of local government at work will be found in Elcock (1982) *Local Government*; the case for local democracy is argued in Jones and Stewart (1983) *The Case for Local Government*; the case for the Thatcher government's approach is argued in N. Ridley (1988) *The Local Right: Enabling not Providing*, and a discussion of postwar changes will be found in Young and Rao (1997) *Local Government since 1945*.

15

THE EUROPEAN COMMUNITY
AND UNION

The development of the Community

The European Community grew out of the European Economic Community, which was put together between 1955 and 1957 and came into operation in January 1958. The original members were France, Italy, West Germany, Belgium, Holland and Luxembourg. The motives for the move were three in number.

The first motive was to establish an organization within which Germany could be brought back into the community of nations and bound to its fellow members in such a way as to eliminate any chance that a revived German nation might again be a threat to European peace. France, which had been invaded by Germany three times in eighty years, was particularly affected by this motive.

The second motive was to promote economic growth by establishing a large common market, with freedom of movement for goods, services and labour within its borders. The third motive was to encourage the modernization of farming methods within the six nations without driving small family farms into bankruptcy, and by so doing to make western Europe largely self-sufficient in the production of food, with the exception of foodstuffs that could be produced only in the tropics.

Some of the politicians involved in the formation of the Community looked forward to the creation of a United States of Europe, based on a federal constitution. The majority thought this unrealistic, however, and opted instead for the establishment of a framework within which the development of functional co-operation would establish the habit of working together, break down suspicions and antagonisms between the nations, and build a new sense of European identity among the general public.

The United Kingdom was invited to join the Community, but opted out of the negotiations at an early stage. One reason for this was scepticism about the probable success of the venture. Another reason was that Britain had world-wide trading and diplomatic interests which it felt would be undermined if it threw in its lot with the other six European nations. In the 1950s most British trade was with the Commonwealth and America, not with Europe, and Britain enjoyed cheap food as a consequence of long-term trading agreements with Commonwealth countries. It also valued the special diplomatic relationship that was thought to exist with the United States. As the only European state that had enjoyed a victorious war without being invaded, and as the richest European state apart from neutral Switzerland and Sweden, Britain felt no need to jeopardize its existing international relationships by joining a European union with an unknown future. This was a short-sighted view from which the country has suffered ever since, but it was not controversial at the time.

The British attitude changed quite quickly after the Community came into being. By 1960 both France and West Germany had caught up with Britain in their standards of living, it had become clear that the Common Market (as it was then usually called) was economically beneficial to its members, and the British had become aware that their annual rate of economic growth was lagging behind that of their European competitors. It also became clear that the pattern of world trade was changing to Britain's disadvantage. Britain's export trade was heavily dependant on shipping basic manufactured goods like cotton textiles and automobiles to Third World countries, but this market was shrinking as the importing countries developed their own industries and as Japanese products became available at prices that the British exporters could not match. It looked as if the future lay with higher quality exports to European markets. In 1961 the British Conservative government applied to join the Community.

This application was vetoed by France, on the stated ground that Britain was more mid-Atlantic than European in its outlook. An unstated reason was the French fear that Britain might be an effective rival to the position of dominance that France then enjoyed within the Community. The Labour Party opposed British entry in 1961, but changed its mind when it came into power and launched a second application in 1967. This was also vetoed by France, to the regret of the other members, but was followed by a third application in 1969. In 1971 the new Conservative administration, led by a committed European in the person of Edward Heath, renewed the application, and this time it was accepted. Britain became a full member in January 1973. Denmark and Ireland joined at the same time, their dependence on exports to Britain making this move essential for them.

This renewed application was controversial within Britain, as Labour had changed its mind once again and now opposed entry. Both parties were divided, however. In the crucial vote on entry in the House of Commons, thirty-nine Conservative MPs defied their party whips to vote against entry, a move that would have prevented British membership had not sixty-nine Labour MPs defied their whips to vote in favour of entry. The terms of entry that Britain secured were not very favourable, as it was in a weak bargaining position and was quite unable to secure changes in Community policies that it disliked, such as the agricultural policy. The timing also proved to be unfortunate, as the British plan for an export drive to Europe was halted in the autumn of 1973 by the crisis caused by the fourfold increase in the price of oil imposed by a coalition of Arab states. An Italian commentator said that Britain joined the Community 'too late, too expensively, at the wrong moment ... reluctantly and somewhat squeamishly' (Barzini 1983: 60).

Since British entry the Community had been enlarged again, with the admission of Greece in 1981, Spain and Portugal in 1986, and Sweden, Finland and Austria in 1995. It now contains a population of just over 370 million people.

Community institutions

The European Community is a unique organization, entirely without precedent. On the one hand, it is not a state, not even a loose kind of federation. A state has authority to exercise direct control over the behaviour of its citizens, to tax their incomes, to conscript them for military service, and on occasion to put them in prison. The Community does not have any of these powers. On the other hand, it is a far stronger body than the United Nations, which relies on the voluntary co-operation of its members and cannot even compel them to pay their annual subscriptions, let alone give orders to them.

The most influential permanent organization of the Community is the European Commission, a body of about 13,000 civil servants directed by the seventeen Commissioners, who are appointed by the member states with two coming from each of the five large states and one from each of the seven smaller states. The Commissioners serve for renewable terms of four years and they each have a portfolio, being responsible for agricultural policy, regional policy, competition and so forth. They are expected to serve the interests of the Community as a whole rather than the interests of their own countries, and their behaviour corresponds partially, but not entirely, to this expectation. British governments have always appointed one Commissioner from each of the two main parties. One of the Commissioners serves as President of the Commission, being appointed for two-year terms by the Council of Ministers. The normal pattern has been for each President to serve for four years, although Walter Hallstein's reappointment after two years was vetoed by the French government while Jacques Delors' appointment was extended for a fourth term in 1992.

The tasks of the Commission are to draft regulations, directives, decisions and recommendations; to prepare the Community budget; to implement and administer those aspects of Community policy that are managed collectively rather than by the member states; and to act as a broker between national governments in working out the compromises on which Community policy depends. If a member state fails to comply with a regulation, directive or decision, the Commission can take the issue to the European Court of Justice for resolution.

The body responsible for drawing up treaties, framing Community policies and approving Community legislation is the Council of Ministers, consisting of one minister from each member state. When this meets in general session the twelve foreign ministers attend. At other meetings, known as technical meetings, the Council considers specific topics, such as agricultural policy or industrial policy. On these occasions the member states are represented by the ministers responsible for that area of policy. The Council of Ministers used to require unanimous agreement for major policy decisions, but since the passage of the Single European Act in 1986 (which came into force in 1987) agreement can be reached by a qualified majority. The present position is that Britain, France, Germany and Italy have ten votes each, Spain has eight, Belgium, Holland, Greece and Portugal have five each, Austria and Sweden have four each, Denmark, Ireland and Finland have three each, and Luxembourg has two. There are therefore eighty-seven votes to be counted, and, while there are three different ways of defining the needed majority, according to the nature of the issue, the highest of the three hurdles requires the support of sixty-two votes for a measure to be approved. Unanimity is still required for some issues, such as taxation, major changes of policy or the admission of a new member state. In addition a state can also veto any other proposal that is deemed to be contrary to a vital national interest, but this is not a power that can be used unless the other members of the Council are willing to accept it as reasonable.

The Presidency of the Council of Ministers rotates between its members in turn, with each President holding office for six months.

The work of the Council is supported by a body known as the Committee of Permanent Representatives (Coreper) which is composed of the permanent ambassadors of each member state to the European Commission. This in turn has specialized committees working with it, so that a considerable bureaucracy is involved. And while the Council meets once every few weeks, the Coreper meets two or three times every week.

While the Council is the top body within the European Community, it should not be regarded as equivalent to a cabinet in a national system of government. Cabinets are collegial bodies of like-minded ministers, who take collective responsibility for their decisions. The Council, in contrast, is a forum in which national representatives meet to protect their varying national interests and to reach compromises whenever this proves possible. Each minister on the Council is answerable to his or her own national government and parliament, not to the European Parliament.

Proposals coming to the Council are passed to the British Parliament for scrutiny and each House has a specialized committee responsible for this. In practice, the House of Lords committee has more time and takes more trouble over the scrutiny than the House of Commons committee. Parliamentary questions on the proposals may be put to the relevant minister, and British ministers will not agree to a proposal on Council before the British Parliament has had time to scrutinize it. The British representative is not bound to act on parliamentary instructions, however, as it is understood that he or she has to have a fairly free hand in the bargaining that takes place at Council meetings.

The European Parliament is a large body of 626 members, who are directly elected in the various member states. It has a semi-circular chamber, in the general continental pattern, where the members (the MEPs) sit in ideological groups, not in national groups. Forming these ideological groupings has not proved easy, except for the social democrats, and there are now nine groups in operation. Britain has eighty-seven MEPs. The Labour Party representatives sit in a group with social democrats from other countries but the Conservatives sit almost alone, as the right-of-centre MEPs have never been able to agree on an international grouping and are actually divided between four groups.

The powers of the European Parliament are limited. Unlike national parliaments, it is not a legislative chamber. It has power to approve or reject the Community budget in its entirety, but no power to make detailed changes except over the so-called 'non-compulsory' sections of the budget, which account for only a small proportion of total expenditure. It can dismiss the seventeen Commissioners as a block, provided it has a two-thirds majority for this course, but it cannot dismiss any individual Commissioner. It does, however, scrutinize and comment on the work of the Commission, having a number of specialized committees for this purpose.

It would seem from this list of powers that the Parliament is little more than a talking shop, but in recent years it has had some limited success in extending its influence. It has frequently made proposals to the Commission for modifications or extensions of policy, and Juliet Lodge has estimated that about a fifth of these proposals have led to some kind of executive action, though not necessarily the precise action recommended (see Lodge 1989: 66). It has secured the right to consider legislative proposals before they are debated in the Council of Ministers, and the Single European Act provides that some categories of legislation, if rejected or amended by an absolute majority of MEPs, can be enacted only if subsequently passed by a unanimous vote in the Council of Ministers. In the first five years of this rule, all but one of the pieces of legislation rejected by the Parliament were reinstated by a unanimous vote on the Council, the exception being a regulation about occupational health, over which a compromise was reached. The Parliament has a low reputation among the British public, partly because its proceedings are rarely reported by the mass media, but it has become a more influential body than is commonly assumed, and its influence is growing.

There is also the European Court of Justice, with one judge from each member state, which has the task of ensuring that Community laws and directives are obeyed. This is a somewhat unpopular body in Britain, because its occasional judgments against British practices are resented, but this reflects nationalistic attitudes rather than informed criticism. The record shows that between 1973 and 1997 the British government was prosecuted only 39 times, as against 305 prosecutions launched against Italy, 182 against Belgium, 141 against France, 133 against Greece (which joined only in 1987) and 95 against Germany. British civil servants are more punctilious than others in enforcing the rules, so Britain has a better record than any member except Denmark.

Yet another major institution is the European Council, a conference of the heads of government in the member states, which meets twice a year to discuss general questions of policy and to formulate plans for the future development of the Community.

This brief sketch of the main institutions of the European Community indicates that it is essentially a bureaucratic rather than a democratic organization. It suffers from what is commonly described as a 'democratic deficit'. The engine of the organization is the Commission, which is an impersonal bureaucratic machine. The European Parliament is democratically elected, but it cannot control the Commission. Elections to the Parliament generally reflect public support for the domestic parties which sponsor candidates, rather than hinging on the work of the Parliament itself or the activities of other Community institutions. The Council of Ministers has wider powers than the Commission and it provides an indirect form of democratic control in that its members are answerable to their national parliaments. However, Council meetings are held behind closed doors, and it is not thought appropriate for national parliaments to question their representatives about what happens at Council meetings.

This said, it should be added that the democratic deficit worries the British more than the people of most other states. The reason for this is that the British parliamentary system produces majority governments pursuing policies that have been, for the most part, put to the electors at the preceding general election, so that the government of the day can claim a popular mandate for them. In any case, the governing party cannot escape responsibility for the policies when it next goes to the polls. Most other member states have multi-party systems and coalition governments, so that formulating policy is a matter of compromise behind the closed doors of the Cabinet and the line of responsibility for the policies adopted is not nearly so clear as it is in Britain. The people in states with this kind of system are more willing than the British people are to accept a process of constant compromise as a substitute for mandates and direct responsibility, and the Community certainly provides for constant compromise.

Community policies

The main policies of the Community can be summarized under five headings. The first objective was to establish a free trade area with a common external tariff. This was achieved in the 1960s, and it was also quickly accepted that the Community should negotiate as one when dealing with other countries about matters of international trade. In the recent GATT round of negotiations, lasting from 1987 to 1992, the Community appointed one of its Commissioners to deal with the Americans and the rest of the world. As a corollary of this, the Community has attempted to eliminate non-tariff barriers to trade between member states. When Germany tried to ban imported beer on the ground that it did not meet German standards of purity, the European Court of Justice stopped this as an unreasonable interference with trade. The Court took a similar decision when Italy tried to ban imported pasta on the ground that it did not meet Italian standards.

A second objective is known as harmonization, the aim being to provide a level playing field for trade in goods and services. Under this heading the Commission has proposed various measures that have caused annoyance in Britain. The first, suggested a few months after Britain joined, was the proposal that British brewers should be made to stop producing traditional British beer and switch to continental-style lager. Another was the proposal that British ice cream should no longer be called ice cream, on the ground that it often contained non-milk fats. A third was the proposal that British chocolate should no longer be called chocolate, on the ground that it was made in a slightly different way from continental chocolate. These proposals were all vetoed or circumvented, but not without leaving the British public with the feeling that the Commission was a petty and interfering body.

Under the heading of harmonization, progress has also been made towards the acceptance throughout the Community of professional qualifications granted by any member state. These include qualifications for university entrance, and there has recently been an increase in the mobility of students between European universities.

A third objective has been the modernization of agriculture, by means of the Common Agricultural Policy (CAP). The essence of this policy, largely drafted by the French to help their sizeable and then inefficient farming industry, was the establishment of guaranteed prices for agricultural products at a level substantially higher than the world price for such products. If farmers fail to sell all their produce at or above the guaranteed price, the surplus is bought by the Community. At the same time, sizeable levies are imposed on agricultural produce coming from outside the Community, so that it does not undercut Community produce.

This policy has been entirely successful in meeting its objectives, but at a heavy cost. It has always absorbed well over half of the Community's budget. Farming methods have been greatly improved, marginal land has been culti-vated, and the Community now produces more food and wine than its citizens can consume. The surplus has been stored in great barns and tanks, and become known as the butter mountain, wine lake and so forth. It is then dumped on overseas markets at very low prices, thus eating into the traditional markets for American, Canadian and Australian agricultural exports, to the consider-able annoyance of those countries.

A fourth objective has been the regulation of fishing within the 200 mile limit round the coasts of the member states. Maximum catches have been agreed upon for each type of fish and national quotas for the various fishing fleets have been imposed. The waters are policed by vessels owned and oper-ated by member states, but sponsored and paid for by the Community. Negotiations over fishing rights in other waters, such as the Grand Banks off Newfoundland, are conducted by a single delegation representing the Community as a whole.

A fifth objective, developed later than the others, has been to help depressed regions out of a Regional Fund and to provide aid in meeting specific social problems out of a Social Fund. In recent years the Regional Fund has provided a good deal of help to the poorer regions of the United Kingdom. In the years 1979–87 British regions received £2.8 billion (see Lodge 1989: 179), 73 per cent of which went towards infrastructure, and the annual payments are tending to increase. The Social Fund has been used mainly to subsidize arrangements for vocational training and retraining.

Community finance

It should be noted that the total Community budget, though often criticized as extravagant, is relatively small compared with national budgets. In 1992 total Community expenditures amounted to only 1.2 per cent of the gross national product of the member states, while these states were spending over 40 per cent of their national income on the multifarious activities of their own national and local governments. In December 1992 it was agreed by the European Council that a sizeable fund should be created to help the 'poor four', namely Ireland, Greece, Spain and Portugal, but even with this the total budget will grow only slowly, to 1.27 per cent of gross national product by 1999.

The Community has four sources of income, which are collected as of right and are not dependent, as contributions to the United Nations and its agencies are, on the goodwill of the member states. First, it imposes and collects customs duties on goods imported into the fifteen member states. Secondly, it imposes and collects agricultural levies on imported agricultural produce, such as New Zealand lamb or Australian fruit. Thirdly, it takes a fixed proportion of the value added tax that each member state is required to levy. This is not a fixed proportion of the total VAT collected in the state, but an amount equal to a VAT rate of 1.4 per cent. Fourthly, in 1988 the Community prepared to meet a threatened budgetary shortfall by introducing an annual levy on national governments which would cover the difference between total revenue from the first three sources and total projected expenditure, the levy being divided between member states in strict proportion to the size of their gross national products. In 1989 this levy amounted to 8.7 per cent of total Community revenue.

It should be added that there has been only one case of a member state holding back its contributions to the budget, that being in April 1983 when Britain held back the money collected in Britain but due to the Community. The European Court of Justice promptly declared that Britain would have to pay interest on the overdue amount, and Britain quickly paid up.

On the expenditure side, the bulk of the Community's budget has always gone to agriculture. The CAP has been extraordinarily expensive, taking over three-quarters of the budget in the early years. The proportion has since fallen a little, mainly because of the development of the Regional and Social Funds, but is still large. In 1988 the CAP took 68.7 per cent of total expenditure, compared with 7.7 per cent for the Regional Fund, 6.8 per cent for the Social Fund, and 16.8 per cent for administration and miscellaneous expenditures (Shackleton 1989: 136).

From statistics published by the Commission up to 1988, it has been possible to calculate the difference between each state's contributions to the budget and its receipts from Community expenditure. These showed that from 1958 to 1972 Germany made a loss while the other five members made a profit, while from the date of Britain's accession in 1973 to 1988 Germany and Britain made a loss while all the others normally made a profit.

The Germans did not object to this state of affairs, partly because they were grateful to their partners for welcoming them back into the community of nations so quickly after they had ended the war in defeat and disgrace, partly because the Community has opened a wide market for German industrial exports, and partly because Germany was in any case the richest nation in the Community from 1961 onwards.

The British did object, however, because they were one of the poorer member states, and when Margaret Thatcher became Prime Minister in 1979 she started a vigorous campaign to secure a reduction in Britain's contribution to the budget. This campaign caused a certain amount of bad feeling in the Community, but in 1984 it was rewarded by success. It was agreed that Britain's VAT rate payable to the Community 'should be decreased by an amount corresponding to two-thirds of the difference between its percentage share of Community VAT resources and its percentage share of total allocated expenditure' (Shackleton 1989: 131). In practice, this cut the revenue from VAT that had to be handed over by almost exactly half. This arrangement is known as the British rebate, and it cannot be changed or abolished without Britain's agreement.

Since 1988 the profit and loss account for member states has been a little more difficult to calculate, but not impossible. The figures show that the financial balance has changed greatly in the 1990s. As more weight has been put on relative prosperity, and as much more money has been devoted to the poor four, more states have joined Germany and Britain as net contributors instead of beneficiaries. The 1995 statistics and 1996 estimates showed that Germany was still contributing most, more than twice as much as Britain in per capita terms, with substantial contributions also coming from France, Italy, Holland and the three newest members, Sweden, Austria and Finland. Only the poor four and Denmark (wealthy but highly agricultural) were substantial beneficiaries, with the figures for Belgium and Luxembourg being rather uncertain but adding up to contributions (*The Economist*, 23 November 1996).

Another change has been that Germany has ceased to be the wealthiest country in the Community since reunification in 1990 added the poor provinces of East Germany to the wealthy ones of West Germany. By 1997 it was no more than fourth in income per capita, and by some calculations only sixth. In these circumstances it is natural for the German government to have become dissatisfied with the existing financial rules, and at the general review that is planned for 1999 it is certain to press for a thorough revision of them. As all states will have differing interests to protect in this review, it is bound to be a complex bargaining session and its outcome is impossible to predict at the time of writing.

The impact of membership on Britain

In constitutional terms, the immediate consequence of Britain's entry into the Community was to deprive the British Parliament and British laws of the supremacy they had previously possessed. Under the terms of the European Communities Act, passed by Parliament in 1972 as a necessary condition of joining the Community, European regulations and directives take precedence over British laws, and should be enforced by British courts. Technically, Parliament could at any time repeal this Act, so it can be said that it has not surrendered its legal sovereignty, but this would mean withdrawal from the Community and so long as this step is not taken Community law has an overriding validity. In practice, this does not mean that any substantial proportion of British law has been invalidated, because Community laws deal mainly with economic matters that were not previously regulated by law in Britain.

The impact of membership on the administrative system has been considerable. It means that the Foreign and Commonwealth Office has lost the near-monopoly of diplomatic activity that it previously enjoyed. Many British departments of state are in constant touch with sections of the European Commission, and officials from these departments frequently visit Brussels to participate in committee meetings. Numerous British citizens work as Commission officials, some of them being British civil servants on leave while others were recruited directly to Brussels. The more important British interest groups, such as the National Farmers' Union, now lobby the Commission and have an office in Brussels as well as one in London. Relations between London and Brussels are no longer regarded as an aspect of foreign affairs, on a par with relations between London and Washington, but have become part of the machinery of British government.

The economic impact of membership has been considerable. In 1997 57 per cent of British exports went to other member states, compared with only about 30 per cent of exports going to those states in 1972. The British pattern of imports has been similarly affected. The British buy European beet sugar instead of West Indian cane sugar, French butter instead of New Zealand butter, European fruit instead of Australian and South African fruit. The number of French and German cars on British roads far exceeds the number of Japanese cars. The overall impact of membership on the standard of living is impossible to measure, but the business community and most economists strongly support

Table 15.1 Percentage of the British population thinking the European Community is a 'good thing'

Year	%
1973	31
1977	35
1981	26
1985	38
1989	50

Source: Franklin 1990: 14.

continued membership. In the highly unlikely event of British withdrawal, it would be difficult to replace lost European markets for British exports by expanded markets in other continents.

The impact of membership on British public opinion has been variable. The immediate and noticeable impact of membership was an appreciable increase in food prices. The VAT, which Britain had to impose by Community law, has never been a popular tax. As already noted, some Commission proposals about British food, made in the interests of harmonization, have been resented. British people in the hotel and catering trades have not been pleased by the Commission's insistence that prominent notices should be displayed in British seaside resorts to warn visitors about the polluted state of the beaches. Among the general public, scepticism about the European Community has always been more common than enthusiasm for it.

Opinion polls show that active support for British membership has been largely confined to the business and political élite, though there has been no active campaign against it since 1975. The figures in Table 15.1 indicate a very gradual move towards acceptance by mass opinion that membership may be advantageous, but support has declined again in the 1990s.

Maastricht and Monetary Union

The Maastricht Treaty, which was signed in 1991 and came into force in 1992, has been briefly outlined in Chapter 5. As noted there, it is a long, complex and badly drafted treaty. Since 1992 it has created difficulties for the governments of several states and has led to a series of problematic questions. These difficulties and questions will now be summarized, beginning with the move towards Economic or Monetary Union (EMU) and continuing with the problems of securing unity in the fields of foreign affairs, defence and various aspects of what are now domestic affairs.

The move towards EMU had begun with the adoption in 1979 of the Exchange Rate Mechanism, whereby the exchange rates of member states would, so far as possible, be kept within a narrow band. Greece and Portugal never joined this arrangement and Britain kept aloof from it until 1990. In 1992 this mechanism came under great pressure and failed to work in the way that had been intended. An adjustment of German interest rates caused pressure on the weaker currencies within the Community; intervention by the German central bank managed to keep the value of the French franc within the agreed limits; but Spain had to devalue the peseta and Italy and Britain were forced to with-draw from the mechanism altogether.

The adoption of the Single European Act in 1986 provided for the removal of various non-tariff barriers to free trade so as to establish a completely inte-grated common market, and these changes were generally adopted by 1993. Then the Maastricht Treaty of 1991 included the Social Chapter (from which Britain opted out) that pushes member states to adopt standardized rules about labour relations, maximum hours of work and similar matters. The most problematic aspect of the whole move towards EMU, however, is the commit-ment in the treaty for the establishment of a single European currency and central bank by January 1999, provided that member states satisfy certain conditions.

The conditions are very stringent. The first of them is that the national rate of inflation should be no more than 1.5 per cent above the average of the three lowest rates within the Community. Secondly, long-term interest rates should be within two percentage points of the average of the three members with the lowest rates. Thirdly, the national budgetary deficit should be less than 3 per cent of gross domestic product (GDP). Fourthly, the national debt should not exceed 60 per cent of GDP. Fifthly, the national currency should not have been devalued during the previous two years and must have remained within the fluctuation margins of the Exchange Rate Mechanism. The strin-gency of these conditions is made evident by the fact that, at the time they were written into the treaty, Greece and Portugal satisfied none of the five, Italy and Spain satisfied only one, and Holland satisfied only two (see *The Economist*, 14 December 1991). The makers of the Maastricht Treaty, essen-tially Germany, France, and the three Benelux countries and the European Commission, were banking on a rapid convergence of European economies, fiscal policies and financial indicators during the following years.

In the event, such convergence as there was took most of the member states away from the criteria rather than towards them. Unemployment rose, welfare costs and budgetary deficits rose with it, and by 1995 both Germany and France were failing the tests they had set themselves. By January 1996 the minuscule state of Luxembourg was the only one of the fifteen that satisfied the criteria for a single European currency established by the Maastricht Treaty. An inter-national survey showed that America, Canada and Japan could not have met the tests either, and that Singapore was actually the only advanced industrial society that could (see London *Sunday Times*, 14 January 1996). It was clear that either the criteria must be greatly relaxed or the whole enterprise must be postponed or abandoned.

This dilemma posed particular problems for France and Germany, that were both determined not to abandon the project. The French government launched a policy of cutting social services to reduce its annual budgetary deficit, which led to widespread protests and demonstrations and to the defeat of the ruling right-wing coalition in the parliamentary election held at the end of May 1997. The German government, which had secured agreement that the new European central bank would be housed in Frankfurt and which clearly hoped to dominate Europe in economic and fiscal matters, found itself facing internal divisions and challenges. Repeated public opinion polls from 1995 to 1997 revealed that between 60 and 70 per cent of German electors were opposed to a single European currency, because they preferred to keep their strong D-mark and did not want their country to be forced to support the less stable economies of other member states. The powerful Bundesbank, which is not controlled by the German government, shared these concerns and insisted that there must be absolutely no weakening of the criteria that had been set. The German Finance Minister, Theo Waigel, went further than this, declaring in September 1995 that there should be a supplementary agreement reducing the maximum permitted budgetary deficit from 3 per cent of GDP set by Maastricht to only 1 per cent. He subsequently advocated a system of central control whereby countries that participated in the single currency would be automatically fined very large sums by the European Commission if they subsequently exceeded the set limits for deficits, and this system was embodied in the Stability Pact that was accepted by all heads of government in their Amsterdam conference of June 1997.

The clear implication of this stand by Waigel and the Bundesbank was that the launching of the single currency should be postponed until the member states tightened their budgets, reduced their rate of inflation, and (in most cases) actually managed a budgetary surplus to reduce their national debts. However, the whole idea of a postponement has been fiercely opposed by Helmut Kohl, the German Chancellor, on the ground that unless the target date is met the whole drive towards European integration will be weakened. In this stand Kohl is affected by his fear that the extreme right in his country might revive an aggressive form of German nationalism, which could again threaten the peace of Europe. In this he has been vigorously supported by his predecessor as Chancellor, Helmut Schmidt, who said in 1997 that postponement might lead to disillusionment with the whole concept of European unity, raising the dire possibility that Germany might once again find itself isolated in a hostile continent. This kind of fear had influenced Mitterand and also Edward Heath, who stated in 1997 that his determination to lead Britain into the Community in 1973 had arisen largely from his horrific experiences as an army officer in the Second World War. These attitudes are understandable, but are not generally shared by a younger generation of politicians and voters who were born after 1945.

At the time of writing it is impossible to predict what will happen. By June 1997 it seemed that by creative accounting, by some relaxation of the Maastricht criteria, and by turning a blind eye to Belgium's national debt, it might be possible for the Community to deem that twelve of the fifteen states were qualified to join, the exceptions being Greece, Italy and Spain. This would be paradoxical in that the governments and people of Greece, Italy and Spain are all strongly in favour of joining, while Britain, Denmark and Sweden are very unlikely to do so, at least by 1999. If Kohl is re-elected to office in the German general election scheduled for 1998, which is not certain, it may be that the single currency will be launched on time with seven or eight participants.

For Britain, there are arguments both for joining and for staying out. Joining would facilitate across-border business, as variable exchange rates enhance the risk involved in signing long-term contracts with fixed prices. The largest British manufacturing firms will undoubtedly press the government to join. Another strong argument in favour is that foreign firms that have opened or taken over plants in Britain, to take advantage of relatively low labour costs combined with an abundance of skilled workers, might move to the continent if Britain stayed out while most other states in the community joined. Japanese firms have larger investments in Britain than in the other fourteen states put together. Nissan and Toyota, in particular, have very large plants in Britain that might be at risk, as Toyota's proposed third plant there would certainly be. The same argument applies to German investments in Britain, notably by Bosch, BMW and Siemens. The future size of the British aircraft manufacturing industry might also be jeopardized. Germany might pull out from the commitment to buy and partly manufacture the proposed Eurofighter, in which British Aerospace has a 40 per cent stake.

The main contrary argument, in economic terms, is that if Britain were to join it would lose control of both interest rates and the value of its currency. Every economy experiences fluctuations, and the ability to vary the basic rate of interest is the best immediate way of dampening down inflation during times of boom or stimulating the economy in times of recession or impending recession. If the rate in Britain were to be controlled by the European central bank in Frankfurt the rate would be determined not by British interest and needs but by some estimate of overall European interests and needs. Further, a deterioration in the British balance of trade can now be met by a natural or planned devaluation of sterling, to make British exports more competitive in overseas markets. Joining the single currency would mean that such a deterioration would lead to lower wages or (more likely) higher unemployment.

There is also a powerful political argument, namely that joining the single currency would be an important step towards British absorption into a federal or quasi-federal form of European government, which few British people want. Staying out, on the contrary, would lead to acceptance of a more flexible, multi-speed European Union, in which some countries would be more integrated than others. The only reasonable conclusion to these arguments is that the establishment of a single European currency would be bad news for Britain, whether the country participates or not.

The second and third pillars

As noted in Chapter 5, the Maastricht Treaty does not mean that the European Community has been replaced by the European Union, only that the Community has become part of a much looser entity called the Union. The other two 'pillars' have been created largely with an eye to the future; neither the European Parliament nor the European Court of Justice has jurisdiction over their activities, though the Parliament has to be informed and on some issues has to be 'consulted'; and, although the European Commission is somewhat involved with them in a minor 'associated' role, it has no right of initiative in foreign and security policy.

The plan for foreign affairs is, so far, little more than an institutional re-arrangement of the practice, known as European Political Co-operation, that was started in 1970 and commits member states to holding regular meetings designed to harmonize their foreign policies. Before Maastricht, these meetings had their own secretariat and were, in a formal sense, distinct from the meetings of the same ministers in the Council of Ministers. Now they are formally linked to the European Community and this secretariat has been merged with the secretariat of the Council of Ministers. In terms of achievements, the harmonization process has produced numerous declarations of common attitudes, but few examples of common action.

The declarations have covered a wide range of issues, including Arab–Israeli relations, the situation in Cyprus, the Soviet invasion of Afghanistan, the war between Iraq and Iran, negotiations over disarmament in Europe, and the violent internal conflicts in Cambodia, El Salvador, Chile and Sri Lanka. The first important example of common action occurred in 1982, when all member states agreed to a British request to ban imports from Argentina and to stop supplying that country with arms or military equipment during the conflict over the Falklands. That was a distinct help to Britain, in view of the importance of the Argentinian market for French arms, aircraft and military equipment. The second important example occurred in 1997, when all states agreed to a German request to follow Germany's example by withdrawing their ambassadors in protest against the Iranian government's practice of organizing terrorist activities in western Europe from its embassy in Bonn. This was more of a symbolic gesture, as trade with Iran was not affected, but it may have influenced voting in the presidential election in Iran that followed four months later, when a fairly moderate politician was elected instead of the extremist Islamic militant who had been the leading contender.

The Maastricht Treaty introduced the possibility of qualified majority voting in the council responsible for the Common Foreign and Security Policy, but the procedure for this (set out in Article J3) has been described by two experts as being 'so hedged about with conditions that it seems unlikely the opportunity to take a decision by this means will ever arise' (Edwards and Nuttall, in Duff, Pinder and Pryce 1994: 96).

214

As this implies that joint action requires unanimity, it seems unlikely that there will be much joint action in the near future. The only states with world-wide interests are Britain and France, and their interests and policies have usually differed. The main British concerns outside Europe are to retain their close relationship with the United States and their friendly relationships with the other members of the Commonwealth. The French have always wanted to keep their distance from the United States, have their own former colonies to look after and go to astonishing lengths to maintain French as the second language at international gatherings, although it is only the ninth language in the world in terms of the number of people speaking it. Germany shares Britain's concern to keep the USA committed to western Europe, and benefits from the presence of US bases on German soil, but on other issues is more likely to side with France than with Britain because of the working partnership between Germany and France in most areas of European Union policy-making. Eleven member states belong to NATO, while the other four (Ireland, Sweden, Finland and Austria) are determined to maintain their neutrality in East–West issues. Britain and Greece have differed over Cyprus ever since British troops had to fight a prolonged campaign in the 1950s against a Greek-Cypriot terrorist organization wanting political union with Greece. France is more openly pro-Arab than the other states because of its historical involvement with Lebanon and Syria. Spain and Britain have a strained relationship over fishing rights, with a tendency to arrest each other's trawlers, which culminated in a British veto of joint European action proposed against Canada when a Canadian warship arrested a Spanish trawler in 1995. All these differences are unlikely to fade away quickly.

The proponents of a common foreign policy often point to the success of a united front in matters of trade in bargaining with the Americans over the GATT reforms, but there are contrary examples. When west European states that fish on the Grand Banks of the north-west Atlantic were represented by only one person in the negotiations of 1994–5, the final agreement, which restricted their fishing quota to only a small fraction of what they would have been entitled to on the basis of tradition, was taken by seven votes to six, with the European Community in the minority. If the several European states involved had kept their individual votes this could not have happened. Equally, a common foreign policy would presumably cut their permanent members of the UN Security Council from two to one, or from three to one if Germany is admitted to that exclusive club.

The hope of integrationists for a common defence policy is also surrounded by questions. Until the end of the Cold War western Europe was defended by NATO, under American leadership, and by the nuclear deterrent. Since 1990 western Europe has had no common enemy to push it towards unity, and the only foreign war in which European forces have been involved was the Gulf War of 1990–1, when British and French troops and aircraft joined the American-led coalition to drive Iraqi forces out of Kuwait. Since the end of the war, the British and French air forces have joined the US air force in patrolling the no-fly zones over Iraq.

Apart from this, European forces have been active only in internal security, notably Northern Ireland, and in a number of humanitarian and peacekeeping missions under UN auspices. In these the activities of the states have varied widely. The British have been constantly engaged in Cyprus, partly to keep the Greeks and Turks apart and partly to protect their air base, which serves as a convenient staging post to the Middle East and has been frequently used by the US air force as well as the British. The Belgians and Italians sent troops to Somalia, to join the American and Canadian contingents. When the break-up of Yugoslavia, encouraged by Germany because of its historic friendship with the Croatians, led to civil war in the eastern tip of Croatia and all over Bosnia, France, Britain and Canada were the only states to send sizeable contingents of troops to distribute food and medical supplies. When the conflict in Bosnia turned into full-scale civil war, the French and British forces were greatly increased (and suffered about seventy deaths in the struggle), while much smaller units from Holland, Spain, Russia and one or two non-European states joined in as well. Since the Dayton peace accord was signed in September 1995 Bosnia has been divided into American, British and French zones, under the auspices of NATO rather than the UN, and the other contingents have withdrawn.

In 1994 the massacre of Tutsis by Hutus in Rwanda led the UN to appeal for other African states to send troops in, but none responded. Only France sent troops into the area, and then not into Rwanda itself (where they would not have been welcome) but into eastern Zaire, where they organized camps for Hutu refugees and (with tragic later consequences) provided the Hutu militia with arms. After the fighting had ended, the British sent trucks and a contingent of army mechanics to repair both them and thousands of other vehicles, to help get the country back on its feet. No other European countries helped.

In March 1997, when Albania relapsed into anarchy, there was debate at a meeting of European Union (EU) foreign ministers about a proposal to send in thousands of troops to restore order, in answer to a request from the Albanian President. This idea was supported by Denmark, France, Italy and Greece, but a majority of governments, led by Britain, Germany and Sweden, were against it, on the ground that it was no business of the EU to support an unpopular and failing foreign government against a popular uprising. In April Britain and the USA sent very small specialized units (of the British SAS and the US Marines) to secure control of Albania's main airport and evacuate their nationals, but this mission was completed in a few days. In May, when fighting had ended, the Italian government organized a small contingent of troops to supervise the distribution of food to groups and institutions that were unable to get it for themselves, such as old people's homes. This was not done under EU auspices, and the participants had varied motives. The Italians and Greeks wanted to avoid their countries having to accept large numbers of Albanian refugees; the French wanted to show the Americans that Europe could some-times do things without US help; and Romania sent a few score men to remind the western powers that it has applied for EU membership.

In spite of this obvious lack of a united purpose, European integrationists have continued to nurture hopes of joint action on defence. To this end, the Western European Union (WEU) has been revived to serve as an alternative to NATO. The WEU was established in 1955 'as a loosely structured, essen-tially consultative, primarily defence-orientated organisation that . . . permitted West German Rearmament and . . . enabled West Germany to become a member of NATO' (Nugent 1991: 40). This aim achieved, it continued as a shadowy and superfluous entity until it was brought back into play after the Maastricht Treaty was signed. Nominally under its auspices, there has been established a very small unit of French and German troops that train together and might one day (it is thought) form the nucleus of a European army. European integrationists hope that by 1999 the WEU might be merged with the EU itself and eventually be persuaded to accept majority voting on defence policy. However, this whole plan suffers from three serious weaknesses. The first of these is that membership of the two organizations is far from identical; the four EU members that are not NATO members, along with Denmark, attend WEU meetings only as 'observers', while twelve states that are not members of the EU participate in the WEU as 'associate members' or 'asso-ciate partners'. The second is that majority voting on defence policy will not be accepted in the foreseeable future, and in any case could hardly be binding as no country would be willing to risk the lives of its soldiers on a mission with which it disagreed. The third is that the EU's activities regarding foreign policy and defence policy 'enjoy neither popular understanding nor popular support' (Edwards and Nuttall, in Duff, Pinder and Pryce 1994: 103). At the 1997 conference of governmental heads in Amsterdam it was therefore decided not to pursue the proposal for a merger.

The activities under the third 'pillar' of the EU, namely justice and home affairs, can be dealt with much more briefly than foreign policy and defence policy have been. One set of problems relates to the introduction of a common policy regarding the need for visas for citizens of other states wishing to visit EU countries, the abandonment of border controls within the EU, and the eventual acceptance of a common European citizenship.

On the question of visa requirements, general agreement was reached, together with provisions for 'a Community response to emergencies in other countries causing a sudden influx of people' (Anderson, Boer and Miller, in Duff, Pinder and Pryce 1994: 116). However, when a Canadian warship arrested a Spanish trawler in 1995, Spain and France unilaterally demanded visas for Canadian visitors to their countries. The abandonment of border controls was accepted by the original six members of the Community in the Schengen Agreement of 1990, before Maastricht, but it was unilaterally broken by France later because of the threat of terrorist attacks by Islamic fundamentalists. Britain has made it clear that it will not accept EU rulings about border controls so long as IRA terrorists remain a threat, and Ireland has to go along with this to maintain its open border with Britain. At the 1997 Amsterdam conference it was agreed that Britain and Ireland could opt out.

The question of common rules for citizenship is more difficult, because several member states are attached to their own unique rules for historical or cultural reasons. France insists that immigrants should demonstrate an understanding of French culture before being granted citizenship. Germany will grant citizenship only to applicants with German blood, thus excluding guest workers from Mediterranean countries and their descendants, though they may have lived in Germany for fifty years and be permanently settled there. At the same time, Germany grants citizenship to people who have lived in other countries for many generations, and have other nationalities, if they can demonstrate that they have German blood in their veins. Britain has three kinds of citizenship as a consequence of its Imperial history, one of which grants an unqualified 'right of abode' in Britain while the others do not. It is not likely that these special national requirements will be easily or quickly surrendered. The EU has also wanted all states to adopt identical immigration rules, but this proposal was rejected by Britain and has not been pressed further.

Another wish of European integrationists is for the EU to establish common policies and institutions regarding security, policing and judicial procedures, but these objectives are not likely to be attained quickly. European states threatened by terrorism have had joint consultations for years, and, as these consultations and counter-terrorist precautions following from them are necessarily secret, there seems little point in subjecting them to the Brussels bureaucracy. In regard to policing, an international agency for mutual help has existed for many years in the form of Interpol, located in Lyon. This is useful for communication between countries remote from one another, or where language difficulties hinder direct communications, but is much less useful within western Europe. A British police officer told this author that 'if western European police forces seriously want our help, they get straight on the blower to us, as we do to them, so European enquiries routed through Interpol are usually a waste of time'. That interview took place in the 1960s, and fax machines and E-mail have of course made direct communications even easier now.

However, significant moves have been made to establish a European centre for the exchange and analysis of police and customs intelligence regarding cross-border crimes within the EU. In June 1993 ministers agreed to set up a European Police Drug Unit (EDU) to deal with illegal drug trafficking between two or more member states, and this began work in The Hague in February 1994. In March 1995 the EDU's mandate was extended to cover illegal trade in radioactive and nuclear materials, illegal immigration networks and cross-border traffic in stolen vehicles, and in September 1996 (following the discovery of an international paedophile ring by the Belgian police) it was agreed to extend the mandate further to cover trafficking in human beings.

In July 1995 the European Commission proposed to establish a European Police Unit (Europol) with greater powers than the EDU (which would be absorbed by it), but this proved to be more controversial. No member state ratified this proposal until Britain did so in December 1996, and it is not clear how soon widespread agreement will be secured. However, it may be an important development in the long run, and the fact that Britain was the first state to agree to it is an exception to the rule that the British have always dragged their feet in the moves towards European integration.

The proposal to establish common criminal laws and judicial procedures is much more ambitious and less likely to be accepted and implemented in the near future. The harmonization of criminal law in fifteen or more states would be immensely difficult and take years of work. The proposal to adopt standard judicial procedures would meet with fierce opposition from the entire legal professions of the countries that would be forced to transform their systems and retain all their judges and lawyers. The arguments in favour of harmonization in the legal field are impressive, but the obstacles in the way of legal and judicial unity are formidable in the extreme.

Enlargement and the future

By 1996 thirteen more states had applied for membership of EU. Three of these are in the Mediterranean area, namely Cyprus, Malta and Turkey, though the Turkish application has been put on hold for the time being. The other ten are in eastern and central Europe, namely Bulgaria, the Czech Republic, Estonia, Hungary, Latvia, Lithuania, Poland, Romania, Slovakia and Slovenia. The possibility that the EU might be enlarged from fifteen members to twenty-seven, or even twenty-eight, raises a number of difficult problems, some institutional and others financial.

One problem is the number of European Commissioners that would be appointed if the existing rules are maintained. The belief in Brussels is that the present number of twenty is quite high enough, and that to have thirty-two would make the Commission unwieldy and create difficulties about the division of functions and powers between its members. However, no state or applicant is likely to be willing to surrender the right to appoint a Commissioner, and the five largest states will not easily surrender their right to have two.

Another institutional problem is that of weighting votes in the Council of Ministers and, much more difficult, the argument about retaining or abandoning the right to veto some kinds of decision. The larger states already think that the weighting gives too much influence to the smallest ones, and would not want to see small (and poor) new member states given the same kind of privileges that Luxembourg, Ireland and Portugal have. The admission of new states would be bound to open this whole question to contentious debate and bargaining.

On the veto power, both in the Council of Ministers and in the European Council of governmental heads, some countries would like to see it abolished (except perhaps for defence), while British leaders have repeatedly made it clear that they will not accept this. However, it should not be thought that Britain will necessarily be alone on this issue, because other states have also used their veto power (or the threat of it), and on several questions that have greater international significance than the ones on which Britain has stood fast. Thus Greece, with its longstanding hostility to Turkey, has for years vetoed the grant that was due to Turkey under the EU's policy of giving a fair proportion of its foreign aid to Mediterranean countries, has vetoed the proposal to admit Turkey to the free trade arrangements that apply to several other countries, such as Norway and Switzerland, and vetoed for some time the EU proposal to recognize Macedonia as an independent state. It would clearly veto discussions on the admission of Turkey to the EU, and it has threatened to veto discussions on the admission of Cyprus. In 1992–3 Italy vetoed some new budgetary plans for the EU until it was granted a higher quota for milk production and also given an assurance that it would not be prosecuted for previous cheating on its milk quota. In 1994, when terms for the admission of Sweden, Finland and Austria were generally agreed, the Spanish government suddenly announced that it would veto their admission unless the deal by which Spain had been admitted in 1986 were revised to allow its fishing fleet to fish in British and Irish waters. In 1996 France vetoed the proposal to extend free trade privileges to South Africa.

It does not follow that these four countries will automatically take Britain's side on the issue, but it does follow that there will be some very hard bargaining over the question of what proposals can be vetoed and what cannot.

The whole question of EU financial commitments will also be a stumbling block for plans of enlargement, for the new applicants are all much poorer than the existing members, and will place a heavy burden on the EU budget unless important changes are made. In 1996 the average Gross Domestic Product (GDP) per capita in the fifteen member states was $18,170, whereas none of the thirteen applicants had equivalent figures of more than $6,000 apart from the Czech Republic ($7,910) and Cyprus ($10,260) (see *The Economist*, 3 August 1996). The wealthier states are likely to insist that changes be made to the present financial arrangements in the EU before the applicant states are admitted. As about 50 per cent of EU expenditure currently goes on the CAP and between 30 and 40 per cent of the 'structural fund', designed to help the poorer member states, and as all the applicants would quality as large beneficiaries under both heads, either one or both of the formulae for expenditure under these heads will have to be revised to make the admission of the applicants a feasible operation in financial terms.

Expenditure on the CAP is clearly, by logical standards, far too high. The policy has achieved its objectives. European agriculture has become much more efficient than it was in the 1950s, the EU has become a major exporter of foodstuffs and there is now such a surplus production of fruit and vegetables that large amounts of them are bought and immediately destroyed – 2.6 billion tons in 1994–5. The financial incentive to farmers to increase their production has led to environmental damage, the expenditure is a burden for the EU and European consumers are forced to pay prices for their food that are much higher than world prices. In December 1995 the European Commission, asked to write a report on the problems of enlargement, reported that 'the status quo for the CAP is not desirable'. Changing it so as to reduce its costs will, however, meet with objections from the French, who designed the CAP and whose farmers constitute a powerful political lobby, and from other countries that benefit greatly from it, such as Ireland, Denmark and Greece.

Changing the formula for the distribution of structural and cohesion funds also presents problems. A small proportion of these funds go on particular projects for disadvantaged areas, as the city of Hull got a grant to build a shopping mall over part of its docks when its large fishing industry collapsed following the extension of Iceland's territorial limits. However, most of these funds go in the form of equalization grants to the four states whose GDP per capita is less than 75 per cent of the EU average. The new applicants have an average of about 26 per cent of the EU average, so under the present formula they would qualify for enormous grants continuing for decades to come. If the qualifying point were reduced from 75 to 60 per cent to help pay for these, Ireland, Spain and Portugal would immediately be excluded from assistance. The Commission's report stated that 'member states in receipt of structural funds cannot expect to obtain existing amounts indefinitely', and while this is fair enough it serves as a clear warning to the present recipients that they will lose financially if they vote for enlargement. It only needs one of them to cast a veto.

It is obvious that the problems of enlargement are very serious. The Commission report stated that 'each applicant country should be treated individually on its merits', and one quite probable result of the coming review at meetings of the Intergovernmental Conference is that many applications will be postponed for the time being. The application from Cyprus presents two problems, one being the ethnic conflict in the country and its partial occupation by the Turkish army, the other being the Greek threat of a veto either of Cyprus' admission or of all the other applications if Greek conditions are not met. Bulgaria, Romania and Slovakia may be put off because they cannot fully satisfy the EU's conditions that all member states must be stable democracies. Estonia, Latvia and Lithuania will probably be put off because the larger member states, such as Germany, France and Britain, will not want to accept responsibility for getting involved in possible conflicts between Russia and former Soviet republics. That leaves Poland, Hungary and the Czech Republic, whose admission is strongly favoured by Germany, because it is Germany's major trading partner in western Europe, and by Britain, for reasons of sentiment and personal ties. These three countries are now being incorporated into NATO, so the EU would not be saddled with any implied obligation to help with their defence in case of future conflicts. The other two current applications are Slovenia and Malta, small countries about whose admission there seem to be no strong arguments either way.

It therefore seems likely that these five applications will be considered first, but the questions of institutional reform and financial reform remain major obstacles to any quick decisions.

Decisions taken in the years between 1997 and 2002 seem to be crucial for the future of the EU. In the forty years since 1958 it has achieved its three original objectives, namely peace in Europe, a large common market and the modernization of agriculture. Most British politicians and people would now like it to rest on its laurels and simply tidy its administration, reduce agricultural prices, and stop the large wastage of funds that now occurs as a result of semi-corrupt practices. However, the belief among many continental politicians and nearly all the bureaucrats in Brussels is that it must quickly press on towards the further objective of what the preamble of the Treaty of Rome called 'an ever closer union among the peoples of Europe'. A popular remark in Brussels is that the EU is like a bicycle in that it must keep moving forwards or it will fall over. Elaborate plans are constantly being hatched to further complicate its already over-complex system of decision-making and to further weaken the power of national governments. Some bureaucrats would like to put an end to the nation-state altogether. In the spring of 1997 one British newspaper published a map that was circulating in Brussels offices, but not intended for publication, showing a plan to put an end to the United Kingdom as such by dividing it into regions that would be controlled directly by the European Commission. One region would consist of Kent and Sussex in south-east England, combined with Normandy and an area north-west of Normandy in France. Another region would consist of Lancashire, Northern Ireland and a chunk of the Irish Republic.

It is not clear how much support this kind of plan would get if it were put forward officially. The Benelux countries would probably approve of it, together with Chancellor Kohl. But President Chirac, though in favour of closer integration, has made it clear that he wants the EU to be a community of nations, not a federal union, and Kohl's successors may not share his commitment to a completely unified Europe.

Only two things can be said with certainty at this time. One is that the last three years of the millennium, and perhaps the first two of the next, will be occupied by a seemingly endless set of negotiations, like a game of chess played by fifteen rival players. The other is that the 250 million electors of the member states will be left out of the negotiations and unable to exert much influence on them except by the indirect method of throwing out national governments whose policies they dislike. This could happen, of course, if the timing is right. In May 1997 the Maastricht Treaty played a large part in the defeat of Major's government, while the French government's attempts to reduce the deficit so as to qualify for the single European currency were largely responsible for its replacement in June 1997. But elections are held only once in four or five years and not all countries will be holding one in the critical period.

The polls have repeatedly shown that the bureaucratic and political elites who are pushing Europe towards greater integration have failed to carry more than a minority of the people with them. There are only very limited signs of a supranational identity emerging. A poll in the mid-1980s which asked how often people saw themselves as citizens of Europe produced the answer 'often' only from 8 per cent of British respondents, 15 per cent of Germans, 18 per cent of Italians and 21 per cent of the French, while 74 per cent of the British, 45 per cent of the Italian and 40 per cent of the French replied 'never' (Hewstone 1986: 33). There is no evidence that these attitudes have changed significantly, because national loyalties and sentiments are very strong in Europe. The French, Germans, British and Italians are all in their varied ways chauvinistic peoples, with different histories, achievements and cultures to be proud of. When the French government urged its people to give a positive vote in the referendum to ratify the Maastricht Treaty, the major argument was not on the lines of 'we are all Europeans now', but that the threat of German domination would be reduced by having Germany bound tightly by Community rules. A Eurobarometer poll early in 1997 showed that in six member states (Sweden, Denmark, Finland, Britain, Austria and Germany) the electors who were hostile to the plan for a single European currency outnumbered those who favoured it. It also showed that 'although in most member countries a majority still believe the EU to be a good thing, the margins in favour are falling steadily' (*The Economist*, 31 May 1997). A 1996 NOP poll in Britain revealed that only 30 per cent of respondents believed that EC and EU membership had been 'good for Britain' and 20 per cent had no view (*Sunday Times*, 17 March 1996). In 1997 *The Economist*, a generally pro-European journal, concluded that 'the EU's deepest problem of all is the disenchantment of its citizens' (*The Economist*, 31 May 1997).

Further reading

A useful guide to EC institutions before Maastricht is Nugent (1991)*The Government and Politics of the European Community*; the best detailed guide to the politics of the EC is Lodge (1989) *The European Community and the Challenge of the Future*; a concise history and analysis of the attitudes of British governments will be found in George (1991) *Britain and European Integration Since 1945*; the best guide to the complexities and implications of the Maastricht Treaty is Duff, Pinder and Pryce (1994) *Maastrict and Beyond*.

16

CONDUCTING FOREIGN POLICY

Control of foreign policy

The conduct of foreign policy is in the hands of the Foreign and Commonwealth Office, which has had that title since the previously separate Department of Commonwealth Relations was merged with the Foreign Office in 1968, but will henceforth, for simplicity, be referred to by its traditional and familiar title of the Foreign Office. The Foreign Office is second in importance only to the Treasury in the British administrative hierarchy, and the views of the Foreign Secretary carry great weight in Cabinet discussions.

The Foreign Secretary, like the Chancellor of the Exchequer, keeps in close touch with the Prime Minister, who may be called upon to answer parliamentary questions dealing with foreign affairs in the weekly sessions of Prime Minister's Question Time and who often deals directly with other heads of government on critical issues of policy. In the middle of the nineteenth century Foreign Secretaries such as Palmerston and Lord John Russell could conduct foreign relations in considerable independence of their Prime Minister (see Vital 1968: 54), but this has not been possible in the twentieth century and is unthinkable today. In critical periods postwar Prime Ministers have even taken foreign policy largely into their own hands, as Eden did over the nationalization of the Suez Canal, Heath did during Britain's negotiations to join the European Community, and Thatcher did when Argentina invaded the Falkland Islands. Six of the eleven postwar Prime Ministers have at one time or another taken charge of particular diplomatic issues.

To say this is not to suggest that the Foreign Office has been elbowed aside on these occasions. The British Prime Minister is not in the position of the US President, who has a very sizeable personal staff in the White House and is able to appoint personal emissaries whose powers may overshadow those of the Secretary of State, as Henry Kissinger's powers did for several years. The Prime Minister has only a minimal staff at 10 Downing Street and until 1982 was entirely dependent on Foreign Office staff for advice and assistance in regard to diplomatic affairs. Since 1982 there has been a special diplomatic adviser in the Prime Minister's Office, a development which was intended and was seen as something of a rebuff to the Foreign Office, but the advisers have been people who have spent most of their careers in the diplomatic service and the importance of this move should not be exaggerated. Thatcher also showed an increasing tendency to engage in personal diplomacy in the late 1980s, as she became the most senior of the world's leaders and enjoyed a close friendly relationship with President Reagan, but the effective conduct of foreign policy requires a considerable staff and that staff is provided by the Foreign Office.

The Foreign Secretary is assisted by three ministers of state and three parliamentary under-secretaries, so the ministerial team is a strong one. The Diplomatic Service is also strong. It is considerably larger than the diplomatic services of other states of similar size and power, such as Germany, France and Italy. Its members are recruited separately from the members of equivalent ranks of the home civil service, and as entry standards are very high the Foreign Office prides itself on hiring the *crème de la crème* for its staff. There is substance to this claim; the Foreign Office has been criticized for its lack of long-term planning, but hardly ever been criticized for poor execution of policy. When Argentina invaded the Falklands, Britain needed a two-thirds majority vote in the UN Security Council to condemn the invasion. The odds were heavily against this, but the British mission achieved it. A senior American delegate described this feat as 'a stunning example of sheer diplomatic professionalism' (Hastings and Jenkins 1983: 101).

The influence of parliamentary and public opinion

Parliament exerts influence over foreign policy in the same way as it exerts influence over domestic policy; through parliamentary questions, debates on policy issues, and the potential sanctions of being able to force a ministerial resignation or to pass a vote of no confidence in the government's handling of foreign affairs. In practice, however, most MPs are less interested in foreign affairs than in home affairs. The average voter has little interest in foreign policy and it is rare for MPs to be subject to constituency pressures in this field. It is relatively difficult for MPs to acquire an expert knowledge of diplomatic matters and there is little incentive for them to do so. The normal timetable of the House of Commons provides for the Foreign Secretary (or a deputy, if the Foreign Secretary is in the House of Lords) to answer questions only once every three weeks.

This relative quiescence of Parliament is encouraged by the fact that the political parties have rarely disagreed over foreign policy. There have been running disagreements within the Labour Party over nuclear arms, but when in power the Labour Party has followed the same policy as the Conservative Party on this issue. The only two occasions since 1945 when there has been outright disagreement between government and Opposition over foreign affairs were over the Suez invasion in 1956, and in 1971–3 over Britain's application to join the European Community. The conflict over Suez was short-lived, as the invasion was called off within two weeks. The frontbench conflict over the European Community was moderated by the fact that both main parties were divided on the issue, to such an extent that the government's narrow margin of support was actually given to it by Labour dissidents.

A different kind of example of parliamentary influence was provided by the emergency debate that took place immediately following the Argentinian invasion of the Falkland Islands. In this debate the vehement demands for a strong British response, coming from all parts of the House and from the Leader of the Opposition, virtually compelled the government to make immediate plans for a British task force to re-take the islands. These demands were not unwelcome to the government, but the political situation in the following weeks would have been very different if the main political parties had taken conflicting views on the issue.

The fact that the government can normally expect to get parliamentary support for its foreign policies does not mean that Parliament can be taken for granted. In times of crisis, parliamentary questions and debates can be very penetrating. This has been true of all of the critical issues that have arisen in the postwar period, including British policy in Palestine, the emergency in Malaya, the Berlin blockade, the Mau Mau campaign in Kenya, the Korean war, the conflict with Egypt over the Suez Canal, relations with Israel and the Arab states, the violent confrontation with Indonesia, the civil war in Nigeria, Rhodesia's unilateral declaration of independence, relations with the European Community, the dispute with Iceland over fishing limits, and the crisis over the Falkland Islands. The Foreign Secretary and the Minister of Defence have to be prepared to answer parliamentary questions day after day when crises are in progress. Their situation stands in sharp contrast to the easy time that the US Secretary of State and Secretary of Defense had in regard to Congress during the Vietnam war, for neither of them had to submit to congressional questioning between October 1964, when Congress authorized the dispatch of American forces to Vietnam, and February 1968, when it became apparent that the Americans were unable to defeat the Viet Cong.

If parliamentary criticism of the government reveals weaknesses in governmental policy or behaviour that cannot be disguised, the Foreign Secretary may feel obliged to resign. This was illustrated dramatically in 1982, when the Foreign Secretary, though himself in the House of Lords, felt he had to resign in response to forthright criticism from backbench Conservative MPs in the 1922 Committee of the failure of the Foreign Office to predict that Argentina would invade the Falklands. The failure was not Lord Carrington's fault, but Foreign Office policy had ended in disaster and Carrington felt honour bound to accept responsibility for this. Two other Foreign Office ministers, themselves in the Commons, resigned with him.

Since 1979 the House of Commons has had select committees on both foreign affairs and defence, as noted in Chapter 12. These are small specialized committees with wide powers to investigate and report on aspects of policy and administration within their fields. They have not yet had any marked influence on policy, but the Foreign Affairs Committee played an important role in 1980–2. At that time the Canadian government asked Parliament to approve a set of amendments to the British North America Act of 1867 which included a proposal to transfer all subsequent powers of amendment to Canada. These amendments were opposed by the majority of the Canadian provinces and this rather delicate issue was immediately referred by the House of Commons to its committee, which heard evidence from experts on constitutional law. After considerable study and debate, the committee unanimously recommended that the Canadian proposals be rejected because they did not have support from sufficient provinces. After protracted controversy within Canada, the proposals were amended in ways that satisfied all but one of the provinces. The amended proposals then went through Parliament without difficulty. The Foreign Affairs Committee was invaluable in this affair, not only because it was able to call expert witnesses and prepare an incisive report but also because it enabled the House of Commons to avoid having an embarrassing debate on the floor of the House that might have had a damaging effect on Anglo-Canadian relations.

Outside Parliament, there are numerous pressure groups that seek influence over foreign policy. At one level, there are élite institutions like the Royal Institute of International Affairs, the International Institute of Strategic Studies, the Royal United Services Institution and the Foreign Affairs Club. They help to shape informed opinion about diplomatic issues, which is also shaped by (and reflected in) *The Times*, *The Economist* and the several other intellectual journals and newspapers.

Alongside these groups with a general concern for the national interest in foreign relations, there are several organizations with a more particular focus, often supported by business firms that have an interest in particular parts of the world. Among these are the China Association, the Sino-British Trade Council, the South Africa Club, the West Africa Committee, the British Atlantic Committee, the Anglo-German Association and Britain in Europe. Such groups sponsor meetings with an educative effect and also press information and views on senior Foreign Office officials and interested backbench MPs.

In addition to these groups with a geographical focus, there are also groups with a particular slant on foreign affairs. There are, for instance, several groups concerned with British aid to the Third World, whose activities in Britain are co-ordinated by the Voluntary Committee on Aid and Development. There is the British Council of Churches, which promotes various Christian causes in relation to foreign policy. There is the United Nations Association, whose activities are mainly educational; Amnesty International, whose varied activities are designed to help political prisoners abroad; and the Corporation of Foreign Bondholders, whose members have special interests to be defended. All such groups communicate their views to the Foreign Office and to sympathetic MPs.

At the level of mass opinion, pressure groups tend to be radical in outlook and to be more interested in defence issues than in foreign policy as such. The largest of them is the Campaign for Nuclear Disarmament (henceforth CND), that has been in business since the late 1950s and in its more successful phases has enjoyed the support of tens of thousands of active sympathizers. CND and various allied groups have gained a great deal of publicity for their cause over the years, though without ever persuading more than a minority of the public to accept their point of view. The polls have varied from time to time, but in the late 1980s they suggested that about 15 per cent of the electors accepted the arguments for unilateral nuclear disarmament by Britain. There is no evidence that the Ministry of Defence or the Foreign Office have ever modified their policies to take account of the pressures generated by these groups.

Issues in foreign policy

For the past two centuries Britain's foreign policies have been deeply influenced by economic and geographical factors. Since the Industrial Revolution transformed British society and led to a rapid increase in its population, Britain has been dependent on imported foodstuffs and raw materials to feed its people and supply its industries. Needing to get these goods from remote parts of the world, it has also been dependent on trade routes and freedom to navigate the seas. At the same time, its position as a group of islands has protected it from invasion by foreign armies. So long as the Royal Navy had control of the seas, Britain was safe. Its traditional policy has therefore been to avoid fixed alliances that would restrict its freedom of action, while intervening in European affairs when this seemed necessary to prevent any one rival power becoming supreme among its neighbours.

These policies were pursued successfully from 1815 until 1914. In the period between the wars Britain was much weaker in terms of both economic power and defence capacity, but the diplomatic implications of these weaknesses were disguised by the isolation of the United States, the Soviet Union's domestic problems, and the confused state of European relationships. It was not until 1945, that, with the British economy ruined by the war and the emergence of the United States and the Soviet Union as superpowers, it became clear that the United Kingdom could no longer sustain the role of a great world power, independently responsible for its own defence.

Since 1945 British diplomacy has been dominated by three problems: the need to maintain the American commitment to the defence of western Europe; the need to dismantle the colonial empire; and the need to establish new relationships with its European friends and allies. In summary, it may be said to have been successful in dealing with the first problem; fairly successful in dealing with the second; and rather unsuccessful in dealing with the third.

A frank discussion of Anglo-American relationships is often confused by a cloud of wishful British thinking about the 'special relationship' that is said to exist between the two countries. In fact, British friendship and co-operation, though important to the United States, is no more important than the friend-ship and co-operation of Germany, Italy or France. Much is often made of the friendly personal relationships that have existed between Macmillan and Kennedy or Thatcher and Reagan, but these are balanced by the poor relation-ships that obtained between Eden and Eisenhower or Wilson and Johnson. American foreign policy was actively hostile to British interests over the Suez crisis, was apparently neutral over the confrontation with Indonesia and was only hesitantly supportive over the Falklands crisis. There is evidence of a close relationship in the exchange of international intelligence, in numerous acad-emic exchanges and in certain kinds of co-operation in the training of naval, military and air force personnel, but at the diplomatic level talk of a special relationship is generally unhelpful.

If this is discounted, the fact remains that Britain was entirely successful, in conjunction with West Germany and other allies, in maintaining the American commitment to an active and immediate defence of western Europe against Soviet aggression. This was a very expensive commitment for the USA, with over 300,000 military personnel (roughly the strength of Britain's entire armed forces) stationed in Europe. As the Soviet Union was the only clear threat to British security between 1945 and 1990, the maintenance of this commitment was vital to Britain. It is partly for this reason that the British government has, perhaps unnecessarily, made occasional gestures that look like subservience to American policy, such as the partial boycott of the 1980 Moscow Olympic Games, verbal support for American policy towards El Salvador and the decision to allow American planes to bomb Libya from bases on British soil.

The process of decolonization undertaken by Britain after 1945 was managed speedily and quite effectively. In 1947 India and Pakistan were created as inde-pendent states and in the same year it was decided to move the African colonies towards independence as soon as practicable, beginning with the colonies in West Africa because they had no British settlers to complicate the procedure. The East African colonies followed quickly thereafter and it was only in Central Africa that serious difficulties emerged.

There, the colony of Southern Rhodesia (subsequently called simply Rhodesia and now called Zimbabwe) had been governed for decades by representatives of the white settlers, who numbered about 210,000 in the 1960s, without any share in political power being given to representatives of the native African population, who numbered nearly 4 million. After it became clear that the British government proposed to extend the franchise to Africans, the settler government made a unilateral declaration of independence in 1965. The British government could not prevent this without using armed force, which no parlia-mentary party was willing to support. Sanctions were imposed and made international, but these proved to be as ineffectual as economic sanctions invari-ably are. It was not until the adjoining Portuguese colony of Mozambique became independent in the hands of a radical government, and started to give active assistance to black guerrilla bands operating in Rhodesia, that the white government agreed to a British proposal, worked out at the 1979 Commonwealth Conference, to hold free elections with the franchise extended to all adult citizens. The result was the independent state of Zimbabwe, with the settlers holding only a few guaranteed seats in its legislative assembly.

In certain other colonies there was violence before independence, but successive British governments, whether Labour or Conservative, dealt with these problems in a highly pragmatic way. When British forces in Palestine had to cope with Jewish terrorists as well as with Arab terrorists, the British abandoned the colony (strictly speaking a Mandated Territory) precipitately, leaving chaos behind them. When the British got tired of dealing with Greek Cypriot terrorists in Cyprus, they negotiated a settlement that gave Cyprus independence while leaving Turkey with the right to intervene militarily if the Turkish minority were threatened by Greeks, as subsequently occurred. When rebel forces in Aden proved particularly awkward, the British withdrew speedily.

In Kenya, with a sizeable number of British settlers to be protected, the government engaged in a three-year struggle against Mau Mau terrorists. This campaign was waged largely by native troops and police and was entirely successful. It was only in Malaya that the British army had to be used in a prolonged fight against rebel forces, and British governments had a good reason for pursuing this struggle. Whereas most colonies were of limited economic use to Britain, the rubber industry made Malaya extremely valuable. By some estimates, the profits Britain derived from Malaya exceeded the profits from all the other forty or more colonies put together. With a good deal to fight for, British troops conducted a small-scale but prolonged campaign against a sizeable band of Chinese terrorists, aided substantially by the fact that the Malays, who comprised 50 per cent of the population (against 40 per cent Chinese), were entirely on the British side. After eleven years of struggle, the terrorists were completely defeated and the British subsequently handed over a peaceful country to an independent government composed of an alliance of Malay, Chinese and Indian leaders.

Other colonies were moved towards independence without serious trouble, the only areas retaining colonial status in 1998 being the Falkland Islands and eleven territories with very small populations.

In the context of this chapter, one way of viewing the impact of British membership of the European Community is to consider its impact upon the making of foreign policy within Britain. This impact has had two clear effects. One is to increase the influence of the Prime Minister, who quite frequently has to speak for Britain at Community meetings. The other is to involve government departments other than the Foreign Office and the Ministry of Defence in diplomatic negotiations. Ministers and officials of the Ministry of Agriculture and the Department of Trade and Industry, to name only the two most obvious examples, are constantly in touch with their opposite members in the Brussels bureaucracy and in other European governments. In 1977 the Central Policy

Review Staff found that only 46 per cent of the personnel working in Britain's external relations were employed through the Foreign Office 'and only 14 per cent were members of the Diplomatic Service' (Clarke 1988: 80–1). The growing importance of European Community activities means that this percentage has probably declined since 1977, and will decline further.

Policy since the end of the Cold War

Questions of foreign policy have become slightly more complex since the end of the Cold War in 1989–90. As the United States is now the only super-power, its policies tend to dominate international relationships, and, as they are not always the policies that European states welcome, this places Britain in an occasionally difficult position as being (in de Gaulle's words) essentially mid-Atlantic in outlook.

The main feature that distinguishes American approaches to foreign policy from European approaches is the American tendency to be more ideological, idealistic and moralistic then Europeans. This sometimes has consequences that are clearly good or clearly unfortunate, and sometimes consequences that are just rather awkward.

To take the clearest examples first, the most unfortunate was the American decision to go to war in Vietnam instead of accepting that the communists and nationalists under Ho Chi Minh were bound to take over the country, as the French had done after their army there was defeated at Dien Bien Phu in 1954. The contrast between European and American attitudes was particularly sharp on this occasion. The French had very direct interests in Vietnam, both because it was part of Indochina, which had been a French colony for gener-ations, and because the French had sizeable commercial interests there. The Americans, on the other hand, had no direct interest in Vietnam, and went to war simply for ideological reasons. The result, as everyone knows, was a disaster for Vietnam, Cambodia and America itself.

In contrast, the finest postwar example of American idealism in international affairs has been their policy in the Middle East. The United States is the only country that has consistently protected Israel's legitimate interests over the five decades of that country's embattled existence, and has also done more than any other country to promote peace between Israel, the Palestinians and the surrounding Arab states. It has given more financial aid to Egypt than to any other country apart from Israel, and this far-sighted policy was rewarded when Jimmy Carter and his colleagues engineered the Camp David accord between the two previously warring countries in 1978. Years later, after the Norwegian initiative in launching and nurturing secret negotiations between Israel and the PLO, President Clinton succeeded in persuading Yassar Arafat of the PLO and the Israeli Prime Minister Rabin to sign a peace agreement in 1995. The US government has also made energetic efforts to persuade Syria to moderate its anti-Israeli policies, and to this end Warren Christopher made twenty-seven trips to Damascus during his four years as Secretary of State. At the time of writing the peace process has been interrupted, but this is not America's fault. Beside this record, the policies of the member states of the European Union have seemed somewhat selfish.

The less dramatic but more awkward questions have arisen over Cuba, Somalia and Bosnia. The absurd American vendetta against Fidel Castro and his regime has never had any support from Britain, Europe or the rest of the world, and it became a serious problem in international relations in 1996. The US congress then passed the Helms–Burton Act, designed to punish non-American citizens and firms that had invested money in Cuba in the previous three decades by allowing them to be sued in American courts. This led to protests by both the British government and the EU as a whole, who took the issue to the World Trade Organization with a demand that the USA should be punished for an illegitimate attempt to interfere with world trade, of which it was clearly guilty. This Act of Congress was quickly followed by another, authorizing severe punishment in US courts for European or other firms which invested money in Iran, which congress regarded as a rogue state responsible for international terrorism. This led to a reprimand by the Foreign Office, stating that it was entirely unacceptable for the USA to claim extra-territorial jurisdiction for its laws. In the event both these transatlantic conflicts were defused by diplomatic pressure from Britain and Brussels, as a result of which the implementation of the offending Acts of Congress was put on hold by President Clinton. However, as Sir Leon Brittan (the EU Commissioner for Trade) pointed out in 1997, 'the bomb pin might still be pulled out'.

The American tendency to view foreign policy in moralistic terms – to put it crudely, in terms of good guys versus bad guys – also had an unfortunate effect on the UN mission to supply food to Somalia. This was an exception-ally difficult mission, as Somalia had no effective government, police or judicial system, so that it was effectively in a state of anarchy. The capital, Mogadishu, was the scene of conflict between well-armed gangs, and at a late stage in the mission the US Commander of the UN forces decided to arrest the leader of the most powerful gang, a man called Mohammed Aideed. As this intention was publicized in advance by one of the US staff, Aideed's men ambushed and killed the soldiers who went to get him. The Americans responded by sending helicopter gunships to bomb what was thought (mistakenly) to be Aideed's headquarters, and there followed a pitched battle in which eighteen American and about forty Pakistani UN troops lost their lives, together with an unknown number of Somalis. The overall consequence was that a largely successful mission to relieve famine will go down into history as a UN failure.

Another example is the civil war in Bosnia. The decision to recognize the provinces that broke away from Yugoslavia, promoted by Germany and accepted by the EU, the USA and the UN, had unhappy consequences. Slovenia presented no problems because it has no serious ethnic conflicts. Croatian inde-pendence led to fighting in its eastern tip, which has a Serbian majority, and it would have been better if a referendum had been held before statehood was recognized. Bosnia should not have been granted statehood at all, as its people are not united by a common ethnicity, religion, language or history, and therefore have none of the normal bases of nationhood. A form of civil war broke out quickly, and the UN sent a large peacekeeping mission to protect civilians and ensure that humanitarian relief in the form of food and medical supplies reached those who needed it. The mission was originally composed of British, French and Canadian troops, though they were joined by smaller contingents from several other nations as the situation in Bosnia deteriorated. The mission was extremely expensive over the three and a half years of its life, saving tens of thousands of civilian lives but placing a great strain on UN finances and costing the lives of thirty-six British and a similar number of French soldiers. The trouble was that there was no peace to keep in Bosnia, and the fighting did not cease until the USA stepped in, flying the political leaders to a conference at an air base in Dayton, Ohio, and threatening them with aerial bombardment unless they signed an armistice.

The UN peacekeeping mission was then, in the autumn of 1995, replaced by a NATO force of US, British and French troops, with the other contingents withdrawing. This co-operative arrangement has worked well, with Bosnia divided into three zones, a British general in overall command of the ground forces, and an American admiral in charge of the entire mission. This military co-operation has not been paralleled by complete political agreement, however. The British and French forces have constantly, from 1992 onwards, been neutral as between the three warring parties, the Croats, Bosnian Serbs and Bosnian Muslims, and careful not to cross what General Rose, who was in charge for a time, called 'the Mogadishu line'. The Americans, in contrast, have always sympathized with the Bosnian Muslims and, to a lesser extent, the Croats, against the Serbs, who are regarded as aggressors who should be punished. Before the Dayton peace agreement, the Americans quietly arranged for small arms to be supplied to the Muslims by Arab states. Since Dayton, US agencies and firms have supplied the Muslims with heavy weapons such as artillery and armoured vehicles, and an organization in Virginia, private but directed by retired US generals, has provided extensive training for the Muslim army. The consequence is that, if civil war breaks out again when the NATO forces leave, the conflict will be more violent and the Muslims may be on top.

While many Europeans believe that the partition of this infant state called Bosnia offers the best hope of long-term peace, the Americans are quite determined that Bosnia should be maintained as a multi-ethnic state. They also appear determined that the political and military leaders of the Bosnian Serbs should be arrested and tried for offences against human rights, a policy that seems unlikely to persuade the Serbs to co-operate peacefully in a united Bosnia under largely Muslim leadership. The Assistant Secretary of State who was largely responsible for the Dayton armistice has publicly sneered at the European powers for being unable to cope with a European problem.

To this sneer the French and British have had different reactions. The French think that it strengthens the case for a joint European defence organization, to which end they want the WEU brought into the EU and defence policy to be subject to qualified majority voting. The British disagree. They are in principle unwilling to see their defence policy taken out of their hands, and they note that only Britain and France of the fifteen EU states have been willing to send sizeable army groups abroad, while Germany, which has most voting power in the EU, has not. They also believe it essential to keep the USA involved. In a major statement of policy in April 1996, the Foreign Secretary, Malcolm Rifkind, declared that 'when the international community faces a crisis on the scale of Yugoslavia's collapse, direct US involvement is indispensable – especially if military action is required. A "European solution to a European problem" was never a realistic option".'

It seems, therefore, that de Gaulle was correct in placing Britain as 'mid-Atlantic' in outlook. Like it or not, one of Britain's most important diplomatic roles for the next few years is bound to be that of acting as a kind of intermediary between Europe and the United States.

Further reading

The best account of the policy-making process is that given in Wallace (1977) *The Foreign Policy Process in Britain*; a good set of case studies of parliamentary influence will be found in Carstairs and Ware (1991) *Parliament and International Relations*; the clearest account of the postwar history of foreign relations is still that in Northedge (1974) *Descent From Power*; and more recent discussions will be found in Freedman and Clarke (1991) *Britain in the World*, and in Smith, Smith and White (eds.) (1988) *British Foreign Policy*.

Part V

THE CITIZEN AND THE GOVERNMENT

17

CITIZENS' RIGHTS AND THE LAW

In Part III of this book we considered the roles played by citizens as voters, as party members and as members of pressure groups, and discussed the opportunities open to citizens to stand for election. In these chapters the citizen was viewed as an active or potentially active participant in the political process. This final part of the book will deal with the position of the citizen in his or her more passive role as a person who is governed. In the present chapter we shall consider his or her individual liberties and rights in relation to the administration and the agencies for law-enforcement. Finally, in Chapter 18 an attempt will be made to assess the merits and problems of British government in the present period.

The rights and liberties of the citizen in Britain will be discussed in the following order: first, the basic civil rights of free speech and freedom of political action; secondly, the nature and role of the police and judiciary; and thirdly, the rights of the citizen in relation to government departments and other administrative authorities.

The basic civil liberties

British civil liberties rest on a different basis from those in most other democracies. Elsewhere, civil rights are normally specified in writing, either in constitutional declarations of rights or in provisions of the legal code of the country. In the United States the fundamental civil liberties are set out in the constitution, the ten constitutional amendments that were added in 1791 (which are collectively known as the Bill of Rights) and the amendments that were passed after the Civil War with the intention of extending equal rights to blacks. In France civil rights were first specified in the Declaration of the Rights of Man and the Citizen of 1789, and the continuing French attachment to these rights is shown by the references to the declaration in the preambles of the constitutions of both the Fourth and the Fifth Republics. In other countries guarantees of rights are much more recent, depending on the dates on which regimes purporting to be liberal were first established.

The position in Britain is different because Britain has not gone through the common experience of overthrowing an oppressive system of government by force of arms and establishing a constitutional regime more or less *de novo*. Britain has enjoyed the rule of law for at least three centuries, since long before its political system was in any sense democratic, and the rights of citizens have been established not by the declarations of politicians but by the decisions of judges, interpreting the Common Law of the land. It follows that one could search the Statute Book in vain for acts conferring upon citizens the rights of free speech, freedom of association or freedom of movement. These rights rest simply on the age-old assumption by British courts that citizens are free to do as they like provided they do not commit any specific breach of the law. A consequence of this situation is that the extent of civil rights can be assessed only by considering particular types of freedom and particular limitations that have been established over the years on the exercise of these freedoms.

To begin with freedom of spech, it is assumed by the courts that anyone is free to say or write what he or she likes provided it does not break the laws designed to protect the rights and security of fellow-citizens. The laws of libel and slander are one check on this freedom; if a statement is made by A about B that is untrue and defames B's character, B may sue A in the civil courts and may be awarded substantial damages if he or she wins the case. But it is not libellous to publish a true statement unless malice can be established; nor is it libellous to hold a person up to ridicule, as is done in satirical programmes on television; nor is it libellous to say that a manufacturer's products are useless, as is done by consumers' associations.

A case lies for libel or slander only if an individual is named. What protection does the law afford to a group of citizens who are the collective victims of defamatory statements? One possibility is that the Director of Public Prosecutions may launch a prosecution for seditious libel but the last occasion on which this was done was in 1947

Another possibility, if the statement is made in a public place, is that the speaker might be prosecuted for using insulting language. This was done in 1937, when a fascist speaker in the East End of London was successfully prosecuted for a speech at a public meeting in which he said that 'Jews are the lice of the earth and must be exterminated from our national life'. But the police generally lean over backwards to avoid prosecuting political speakers, no matter how offensive their remarks.

The legal situation has been somewhat changed by the passage of the Race Relations Act of 1965, which makes it a criminal offence to stir up racial hatred in a public place by written or spoken words. This led to a good deal of comment arising from the ingrained British dislike of anything approaching political censorship, and *The Times* observed that

the clause can be seen to set the criminal law moving once again towards a position from which it has been retreating in Britain for about 300 years: judging the criminality of utterances by reference to their subject matter and content rather than by reference to their likely effect on public order.

(The Times, 8 April 1965)

However, the British police share the values underlying this comment, and few cases have so far been brought under this section of the Act. Of these the most publicized case was against a speaker at a public meeting who described coloured immigrants as 'niggers and wops' and made some singularly unpleasant remarks about them. At the trial the jury failed to agree, and at the retrial the speaker was acquitted.

Other restrictions on freedom of speech are the laws against blasphemy, obscenity and incitement to violence. The law against blasphemy is a relic from earlier times that is now virtually obsolete. The law against obscenity has been liberalized by the passage of the Obscene Publications Act of 1959, under which a charge of obscenity can be successfully countered by proving (with the aid of expert witnesses) that the publication has literary merit. It was on this ground that the publishers of the unexpurgated edition of *Lady Chatterley's Lover* successfully withstood a prosecution alleging that this was an obscene publication. The law against incitement to violence will be discussed below, in connection with public meetings.

Another basic liberty is that for people wishing to demonstrate their views on a political issue to march in procession bearing placards. For many years members of the labour movement have done this on May Day. In the 1930s unemployed workers drew attention to their plight by marching from the north of England to London. In the 1960s tens of thousands of people marched about the country to indicate their dislike of nuclear weapons.

People are entitled to do this because the Queen's highway exists to facilitate travel from one place to another, and as each citizen enjoys the right to use the highway it necessarily follows that 10,000 citizens have the right to do so together. They have to be careful about stopping, because that may constitute obstruction, but so long as they keep on the move they are, with certain limitations, within the law.

There are three limitations on this right, one dating from the eighteenth century and two fairly new. The first is that no processions or public meetings may be held within one mile of the Houses of Parliament while Parliament is in session. In practice it is common for meetings to be held with official permission in Trafalgar Square, but the one attempt made in recent years to move off from the square towards Parliament was briskly and effectively broken up by the police. The second limitation arises from the Public Order Act of 1936, which was passed because of the disorders caused by fascist meetings and processions in London. The Act gave any chief of police power to change the route of a procession if there was reason to think that it might otherwise lead to serious disorder, or to impose other conditions on the marchers to prevent disorder. Since then most organizers of marches have given the police notice of their intentions.

239

This limitation was strengthened by the Public Order Act of 1986, which compels organizers of processions to notify the police of their intentions a week in advance and empowers the police to ban a procession if they think it poses a threat to public order. This means that processions now take place only with police permission, but in practice this permission in invariably granted. Police officers share the general public tolerance for this form of political activity, and in addition know well that if they were to issue a ban that was ignored they would be faced with the unpleasant choice of either looking silly or having to use force themselves to stop the procession.

A similar basic freedom is that of holding political meetings. Since individuals are free to talk with one another, it follows that large numbers of them are free to gather together in a public meeting, provided they can find a place to meet. If they can hire premises, there is no problem. If they gather on the public highway, however, they will be guilty of obstruction, unless they have police permission. As motorists know to their cost, the highway is intended only for movement, and a motorist who parks in a cul-de-sac is technically guilty of obstruction although a procession of demonstrators holding up traffic on a main road is innocent of any such thing. It is commonly thought that people enjoy a legal right to hold meetings in public parks, but in fact meetings of this kind are dependent on the permission of the authorities who control the parks: the Department of the Environment in London and local authorities elsewhere. However, in practice such permission is fairly freely granted and, one way or another, groups who wish to hold a public meeting rarely find it difficult to do so.

The general principle governing public meetings is that people may say what they like provided it is not likely to lead to a breakdown of public order. If this likelihood arises, the police may ask the speaker to desist or in some circumstances they may arrest him or her. The offences with which they may be charged include disturbing the peace, inciting others to commit a breach of the peace, behaviour with intent to provoke a breach of the peace, behaviour whereby a breach of the peace is likely to be occasioned, insulting behaviour and (if they refuse a request to stop) obstructing police officers in the execution of their duty. As a form of shorthand it is convenient to group these offences under the heading of incitement to violence.

The law regarding incitement to violence is generally administered in a liberal way, though the following examples show that there is a slight area of uncertainty at the margin. In 1914 George Lansbury was arrested after a meeting at which he had urged suffragettes to continue their militant tactics and was subsequently found guilty of inciting others to commit breaches of the peace. In 1961 Bertrand Russell and other leaders of the Committee of One Hundred were condemned on the same charge when they tried to hold a meeting in Trafalgar Square without official permission, though on other occasions members of this committee advocated civil disobedience without prosecution.

Another interesting example is that of the series of fascist meetings in Dalston, north London, in 1947. These were held in a cul-de-sac with police permission, but they caused violent reactions from the audience, many of whom came to the meetings with the express intention of breaking them up. The speeches were full of abusive and provocative anti-Semitic remarks, which could be regarded as an incitement to violence when uttered in an area with some Jewish residents. But all the violence was directed towards the speakers and the police took the view that, although speakers should be prosecuted if they incite the audience to violence against a third party, they are entitled to take the risk of provoking violence against themselves. It was felt that the traditional right of uttering unpopular opinions should be defended, and in the later meetings of the series the speakers were accordingly surrounded by a cordon of policemen facing outwards towards the audience. On the other hand, in 1963 a fascist speaker in another area was successfully prosecuted for provoking a breach of the peace among an audience that was almost entirely hostile to him, and it is clear that the application of the law in this field depends very much on the attitudes of the police.

A fourth basic freedom is that of political association. There have been no restrictions on the organization of voluntary associations in Britain since the repeal of the Combination Acts in 1824. Trade union leaders had to engage in a long struggle to secure immunity from court actions over the organization of strikes that have an injurious effect on the interests of other people, but the right to form unions has not been curtailed and pressure groups and political parties have been completely free from legal restrictions. As noted in Chapter 6, political parties are not known to the law and their organization and activities are entirely untrammelled. The Communist Party was never banned, as it has been in Germany and some other democratic countries. Neither was the British Union of Fascists declared illegal, though during the last war some of the leading members of the union were interned because the government regarded their loyalty to the nation as suspect.

What is almost equally important, individual members of parties have not suffered persecution or hardship on account of their views. Britain has never seen anything like the McCarthyite period in the United States, when people were driven from their jobs and sometimes driven to suicide by the lack of tolerance for their suspected sympathies or connections (past or present) with the Communist Party. Nor would the British accept as normal a variety of practices that are so accepted in the United States, such as the screening of applicants for a wide variety of posts that could not possibly be 'classified' for security reasons, or the occasional suspension of teachers for expressing heretical views on political or religious matters.

Of course, the British government has to exercise some control over internal security. In 1948 the development of the Cold War led the government to initiate a new policy of screening civil servants in posts involving security risk. Five years later it was reported that 17,000 officials had been screened, which was rather less than 3 per cent of the total number of civil servants at that time. Of these 111 were regarded as possible risks to security and 9 were still under consideration. Of the 111, 69 were transferred to equivalent posts else-where in the civil service, 19 resigned and 'only twenty-three were dismissed, and these because their qualifications were such that they could be employed only in secret work' (Street 1963: 222). In the two years following there was only one resignation and three transfers. This is not a disturbing record, and there is no evidence or suggestion that civil servants with extreme political views suffer in their careers if they are engaged in non-secret work. Outside Whitehall, the only reported case of an individual being penalized on political grounds occurred in 1956 when a lawyer working for Imperial Chemical Industries was dismissed because the government refused to place secret contracts with the firm unless he were denied access to the secrets. The case created such a furore in Parliament and the press that it is unlikely that any similar incidents will occur.

These facts underline the general tolerance of British society, as does the unemotional way in which the British receive news that scientists or public servants have given secrets to potential enemies. The cases of the traitors Klaus Fuchs, Nunn May and Burgess and Maclean created interest, a measure of understanding and in the last case a good deal of amusement, but little or no sense of moral indignation. Maclean's family went to join him in Moscow, Fuchs was allowed to work for East Germany after he was released from prison, and Nunn May was offered a post in industrial research a few weeks before his sentence ended.

The British take their liberties and their tolerance so much for granted that they do not always realize how rare these conditions are in the world or how much they contribute to the quality of British life. They are among the most precious fruits of three centuries of political stability and security.

A fifth basic freedom is freedom from arbitrary arrest and imprisonment. This is a field in which it is difficult to be specific in short compass because of the complexity of the law and the very large number of relevant cases that could be cited. However, it is possible to establish one or two general points.

In the first place, it is a principle of British law that all persons are presumed to be innocent until they are found guilty by a court. This has various impli-cations. For instance, it implies that persons suspected of a crime should not be physically harmed by the police before they are brought to trial. The exten-sive guarantees of fair treatment by American law are of no use to those who are killed while being arrested, to say nothing of the fact that innocent pedes-trians may be killed or wounded because police bullets miss their mark. Very few incidents like this have happened in Britain because, at least until the late 1970s, British police have been unarmed. This makes them almost unique among the police forces of the world, and has been possible only because of the relative lack of violence in British society. Unfortunately, the situation changed during the 1970s. It became necessary to train special squads of police marksmen to protect embassies and airports against international terrorists, and the considerable growth in the propensity of armed robbers to open fire on the police forced the authorities to adopt the policy of issuing guns to the police in dangerous situations. At the time of writing about 20 per cent of the British police are trained marksmen, to whom guns may be issued in special circumstances on the authority of a senior officer. However, arms are not carried normally and when they are issued the police have to account for every bullet used.

Secondly, the principle implies that people should not be detained without trial. In fact, a person other than a suspected terrorist cannot legally be detained in Britain unless he or she is charged with a specific offence, and if they are then kept in custody they must be brought before a magistrate within twenty-four hours. In the great majority of cases they will then be released on bail until the time of their trial. Since November 1974 (the month when IRA bombs killed more than twenty people in a Birmingham pub) it has been possible for the police to detain suspected terrorists for questioning for up to four days without charging them, a power that was declared excessive by the European Court of Human Rights in 1988. Notwithstanding this judgment, the British government has insisted on maintaining the power, using (for the first time) its right of 'derogation' in respect of judgments by the European Court.

Thirdly, the principle implies that there should be some method whereby a person kept illegally in custody may secure his or her release. This method is the writ of *habeas corpus*, which can be issued by any High Court judge at any time, on his being informed that a person is being kept in custody without authorization. An application for such a writ takes precedence over all other business in court and application may also be made directly to a judge in chambers. This writ, incidentally, is of use not only against detention by the police but also against detention in, say, a mental home.

Another principle is that 'the Englishman's home is his castle'. The police are entitled to enter a house only if they have a search warrant after making a sworn statement regarding the need for it, unless they are in hot pursuit of a criminal. If the police exceed their powers they can be sued for damages. Thus, in the case of *Peters* v. *Shaw* (1965) a merry-go-round proprietor sued a policeman who had entered his caravan without permission while looking for persons suspected of committing a felony on the fairground; the proprietor was awarded damages and costs against the policeman (*The Times*, 6 May 1965). In another case a policeman entered a garage to inquire about a lorry there, which had previously been obstructing the highway. The owner ordered the policeman off the premises, but instead of leaving immediately he started to produce a document to prove he was a police officer. The owner then ejected him by force, was prosecuted by the policeman for assault, but was acquitted because the policeman had no right to stay on the premises after he had been told to leave (Street 1963: 24).

Another principle is the right to a fair trial before an impartial judge or jury. British judges are appointed for life from the ranks of successful barristers, so that they cannot be subjected to any kind of political pressure. The right to trial by jury has been firmly established for a very long time, and juries are independent bodies who cannot easily be bullied or persuaded into taking a decision that they do not consider right. There have been numerous cases, from the eighteenth century onwards, of juries acquitting an accused person in spite of the strongest advice given by the judge that the facts pointed towards a conviction. Further provisions designed to ensure a fair trial are the provision of legal aid to persons who cannot afford to pay for representation by counsel and the right of appeal to the Court of Appeals and, with permission, to the House of Lords (where the case is heard by a small group of Law Lords appointed for this purpose).

Of course the police have some powers not granted to ordinary citizens, but these are strictly limited. They have no right, for instance, to take people to a police station or detain them there for questioning, against their will, unless they arrest them. The papers frequently report that a person has spent some hours at a police station 'assisting the police with their inquiries', but this happens either because the individual wishes to co-operate with the police, or because they think it will pay them to appear to co-operate with the police, or because they do not know their rights and were not told of them. It should not be thought that British police behaviour is always beyond criticism when dealing with suspected criminals.

The difficult period is that between the time when a suspect is taken to the police station for questioning and the time when he or she appears in court. In this period the behaviour of the police is supposed to conform to a pattern codified in the Police and Criminal Evidence Act of 1982. According to this ideal pattern, the police must permit suspects to call a lawyer unless this is likely to interfere with the administration of justice; must respect their right not to answer questions unless they freely choose to do so; must ensure that they are provided with reasonable comfort and refreshments; must not tell the suspects that the police believe them to be guilty; must not use threats or promises or any undue pressure to induce the suspects to make a statement; and must give the suspects a clear warning that any statement they make may be taken down and used in evidence.

The police have to deal with some pretty rough characters in circumstances of considerable tension, and it would be surprising if this code of conduct were always followed exactly. In practice it is clear that the police sometimes trade on the ignorance of the people they examine and sometimes engage in verbal bullying or cajolery in order to secure information, or even a confession, on which they can base a charge. Occasionally they also resort to intimidation and the milder forms of violence. Moreover, there are grounds for believing that police behaviour has deteriorated in recent years. Given the general increase in violence during the 1970s and since, this is not surprising. The police now have to cope with violent political demonstrations, armed robbers and terrorists bent on murder. There have been far more injuries and deaths among police officers than previous generations had to accept. In any assessment of police behaviour it is essential to realize that the great majority of the police are not heroes or saints, not bullies or pigs and not disembodied instruments of the law, but men and women doing a difficult job whose performance is inevitably influenced by the cumulative impact of their experiences.

The rules of police conduct should not therefore be taken as an infallible guide to practice. Their value is that they constitute a norm to which appeals can be made. If the police deviate from them, the matter may be raised in court. If the defence can show that a statement was involuntary in the sense that it was induced by threats or promises, the jury is apt to dismiss the statement as being of no value; and if it is the basis of the prosecution's case the result is likely to be an acquittal.

Some recent restrictions

In the 1990s increased public anxiety about what was perceived as a decline in law and order led the Home Secretary to strengthen police powers by several measures, culminating in the Criminal Justice and Public Order Act of 1994. The police were given authority to tap private telephones without having to go through the formalities that were previously required to get permission for this, and to stop and search people in the street without having to show that they had 'reasonable cause' to suspect them of carrying drugs or stolen goods. They were also authorized to stop and if necessary arrest political demonstrators who were interfering with the rights and amenities of citizens, such as environmentalists who blocked traffic to prevent new roads being built and opponents of hunting who had the habit of upsetting the hunt by spraying scent in the nostrils of foxhounds. Another power given to them was that of moving on, and if necessary arresting, the tens of thousands of unemployed people who move around the country in converted vans and buses and gather in large encampments that annoy local residents by their noise and refuse.

These are sweeping powers, but their implementation depends entirely on the attitudes of police and magistrates, who tend to be more tolerant than the minister himself was. Shortly after the 1994 Act was passed, a sizeable body of protesters gathered in the garden of the private house of the Home Secretary and clambered all over his roof, without hindrance by the local police. They were present to stop actual damage to the minister's property, but they did not feel it right to stop the demonstration. A few country police forces have come down hard on hunt saboteurs, but most have not. A senior police officer in Surrey said that 'We are coming under pressure from the hunt to use the Act to finish off the sabs, but we don't think it will. We think it will antagonise them and make the situation worse.' A few police forces have made groups of 'travellers' move on, but most have not. In the first year of the Act 545 arrests were made but they led to only twenty-eight successful prosecutions. When magistrates did convict people they were unwilling to impose heavy punishments. The Act provides for fines of up to £2,500 and imprisonment of up to three months, but the maximum fine imposed on the twenty-eight offenders was £200 and nobody was jailed (see *The Economist*, 11 November 1995). These figures seem to confirm that the attachment to freedom and tolerance is deeply entrenched in British society.

The police and the judiciary

The police deserve a further word, because in any advanced society they constitute what might be called the sharp end of the state, whose activities constantly bring citizens up against the fact of political authority. One deals with the tax inspector once a year, but one encounters police officers on the street almost every day. Two particular reasons for considering the organization and behaviour of the police are that the British system of policing differs from the systems of most other democracies and that the conduct of the police is more a matter of controversy in the 1990s than at any previous time in the twentieth century.

In Chapter 14 it was observed that the British system of local government lies somewhere between that of France, which is highly centralized, and that of the United States, which is highly decentralized. The same observation can be made about the British system of policing. France has thirteen national police forces, each specialized in function and all ultimately controlled by the Minister of the Interior. Local branches of these forces are supervised by departmental prefects, who are ministry officials. In contrast, the United States has a fairly small national force, the Federal Bureau of Investigation, which deals with only a limited category of offences. The great bulk of police work in America is handled by fifty state forces and about 40,000 city and county forces, each of them controlled by the representative political authorities of the area concerned, such as the city or county council.

Britain, on the other hand, has no national police force but fifty-one largely autonomous regional forces. Operational control of each force is in the hands of the Chief Constable (or Commissioner of Police in Greater London), though there is also a regional police authority that has certain limited administrative powers. In Greater London the Home Secretary is the police authority.

The organization of each force has to comply with national regulations, drawn up by the Home Secretary in consultation with the Police Council (a body composed of representatives of the police authorities and the police themselves). Expensive pieces of equipment, such as a national computerized records system, are provided by the Home Office.

Each police authority is made up partly of people nominated by the local authorities in the region (who comprise two-thirds of the authority's members) and partly of local magistrates (who comprise the remaining third). The powers of the authority are to appoint the Chief Constable and his or her immediate deputies (subject to the approval of the Home Office); to approve the budget submitted by the Chief Constable; to provide buildings and equipment for the force; to call on the Chief Constable to submit reports on policing in the area (subject to their right to refuse a report if they think it unnecessary for the proper use of the authority's supervisory powers); and to request the retirement of a Chief Constable on grounds of inefficiency (subject to the agreement of the Home Secretary).

These powers are strictly limited, as the underlying principle of police organization is that the Chief Constable in each area should be autonomous in all operational matters. The function of the police, it is constantly asserted, is to enforce the law and maintain the Queen's peace, not to serve the interests of local politicians or the national government. The fact that area police authorities have some control over the budget does not permit them to acquire a degree of operational control through this means. Staffing and salary levels are effectively controlled by the Home Office, and negotiations between Chief Constables and police authorities over budgetary matters relate to more marginal questions, such as expenditure on vehicles, office equipment and uniforms.

This autonomy of the police is fiercely defended by senior police officers, who believe it to be one of the great strengths of the system that the police are both independent of political control and known by the public to have this independence. An interesting example occurred in Manchester in 1981. Following extensive riots in the city, the police authority asked the Chief Constable to attend a meeting of the authority to explain the actions of the police in dealing with the riots and to answer questions. The Chief Constable refused, on the ground that this would compromise his autonomy in operational matters. He submitted a written report instead.

How do the police use the very considerable discretion that their autonomy gives them? According to Sir Robert Mark, Commissioner of the Metropolitan Police from 1972 to 1977, the police 'reflect society as a whole' and 'discharge the communal will, not that of any government minister, mayor or public official' (Mark 1977: 12). It is to be presumed that they understand the communal will through their experience and intuition. A better way of putting this might be to say that the police try to reflect current social values, partly because they regard this as their duty and partly because they wish to maintain what is commonly called 'the British police advantage', namely that they enjoy the sympathy and support of the majority of the population.

Certainly the police reflect social values, which are probably those of the majority, in the priority that they give to dealing with differing types of offence. For instance, they give high priority to dealing with cases of blackmail, personal violence, robbery and the distribution of hard drugs; low priority to sexual offences, the sale of pornographic literature, under-age drinking and motoring offences other than those leading to personal injury. Being anxious not to alienate the motoring public, they rarely prosecute people for speeding. When radar traps are set, they are often preceded by a sign at the side of the road giving advance notice of them to watchful drivers. Breathalyser tests are conducted, but motorists are not stopped unless some other offence (such as driving without due care) is suspected. Illegal parking has to be punished to avoid congestion, but the main responsibility for this has been hived off to a separate body of officials known as traffic wardens, who are notably less popular than the police.

The police are also careful not to intervene in disputes that can be categorized as private. They are extremely reluctant to intervene in family disputes. Unlike the police in many other countries, they refuse to clear university campuses of students engaged in sit-ins and other demonstrations. They do not keep order at sporting events unless hired to do so (at so much an hour) by the sports club involved. They try not to become involved in industrial disputes, and have been reluctant to deal with mass picketing except when it is likely to provoke personal violence.

By exercising their discretion in these and similar ways, the British police were until recently very successful in maintaining public trust and support. An international survey conducted in 1959 and 1960 showed that 74 per cent of British people expected that the police would give serious consideration to their point of view in an encounter, compared with 59 per cent in West Germany, 56 per cent in the United States, 35 per cent in Italy and 12 per cent in Mexico. Moreover, Britain was the only one of these countries in which the expectations were just as favourable among people who left school at 14 or 15 as they were among the better educated (Almond and Verba 1965: 66). In 1972–5 an elaborate study sponsored by the London School of Economics showed that over 90 per cent of adults in London, and over 80 per cent of teenagers, declared that they respected, trusted and liked the police.

More recently, the police have been put under pressure by an increase in crime, an increase in the incidence of violence in society, and several revelations of police misconduct. In 1984 a national MORI survey revealed that only 61 per cent of people 'generally trusted' the police to tell the truth; a sharp decrease in the figure of 90 per cent for the early 1970s, though a much higher figure than that yielded for trust of trade union officials (18 per cent) or government ministers (16 per cent) (see *Sunday Times*, 8 January 1984). In 1989 a MORI poll showed that only 43 per cent of the public had 'a great deal of respect' for the police, while 41 per cent had 'mixed feelings' and 14 per cent had 'little respect'.

Since 1989, public confidence in both the police and the courts has suffered a series of blows. First, in 1989, it emerged that six IRA suspects convicted of setting bombs that killed twenty-one people in Birmingham pubs were actually innocent, their convictions having been secured on the basis of forensic evidence that, years later, was shown to be unreliable, plus confessions that had been secured by improper means. Immediately following this, reviews conducted by the police and by Home Office lawyers led to three other convictions being overturned, one involving IRA suspects said to have planted a bomb in a pub in Guildford, one of an Irish family said to have operated a bomb factory, and one of a black man (recently released from prison after serving nine years for killing a policeman) who was said to have murdered another policeman during a riot. In each case the police were said to have relied too much on circumstantial evidence or to have been careless in their procedures. A further shock was delivered when it emerged that the West Midlands Serious Crime Squad, responsible for Birmingham and district, had planted evidence or fabricated confessions in twenty-three other cases in the 1980s, not involving Irish defendants or members of ethnic minorities but simply as a short cut to obtain convictions of suspects whom the police felt sure were guilty. The Squad was immediately wound up, but questions remained about court procedures that had denied justice to the defendants.

Following these revelations, a Royal Commission on Justice was appointed in 1991, with very wide-ranging terms of reference, under the chairmanship of a distinguished sociologist. Much was expected of this Commission, including the possibility that it would recommend the abolition of the adversarial system of court procedure and its replacement by a version of the system developed in France and used in most other European countries, where the defendant is interrogated by a panel of judges as well as by counsel for the prosecution and defence. In this system a trial is not regarded as a competition between prosecution and defence, with the judge trying to ensure fair play, but as an opportunity for all concerned to discover and reveal the truth. When the Commission's report was published in 1993, however, it was not nearly so radical, though it recommended a large number of smaller reforms.

The most surprising of its recommendations was the establishment of an entirely new body, not to be composed of judges, that could sit on top of the existing hierarchy of courts to hear appeals against criminal convictions for serious crimes. The government accepted this, and in 1996 they set up the Criminal Cases Review Commission, chaired not by a lawyer but by a distinguished university head whose own disciplines were engineering and physics. It was reported in April 1997 that 251 appeals for review had been received in the first week of operation of the commission, 210 of them from the files of the Home Office, and that hundreds more were expected in the following twelve months. At the time of writing the Commission has not developed clear criteria for distinguishing between important appeals and frivolous or outdated ones, nor has it been able to appoint enough skilled investigators and lawyers to reduce the backlog quickly. It is therefore too early to assess the overall effects of this new institution of government, whose work seems likely to arouse one controversy after another. If it is able to overturn wrongful convictions it will be a very valuable instrument of justice, but the more successful it is then the more likely it is to further undermine public confidence in the police and the judicial system.

The judiciary in England and Wales comprises about 30,000 magistrates and 500 judges. The magistrates are unpaid and are not qualified lawyers, though they receive a certain amount of legal training after appointment. They are volunteers drawn from the local community, usually nominated by civic bodies or local branches of the political parties, and formally appointed by the Lord Chancellor. They normally sit in panels of three and the only general criticism that has been made of their work is that the severity of the sentences they pass varies rather widely from area to area. They try minor offences themselves and conduct the preliminary hearing of more major offences, normally the day after the arrest is made. Provided that the magistrates are satisfied that there is a case to answer, the defendant is committed to trial at a higher court, with or without bail.

The judges are appointed, by a rather secretive process, from the ranks of successful trial lawyers. The appointment is made by the Lord Chancellor on the advice of a panel of senior (but anonymous) judges. No politician or civil servant is a member of this panel, so the process is essentially one of co-option. The appointment is for life, to ensure the independence of the judges from political or other pressures. Only one judge has ever been dismissed for corruption and that was in 1830.

The independence of judges has not been questioned, and they have hardly ever been accused of political bias. Questions have been raised, however, about their unrepresentative character in terms of social class and lifestyle. The overwhelming majority of them (perhaps 90 per cent) come from prosperous upper- or upper-middle-class families and all of them have enjoyed large incomes as successful lawyers before being appointed to the bench. Another, though more muted, criticism has been that they are overwhelmingly male and white. However, it is not at all clear how this state of affairs might be changed. Nobody wants judicial appointments to be made on a partisan basis, as would be apt to happen if a committee of Parliament were to be given power in this field. Nobody wants judges to be appointed because of their sex or ethnicity, which would weaken their authority. But the whole method of appointment might possibly come under review if judges make a series of unpopular decisions when they acquire the responsibility of hearing cases under the European Convention of Human Rights.

The independence of judges from political pressure has been emphasized in recent years by their refusal to modify their sentencing to conform with strong requests from the minister responsible for justice, the Home Secretary. In the 1980s a liberal Home Secretary, Leon Brittan, urged them to give shorter jail sentences in view of the overcrowding of jails and the evidence that imprisonment very rarely reformed the prisoners. The judges resented this interference with their discretion and refused to modify their policies. In the 1990s a less liberal Home Secretary, Michael Howard, urged them to give longer sentences and attempted to persuade Parliament to emulate the Californian innovation of prescribing minimum sentences, perhaps including imprisonment for life, after repeated convictions for certain categories of crime. The Lord Chief Justice made a vigorous public attack on this proposal, following which the House of Lords watered down the proposed legislation.

Another recent development is the growth of judicial activism, in the form of an increased readiness to challenge the behaviour of ministers and even the decisions of Parliament. The British tradition has always been that the courts should accept ministerial discretion in applying the law unless it was blatantly unreasonable. In the 1990s this has changed. In 1993 the House of Lords ruled that, despite the existing state of the law, prisoners who allege that they had been ill-treated by warders could sue the Home Office for compensation. In 1993 also, the Lords ruled that the Inland Revenue must repay a building society £76 million in overpaid taxes, despite the fact that it had no statutory obligation to make any repayments. In 1994 the High Court ruled that the Foreign Secretary's decision to provide £234 million over fifteen years from the overseas aid budget to help build a dam in Malaysia was illegal, as the dam would be of dubious economic benefit to that country and would damage its environment. The money had been promised as part of a deal whereby Malaysia would buy very large quantities of British arms, so it had to be paid, but the court's decision meant that it had to come from other government funds, without damage to the budget earmarked for overseas aid. In 1995 the Lords ruled that the Home Secretary had gone beyond his powers in changing the rules regarding the payment of compensation for criminal injuries without consulting Parliament. There were twelve other cases between 1992 and 1997 in which the courts overturned decisions by Michael Howard, the Home Secretary.

An even more innovative example of judicial activism occurred in 1995, when in three successive court cases the judges refused to accept the legitimacy of an Act passed by Parliament. At issue was the decision to refuse welfare benefits to immigrants who had applied for political asylum after they had secured entry to the country for some other stated purpose. The most senior judge justified the ruling by stating that

> Parliament cannot have intended a significant number of genuine asylum seekers to be impaled on the horns of so intolerable a dilemma: the need to abandon their claims to refugee status or alternatively to maintain them as best they can but in a state of utter destitution.

As Parliament had actually had just that intention, as a way of forcing asylum seekers to state their claims at the port of entry, this ruling was in fact a refusal by the judges to accept the sovereignty of parliament that has been a basic principal of the British constitution for three centuries. They took this drastic step because they clearly believed that Britain needed a Bill of Rights to check parliamentary power if it violated the reasonable rights of the individual.

The country is now about to get such a provision, as the Labour government elected in 1997 has promised to incorporate the European Convention for the Protection of Human Rights into domestic law. This convention was drawn up in the late 1940s and ratified by the British Parliament in 1950, though Britain did not follow the example of most other states that ratified the convention, which promptly added its provisions to their own law. The European

Court of Human Rights was soon established to investigate cases of alleged violation brought by citizens of those countries that permitted their citizens to take cases to the court. Britain, with its longstanding commitment to the sovereignty of Parliament and its dislike of abstract principles, was not among these for several years, but in 1966 it was agreed that British residents could take cases directly to the European Court if they so wished.

Not many have done so over the years, but by 1997 the Court had found that governmental agencies had violated the European Convention on thirty-seven occasions. These decisions were not binding, for the European Court (which has no connection with the European Union) has no power to enforce its judgements, but they created a strong moral and political obligation for the British government to rectify whatever had caused the adverse judgments. Two of them caused interesting dilemmas.

One was that the rights of parents had been violated when their son had been subjected to corporal punishment in school without his parents' permission. The problem was that educational authorities and teachers' unions in Britain believed strongly that school discipline could not be maintained unless teachers had the possibility of resorting to corporal punishment in extreme cases of bad behaviour. After much discussion, the minister proposed and the House of Commons agreed that all parents of children in state schools should be asked to sign a statement indicating whether they did or did not wish their children to be exposed to the possibility of corporal punishment. However, the House of Lords rejected this proposal and substituted an outright ban on corporal punishment in state schools.

The other case involved Ernest Saunders, who as chief executive of Guinness had organized a brilliant manipulation of stock market prices that enabled his firm to buy a controlling interest in the Distillers Company (the largest producer of Scotch whisky) at far less than a fair price. The manipulation was investigated by Department of Trade inspectors, who forced Saunders to open his books and answer all their questions on pain of imprisonment if he refused. Transcripts of the interviews were subsequently used by the prosecution in his subsequent criminal trial for fraud, at which he was sentenced to five years in jail. After his release, Saunders appealed to the European Court on the ground that he had been deprived of a fair hearing because his right of silence had not been respected, and the Court upheld his appeal in September 1994. The government believes that Department of Trade inspectors have to have this power of compulsion, which the police do not have, in order to investigate complicated cases of fraud, but, since the ruling, evidence secured in this way has not been used in criminal prosecutions.

Another decision that surprised British authorities was made in 1995, when the Court ruled that the killing of three IRA terrorists by SAS men, in Gibraltar in 1988, had been unlawful, on the ground that better advance intelligence should have made it possible for the terrorists to be arrested rather than killed. The decision was reached by a vote of ten judges to nine, and the Court refused to award damages to the families of the dead terrorists because it acknowledged that the killings had foiled a bombing plot. The decision was therefore both marginal and equivocal, but it infuriated British politicians and led some who disliked the idea of a Bill of Rights in principle to accept that, since the country was stuck with this one, it had better be implemented by British judges than by foreigners. There are, however, constitutional problems about incorporating the European Convention into British law, which will be mentioned in Chapter 18.

The citizen and the administration

The rights so far discussed in this chapter are essentially rights to be left alone by agents of the state. The development of social and economic legislation in the twentieth century has given citizens rights of a different kind: the right to a pension, to benefits while unemployed or sick, to housing at a controlled or subsidized rent, to tax relief in respect of some kinds of expenditure. The disputes about rights of this kind could not appropriately be settled by the ordinary courts, for a variety of reasons. First, the courts would be hopelessly clogged by the vast number of cases that arise. Secondly, the citizen needs a remedy that is quicker and cheaper than court procedure makes possible; it would be useless for an unemployed person to have to hire a lawyer to make a claim for a few pounds' benefit. Thirdly, the issues are administrative rather than judicial; it is desirable for those hearing the case to have some technical knowledge and it is often thought appropriate for them to be guided by depart-mental policy when reaching decisions.

For these reasons, disputes of this kind go not to the ordinary courts but to a variety of administrative tribunals. It is almost impossible to generalize about the composition and procedure of these tribunals because they are so varied. Some are chaired by lawyers, others by ordinary administrators. Some contain members appointed to represent interested groups such as trade unions or employers, while others do not. At some the appellant may be represented by a lawyer, at others he or she may bring a friend but not a lawyer.

This kind of variation is confusing but may be inevitable if each body is organized to deal with a particular set of problems. By and large, the tribunals are quick and cheap, and the people who have most to do with them are not dissatisfied. Tribunals are obliged to inform appellants of the reasons for their decisions and also of the possibilities for further appeal. The most common situation is that it is possible to appeal to a court on points of law but further appeals on questions of fact or interpretation have to go to another adminis-trative tribunal or to the minister himself. As this second kind of possibility violates the legal principle that no person should be a judge in their own case, the government was persuaded in 1965 to establish a new channel whereby aggrieved citizens can appeal against the decisions of civil servants.

This new channel is an adaptation of the system long used in Denmark and Sweden whereby an officer known as an Ombudsman can investigate allegations of maladministration. In Britain the officer is entitled the Parliamentary Commissioner for Administration, the difference between this position and that of the Scandinavian Ombudsman being that the Commissioner acts only on the request of an MP. Citizens wishing to complain must therefore find an MP (not necessarily their own) who is willing to pass the matter on to the Commissioner. The latter has power to call for oral or written evidence and to examine departmental files. If they find that the complaint is justified and the department responds to their invitation to put the matter right, that is the end of the matter. If the department does not so respond, the Commissioner reports the whole matter to Parliament, which has a select committee to consider such reports.

This constitutional innovation is almost universally regarded as having been successful. The work of the Commissioner has led to a significant extension of the rights of the citizen in relation to the administration. As a consequence of this success it was decided in the 1970s to appoint commissioners with similar powers to deal with complaints about the National Health Service and the activities of local authorities.

Another innovation was introduced in 1991, on the personal initiative of John Major. This was the Citizen's Charter, designed to improve the delivery of public services, with particular reference to education, health services, public housing and transport.

In education, it was provided that there should be regular and independent inspection of all schools, with the results reported to parents. The test and examination results achieved by pupils are now summarized in a standardized way so as to facilitate comparison between schools, and the summaries published so that parents have more information than hitherto about the performance of schools in their neighbourhood. Advice is available to parents about how to move their children from one school to another.

In health care, all family doctors are required to produce pamphlets on the services they offer; the procedure for changing doctors has been simplified; doctors are required to carry out free health checks on all new patients and annual health checks on patients over 75. Comparative information on the performance of hospitals is publicized; and out-patients given individual appointments instead of all being called at nine o'clock and then treated in turn over the next three hours.

Tenants of council housing have been given extended rights to repair their own houses or flats, and encouraged to exercise their right, through a ballot, to effect the transfer of their properties out of the hands of municipal and county councils into the hands of housing associations or, in some circumstances, private landlords.

In the field of transport, the Charter had led to somewhat cleaner trains and the provision of more motorway service areas. It also led the Ministry of Transport to set up a 'hot line' by which motorists could complain directly to the ministry if they were annoyed by the existence of apparently unnecessary red plastic cones blocking traffic lanes to facilitate road repairs that were not being carried out. After three years the Ministry had to admit that the 17,700 complaints received on this score had led to cones being moved only five times, and this statistic produced a degree of public cynicism. All in all, however, the Citizen's Charter has to be counted as a moderate success in reducing the frustrations of citizens in relation to the bureaucracy.

Further reading

For the legal basis of British civil liberties see Robertson (1989) *Freedom, the Individual and the Law*; for a practical guide see Hurwitt and Thornton (1989) *Civil Liberty: The NCCL Guide*; for the position of the Parliamentary Commissioner for Administration see Stacey (1971) *The British Ombudsman*; for a discussion of the criminal justice system see Reiner and Cross (1991) *Beyond Law and Order: Criminal Justice Policy and Politics into the 1990s*; on the role of judges see Waldron (1990) *The Law*; for warnings about judicial activism see Rozenberg (1996) *Trial of Strength*.

18

MERITS AND PROBLEMS OF BRITISH GOVERNMENT

It seems appropriate to conclude this book with a brief discussion of the merits and contemporary problems of British government. This chapter will deal in turn with the representative process, the constitutional questions that have recently emerged and the question of Britain's future as a member of the European Union.

The representative process

If the British representative process is compared with those of other liberal democracies, it comes out rather well. There is, in the first place, a high level of public participation in politics. Party membership figures are higher than those in most other democracies. The Conservative Party's membership (until the 1990s) has been equalled only by the German Social Democratic Party and what used to be called the Italian Communist Party. Turn-out figures at national elections are also quite high, being significantly higher than the average turn-out for an American Presidential election and over twice as high as the turn-out in mid-term Congressional elections. The parties produce a vast number of policy statements, pamphlets and notes for speakers on a regular basis and not just during election campaigns, so that the level of political knowledge among party supporters is reasonably high. Both main parties have ideological discussion and pressure groups within their ranks, the Bow Group and the Monday Club in the Conservative Party, the Campaign for Social Democracy and other variously named groups on the Labour side.

General elections are fairly conducted, with strict (and low) expenditure limits that prevent wealth being a significant advantage. Television advertising cannot be bought, and both publicly owned and commercial television channels operate under orders to give equal coverage to each of the main parties during campaigns. All parties publish election manifestos setting out the policies they would promote if they were to be given a parliamentary majority, and campaigning focuses on these proposals, and on the existing government's record, with very little attention being devoted to questions of personality. In the twentieth century Britain has never had a general election remotely like the 1992 Presidential election in America, where the central feature of the Republican campaign was an attack on alleged defects of character in the Democratic candidate.

Membership of pressure groups is high, the financial resources of the groups are (as noted in Chapter 7) rarely a dominant factor in their success or failure, and spontaneous public campaigns can be effective. The campaigns about the location of a third airport for London have been mentioned in Chapter 7. Another example was the success of the group called Anti-Apartheid in inducing the government to ban sporting contests with South Africa for many years. Yet another was the remarkable success of a public demonstration in London, organized at only two or three days' notice, which persuaded the government in October 1992 to put into cold storage the plans it had announced only a week earlier to close down half of the country's coal mines.

Another feature of British political life that can be counted an asset is the way in which the parliamentary system provides for the recruitment of politicians and party leaders. Bright young people can and do get into Parliament at an early age, often in their late twenties or early thirties. However, they normally have to serve an apprenticeship of many years in Parliament before they achieve high office, so that their skills have been honed and their qualities publicly tested before they make it. There is no parallel in Britain to the situation in the United States, where the Presidency can go to a retired general like Eisenhower or a nationally unknown politician like Carter. The United States does not have a parliamentary system, of course, but Canada is an example of a democracy that has a parliamentary system and signally fails to use it for the selection and training of leaders. Of Canadian Prime Ministers since 1945, Pearson and Mulroney had no parliamentary experience when they took office, while Mackenzie King had less than a year and Trudeau only seventeen months. The case for the British tradition in this respect is not only that leaders will have proved themselves in the cut and thrust of debate, but also that long experience of dealing with the problems of constituents will have given them an understanding of the way in which ordinary citizens have to cope with the impact of government on their personal lives.

Parliament itself is generally, and probably rightly, held in high esteem in Britain. Debates are lively, with speeches that are (by comparative standards) short, informal, pointed and frequently interrupted. Backbenchers do not act as rubber stamps for their leaders' proposals, as they do in Canada and some other democracies. In the past there have been very reasonable complaints about the lack of facilities provided for MPs and the lack of specialized committees to review policy, but since 1979 these complaints have been met. The House of Commons has to be given high marks and even the House of Lords does a reasonably useful job, as noted in Chapter 4.

There is a very reasonable theory that in an ideal two-party system the policies of the parties should converge towards the centre, being driven there by the need to appeal to uncommitted voters. In the later 1970s and early 1980s the British parties greatly diverged from this model, but in the late 1990s they have returned to it. The fear expressed in the late 1980s and early 1990s that Britain was becoming a state of single-party dominance was banished by the 1997 election. The fear that the new Labour government would be gravely weakened by the inexperience of its leaders after eighteen years in opposition has been banished by its performance in its first months of power.

For this last matter senior civil servants must take much credit. The British tradition is that, when a forthcoming general election seems likely to produce a change of government, top civil servants hold a series of discussions with opposition leaders, designed partly to brief the latter on the problems they will face if they take office and partly to inform civil servants of the policy priorities of the opposition. In consequence, the transfer of power is always extremely smooth. The new ministers will know what problems they will face and senior civil servants will be well prepared to assist their new masters to introduce new policies and to draft the legislation needed to implement them.

This tradition was perfectly reflected in the transfer of power in 1997. Within a few days of taking office, the new Chancellor of the Exchequer announced an emphatic change by giving the Bank of England complete independence from the government. This reform had been thoroughly discussed with Treasury officials before the election, and the new Chancellor had also prepared himself for it by holding private discussions with the head of the Federal Reserve Bank in Washington. Within six weeks of taking office, the new Prime Minister had a mastery of the issues surrounding Britain's role in the European Union that enabled him to protect British interests superbly well in the Amsterdam conference of heads of government. In all these ways, the British system of government works excellently. There are, however, a number of constitutional problems it now faces.

Constitutional problems

Britain's unwritten constitution has served the country well for three centuries, having been adapted to changing needs by a long series of *ad hoc* measures and quiet changes of practice. However, since the 1970s new questions and problems have developed that have led the majority of respondents in public opinion polls to express a preference for the adoption of a written constitution with a specified procedure for its amendment. There is no agreed method by which a written constitution could be drafted and adopted, and this sentiment reflects public disquiet with aspects of the present constitutional arrangements rather than an actual movement for reform, but the reasons for disquiet deserve brief mention.

To begin at the top, in constitutional terms, there is disquiet about the role and privileges of the monarchy. While there is no republican movement as such, there exist varied concerns about the expense of the monarchy, the possible powers of the monarch in a constitutional crisis, and the suitability of

Prince Charles as the next king. The trouble is that there is no official forum in which these concerns can be discussed. A fair number of MPs would like them to be raised and discussed in the House of Commons, but it is very difficult to get them on to the agenda there. Questions in Parliament can deal with almost any imaginable topic apart from the monarchy, for one of the written rules governing Question Time is that 'No question can be put which brings the name of the Sovereign or the influence of the Crown directly before Parliament, or which casts reflections upon the Sovereign or the royal family' (quoted in Franklin and Norris 1993: 67).

Another topic is the reform of the House of Lords proposed in the 1997 Labour Party manifesto. The plan is first to remove the hereditary peers from the House, then to amend the system of appointing life peers, and subsequently to appoint a committee of both Houses of Parliament to consider and propose further possible reforms. In terms of practical politics this seems quite a workable plan, but in terms of constitutional theory it is odd that a temporary majority in the lower house should be able to remove two-thirds of the members of the upper house without any special procedure being required. It could not happen in any other democracy.

Other proposals in the manifesto, under the heading of devolution, are odder still. In 1979 a detailed plan for a Scottish Assembly was put to Scottish voters in a referendum, got a bare majority of 33 to 31 per cent of the electorate, but failed to receive the support of 40 per cent as required by the Act. A similar proposal for a Welsh Assembly, albeit with fewer powers, was rejected by four-fifths of the Welsh voters. Now it is planned to revive the proposal for a Scottish Assembly, but with two referendums in Scotland, the first on outline plans and the second (if there is an affirmative vote in the first) on the crucial question of whether the Assembly should or should not have taxing powers. No special majority will be required in either. Then there would be a referendum about the proposal to create a Welsh Assembly and later still there would be an opportunity for the various regions of England (however defined) to decide by local referendums whether they wanted regional assemblies also. There would be no opportunity for the people of England to decide whether they want an English Assembly, which would be the only logical counterpart to Scottish and Welsh Assemblies. This has apparently been ruled out by party leaders.

If this entire scheme were to be put into practice the result would be that the United Kingdom would be converted into a quasi-federation in which the powers of the component units would be widely unequal. Leaving aside Northern Ireland, Scotland would have extensive powers, Wales fewer powers, the regions of England that voted for assemblies would have fewer still, and the other regions of England would be directly governed from London. Such a system would obviously be a constitutional monstrosity, but that is what is envisaged.

In practice, it seems rather unlikely that this will come about. If voting in the 1979 referendums and more recent polls are a guide, the Scots would vote for a Scottish Assembly but the Welsh and the English regions would not follow suit. However, that outcome would also be highly controversial. If there were no difference in the powers of Scottish MPs at Westminster, this would mean that Scottish MPs could help to determine the nature of education in English schools but English MPs would have no power to control or even discuss the nature of education in Scottish schools, which would be a matter reserved to the Scottish Assembly. Other topics would be in the same position. This would be unfair to the English, but is probably unavoidable. If Scottish MPs in the UK Parliament were unable to vote on matters controlled by the Scottish Assembly, the result might be that a Labour government with an overall majority would find itself in a minority when Scottish MPs were excluded from the vote, and this would be constitutionally unworkable. It is by no means an extreme hypothesis, for of the seven post-war elections that have yielded Labour victories, only three (in 1945, 1966 and 1997) have produced Labour majorities in England.

While there is no obvious way of preventing this anomaly, there is a clear precedent for reducing its unfairness. When the Northern Irish Parliament was functioning, from 1922 to 1972, that province's representation in the UK Parliament was reduced to two-thirds of the number of seats that its population entitled it to. This has been regarded as a workable compromise and has been supported by all British parties. If the same formula were applied to Scotland this would give it thirty-nine seats, as under present electoral arrangements Scotland is seriously over-represented in Parliament. In the government's White Paper of June 1997 it was accepted that there should be some reduction in the number of Scottish seats, but recommended that an exact proposal should be left to a new Scottish boundary commission, to be appointed in 1999.

Another constitutional dilemma is presented by the proposal to incorporate the European Convention on Human Rights into British law. The problem about this is that, under present British rules, no Parliament has the power to bind its successors. It follows that a later Act which infringed the Convention on Human Rights would have to take precedence over the Act which adopted the Convention. This could be largely overcome by copying the 'notwith-standing' rule added to the Canadian constitution in 1982, when the Canadian Charter of Rights was adopted. Under this rule, any of the eleven Canadian legislatures can add a clause to a Bill stating that it must take effect notwith-standing the Charter of Rights. If no such clause is added, the implementation of the legislation can be invalidated by the courts if they decide that it infringes the Charter. This arrangement raised eyebrows at first, but the clause has rarely been used except in Quebec and is not now regarded as controversial. If adopted in Britain it would deal with the problem of parliamentary sovereignty, but it would not have the finality that it has in Canada, as it would still presumably be possible for an aggrieved person to appeal to the European Court in Strasbourg on the ground that a British Act infringed the European convention, notwithstanding the notwithstanding clause that had been added to the Act.

It should also be noted that the incorporation of the Convention into British law would increase the power of British judges and bring them more frequently into conflict with the administration, a development that might raise questions about the appointment of judges.

Britain's future in the European Union

This is not only one of the most important questions now facing the country, but also one of the most confusing questions. The basic problem is that the development from the original Common Market established in 1956 to the quasi-federal union now being promoted by its leading members has been an uneven and complicated development, very poorly understood by most citizens. There has been nothing remotely like the Philadelphia Convention of 1787, in which elected representatives from the thirteen states came together and drew up plans for a federal constitution in more than three months of open debate, with the proceedings being published. There followed several more months of open debate in the various states, conducted by speeches, pamphlets and articles, the overall result being a democratic and lasting constitution established by a democratic process.

In contrast, the promoters of European integration have always preferred to keep the debates in the hands of political and administrative élites, with no serious attempt to involve the general public. In his last weeks as Foreign Secretary, Malcolm Rifkind told a Dutch audience on 19 March 1997 that 'Europe does not just belong to politicians' and it was high time to involve the people by having a clear debate about the choices facing the continent. Unfortunately, he continued, he had been told that 'it is too late for such a fundamental debate: that it took place, or should have taken place, several years ago; that the decisions have been taken'. This was an entirely reasonable complaint, as was his subsequent complaint that the proponents of further integration were being unrealistic in their refusal to admit that what they proposed was a federal union, a United States of Europe. The consequence of all this is that the citizens of the fifteen states are being propelled towards membership of an untidy kind of federal system without their general agreement. Polls show that less than half of them believe that the European Union is, in general terms, a good thing, and it is safe to conclude that a much smaller proportion believe that a federal Europe would be desirable. It would perhaps be too derogatory to describe the whole process as 'federalism by stealth', but it seems reasonable to describe it as 'quasi-federalism by elitist manipulation'.

However this may be, there are still important choices to be made by the British government. As withdrawal from the European Union does not appear to be a sensible option, the question of sovereignty is somewhat outdated. It seems to this author that a much more crucial question is that of the extent to which the emerging system of government within the Union can be described as democratic. For a system to qualify for that description, three conditions need to be met, as follows:

1   The process of decision-making should be well understood and reasonably open.
2   There should be free and constant debate so that the public can influence decisions, either directly or through the law of anticipated reactions, which will affect a government wishing to be re-elected.
3   There should in fact be free and fairly frequent elections so that the people can choose who will govern them.

By these criteria, the main problem of the European Union is that its decision-making procedures are so complex that relatively few electors understand them. The steps by which new laws and regulations are made can be summarized as follows:

1   Proposed laws are drafted by the European Commission, meeting behind closed doors.
2   The drafts are sent both to the European Parliament and to the Council of Ministers, but the Parliament is little more than a forum for debate and on the few occasions when it has objected to a proposal its objections have nearly all been over-ruled by the Council of Ministers.
3   Nine-tenths of the proposals sent to the Council never actually reach it, as they are decided by COREPER, the committee of ambassadors and bureaucrats that is in almost permanent session, and there is an increasing tendency for the most problematic of the remaining 10 per cent to be referred by the Council to the biannual meeting of the heads of government.
4   The remaining proposals (say about 8 per cent of the total) are settled by the ministers, either by consensus or by a veto or by weighted majority voting, but there are three different formulae to determine what constitutes a majority, depending on the nature of the issue, and the meetings of the Council are not reported.

A relevant question is that of how many electors understand this process well enough to be able to exert an influence on it or (in the case of lawyers) to advise their clients how to do so. In each member state this knowledgeable group will be made up of several hundred politicians, a larger number of senior civil servants, and specialized lawyers, journalists, business executives and academics. The best speculative estimate this author can give is that, in present circumstances, this would probably come to a total of between 10,000 and 20,000 in each of the fifteen states. Taking the more generous figure, this would add up to a grand total of about 300,000 potential political actors, which is certainly an appreciable number but only a little more than one tenth of 1 per cent of the total electorate of about 250 million.

If it is also appreciated that the only body for which there is direct voting, namely the European Parliament, has by far the least power of the various institutions involved, it has to be concluded that the European Union is far from meeting the conventional criteria of what constitutes a democratic system of government. It is certainly not a dictatorial system, and it might be described as well-intentioned, economically beneficial, open to pressure from organized groups, and respectful of individual liberties. At the same time, it is also highly élitist, highly bureaucratic and highly secretive. It is an entirely novel kind of political entity, and it is inevitable that most British voters should find it bewildering and somewhat alien. It seems likely to continue to play a large and uncertain place in British political debates in the coming years.

Further reading

For a good account of Britain's constitutional problems by a lawyer see Oliver (1991) *Government in the United Kingdom*.

Appendix

NOTES ON THE POLITICS OF NORTHERN IRELAND

(1) The character of politics in Northern Ireland differs sharply from the character of politics in the remainder of the United Kingdom. While in Britain power alternates between the two main parties, in Northern Ireland the Ulster Unionist Party enjoyed power continuously from 1922 to 1972. In Britain, religion is of little political significance whereas in Northern Ireland it dominates the political scene. In Britain the main opposition parties are completely loyal to the constitutional system whereas in Northern Ireland their aim is to transform or overthrow it. Above all, British politics has been largely free from violence whereas Northern Ireland has been the scene of violent protests, political assassinations and intermittent guerrilla warfare for the past seventy years.

(2) The extraordinary character of Irish politics can be explained only in historical terms. While political attitudes in other countries are influenced by history, political attitudes in Ireland seem to be imprisoned by it. For this reason some of the main events in Irish political history will be outlined in the following paragraphs. For reasons of space, the treatment will be sketchy, and paragraphs will be numbered to emphasize this.

(3) Ireland was dominated by England from the twelfth century to the twentieth century. There was never an independent Irish state until 1921. There were local communities and local rulers, provinces and provincial governors, but the sovereign of Ireland – in so far as it could be said to have a sovereign – was the King of England. The Roman Catholic religion of the Irish people was not affected by the Reformation, but in the late sixteenth and seventeenth centuries a substantial number of Protestant settlers migrated to Ireland from Britain, settling mainly in the northern part of the country.

(4) In 1641 the 'Ulster Rising' occurred. This was a revolt of the native Irish against British government and against the Protestant settlers in the northern counties (nine of which constituted the Province of Ulster). It was a bloody affair, and troops had to be sent from England to suppress it. The Catholic King Charles was weakened doubly by this episode. In the first place, the rebellion increased anti-Catholic feelings in England. Secondly, the need to finance a military expedition forced Charles to convene Parliament, which set in train the events leading to the English Civil War.

(5) After the Civil War Cromwell's army took their revenge against the Irish. In particular, they attacked the Catholic Church, killing priests and despoiling the churches. However, after the Restoration in 1660 there was a reversal of fortunes. Ireland became a Roman Catholic country once more, an Irish army was recruited that was almost entirely Catholic in composition, and all Protestant judges, officials and aldermen were thrown out of office.

(6) In the bloodless revolution of 1688 James II fled from England without putting up a fight against William of Orange, his invading army and his English supporters. However, in Ireland only the Protestants recognized William and Mary as legitimate rulers. In March 1689 James landed in Ireland from France and took command of the Irish army, and what was in effect a war for the English throne was then fought out on Irish soil. An attack on Londonderry was frustrated by the courage of the Protestant minority in the city – an event that has been celebrated annually ever since by the 'Apprentice Boys' March' – and on 1 July 1690 James came face to face with William in the Battle of the Boyne. In this famous encounter James's Irish and French troops were defeated by a mixed force of Ulster Protestants, Scots, Englishmen, Dutchmen and Danes and this victory ensured the supremacy of the Protestant religion in Britain.

(7) From 1690 to 1800 Ireland was ruled by its Protestant minority through a Parliament in Dublin. This Parliament was notable for the 'Penal Laws' with which it discriminated against Roman Catholics. Under these laws, Catholics were not allowed to bear arms, Catholic priests were forbidden to celebrate mass, and Catholics were not permitted to send children abroad to be educated (to stop them going to continental seminaries). In an attempt to help Protestant landowners extend their estates, Catholics were not permitted to buy land, except on a lease of up to thirty-one years, and were not permitted to bequeath their land by will. When a Catholic landowner died his land was divided equally between all his sons, which in a country of large families ensured the fragmentation of Catholic estates. And, as a final twist of the knife, it was decreed that if the eldest son of a Catholic landowner joined the Protestant Church he would immediately be given ownership of the whole estate, with his father remaining simply as tenant for life and his brothers disinherited.

Edmund Burke said that this period degraded the character of the Irish Catholic peasant, and an Irish historian has elaborated the same view:

> His religion made him an outlaw ... and whatever was inflicted on him he must bear, for where could he look for redress? To his landlord? Almost invariably an alien conqueror. To the law? Not when every person connected with the law, from the jailer to the judge, was a Protestant ...
>
> In these conditions suspicion of the law, of the ministers of the law and of all established authority worked into the very nerves and blood of the Irish peasant, and since the law did not give him justice he set

up his own law. The secret societies which have been the curse of
Ireland became widespread . . . dissimulation became a moral necessity
and evasion of the law the duty of every God-fearing Catholic.

(Woodham-Smith 1962: 27–8)

(8) In 1800 Ireland was made an integral part of the United Kingdom and
a sizeable contingent of Irish MPs arrived at Westminster. The Penal Laws
were gradually abolished and Catholics achieved equality of status with
Protestants. The last decade of the nineteenth century saw the growth of the
Irish nationalist movement, and the question of Irish Home Rule became a
lively issue in British politics.

(9) In 1912 Asquith's Liberal government introduced a Home Rule Bill that
was designed to give a substantial measure of internal self-government to the
whole of Ireland, under the control of an Irish government and Parliament in
Dublin. The Ulster Protestants objected passionately to this proposal, being
totally unwilling to accept the rule of what would inevitably be a Roman
Catholic regime. As loyal subjects of the Crown they claimed that the United
Kingdom government had no right to place them at the mercy of their historic
enemies. In this they had the support of British Conservative leaders and large
sections of British public opinion. An armed fighting force, under the title of
the Ulster Volunteers, was established to resist the proposed change by force
and it is possible that a civil war would have developed had not the outbreak
of war with Germany given the British government the opportunity to put the
whole reform into cold storage.

(10) Frustrated by these events, the Irish nationalists turned from moderate
leaders to extremists. In 1916 a group of the latter staged the 'Easter Rising' in
Dublin, seized the main Post Office, and proclaimed an Irish Republic. The rebellion was quickly put down by British troops, and sixteen of its leaders were
executed for treason. The executions were, however, a gift to the nationalist
cause, for the dead men were regarded as martyrs, their role was commemorated
by Irish poets, and the nationalist movement gained immensely in strength. In
1918 the nationalists successfully sabotaged a British attempt to impose conscription on Ireland and in 1919 they launched a general insurrection.

(11) In 1921, after nearly two years of fighting, a treaty was concluded
between the British government and the nationalist leaders whereby the twenty-
six mainly Catholic counties of Ireland were granted political independence as
the Irish Free State, while the six predominantly Protestant counties of the
north-east remained as part of the United Kingdom, though with their own
Parliament in Belfast to legislate on domestic affairs. In view of the militant
determination of the Protestants this partition of the country was almost
inevitable; the British government could hardly expel a million loyal citizens
from the United Kingdom against their wishes, and any attempt to do so
would have led to a continuing civil war in Ireland between Protestants and
Catholics.

(12) Unfortunately, the Province of Northern Ireland was (and is) by no means homogeneous in its population. In 1921, 34 per cent of the inhabitants were Catholics; in 1951 the proportion was 35 per cent; and in 1991 it had risen to 38 per cent. The two communities are highly segregated. For the most part, they are served by different schools, which are equally supported by government funds. The schools used to teach history in different ways, so that children were socialized into conflict. They play different games, so that Catholic and Protestant children rarely meet on the sports field. There is considerable segregation in areas of residence and in clubs and pubs visited. There is little intermarriage, which is condemned by both communities. Looked at in a sociological perspective, Northern Ireland is more like a bi-tribal society than a society divided between two branches of the Christian religion. Like tribes, each community in Northern Ireland has its own myths and heroes, its own songs and its own symbols – the orange and green sashes, the Union Jack and the Irish tricolour. The Protestants also have ritual marches, which by celebrating past victories are designed to rub salt in the wounds of the other side.

(13) In an open society (i.e. one not governed on totalitarian lines) that contains more than one religious or ethnic community there are only three possible patterns of political behaviour. One pattern may be called the politics of integration, in which the differences between religious and ethnic groups have no direct bearing on the competition for political power. A good example is England, where there are only a handful of parliamentary constituencies in which a candidate's religion has any perceptible effect on his electoral support (these all being constituencies with a considerable number of Irish electors). A second pattern is best called the politics of accommodation. In this kind of system a deliberate and conscious attempt is made to ensure that each community or group has a reasonable share of political power. In Canada, for instance, there is a firm convention that, no matter which party holds office, the federal cabinet should contain so many French-speaking Catholics, at least one English-speaking Catholic and representatives from each province of the country. The third pattern is the politics of group dominance, in which each community or group is associated with its own political party and a policy of 'winner takes all' is adopted.

(14) From the beginning, politics in Northern Ireland followed the pattern of group dominance. The Ulster Unionist Party, which has close relations with a Protestant society called the Orange Order, won every general election and made no attempt to share any of its power with Catholics. At the same time, Catholic politicians made no attempt to win the support of Protestant voters and deepened the antagonism of the Unionists by refusing to recognize the legitimacy of the Belfast regime. For fifty years Northern Ireland had a political system in which a permanent majority nursed their power and a permanent minority nursed their grievances.

Until 1973 the Protestants were always more united than their opponents. The Ulster Unionist Party was well organized and well financed, benefited from the fruits of office and had the advantage of a clear objective: to maintain the constitutional position. This was advantageous to Northern Ireland in some ways, for over a whole range of social affairs the Belfast Parliament had the option of either adopting British legislation or introducing its own variations. By normally adopting British legislation on social and economic affairs the Unionists not only deprived their opponents of the possibility of appealing to the voters with a programme of progressive social policies but also ensured a very heavy concealed subsidy from the British taxpayer.

The Catholics, in contrast, have always been somewhat divided. It is demoralizing to be in a permanent minority and not surprising that Catholics have differed among themselves over tactics. Should they, for instance: (a) fight elections and if successful put up a vigorous opposition in Parliament; (b) fight elections but if successful boycott Parliament; (c) boycott elections; (d) offer passive resistance to the Belfast regime; (e) take every step, including violence and terrorism, to erode the authority of Belfast; (f) engage in guerrilla warfare with the hope of internationalizing the conflict and securing the intervention of the Irish Republic? All six tactics have had their supporters and these differences of view have fragmented the political activities of the Catholics. This has been reflected in the multiplicity of political organizations supported by the Catholic community, which in the postwar period have included the Nationalist Party, the Republican Party, the Social Democratic and Labour Party (SDLP), the Civil Rights Association and both the Official and Provisional wings of Sinn Fein.

(15) On the most important issue, all the Catholic parties have been united; they have all committed themselves to the unity of Ireland as the only proper solution to the problems of their community. However, on this matter they have not represented the views of the majority of Catholic electors, as revealed by public opinion surveys. The Catholics of Northern Ireland, though on average slightly poorer than their Protestant neighbours, are nevertheless better off in material terms than they would be in the Irish Republic. Northern incomes are swollen by large British subsidies to industry and the social services. It is probably for this reason that only a minority of Catholic electors have favoured an end to partition. A 1979 survey by the Economic and Social Research Institute of Dublin showed that 39 per cent of Catholics in Northern Ireland favoured unification while 49 per cent preferred to stay in the United Kingdom (O'Brien 1980: 81). The knowledge that Catholic political leaders have misrepresented the views of the Catholic community on this vital issue increases the contempt with which these leaders are regarded by Protestant leaders and strengthens the resolve of the latter not to share political power with the former.

(16) In 1969 Northern Ireland was plunged into political violence. This was started by conflict between Catholic demonstrators and Protestant mobs and has been continued since 1970 by a campaign of terror waged by the provisional wing of the Irish Republican Army (IRA). This underground army, with seventy years of intermittent violence and guerrilla warfare to its credit, is the

most experienced revolutionary group now operating in the world. Its objects are to induce the British to abandon Northern Ireland, to secure the unification of that province with the Republic, and then to overthrow the government of the Republic. It has been an illegal organization in the Republic since 1931, but it has commanded such a mixture of sympathy and fear among the public that successful prosecutions have been rare and in practice it is tolerated by the Dublin government. It is well financed from a variety of sources and is well supplied with modern arms from overseas, its chief recent supplier being the government of Libya.

Since 1969 political violence in Northern Ireland, though consisting mainly of bombings and shootings committed by the IRA, has also involved the assassination of numerous Catholics by Protestant paramilitary forces. Although the British Army has stationed between 10,000 and 30,000 troops there to help the police maintain security, the casualties between 1969 and 1997 amounted to just over 3,200 deaths and 37,000 people injured. In terms of the ratio of deaths to population, this is equivalent to over half a million deaths in the United States.

(17) Because the British government felt that it had to take charge of policy in Northern Ireland once the army was heavily engaged there, and also because it was dissatisfied with the advice on security issues emanating from the Northern Ireland government, that government and the Northern Ireland Parliament were abruptly suspended in 1972. Since then the province has been governed directly from London, apart from the period between January and May 1974 when there was a power-sharing executive in Belfast. Policy is mainly controlled by the Secretary of State for Northern Ireland, who is a member of the British Cabinet and commutes between London and Belfast. The policies adopted by the British government can be summarized under four headings, as follows:

1   An attempt to remedy the legitimate grievances of the Catholic minority.
2   An attempt to minimize violence and pacify the province.
3   An attempt to persuade Protestant and Catholic politicians in the province to share executive power in a Belfast administration responsible for local issues.
4   An attempt to secure the co-operation of the government of the Irish Republic in fighting terrorism and improving the political atmosphere in the North.

(18) British efforts to remedy Catholic grievances began in 1969. The local government franchise was extended to all adult citizens, instead of being dependent on a property qualification. The municipal government of Londonderry, which had been controlled by Protestants as a result of electoral gerrymandering, was transferred to a bipartisan commission. The control of public housing was taken out of the hands of municipalities, which had engaged in sectarian favouritism in allocating tenancies, and given to a non-sectarian province-wide

Housing Executive. The Royal Ulster Constabulary was put under the control of an English Chief Constable and turned gradually into a much more professional force than it had been. The police reserve force, greatly distrusted by Catholics because of its Protestant bias, was disbanded.

The response to these reforms was very discouraging. In London the reforms were regarded as sweeping, rapid and a clear demonstration of the government's fairness. Many Catholic leaders, on the other hand, regarded the reforms as belated concessions made in response to violence, and drew the conclusion that militancy paid dividends. New grievances were quickly discovered. The Catholic members of the Londonderry Development Commission refused to take part in administration. The army, at first welcomed by Catholics as a protection against Protestant mobs, was soon being denounced as an instrument of British oppression. The attempt to remedy Catholic grievances did little or nothing to improve relationships.

(19) The attempt to pacify the province met with an early reversal. In 1971 the British decided (at the suggestion of the Northern Ireland government) that IRA suspects should be interned without trial, as an answer to IRA intimidation of juries that made successful prosecutions difficult to achieve. This measure infuriated the Catholic community and proved to be a sad mistake. Although several hundred IRA members were interned, they were quickly replaced by new recruits and IRA violence became more widespread and indiscriminate as the months went by. The death rate from political violence increased to 467 in 1972. However, the security forces learned from this blunder and by careful intelligence and improved techniques they were able to reduce the violence to more acceptable levels by 1976. In the 1980s the death rate was reduced further, to under a hundred a year. Whereas Belfast was in a state of siege in the early 1970s, with barricades and body searches every few yards in the city centre, daily life in the city has now returned to a more normal condition.

However, it is not possible to defeat the IRA completely, so long as it can attract recruits and provide its members with training, weapons, money and safe houses. As underground armies go, it is a very professional outfit, now organized on a cellular basis to frustrate the efforts of British intelligence. Every defeat produces martyrs who can be compared with the original martyrs of the Easter Rising and serve as an incentive for new recruits to join. Having committed itself to two quite unattainable objectives in the unification of Ireland followed by a revolution in Dublin, the IRA will always have a cause to go on fighting for. It would be foolish to regard it as other than a permanent actor in Northern Irish politics.

(20) Several attempts have been made to persuade Protestant and Catholic politicians to share executive power, so far with only transitory success. In 1973 the Heath government persuaded the Ulster Unionist leader of the time, Brian Faulkner, to form a government of both Protestant and Catholic ministers to take charge of domestic affairs in the province and to answer to a newly elected

Northern Ireland Assembly. Faulkner was denounced by many of his senior Unionist colleagues and his action split the Ulster Unionist Party. Nevertheless, the new government took office in January 1974 and ran the internal affairs of the province, apart from security issues which remained under London control, until May 1974. In that month the province was crippled by a general strike called by the Ulster Workers' Council in protest against the power-sharing arrangement. After electricity and water supplies had been interrupted, and when the sewerage workers threatened to block the sewerage system, Faulkner resigned and the whole government collapsed. The Assembly was then suspended and the militant Protestant groups celebrated their victory.

(21) The government of the Irish Republic is another actor in the ongoing drama of Northern Irish politics. On the one hand, the Republic is a bad neighbour, providing a sanctuary for terrorists and repeatedly refusing to extradite persons wanted for terrorist offences, even if these include murder. On the other hand, the Catholic minority in the North tend to look to Dublin for assistance and the British government needs the help of the Dublin government in dealing with the North.

Various negotiations between London and Dublin produced results that were either negligible or short-lived, until in 1985 the Anglo-Irish Agreement was signed by Margaret Thatcher and the Irish Prime Minister. This Agreement has two main provisions, one of symbolic importance and the other of practical value. The first of these provisions is a declaration by the British government that Northern Ireland could be united with the Republic if a majority of its citizens voted for this course of action, together with a declaration by the Irish government that it would only want unity with the North if this were desired by a majority of northerners. There is no early prospect of the northerners voting for unity, but this provision has the great merit of making clear that the question is entirely one for the citizens of the province to settle and is not an issue between the British and Irish governments.

The other main provision of the Anglo-Irish Agreement was the establishment of an Intergovernmental Conference, composed of senior members of the British and Irish governments, to meet regularly in Northern Ireland to discuss ways of improving the political situation there. The Conference makes recommendations to the British government that the latter may accept or reject. In practice this liaison body serves as a valuable channel through which proposals emanating from the Catholic minority in the North can be supported by representatives of the Republic and passed to London for consideration. Some of these proposals have been rejected, but most have been acted upon. In consequence, Catholics are now permitted to fly the Irish tricolour and to display other flags and emblems as they wish; there are improved procedures for dealing with complaints about police behaviour; and new measures have been adopted to eliminate religious discrimination in employment.

Under the Fair Employment Act of 1989 all employers with over ten employees must register with the Fair Employment Commission, must submit an annual return showing the religious composition of the workplace, must keep a record of all job applications, and must take affirmative action measures if either religious community has less than a fair share of the jobs. An employer who fails to do these things may be barred from receiving any public sector contracts, may be fined up to £30,000, and may have to pay heavy damages to any potential employees who successfully claim that they have been discriminated against. An employer who ignores an order from the Fair Employment Tribunal may be prosecuted in the High Court and fined an unlimited amount or committed to prison.

Yet another provision of the Agreement is that if Unionist and Catholic politicians can agree to share executive power in respect of a particular field of policy – say education or public health – then that field can be excluded from the deliberations of the Intergovernmental Conference. This provision is essentially an incentive to Protestant leaders to move towards a form of political accommodation for the government of the province, as successive British governments have wanted from 1973 onwards. So far there is no sign of the incentive producing results.

(22) In 1994 the British and Irish governments launched an unexpected peace initiative. Their intelligence services had reported in the spring that the IRA was experiencing recruitment problems and some loss of morale. John Major and Albert Reynolds, the Irish Prime Minister, produced a joint statement that they would encourage all-party negotiations for a new settlement in the North if paramilitary forces would commit themselves to a ceasefire. The Protestant paramilitants agreed, providing the IRA would agree, and the IRA did so on 31 August. It was agreed between Major and the Ulster Unionist leader that any recommendations by the negotiating body would have to be put to a binding referendum in Northern Ireland.

This development received enthusiastic support from President Clinton and early in 1995 he invited Gerry Adams, the Sinn Fein leader, to visit him for a talk in the White House. This move infuriated the British government, who regarded it as unduly partisan and knew that Adams would use the visit to gain further financial support from Irish-American sympathizers with the republican cause. Progress lagged in 1995 as the Ulster Unionists demanded that, before negotiations began, the IRA should begin to decommission their offensive weapons, such as Semtex and detonators, as an indication that they had permanently abandoned terrorist tactics. The British government had no choice but to agree, though making it clear that decommissioning should apply to paramilitary groups on both sides, but the IRA refused to comply with the demand.

(23) This deadlock continued until November 1995, when, just two days before Clinton flew over for visits to London and Belfast, Major and the new Irish Prime Minister, John Bruton, announced that they proposed to invite an independent body of distinguished outsiders to advise on the whole issue of decommissioning. Clinton's nominee, retired Senator George Mitchell, agreed to chair this body, and the other members were the retired head of the Canadian army and a retired Finnish Prime Minister. This committee, known as the

International Body on Decommissioning, worked very quickly, with intensive interviews with all parties in Belfast, Dublin and London. On 22 January 1996 their report was published, with the following main recommendations:

1 That all parties to the forthcoming negotiations should 'affirm their absolute and total commitment to democratic and exclusively peaceful means of resolving political issues'.
2 That they should agree to the total disarmament of all paramilitary organizations, this disarmament to be verifiable by an independent commission, and to be engaged in on the basis of legal understandings by both British and Irish governments that nobody would be prosecuted for possessing the arms and that they would not be subjected to forensic examination.
3 That, as nobody interviewed thought it likely that arms would, in practice, be handed in before the negotiations started, it should be agreed that the decommissioning process should be carried out simultaneously with the negotiations.

These recommendations were accepted by both British and Irish governments and were commended by the US government.

(24) On 9 February the IRA gave their response to this plan by detonating a large bomb in the docklands area of London that killed two people and injured forty-three. This unilateral breach of the ceasefire led the British and Irish governments to break off their contacts with Sinn Fein and announce in a joint statement that Sinn Fein could not be included in the forthcoming negotiations unless the ceasefire were restored. The IRA's next move was to detonate an even larger bomb in Manchester's largest shopping centre, which injured 200 people who had to be rushed to hospital.

In the face of these actions, the negotiations began in Belfast in June 1996 without any Sinn Fein representatives. The three members of the International Body on Decommissioning were renamed the Independent Chairmen, and patiently presided over endless discussions of procedure, decommissioning and the agenda that made virtually no progress towards agreement on substantive issues. In March 1997 it was decided by the Chairmen to delay the next meeting of the negotiating body until after the British election.

The Minister for Northern Ireland in the new Labour government, Marjorie (Mo) Mowlam, decided to make a further effort to persuade the IRA to resume the ceasefire, to which end she arranged for three meetings between her officials and IRA representatives. However, after the second meeting the IRA again demonstrated their rejection of the peace process by murdering two community policemen who were not involved in security but were simply patrolling the shopping centre of a small town, on foot, to deal with such offences as shoplifting or the theft of car radios. The third meeting was immediately cancelled.

(25) The only way to understand the policies of the present IRA is in terms of its history. It is in fact a very small body of dedicated revolutionaries, the

product of three splits in the republican movement which have each led the majority of its supporters to accept a degree of compromise, with the current remainder having an attitude that might be called extremism cubed. The first split occurred at the end of the armed insurrection against British rule that lasted from 1919 to 1921. Facing defeat in 1921, the military leader, Michael Collins, went to London to negotiate a peace treaty which he and his colleagues signed. When this was presented to the new Irish assembly for ratification, a sizeable minority, led by Eamon de Valera, walked out because Collins had not been able to secure an all-Ireland republic but had been forced to accept partition, an oath of allegiance to the Crown, and the use by the Royal Navy of four west coast Irish ports to protect convoys in case of war. The minority launched a civil war that killed more people than the insurrection had done, but resulted in victory for the new Irish government. The losers nursed their wounds and boycotted elections.

The second split occurred in 1926, when de Valera organized his supporters into a new political party called Fianna Fail ('Soldiers of Destiny' in English) to compete in elections. Soldiers of Destiny is a peculiar name for a political party, and it was very much an old comrades' association. It was very successful in the 1927 election, gaining over 600,000 votes, and in 1932 became the largest party, putting de Valera into power as Prime Minister for the next twenty-seven years. In that capacity, he was able to secure all republican objectives apart from the incorporation of the North, so that a new constitution was adopted, the concession regarding the Irish ports was cancelled, the country became a republic and remained neutral in the Second World War. Nearly all his supporters abandoned violence, apart from a handful of extremists who vowed to continue the fight. They were dedicated fanatics, willing to risk their liberty and their lives fighting for a lost cause, knowing that if they were killed they would join the honoured ranks of martyrs. To quite a large extent, the modern IRA, which really dates from 1926, is a family affair, with teenage members convicted of terrorist crimes saying that they did it to take revenge on the British for having killed or imprisoned one of their grandfathers or great-uncles. In January 1939, the IRA actually issued a formal declaration of war on the United Kingdom, which has never been revoked.

The third split occurred in 1969/70, when the IRA leadership, resigned to a long and patient struggle until the conditions were ripe for change, was repudiated by an even more militant group of members who vowed to use terrorist methods to destabilize the political situation. This group, calling themselves the Provisional IRA to emphasize their commitment to fulfil the aims of the Provisional Government proclaimed on the first day of the 1916 Easter Rising in Dublin, have taken over the organization. They see no point in peaceful negotiations with their enemies, because they know that these cannot lead to their first and main objective, the unification of Ireland. Their seventeen-month ceasefire was little more than a tactical move.

(26) It does not follow from this that no progress at all has been made in the 1990s. Violence will continue, but in three ways the situation is better now than it was in the 1980s. First, the seventeen months of ceasefire brought large investments to Northern Ireland from overseas. New industrial plants and hotels were built, unemployment was reduced, and there was a dramatic rise in revenues from the tourist trade. Secondly, the end of the ceasefire, which had so raised hopes of a permanent peace, discredited the IRA and Sinn Fein in the eyes of Washington, and perhaps even led to the disillusionment of Irish-American supporters elsewhere.

Thirdly, there have been educational reforms that give promise of a reduction in communal hatred among the rising generation. The government has encouraged the development of non-denominational schools, and although this has been a slow development because nearly all schools were owned by the churches, there were by 1997 twenty-five new integrated schools in operation, all working happily without the playground violence and other problems that had been predicted by sceptics. Perhaps more important, all the churches and educational authorities have been persuaded to accept a Northern Irish version of the new national curriculum that the British government has promoted for all state-supported schools. This means that all children in the North now study the same history syllabus, instead of being socialized into conflict by studying a nationalist version of history in Catholic schools and a unionist version in Protestant schools. In some areas there is evidence of an emerging generation gap, with teenagers reluctant or unwilling to accept the rigid sectarian attitudes of their parents and grandparents. It is only scattered evidence, but it gives hope for the future.

Further reading

For a brief guide to the history of Anglo-Irish relations see Birch (1977) *Political Integration and Disintegration in the British Isles*, chs. 4 and 5; for the best analysis of politics in Northern Ireland up to the violence of 1969 see Rose (1971) *Governing Without Consensus*; for shorter but more up-to-date analyses see Arthur (1984) *Government and Politics of Northern Ireland* and Arthur and Jeffery (1988) *Northern Ireland Since 1968*; for a fascinating essay on the triangular relationship between the peoples of Ireland, Ulster and Britain see O'Brien (1980) *Neighbours*.

BIBLIOGRAPHY

This bibliography includes only the books, articles, reports and papers that have been mentioned in the text or in the lists of further reading.

Alderman, G. (1984) *Pressure Groups and Government in Great Britain* (New York: Longman).

Alexander, A. (1982) *Local Government in Britain since Reorganization* (London: Allen & Unwin).

Almond, G. and Verba, S. (1965) *The Civic Culture* (Boston, Mass.: Little, Brown).

Anderson, M., den Boer, M. and Miller, G. (1994) 'European citizenship and cooperation in justice and home affairs', in A. Duff, J. Pinder and R. Pryce, *Maastricht and Beyond* (London: Routledge).

Arthur, P. (1984) *Government and Politics of Northern Ireland*, 2nd edn (London: Longman).

Arthur, P. and Jeffery, K. (1988) *Northern Ireland since 1968* (Oxford: Blackwell).

Baldwin, R. and Kinsey, R. (1982) *Police Powers and Politics* (London: Quartet).

Barber, J. (1991) *The Prime Minister since 1945* (Oxford: Blackwell).

Barker, A. and Wilson, G. K. (1997) 'Whitehall's disobedient ministers? Senior officials' potential resistance to ministers in British government departments', *British Journal of Political Science*, 27: 223–46.

Barzini, L. (1983) *The Impossible Europeans* (London: Weidenfeld & Nicolson).

Beer, S. H. (1982) *Britain against Itself* (New York: Norton).

Belson, W. A. (1975) *The Public and the Police* (London: Harper & Row).

Benewick, R. J., Birch, A. H., Blumler, J. G. and Ewbank, A. (1969) 'The floating voter and the liberal theory of representation', *Political Studies*, 17: 175–95.

Bennett, C. I. (1992) *Regulating Privacy* (Ithaca, NY: Cornell University Press).

Bevins, R. (1965) *The Greasy Pole* (London: Hodder & Stoughton).

Birch, A. H (1964) *Representative and Responsible Government* (London: Allen & Unwin).

—— (1977) *Political Integration and Disintegration in the British Isles* (London: Allen & Unwin).

—— (1984) 'Overload, ungovernability and delegitimation: the theories and the British case', *British Journal of Political Science*, 14: 135–60.

Blackstone, W. (1809) *Commentary on the Laws of England* [1765], 15th edn (Oxford: Clarendon Press).

Blondel, J. (1963) *Voters, Parties and Leaders* (Harmondsworth: Penguin).

Bogdanor, V. (ed.) (1983) *Liberal Party Politics* (Oxford: Clarendon Press).

Bonham, J. (1954) *The Middle Class Vote* (London: Faber).

Borthwick, R. (1979) 'Questions and debates', in S. A. Walkland (ed.), *The House of Commons in the Twentieth Century* (Oxford: Oxford University Press).

Brown, R. G. S. and Steel, D. R. (1979) *The Administrative Process in Britain*, 2nd edn (London: Methuen).

Buck, P. W. (1963) *Amateurs and Professionals in British Politics* (Chicago, Ill.: Chicago University Press).

Budge, I., McKay, D., Marsh, D., Page, E., Rhodes, R., Robertson, D., Slater, M. and Wilson, G. (1983) *The New British Political System* (London: Longman).

Bulpitt, J. (1983) *Territory and Power in the United Kingdom*, 9th edn (Manchester: Manchester University Press).

Burch, M. and Moran, M. (1985) 'The changing British political élite, 1945–1983', *Parliamentary Affairs*, 38: 1–15.

Butler, D. (1983) *Governing Without a Majority* (London: Collins).

—— (1989) *British General Elections since 1945* (Oxford: Blackwell).

Butler, D. and Kavanagh, D. (1984) *The British General Election of 1983* (London: Macmillan).

—— (1992) *The British General Election of 1992* (London: Macmillan).

Butler, D. and Stokes, D. (1974) *Political Change in Britain*, 2nd edn (London: Macmillan).

Butler, D., Adonis, A. and Travers, T. (1994) *Failure in British Government: The Politics of the Poll Tax* (Oxford: Oxford University Press).

Carrington, Lord (1988) *Reflect on Things Past* (London: Collins).

Carstairs, C. and Ware, R. (eds) (1991) *Parliament and International Relations* (Milton Keynes: Open University Press).

Chapman, B. (1963) *British Government Observed* (London: Allen & Unwin).

Chapman, R. (1970) *The Higher Civil Service in Britain* (London: Constable).

The Civil Service Code (1995) (London: HMSO).

Clarke, M. (1988) 'The policy-making process', in M. Smith, S. Smith and B. White (eds), *British Foreign Policy* (London: Unwin Hyman), pp. 71–95.

Crewe, I. (1996) '1979–1996', in A. Seldon (ed.), *How Tory Governments Fall* (London: Fontana).

Crewe, I. and King, A. (1995) *S.D.P.* (Oxford: Oxford University Press).

Crick, B. (1970) *The Reform of Parliament*, 2nd edn (London: Weidenfeld & Nicolson).

Criddle, B. (1992) 'MPs and candidates', in D. Butler and D. Kavanagh, *The British General Election of 1992* (London: Macmillan).

Crouch, C. (1979) *The Politics of Industrial Relations* (Glasgow: Fontana).

—— (1982) 'The peculiar relationship: the party and the unions', in D. Kavanagh, *The Politics of the Labour Party* (London: Allen & Unwin), pp. 171–90.

Dale, H. E. (1941) *The Higher Civil Service of Great Britain* (Oxford: Oxford University Press).

Dowding, K. (1995) *The Civil Service* (London: Routledge).

Dearlove, J. (1979) *The Reorganization of British Local Government* (Cambridge: Cambridge University Press).

Drewry, G. (ed.) (1985) *The New Select Committees* (Oxford: Clarendon Press).

Drewry, G. and Butcher, T. (1988) *The Civil Service Today* (Oxford: Blackwell).

Drucker, H. (1979) *Doctrine and Ethos in the Labour Party* (London: Allen & Unwin).

Duff, A., Pinder, J. and Pryce, R. (1994) *Maastricht and Beyond* (London: Routledge).

Dunleavy, P. and Husbands, C. T. (1984) 'The social basis of British electoral alignments in 1983', unpublished paper presented to the annual conference of the UK Political Studies Association.

—— (1985) *British Democracy at the Crossroads* (London: Allen & Unwin).

Dunleavy, P. and Rhodes, R. A. W. (1983) 'Beyond Whitehall', in H. Drucker, P. Dunleavy, A. Gamble and G. Peele (eds), *Developments in British Politics* (London: Macmillan).

Edwards, G. and Nuttall, S. (1994) 'Common foreign and security policy', in A. Duff, J. Pinder and R. Pryce, *Maastricht and Beyond* (London: Routledge).

Elcock, H. J. (1982) *Local Government* (London: Methuen).

Ewing, K. (1987) *The Funding of Political Parties in Britain* (Cambridge: Cambridge University Press).

Finer, S. E. (1956) 'The individual responsibility of ministers', *Public Administration*, 34: 377–96.

—— (1966) *Anonymous Empire*, 2nd edn (London: Pall Mall Press).

Franklin, M. (1990) *Britain's Future in Europe* (London: Pinter).

Franklin, M. and Norton, P. (eds) (1993) *Parliamentary Questions* (Oxford: Clarendon Press).

Freedman, L. and Clarke, M. (eds) (1991) *Britain in the World* (Cambridge: Cambridge University Press).

Fry, G. K. (1984) 'The attack on the Civil Service and the response of the insiders', *Parliamentary Affairs*, 37: 353–63.

Fulton Committee (1968) *Report of the Committee on the Civil Service* (London: HMSO, Cmnd. 3638).

Garrett, J. (1980) *Managing the Civil Service* (London: Heinemann).

George, S. (1991) *Britain and European Integration Since 1945* (Oxford: Blackwell).

Gladstone, W. E. (1879) *Gleanings from Past Years* (London: John Murray).

Grant, W. P. (1989) *Pressure Groups, Politics & Democracy in Britain* (London: Philip Allan).

Griffith, J. A. G. (1966) *Central Departments and Local Authorities* (London: Allen & Unwin).

Grove, J. W. (1962) *Government and Industry in Britain* (London: Longman).

Habermas, J. (1975) *Legitimation Crisis* (Boston, Mass.: Beacon Press).

Halsey, A. H. (1987) 'Social trends since World War II', in *Social Trends 17* (London: HMSO).

Hart, V. (1978) *Distrust and Democracy* (Cambridge: Cambridge University Press).

Hastings, M. and Jenkins, S. (1983) *The Battle for the Falklands* (London: Michael Joseph).

Heclo, H. and Wildavsky, A. (1974) *The Private Government of Public Money* (London: Macmillan).

Hennessy, P. (1990) *Whitehall* (Glasgow: Fontana).

Hewstone, M. (1986) *Understanding Attitudes to the European Community* (Cambridge: Cambridge University Press).

Himmelweit, H. T., Humphreys, P., Jaeger, M. and Katz, M. (1981) *How Voters Decide* (London: Academic Press).

Hoskyns, Sir John (1983) 'Whitehall and Westminster: an outsider's view', *Parliamentary Affairs*, 36: 137–47.

Hunt, N. (ed.) (1964) *Whitehall and Beyond* (London: BBC Publications).

Hurwitt, M. and Thornton, P. (1989) *Civil Liberty: The NCCL Guide* (Harmondsworth: Penguin).

Ingle, S. (1987) *The British Party System* (Oxford: Blackwell).

James, S. (1992) *British Cabinet Government* (London: Routledge).

—— (1997) *British Government: A Reader in Policy Making* (London: Routledge).

Jefferys, K. (1993) *The Labour Party since 1945* (London: Macmillan).

Jenkins, R. (1959) 'Obscenity, censorship and the law', *Encounter*, October.

—— (1967) *Asquith* (Glasgow: Fontana).

Jones, G. and Stewart, J. (1983) *The Case for Local Government* (London: Allen & Unwin).

Jowell, J. and Oliver, D. (1989) *The Changing Constitution* (Oxford: Oxford University Press).

Jowell, R. and Airey, C. (eds) (1984) *British Social Attitudes: The 1984 Report* (Aldershot: Gower).

Judge, D. (ed.) (1983) *The Politics of Parliamentary Reform* (London: Heinemann).

Kavanagh, D. (ed.) (1982) *The Politics of the Labour Party* (London: Allen & Unwin).

Kellner, P. and Crowther-Hunt, Lord (1980) *The Civil Servants: An Enquiry into Britain's Ruling Class* (London: MacDonald).

King, A. (ed.) (1985) *The British Prime Minister* (London: Macmillan).

Layton-Henry, Z. (ed.) (1980) *Conservative Party Politics* (London: Macmillan).

Lees, J. D. and Kimber, R. (eds) (1972) *Political Parties in Modern Britain* (London: Routlege & Kegan Paul).

Lees, J. D. and Shaw, M. (eds) (1979) *Committees in Legislatures: A Comparative Analysis* (Durham, NC: Duke University Press).

Leonard, D. (1996) *Elections in Britain Today* (London: Macmillan).

Lodge, J. (ed.) (1989) *The European Community and the Challenge of the Future* (London: Pinder).

McGrew, T. (1988) 'Security and order: the economic dimension', in M. Smith, S. Smith and B. White (eds), *British Foreign Policy* (London: Unwin Hyman).

Mackenzie, W. J. M. and Grove, J. W. (1957) *Central Administration in Britain* (London: Longman, Green).

Mackintosh, J. P. (1977a) *The British Cabinet*, 3rd edn (London: Stevens).

—— (1977b) *The Government and Politics of Britain*, 4th edn (London: Hutchinson).

Madgwick, P. J. (1977) 'Linguistic conflict in Wales: a problem in the design of government', in G. Williams (ed.), *Social and Cultural Changes in Contemporary Wales* (London: Routledge & Kegan Paul).

—— (1991) *British Government: The Central Executive Territory* (London: Macmillan).

Mansergh, N. (1975) *The Irish Question, 1840–1921*, 3rd edn (London: Allen & Unwin).

Mark, Sir Robert (1977) *Policing a Perplexed Society* (London: Allen & Unwin).

Marsh, A. (1977) *Protest and Political Consciousness* (Beverly Hills, Calif.: Sage).

Marshall, G. (1984) *Constitutional Conventions* (Oxford: Clarendon Press).

—— (ed.) (1989) *Ministerial Responsibility* (Oxford: Oxford University Press).

May, Timothy (1984) 'The businessman's burden: rates and the CBJ', *Politics*, 4: 34–8.

Mellors, C. (1978) *The British MP* (Farnborough: Saxon House).

Moran, M. (1989) *Politics and Society in Britain* (London: Macmillan).

Morrison, H. (1954) *Government and Parliament* (Oxford: Oxford University Press).

Northedge, F. S. (1974) *Descent From Power* (London: Allen & Unwin).

Norton, P. (1981) *The Commons in Perspective* (Oxford: Martin Robertson).

—— (1985) 'Behavioural changes: backbench independence in the 1980s', in P. Norton (ed.) *Parliament in the 1980s* (Oxford: Blackwell).

Norton, P. and Aughey, A. (1981) *Conservatives and Conservatism* (London: Temple Smith).

Nugent, N. (1991) *The Government and Politics of the European Community*, 2nd edn (London: Macmillan).

O'Brien, C. C. (1972) *States of Ireland* (London: Hutchinson).

—— (1980) *Neigbours* (London: Faber).

Oliver, D. (1991) *Government in the United Kingdom* (Buckingham: Open University Press).

Pinto-Duschinsky, M. (1985) 'Trends in British political funding 1979–83', *Parliamentary Affairs*, 38: 328–47.

Potter, A. M. (1961) *Organized Groups in British National Politics* (London: Faber).

Radice, L., Vallance, E. and Willis, V. (1990) *Member of Parliament: The Job of a Backbencher*, 2nd edn (London: Macmillan).

Ranney, A. (1965) *Pathways to Parliament* (London: Macmillan).

Reiner, R. and Cross, M. (eds) (1991) *Beyond Law and Order: Criminal Justice Policy and Politics into the 1990s* (London: Macmillan).

Richards, P. G. (1959) *Honourable Members* (London: Faber).

—— (1970) *Parliament and Conscience* (London: Allen & Unwin).

—— (1972) *The Backbenchers* (London: Faber).

Richardson, J. J. and Jordan, A. G. (1979) *Governing under Pressure* (Oxford: Martin Robertson).

Richardson, J. J. and Jordan, A. G. (1987) *Government and Pressure Groups in Britain* (Oxford: Clarenden Press).

Ridley, F. F. (1983) There is no British constitution: a dangerous case of the emperor's clothes', *Parliamentary Affairs*, 41: 340–61.

Ridley, N. (1983) *The Local Right: Enabling not Providing* (London: Centre for Policy Studies).

Robertson, G. (1989) *Freedom, the Individual and the Law* (Harmondsworth: Penguin).

Robson, W. A. (ed.) (1956) *The Civil Service in Britain and France* (London: Hogarth Press).

Rodgers, W. (1983) 'The SDP and Liberal Party in alliance', *Political Quarterly*, 54: 354–62.

Rose, R. (1971) *Governing without Consensus* (London: Faber).

—— (1974) *The Problem of Party Government* (London: Macmillan).

—— (1980a) *Politics in England*, 3rd edn (London: Faber).

—— (1980b) *Do Parties Make a Difference?* (Chatham, NJ: Chatham House).

—— (1983) 'Still the era of party government', *Parliamentary Affairs*, 36: 282–99.

Rose, R. and McAllister, I. (1986) *Voters Begin to Choose* (London: Sage).

Rosebery, L. (1899) *Sir Robert Peel* (London: Cassell).

Rozenberg, J. (1996) *Trial of Strength* (London: Richard Cohen).

Rush, M. (ed.) (1990) *Parliament & Pressure Groups* (Oxford: Oxford University Press).

Sarlvik, B. and Crewe, I. (1983) *Decade of Dealignment* (Cambridge: Cambridge University Press).

Seldon, A. (ed.) (1996) *How Tory Governments Fall* (London: Fontana).

Seldon, A. and Ball, S. (eds) (1994) *Conservative Century* (Oxford: Oxford University Press).

Shackleton, M. (1984) 'Britain and the EEC', in R. L. Borthwick and J. E. Spence (eds), *British Politics in Perspective* (Leicester: Leicester University Press).

—— (1989) 'The Budget of the European Community', in J. Lodge (ed.), *The European Community and the Challenge of the Future* (London: Pinter).

Shaw, E. (1996) *The Labour Party since 1945* (Oxford: Blackwell).

Shell, D. R. (1985) 'The House of Lords and the Thatcher government', *Parliamentary Affairs*, 38: 16–32.

Sisson, C. H. (1959) *The Spirit of British Administration* (London: Faber).

Smith, M., Smith, S. and White, B. (eds) (1988) *British Foreign Policy* (London: Unwin Hyman).

Stacey, F. (1971) *The British Ombudsman* (Oxford: Oxford University Press).

Stephenson, H. (1982) *Claret and Chips: The Rise of the SDP* (London: Michael Joseph).

Street, H. (1963) *Freedom, the Individual and the Law* (Harmondsworth: Penguin).

Theakston, C. (1995) *The Civil Service since 1945* (Oxford: Blackwell).

Trevelyan, G. M. (1929) *History of England* (London: Longmans, Green).

Utley, T. E. (1975) *Lessons of Ulster* (London: Dent).

Vital, D. (1968) *The Making of British Foreign Policy* (London: Allen & Unwin).

Waldron, J. (1990) *The Law* (London: Routledge).

Walkland, S. A. (1968) *The Legislative Process in Great Britain* (London: Allen & Unwin).

—— (ed.) (1979) *The House of Commons in the Twentieth Century* (Oxford: Clarendon Press).

Wallace, W. (1977) *The Foreign Policy Process in Britain* (London: Allen & Unwin).

Wheare, K. C. (1955) *Government by Committee* (Oxford: Clarendon Press).

Williams, F. (1961) *A Prime Minister Remembers* (London: Heinemann).

Wilson, F. M. G. (1959) 'The roots of entry of new members of the British Cabinet, 1868–1958', *Political Studies*, 7: 222–32.

Woodham-Smith, C. (1962) *The Great Hunger* (London: Hamish Hamilton).

Young, K. and Rao, N. (1997) *Local Government since 1945* (Oxford, Blackwell).

Zentner, P. (1982) *Social Democracy in Britain* (London: John Martin).

INDEX